850AA

D0699801

WITHDRAWN
UTSA LIBRARIES

Social Welfare in the Soviet Union

Social Welfare in the Soviet Union

BERNICE Q. MADISON

STANFORD UNIVERSITY PRESS   STANFORD, CALIFORNIA   1968

Stanford University Press
Stanford, California
© 1968 by the Board of Trustees of the
Leland Stanford Junior University
Printed in the United States of America
L.C. 68-17137

To My Parents

Contents

Charts and Tables

Foreword

"From each according to his abilities, to each according to his needs."
This familiar statement of the communist goal is also a description of
what might be called a total welfare state, except that when this blissful
condition is reached, there will be no state.

The achievement of this goal, according to the 1961 program of the
Communist Party of the Soviet Union, is inevitable, but it will come
gradually from socialism through a period of "communist construction." When it has been achieved, the dictatorship of the proletariat will
no longer be necessary, and the state, which since the days of Marx and
Engels has been destined to wither away, will cease to be the instrument
of the proletarian dictatorship. It will survive, however, as the instrument of the classless society until the complete victory of communism,
presumably throughout the world. The Communist Party, which organized the proletarian dictatorship, will not follow the dictatorship
and the state in withering away. On the contrary, during the period of
communist construction its role as "the leading and guiding force of
Soviet society will be enhanced." Although the Party program does not
say so, the social welfare system, described so well by Dr. Madison in
this excellent book, also seems to be destined for a greater role, for during the period of the construction and the final achievement of communism it will be the agency best qualified to see that each receives what
he needs from that which all have contributed according to their abilities.

The importance of the social welfare system in the communist scheme has been overshadowed in the studies by noncommunist writers on Soviet history and institutions by the more spectacular features of Soviet authoritarianism and foreign policies. In the early days of what sympathetic foreign visitors called "the Soviet experiment," the Soviet decrees and policy statements about social welfare were in such apparent harmony with the programs of American progressives, and British and European socialists and social democrats, that these decrees were considered the most notable feature of the Soviet regime, reflecting its aims if not its actual achievements.

The only one of the early studies of the Soviet Union known to me that gives even a brief account of social welfare in tsarist times is *Labor Protection in Soviet Russia* (1928), a small book of 128 pages by George M. Price, M.D. Dr. Madison, recognizing the importance of knowledge of the past to an understanding of later developments, begins her study with a somewhat longer account of social welfare under the tsars.

Social security was an important part of the programs of all socialist parties—Utopian, Marxist, Christian, Populist. As a part of the socialist movement, the Russian Social Democratic Labor Party, which held its first congress in 1898, followed this pattern. Members of the Bolshevik component of that party agreed that social reform was a goal of the social democratic movement, but insisted that something else came first. In the statements made by Lenin and others, means received more emphasis than ends, for the Bolsheviks took the line that while they advocated social reforms, they did so to gain wide popular support for the revolution that would enable them to seize power. This, they claimed, was the only way that real social welfare could be assured. Both before they seized power and since, the Bolsheviks have used social welfare programs as a means of gaining the approval of people in their own and other countries.

In 1899 Lenin wrote an article entitled "Our Program," which was not published until 1925 because the police, attracted as they usually were by articles advocating the overthrow of the government, suppressed the periodical in which it was to appear. In the article Lenin denounced the reformism he saw in the revisionism of Eduard Bernstein (1850–1932), the German social democrat; he argued that it was particularly necessary for Russian socialists to work out the application of Marxist theory independently, for its general precepts must be applied differently in Russia than in Germany, France, or England. In Russia the only way to obtain a permanent improvement in the situation of the workers was by uniting the economic with the political struggle for the purpose of seizing political power.

In his much more famous essay "What Is To Be Done: Dogmatism and 'Freedom of Criticism,' " published in 1902, Lenin again attacked the revisionists' attempt to convert the revolutionary Social Democratic Party into a democratic reformist party. He insisted that while the Party should always fight for reforms, it must subordinate the struggle for reform to the revolutionary struggle for liberty and socialism, that is, to the seizure of political power and the achievement of social reforms implicit in socialism. Lenin argued that in Russia it was not enough to expose conditions that cried out for reforms; the exposure of these conditions and the demands for political and social reforms must not divert the Party from the immediate aim of recruiting and organizing a revolutionary movement strong enough to overthrow the tsarist government.

The 1903 Program of the RSDLP contained more than a dozen demands affecting conditions of labor, wages, social insurance, sanitation and health, new methods of dealing with industrial disputes—all for the declared purpose of saving the working class from physical and moral degeneration and increasing the power of the workers in their struggle for emancipation. Lenin did not mention a specific program of social welfare in *The State and Revolution,* written about two months before the October Revolution of 1917, except to quote Marx's contention that under socialism the worker would not receive the full product of his labor, for it was necessary to create a fund for expansion and replacement of machinery, for the expenses of management, and for the maintenance of schools, hospitals, homes for the aged, and so forth.

Almost immediately after the seizure of power, the Soviet government, as Dr. Madison notes, declared its intention to honor past pledges in the field of social welfare. More significant than this promise were the decrees on these matters issued during the following two months. These decrees constituted, at least on paper, a fulfillment of the Party's pre-revolutionary promises. The decrees, however, could not really be put into effect because the Soviet government did not have the power to enforce the orders even if it had had the necessary financial resources, which it did not have.

Lenin's purpose in issuing these decrees, Trotsky recalls in his *My Life* (New York, 1930, p. 342), was "to unfold the party's program in the language of power." The decrees were, in Trotsky's words, "really more propaganda than actual administrative measures. Lenin was in a hurry to tell the people what the new power was, what it was after, and how it intended to accomplish its aims." Since the Bolsheviks, in those first months, could not know whether they would stay in power or not, "it was necessary," Trotsky says, "whatever happened, to make our revolutionary experience as clear as possible for all men." Other communist parties have used this kind of propaganda by decree—the Chinese in Yenan, the Indians in Telengana and Andhra—to attract support or, if they failed to retain power, to leave a record in the language of power, of what they would have done if their enemies had not prevented them.

Five months after the seizure of power when, as the Bolsheviks put it, the dictatorship of the proletariat was realized and the laying of the foundations of a communist society was begun, the VII Party Congress decided to take the name "All-Russian Communist Party" and to revise and supplement the 1903 program. The new program, adopted a year later in March 1919, included sections on housing, social security, public health—measures, it was claimed, that the establishment of the dictatorship of the proletariat had made possible for the first time. The aim of the new social security system was to bring back "to a life of work any who have been dislodged from work" because of accidents or abnormal social relations.

During the same year N. I. Bukharin and E. A. Preobrazhensky, two veteran Bolshevik theoreticians, wrote *The ABC of Communism*. They intended this to be a textbook for an elementary course in the Party schools, to meet the needs of Party propagandists and agitators, and to provide a commentary on the Party program. Chapter XVIII, "Labour Protection and Social Welfare Work," is a commentary on the section of the Party program with the same title. Social welfare, the authors write in the final paragraph of their commentary, will not be "undertaken by the Party in the spirit of the charity-monger or in a way which will encourage parasitism and idleness" but as the duty of proletarian power to give help where it is needed and to enable persons demoralized by bad social conditions to return to a working life.

At its Fifth Congress (1928) the Communist International (Comintern), founded in Moscow nine years before, extended to all foreign communist parties the principles of social welfare that the Russians had adopted at the VIII Party Congress (1919) as part of the new, Second Party Program. The Constitution of the Union of Soviet Socialist Republics of 1936 ("the Stalin Constitution") contains a section on fundamental rights and duties of citizens; provisions for social welfare are among these rights.

The Third Party Program, authorized by Party congresses in 1939 and 1952, was finally adopted at the XXII Congress in 1961, eight years after Stalin's death and during the supremacy of N. S. Khrushchev. It claimed that the First (1903) Program had been carried out by the Great October Revolution and the abolition of capitalism in Russia; that the Second (1919) Program had been carried out by the complete and final establishment of socialism in the Soviet Union. No mention was made, however, of the drastic revisions of dogmas and policies of earlier programs. The Third Program was declared to be one for the building of a communist society. This meant the extension of welfare benefits promised in earlier programs to the point where public funds would be distributed to members of society "according to need, irrespective of the quantity and quality of their labor."

Such progress toward this utopian goal as the Soviet regime has made through economic growth, technological advance, and social welfare is recognized by the Party as a means not only of gaining or retaining the support of the peoples over whom it rules, but also of bringing "closer the triumph of Marxism-Leninism on a worldwide scale." The ideas of communism, according to the 1961 program, will win the minds and hearts of the masses, "not through war with other countries but by the example of a more perfect organization of society, by rapid progress in developing progressive forces, the creation of all conditions for the happiness and well-being of man...." This heretical revision of a long-revered Marxist-Leninist dogma is not an accurate reflection of present conditions in the Soviet Union, but is significant as an indication of the continuing importance of policies related to social welfare in the ruling circles of the ruling party.

It is an honor to be asked to write a foreword to a very good book, written by an accomplished scholar, who has had exceptional opportunities to use her professional skills in the investigation of an important subject.

HAROLD H. FISHER

May 1968

Preface

This is a book about social welfare in the Soviet Union. Social welfare programs are being instituted all over the world by newly developing countries, and expanded by more sophisticated, industrial societies. Sums spent on welfare measures by the nations of the world have mounted steadily over the years. In the twentieth century in particular there has been a growing recognition that social welfare programs play an important role in meeting needs of particular individuals and groups and in promoting social harmony. Social welfare is not only an effect of social development, but also an influence upon the developmental process.

What is "social welfare"? What is its role in society and in social change?[1] So far no general agreement has been achieved on the answer to these questions, either on a countrywide or a worldwide basis. As yet "social welfare" has not acquired a universal pattern. In each country it is

a dynamic activity that has grown out of, and is constantly influenced by, evolving social, economic, political, and cultural trends, and—for this very reason—can acquire an established pattern only at the price of failing to meet new situations. That is, the character of the services offered, the methods by which they are extended, and the persons eligible to receive them differ not only from country to country but also from place to place and from time to time within each country.[2]

In many countries the term "social welfare" is used both for specific activities and for the social policy of maintenance by the state of a minimum standard of social and economic well-being for the entire population. Thus, "social welfare" cuts across the fields of health, education, labor, and many others, greatly complicating the problem of definition. Further confusion results from the fact that "social welfare" programs are sometimes described in terms of their values to individuals and sometimes in terms of their social functions. Another difficulty stems from the absence of a standardized terminology: the terms "social security," "social services," and "social work" have no established meanings, and are often used interchangeably.

However, efforts to overcome these difficulties at the international level have yielded definitions broad enough to be useful to nations in all stages of social development. For example, one group of nations defines "social service" as

> an organized activity that aims at helping to achieve a mutual adjustment of individuals and their social environment. This objective is achieved through the use of techniques and methods designed to enable individuals, groups, and communities to meet their needs and solve their problems of adjustment to a changing pattern of society, and through cooperative action to improve economic and social conditions.[3]

In another broad definition, "social welfare" is said to include "those laws, programs, benefits, and services that assure or strengthen provisions for meeting social needs recognized as basic to the well-being of the population and the proper functioning of the social order."[4] A recently proposed definition of "social welfare" in the United States is as follows:

> The organized system of functions and services under public and private auspices that directly support and enhance individual and social well-being, and that promote community conditions essential to the harmonious interaction of persons and their social environment, as well as those functions and services directed toward alleviating or contributing to the solution of social problems, with particular emphasis on strengthening the family as the primary social institution in a democratic society.[5]

Such broad definitions cannot be used as a framework for this book. Suffice it to say that a detailed analysis of the measures and programs they encompass could not be presented in a single book of manageable proportions, even if I possessed the competence required to deal with all of them. Nor can a suitable narrower definition be arrived at by an examination of the functions of personnel in the "social welfare" field in different countries. In no country have the functions of these personnel, designated as "social workers" or "social service workers" or "welfare workers," been clearly differentiated from certain functions performed by people in such closely allied fields as medicine, education, law, or religion, for example. In the United States, where social work training has been available for over 65 years, the question of who shall be considered a "social worker" still persists, and it will probably be resolved only when uniform criteria are established for the several levels and types of personnel within the field by a system of licensing. Reports on "social welfare" expenditures prepared by federal agencies enumerate the specific programs encompassed, but they do not lead to a narrowing of the social welfare concept: they include social insurance, public aid, health and medical programs, "other" welfare services (vocational rehabilitation, institutional care, child welfare), veterans' programs, education, and public housing. In addition, these reports point out that while "government actions that promote welfare indirectly by enforcing law and order, fostering economic development, stabilizing prices, etc. are by general consent not regarded as social welfare measures," the "wide borderline area between social welfare and any other measures" is "subject to change."[6] Western scholars who have written on "social welfare" in the Soviet Union have included the following categories: health, education, social security, social insurance, and maternity assistance, as well as "other welfare benefits"—holidays, working conditions and hours, wage policies, housing.[7]

The spectrum of "social welfare" discussed in this book is broader than some would prefer, though narrower than others might choose. The major considerations that entered into the limitation of the discussion were my competence, the amount and quality of the available data, the audience at which the book is aimed, the desire not to duplicate other research already completed or in progress, and the relative importance of the various types of social welfare programs. The social services discussed in this book include the following: (1) family and child welfare services, including services for delinquent youngsters; (2) income maintenance programs, that is, programs that furnish monetary grants or assistance in kind either on a discretionary or nondiscretionary basis; (3) vocational rehabilitation and services for the aged. (With regard to juvenile delinquents, causation and treatment, rather than legal and administrative aspects, are emphasized.) Other social services in the areas of health, education, recreation, labor protection, housing, etc. are referred to whenever necessary to show interconnections, to clarify points, and to provide a balanced presentation.

The book is divided into two parts. Part I opens with a condensed analysis of major welfare developments during the ten centuries that preceded the October 1917 Revolution. An attempt is made to elucidate the basic philosophy that underlay social welfare in tsarist Russia, and to compare Russian welfare practices with those in various other European countries. The analysis is based almost entirely on materials published by Russian scholars during the pre-Revolutionary period, in order to avoid the bias of Soviet writers. By showing the links between the past and the present, it facilitates understanding of post-Revolutionary developments.

Chapters 2, 3, and 4 are primarily an examination of the formation of Soviet social welfare policy up to 1956—the year in which the social welfare system was radically revised by the post-Stalin leadership, and the current program became crystallized. In Chapter 2, the Soviet view of man as a psychosocial being is discussed; the Soviet position concerning the character and function of the family is treated in Chapter 3; and the policies governing the provision of income maintenance are analyzed in Chapter 4. Throughout, care is taken to distinguish between policies of a transitory nature designed merely for political purposes and those based upon a more enduring concept of social welfare.

Several points should be noted with regard to the material on income maintenance in Chapter 4. My intention was to present a balanced picture, that is, to discuss not only social insurance and family allowances, but mutual aid and public assistance as well. To my knowledge, the two latter programs have not yet been seriously studied; in contrast, the Soviet systems of social insurance and family allowances have been competently analyzed by a number of American scholars and administrators. (See, for example, Chapter VIII and Appendix F in Janet G. Chapman's *Real Wages in Soviet Russia Since 1928* and *A Report on Social Security Programs in the Soviet Union,* published by the U.S. Department of Health, Education and Welfare.) Because of the availability of these studies, and because I am neither an economist nor an actuary, my handling of the social insurance and family allowance programs is confined largely to their policy implications. Technical aspects are deliberately avoided, and the details provided are the kind that will help the reader to understand what life is like for those who are covered by these programs.

Part II is an analysis of current Soviet social welfare practice and programs. It opens with an examination of social welfare organization and personnel. Since a social work profession does not exist in the Soviet Union, it was necessary to select from among the public service vocations those that include social welfare activity as a regular part of their functions. The concept of such activity that was chosen as appropriate for Soviet society is that of a service, either professional or nonprofessional, under government or nongovernmental auspices, potentially available to every member of the community irrespective of his means, that assists him to achieve his full potentialities for a productive and satisfying life. With regard to the discussion of social insurance in Chapter 11, again it should be emphasized that only its major features and policy implications are analyzed, and that no attempt is made to deal with the technical aspects of social security.

In Chapter 7 four case studies are presented. They represent the best in Soviet treatment methods. They were translated by me, and although I have made considerable deletions, I have taken care not to alter their substance.

In the concluding chapter, I have attempted to analyze the way in which Soviet social welfare has been shaped by the special nature of Soviet history, ideology, and society, and the manner in which social welfare in turn has influenced Soviet society. Soviet welfare achievements and weaknesses are then compared briefly with developments in the United States and in several European countries. This comparison and assessment provides the basis for a discussion of what the Soviet Union and the United States can learn from each other with regard to social welfare, as well as what the newly developing countries can learn from the Soviet experience.

This book is based on data from two sources: (1) the literature I examined in libraries in the United States and the Soviet Union, as well as material I read in manuscript form, and (2) insight and information I acquired during two trips to the Soviet Union—one of three months duration in 1960–61, the second of four months duration in 1964–65.

During the seven months I spent in the Soviet Union, I visited three republics: the Russian Soviet Federative Socialist Republic (RSFSR), the Ukrainian Socialist Soviet Republic, and the Uzbek Socialist Soviet Republic. In 1959 these three republics contained more than 80 per cent of the total population of the Soviet Union. In these republics I had extended discussions with "social welfare" staff in the Ministries of Social Welfare, Education, and Health; the All-Union Trade Union Organization; the Universities of Moscow, Leningrad, and Samarkand; the Academies of Pedagogical Sciences in Moscow and Tashkent; and the Institute of Defectology and the Institute of Psychology in Moscow. Among the many persons with whom I talked were the Minister of Social Welfare of the Uzbek Republic, the Vice-Minister of Social Welfare for the Ukraine, several leading Soviet authorities on the family, the entire staff of the Institute of Defectology, and the leading staff members of the Institute of Psychology. Our discussions ranged over the entire spectrum of social welfare—the etiology of social problems, philosophy, methodology, administration, staffing, financing, etc.

In addition I visited a number of social welfare agencies, such as institutions for handicapped children (blind, deaf, mentally retarded, orthopedically handicapped, and hard-of-hearing, as well as those suffering from speech defects or from impaired vision), homes for the aged, homes for the disabled, a variety of workshops and enterprises in which handicapped people are employed, local offices supervising benefit payments, nurseries, clinics for women and children, institutions for dependent and neglected children. I was also present at case conferences concerned with child welfare problems, and was able to interview parents. In the course of these visits I talked with administrators, staff members, and clients, and inspected physical facilities. (My fluency in Russian made interpreters unnecessary and permitted direct communication, enriched by the nuances and overtones that are usually lost in translation.) Every discussion or visit was carefully recorded, usually within twenty-four hours of its occurrence.

I encountered certain difficulties in obtaining information. As is well known, Soviet authorities have chosen not to publish certain kinds of statistics, either because they are not gathered or because they might prove embarrassing to the regime. For example, to date no statistics are available on juvenile delinquency, or even on such a relatively simple matter as the average old-age pension. It is therefore either impossible or extremely difficult to measure quantitatively the success or failure of a given policy in a particular area. Like other American scholars, I have had to resort to estimates in those instances in which a quantitative analysis seemed important. The procedures and reasoning upon which these estimates are based are carefully explained, and their limitations are noted.

Soviet studies in the social welfare field are for the most part programs for action rather than analyses of existing models. Among the hundreds of studies I examined, there was not a single one of a comparative, follow-up, or evaluative nature. No annual or any other kind of regularly published reports (except those that give overall figures in relation to a current plan) are available—either at the Union, the republic, or the local level. The literature is completely void of discussion of some welfare programs (adoption, for example) or of meaningful descriptions of operational procedures in many others. There are no case histories of aged and handicapped adult clients. Hence, qualitative judgments in this book have had to be based upon a careful weighing of disjointed, often fragmentary bits of material from a great variety of sources and especially upon my observations in the field. Special efforts have been made to show the reader the considerations that went into the making of judgments.

Obviously, the value of observations and evaluations depends upon a host of factors, including the competence of the observer and the selection of the phenomena to be observed. In this connection, it is perhaps worth mentioning that in most cases I succeeded in establishing a good working relationship with the people I met. Officials and ordinary citizens were often very frank about deficiencies in the regime.

In writing this book I hoped to achieve two things: first, to increase our knowledge of social welfare in the Soviet Union, an aspect of its society that is steadily gaining in importance there as well as everywhere else in the world, and second, to improve our understanding of the special problems faced by underdeveloped countries that wish to attain a reasonably high level of social welfare at the same time as they industrialize, as did the Soviet Union. Most studies of social welfare suffer from too limited a focus, and from considering the various segments of the field in isolation. In this book I attempt to present a comprehensive study of the relation of social services to social change in Soviet society. In view of this desire to achieve comprehensiveness, it was essential to emphasize principles and policy rather than concentrate on detailed descriptions of the provision and operation of services—although these latter are not neglected by any means.

Except where otherwise noted, the translations from the Russian and French are my own.

I hope that despite its limitations and inadequacies *Social Welfare in the Soviet Union* will make a genuine contribution to our understanding of Soviet society, and that it will help those engaged in welfare services everywhere to respond more constructively to the pressures and needs of people in this age of rapid social and economic change.

Acknowledgments

Many people have helped me with this book—so many, in fact, that I cannot begin to name them all. First, there is the Inter-University Committee on Travel Grants, which sent me to the Soviet Union twice. Without these field trips this book at best would have been a mere library study, inevitably limited, for social welfare deals with actual situations and ongoing activities. There are hundreds of Soviet officials, welfare administrators, workers, researchers, and recipients of welfare services who gave unstintingly of their time to answer my endless questions as fully as possible. Limitations of space do not permit mentioning all of them by name, but I wish to express my special indebtedness to T. G. Lazareva of the Russian Academy of Pedagogical Sciences, the agency in charge of overall arrangements for me in the Soviet Union, and Dr. A. I. D'iachkov, Director of the Russian Institute of Defectology, and my official host. Equally important is the U.S. Public Health Service, specifically its Division of Community Health Services, which provided a grant that freed me from teaching and made it possible for me to work without interruption. I wish to thank San Francisco State College, my employer for the past 14 years, for granting me the necessary leave.

It is a pleasure to acknowledge the assistance of my five readers: Drs. David Crystal, Kent Geiger, Harold H. Fisher, and Ernest Witte, and Mr. Robert J. Myers, F.S.A., F.C.A.S., of the Social Security Administration. All read the first part of the book; Drs. Crystal and Geiger read sections of the second part; Dr. Fisher read the concluding chapter. All made criticisms and suggestions; Dr. Geiger's thoughtful comments were especially valuable. In interpreting the data in Table 11, I benefited greatly from the assistance of Mr. Myers. To Dr. Fisher I wish to acknowledge a special debt, not only for his careful reading and detailed suggestions, but for his inspiration and encouragement.

Library personnel in Moscow, Leningrad, Samarkand, Washington, D.C., New York City, and Berkeley, California, were most helpful, and to them I want to express my deep appreciation. I want to thank particularly the librarians at the Hoover Library of Stanford University: their invariably efficient and generous assistance often went beyond the call of duty. I am also grateful to Mrs. Eve Tebow and Mrs. Mary Johnson, who typed and retyped the huge manuscript—always meticulously, patiently, with good humor, and undaunted by the difficult Russian words and titles. And finally I want to convey my thanks to my husband, Michael Schapiro, who was cheerful and uncomplaining during periods when hard work and concentrated effort made me morose and exhausted. He has been a source of strength to me throughout.

To all of these people I feel a deep gratitude. Without them whatever is of value in this book would have been much more difficult to achieve. However, I alone am responsible for whatever is weak or inadequate.

B. Q. M.

PART ONE

SOCIAL POLICY FORMATION
1917–1966

The clergy and beggars, and the unimportant ones, and the poor, and the unfortunate, and the wandering strangers, invite into your house and in accordance with your strength feed them, and give them to drink, and warm them, and give alms from your honest labors, in your house and in your place of business, and on the road: in this way you are cleansed of sins, in this way they appeal to God about your sins.*

I

The Pre-Revolutionary Heritage

According to the available evidence, the Russian state first became involved in social welfare during the reign of the Grand Duke Vladimir, who ruled from 978 to 1015.[1] Vladimir (later named Vladimir the Saint) was converted to Christianity in 988, and thereafter became a zealous philanthropist. In 996 he issued a poor code that made the church responsible for the care and supervision of the poor, sick, aged, and disabled. Resources required to construct and maintain almshouses, hospitals, retreats, and asylums for indigent strangers were to come from the "tenth"—a tenth of the revenues from fines, profits from every tenth week of trading in all cities, and a tenth of the annual production of grain and cattle. This was to be augmented by voluntary "tenths" from God-fearing people, including the ruler. Vladimir's policy dominated Russian welfare practice until the close of the seventeenth century; attempts to relieve poverty were guided largely by the Christian precepts of charity and love and were administered directly or indirectly by the clergy. Tatar rule had virtually no effect upon the system. The khans treated the clergy with genuine respect; indeed, some khans augmented the church funds for the poor.

Most of Vladimir's successors also concerned themselves with charitable works. Ivan the Terrible (1533–84), for example, built almshouses in

* From the *Domostroi*, rules for family life written by the priest Sylvester in the sixteenth century.

many cities, and often distributed alms personally to the inmates, as well as to the poor on the streets. At his coronation Boris Godunov (1598–1605) swore a solemn oath that there would be no poor in his empire, and during the Great Famine of 1601–3 he spent large sums from his own treasury to feed the hungry. Godunov provided employment instead of alms for the able-bodied poor by ordering the construction of stone buildings in Moscow and other cities. The Tsar Aleksei Mikhailovich (1645–76) built special asylums for wounded and aged veterans. (Many wealthy men followed the tsars' example, and were often celebrated for their zeal in charity. Churchmen, anxious not to be outdone, also frequently gained renown for their humanitarian activities.)

On the communal level, assistance was administered by the parish, which acted as the local civil as well as ecclesiastical authority. The clergy devised various forms of aid. "Poor cells" were built at almost every church, and many churches had special asylums for the sick, children, widows, and strangers. Communal aid, however, never expanded beyond a form of local mutual aid. As towns grew, they found their resources insufficient to meet the ever-more complex needs of the increasingly heterogeneous group requiring assistance. The state eventually substituted centrally administered aid for communal assistance.[2]

Probably the most enlightened welfare plan before the eighteenth century was that of Tsar Feodor Alekseevich (1676–82), whose ideas reflect knowledge of policies then in effect in Western Europe. In a ukase on welfare he acknowledged the state's obligation to care for the poor, specified criteria for separating them into categories, and outlined an organizational structure for administering diverse facilities. The ukase also included provisions empowering the authorities to punish those poor who resisted the workings of the relief system: "sturdy" beggars and their children would be sent to workhouses, those who refused would be beaten and exiled to Siberia. Feodor urged that each almshouse for the deserving poor employ a doctor and that needy children be educated—the boys in trades, professions, and sciences, the girls in household tasks. Unfortunately, Feodor died the year this ukase was written, and it never became law; however, it had considerable influence on his son, Peter the Great, though Peter tended to stress its punitive features.

In Russia, as in all early Christian societies, church-administered welfare programs and church-inspired charity failed to provide an effective solution to the problem of poverty. Charity became much like a commercial transaction: the giver bought salvation for his soul from the receiver, without concerning himself with the fact that those too proud to beg were passed over.[3] The giving of alms helped wealthy Russians to ignore the fundamental social and economic problems that, exacerbated by natural calamities, epidemics, and wars, had reduced large segments of the population to starvation. It widened the distances between classes and retarded the growth of social consciousness that is essential if assistance is to be transformed from charity into a rehabilitative social mechanism. A constant imbalance between the enormous need and the few resources available to meet it was made even more pronounced by corrupt administration. As early as 1551 the Tsar complained that almshouse officials made places available for well-to-do "muzhiks with wives," while "the honest beggars, the sick, and the maimed go abroad in the world without care." Such practices continued and became veritable scourges.

Social Welfare under Peter and Catherine

Peter the Great (1682–1725) brought the state more directly into the welfare field. During his reign welfare institutions were created by the state, administered by it, and supported by it. The church eventually ceased to play a controlling role in welfare matters, and communal assistance became a shadow. Almsgiving was restricted to donations to state-run institutions. Peter's welfare activities had four basic aims: relief for the "honest poor," combined with the rooting out of professional begging; providing for veterans; care of illegitimate children; and the securing of increased revenues for charitable purposes.

Peter held that in Moscow and other major cities, church and municipal authorities were jointly responsible for alleviating poverty. He thought the police uniquely qualified to provide work for the able-bodied and administer corrections, while the church could best establish and maintain almshouses, orphanages, and schools. In time, however, the church became the weaker member of the partnership, and control of most charitable establishments was assigned to the police—leading many to equate poverty with criminality. Peter's orders that provincial capitals duplicate the Moscow system of poor relief were only partially carried out, because of chaotic revenue policies and inadequate facilities. In villages, owners of needy serfs were expected to provide work for the able-bodied, and bread and clothing for the disabled; free men were to be aided by the local community.

Peter's activity with regard to "idle" beggars amounted to a cruel and merciless war. He demanded that they be caught and punished by the police; if apprehended a second or third time, they were mercilessly beaten in the public square (this applied also to women and children). Men were then sent to Siberia, and women and children forced to labor in woolen mills. All direct almsgiving was forbidden under penalty of stiff fines; donations were to be given to monasteries and churches instead. These harsh measures, similar to laws passed earlier in every country of Western Europe, did not appreciably diminish professional begging. Low wages, lack of education, wars, and famines bred huge contingents of beggars; thus the Tsar's decrees inflicted terrible suffering on many innocent and helpless people.[4]

Peter's concern for veterans, whose ranks swelled because of his extensive military activity, continued throughout his reign. He ordered the clergy to give some veterans subsistence pay and to give preference to the old and disabled among them in selecting people for almshouse care. He also opened state-maintained asylums for former soldiers and gave employment to disabled officers. In 1717 he introduced a quasi-pension system for such officers and established free infirmaries for all ranks.

Peter was especially sympathetic to the plight of needy children. Those under ten who had no adult responsible for them were placed in the care of foster parents, or were reared in almshouses, the boys being registered for navy service at age ten and the girls trained for domestic service. Perhaps the most daring of Peter's welfare innovations concerned illegitimate children, a completely outcast group in Russia at that time.[5] He decreed that orphanages for them be opened at monasteries, with costs to be covered by government subsidy and private donations. Children were to remain in these asylums until the boys could be apprenticed and the girls married or sent out as domestics. But many died in infancy because their nurses lived outside and could not give uninterrupted care.

Peter's welfare activities entailed sizable expenditures. No privately supported charities existed at that time, and the state and many cities and communes found the financing of welfare too heavy a burden. Peter decided that monasteries, with their untapped wealth, should pay the bulk of welfare costs by allocating to charitable purposes two-thirds of all income that remained after the clergy's needs were satisfied. The fundamental principles of the Petrine welfare system remained in effect and virtually unchanged until modern times: that the "honest" poor must be assisted, aid must be differentiated according to the needs of the recipient, and the central government must promulgate welfare regulations and specify punishments for noncompliance. Peter's immediate successors, the Empresses Anna Ioanovna and Elizaveta Petrovna, could not raise the large sums his measures required; succumbing to pressures from the clergy and the police, they reduced or eliminated many programs. They also softened Peter's rigorously coercive restrictions against mendicancy—chiefly because enforcement was almost impossible. Asylums deteriorated throughout their reigns, primarily because of dishonest and incompetent administrators.

Catherine the Great (1762–96) secularized welfare administration further by assigning responsibility for almshouses, asylums, and veterans' homes to the Economic Board in 1763. She worked closely with the police to establish more workhouses and almshouses, and opened insane asylums in Novgorod, Moscow, and St. Petersburg.* Her major achievements in welfare, however, concerned illegitimate children and the establishment of the principle of public responsibility for dealing with the poor and helpless.

Most of Peter's orphanages had been closed, while the number of illegitimate children had increased, and many were being killed or left to die. Ivan Ivanovich Betsky, who had toured Western Europe studying the care of illegitimate children, petitioned the Empress with a plan for a "home" that would raise these children as useful citizens, the nucleus of a "third estate"—a social class midway between ruling groups and the masses. Financed by general donations as a state agency "eternally under special Monarchical protection," such a "home" was opened in Moscow in 1763. A similar institution was established in St. Petersburg in 1771. Operating as a unit with the Moscow home, it remained the major agency for illegitimate children for the next 153 years. The education offered the youngsters there was influenced by the most advanced ideas of that period; for example, the teaching of prayers, fables, and "devilish superstitions" was forbidden. At maturity, some of the orphans remained as teachers in the homes, and a few studied at the Imperial Academy of Arts; the majority went to work in textile factories.

In an effort to carry out the Empress's wish that "in these children there should be a union between a beautiful mind and heart," Betsky demanded that personnel in the homes be sober, God-fearing, honest, industrious, intelligent, and kind, but not weak. Amusements were to be planned to prevent the children from wallowing in "sadness and misery." Corporal punishment was completely ruled out, and "all the children and their issue were to be free for eternity." Administration was in the hands of a patronage committee composed of persons highly placed in society, which was responsible to the Empress herself. Huge sums were needed for this grandiose scheme; by her own generosity, Catherine encouraged contributions from all classes and even foreigners.

---

* Among beggars, there were many mentally ill persons. In feudal Russia, as elsewhere, the commonly accepted explanations for psychoses were possession by demons, bewitchment, and divine punishment. But as early as the eleventh century "some modest relief and protection was sometimes afforded to the unfortunate insane in the monasteries, where they were . . . likely to be regarded as the involuntary victims of dark powers, whose devils might be exorcised by prayer" (*490*, pp. 12–13). In Russia, the insane were never treated with the cruelty characteristic of many of the European countries. This is probably attributable to the fact that there was no fierce struggle among religions, and particularly that there was no Inquisition that looked upon the strange utterances and behavior of the insane as evidence of heresy (*353*, pp. 11–12; *509*, p. 716).

Other important sources of income for the homes were auctions, lotteries, a monopoly on the manufacture and sale of playing cards, and fines for "all sorts of public disorders."

Despite an auspicious beginning, Betsky's homes were a disastrous failure almost at once. In the first four years, 82 per cent of the children died (98 per cent in 1767). Many infants were already near death when they arrived. There came into being a special group known as "found-ling deliverers"—women who obtained several rubles from unwed mothers in return for promising to take their children to the homes. These women waited until they had gathered a large number of babies before delivering them. When unwrapped, many of the infants could scarcely breathe, having been smothered for days, or they were often in the last stages of starvation. The homes could never attract the needed number of wet nurses, and artificial feeding was necessary. This, and the over-crowding that persisted until almost the end of the nineteenth century, brought infection and the rapid spread of disease. The fearful mortality rate forced Betsky to resort to foster care in rural families for most of the children. In 1837 education was discontinued in the homes; from then on, they were merely transfer stations for children on their way to foster homes in the villages, from which they never returned.

The foster-care program was also a disastrous failure: during its first 32 years, three-quarters of the children died, and another 12 per cent were kidnapped and forced into serfdom by local landlords. Usually only the poorest peasants, eager for the three-ruble monthly payment, were willing to take in children. "Traveling supervisors," employed to in-vestigate the foster homes, were untrained civil servants who did almost nothing to improve the wretched conditions.* Even the children lucky enough to be educated in the homes were often pale, weak, and plagued by disease; Catherine found them "awkward, slow, silent, and morose." The entire program fell into disrepute. A careful study indicates that the derisive label "angel factories" was deserved: in 153 years, more than 76 per cent of the approximately 1.5 million children admitted to the homes died. How many of the survivors entered the "third estate" is not known, perhaps about 25,000; the rest became peasants and factory workers.[6]

Realizing that prior legislation on begging was ineffective, Catherine included a striking innovation in her decree of November 7, 1775—a provision for a Committee on Public Assistance (*Prikaz Obshchestven-nogo Prizreniia*) in each province. The duties of these committees (*prikazy*) multiplied over the years. They were to establish and main-tain elementary and trade schools, orphanages, veterans' homes, hospi-

---

* These facts undoubtedly played a part in shaping the negative attitude toward foster family care that is still prevalent in Soviet society.

tals, almshouses, institutions for the incurably ill, for illegitimate children, and for the insane, workhouses for able-bodied beggars and petty thieves, and correctional institutions. They were also responsible for supervising privately established charities, and for giving noninstitutional relief to the "deserving poor," especially among the military. If necessary, the *prikazy* were to place needy orphans in foster homes for "reasonable" pay, retaining the right to supervise and remove them. Asylums were to be reserved for the needy aged, the maimed, and other "miserable" persons; young persons were to be educated or placed in the homes of "good" people as apprentices or domestics.

The *prikazy,* created as civil rather than as church organs, were chaired by the provincial governors; their six members represented the nobility, the bourgeoisie, and the rural communes. The composition of the *prikazy* emphasized the government's desire for local participation and signified government acceptance, at least in principle, of responsibility for charitable institutions. It was hoped that each province would broaden its welfare undertakings, and that the committees would encourage local engagement in philanthropic activities. The fact remained, however, that the *prikazy* were created by central government authority, offered assistance in the name of the state, and owed no allegiance to the local community. Funds for *prikazy* activities came from varied sources, but were always inadequate. Each *prikaz* was allotted a set sum from the central treasury; money also came from individual donations, fines, unused municipal taxes, revenues from pharmacies licensed by the *prikazy,* special church collections, income from properties owned by the *prikazy,* occasional state subsidies, and interest on loans and investments—the most lucrative source of all.

In 1780, Catherine opened large government-sponsored homes for veterans in the village of Smolnoi and in St. Petersburg and Moscow. These institutions accepted disabled and destitute noncommissioned officers, enlisted men, and soldiers' widows. A special edict originated a pension system for disabled high ranking officers—life stipends related to former earnings and the beneficiary's economic circumstances. Officers' and soldiers' widows and children received some benefits, based on the salary of the deceased for the former, but only two and three rubles per year for the latter.

Catherine modified some of Peter's welfare programs and expanded others. However, rigid class distinctions remained characteristic of welfare practices. The duty of caring for the poor was more firmly placed on local authorities, and a diversified network of specialized agencies was established. Most of these agencies were administered by chief magistrates who, together with the *prikazy,* were answerable to the Economic

Board, the state agency that set public policy for welfare services. In 1802 Alexander I replaced the various boards with ministries; public welfare was placed under the Ministry of Interior where, except for nine years under the short-lived Ministry of Police, it remained until the Revolution.

Social Welfare from Alexander I to the Revolution

The pressing need for new sources of revenue for welfare purposes led Alexander I (1801–25) to encourage the establishment of voluntary charitable societies that he hoped would open untapped sources of revenue and exert a greater rehabilitative influence than government agencies had done. However, he insisted that such societies be creatures of the state and report in detail annually to the Ministry of Interior on their activities and finances. Because of these requirements only eleven societies had been founded by 1862. In 1890 the Ministry injected new vigor into the voluntary movement by issuing a series of basic guidelines and authorizing local police chiefs to approve societies that conformed. Eventually, voluntary societies, regulated by "special law," evolved into semi-public institutions—in some respects quite independent of the state system of assistance, yet administratively and financially tied to it.

Two of these organizations, the Department of the Institutions of the Empress Maria and the Imperial Philanthropic Society, in time developed into huge aggregates. Founded by Maria Feodorovna, the wife of Paul I (1796–1801), the Department's greatest development occurred when the wife of Alexander III (1881–94) increased its revenues substantially by selling titles of nobility to some of the bourgeoisie.[7] The Department's monopoly on the manufacture and sale of playing cards was another important source of revenue. The tsar named the members of its managerial body, and its head held a seat in the Council of State. In 1828 management of the Department was assumed by a Private Chancellery, controlled directly by and answerable only to the tsar. Although no continuous statistics are available for the 121 years of the Department's existence, figures for 1900 show that it administered more than 500 establishments, including 345 welfare institutions (as distinct from those concerned with health or education), most of them for children.[8] Its budget in that year amounted to 13.5 million rubles.[9]

The Imperial Philanthropic Society was created by Alexander I in 1802. Its top administrative council consisted of influential men from the clergy, the military, the nobility, and the wealthy bourgeoisie. Membership in the Society conferred the right to contribute money and to work with clients under direction; it was open to all social classes and both sexes. In 1816 the Society was given permission to operate throughout the country, and was charged with both distributing alms and helping the industrious to extricate themselves permanently from poverty. Again the data available are only fragmentary, but by 1902 the Society was administering 221 charities and serving about 200,000 persons—the majority (177,000) with medical help.[10] The Society attempted to apply some features of the famous Hamburg-Elberfeld system.* In St. Petersburg, for example, poor persons were made salaried investigators to assure an understanding of clients deemed impossible for upper class benefactors. They were expected to ascertain reasons for dependency and the major difficulties of each family's situation. Although these efforts were only partially successful, they did inject new thinking into the welfare field; other types of undertakings—a monthly journal, a welfare library, and a project to help needy writers and artists—failed from lack of support.

Several other voluntary organizations also contributed considerably to social welfare. The Homes for Industry and Workhouse Patronage served 20,000 persons by 1905 in 677 institutions (trade schools for adults, and workhouses, correctional homes, and apprenticeship shops for children). This organization also provided work relief in famine stricken areas on an emergency basis.[11] The Temperance Society occupied itself primarily with educational and recreational activities, and with maintaining teahalls and restaurants as alternatives to taverns. The Red Cross expanded its function of providing nursing care in wartime to include disaster relief in peacetime.[12] Voluntary philanthropy assumed a dominant role in veterans' welfare early in the nineteenth century, when the wealthy were permitted to maintain asylums for invalids and to help support government facilities. Almost all beneficiaries were officers; lower ranks did not become entitled to assistance until 1897, and then only if totally disabled and destitute, and only to the extent of three rubles a month.[13] Voluntary societies showed some concern for prostitutes, but their impact was negligible: only two welfare institutions were opened for them.[14]

Temporary Committees to Deal with Mendicants, composed of officials and citizens named by the Ministry of Interior, were established to classify arrested beggars in relation to their ability to work, then assist them or give them employment. These committees lasted more than fifty years, but quickly degenerated into bureaucratic and punitive agencies that discouraged rather than stimulated community concern for the

---

* This system operated on the assumption that charity should be based on detailed knowledge of the causes, extent, characteristics, and effects of poverty; it had proved remarkably effective in Germany.

poor; by 1855 only 19 of the 423 committees that had been created over a period of 18 years were operative.[15] The Moscow committee was replaced in 1892 by the Government Agency for the Examination of Beggars. Under this agency (which also tried to apply Hamburg-Elberfeld principles) municipal public assistance attained its highest development in Russia. Moscow was divided into 40 "guardianships"; the municipal council granted each a subsidy, and appointed administrative personnel. Almost 1,800 volunteers were allowed to serve, without regard to sex or social class, which made it possible to provide some individual attention for each welfare applicant. But the agency floundered and eventually disintegrated when the volunteers' demand for the right to vote on welfare questions was rejected by the city. Similar agencies created in fifty to sixty cities eventually became adjuncts to the police apparatus.

Despite its extent and variety, voluntary welfare left many gaps. Mentally retarded youngsters were almost entirely neglected until 1894, when Catherine Gracheva opened a small asylum at her home.* A service badly needed for decades—protection of children from abuse and exploitation by employers and parents—was not begun until 1899. Services for children were primarily institutional, and woefully inadequate. In 1914, for example, only 1.6 per cent of all blind youngsters received special institutional care and education—and these learned only rudimentary skills that did not prepare them for earning a living.[16] Of 40,000 deaf children of school age in 1906, only 3,000 were being educated. In 1914 only 2,800 adolescents were accommodated in special correctional facilities; other juvenile offenders were in adult jails. These young people, though primarily dependent and neglected, were classified as "morally defective" and socially dangerous; their treatment consisted of isolation and harsh punishment.[17]

The number of charitable institutions for children in small towns, rural areas, and outlying provinces was negligible; almost without exception, the few that existed provided cheap custodial care in wretched surroundings.[18] Many institutions required the children to do work that bordered on exploitation. Infant mortality in homes for illegitimate children and foundlings was frightening—three times higher than in the general population. Guardianship, foster care, and adoption were also available, but had fallen into disrepute because of high mortality rates and because children often led hard and unhappy lives as wards of exploitative guardians.[19]

Handicapped adults faced an even worse situation. A "Patronage for

---

* Gracheva continued working with the retarded until her death in 1934. Her rich experience was analyzed in her book *The Upbringing and Education of the Severely Retarded Child*, which appeared in 1932 (see 95, p. 20).

the Blind" was not created until 1881—an especially tragic delay because blindness in Russia was widespread and increasing and, in large part, preventable. The Patronage accomplished little; in 1917, it provided assistance and inferior occupational training to less than 1,500 of the more than 250,000 blind persons in the country, 94 per cent of whom remained illiterate.[20] Even fewer facilities were available for deaf-mutes, and these were mostly for the nobility; 98 per cent remained illiterate. Since tsarist law equated the deaf with the insane, and deprived them of legal and civil rights, even the few educated deaf persons were often incarcerated in mental institutions—or driven to vagrancy to avoid this fate.

Perhaps the most important shortcoming of voluntary charitable societies was their failure to institute preventive measures. As representatives of the governing classes, those on the administrative boards refused to challenge the social conditions or government measures that bred and perpetuated the miseries they were supposed to alleviate. For example, alcoholism was widely recognized as a major cause of poverty. Many thought the government liquor monopoly was partly responsible, because it led the government to encourage liquor consumption in order to increase revenues; yet the Temperance Society never advocated abolishing this monopoly. Prostitution was a state-recognized institution that yielded considerable profits in bribes to officials, yet charitable societies did nothing to close the brothels.[21] Nor did charity patrons concern themselves with the inhuman conditions and pitiful earnings of child laborers in what Dostoevsky called "small houses of death." The societies also remained indifferent to the terrible conditions of those apprehended for lawbreaking,[22] though Russian intellectuals repeatedly urged more humane correctional procedures.*

Alongside the voluntary system, the *prikazy* continued to operate. By 1850 *prikazy* had been established in 57 of the 78 provinces. According to the fragmentary and sporadic reports that they began to submit to the central government in 1802, the number of institutions under their jurisdiction rose from 389 in that year to a peak of 827 in 1852, when they served 235,953 persons. Table 1 presents the data available for 1852. Note that the largest expenditure was for medical care; aside from hospital patients, *prikazy* services reached fewer than 25,000 persons. The mortality rates for children differ strikingly—undoubtedly because daily expenditures for government employees' children, for example, ranged be-

---

* The obvious inadequacies of the voluntary system, as well as the often humiliating manner in which meager assistance was offered, made it relatively easy for the Soviet government to abolish all voluntary welfare organizations when it assumed power, and to reintroduce them only under tight state control.

TABLE 1

PRIKAZY INSTITUTIONS IN 1852, BY NUMBER OF INMATES, DISPOSITION, AND COST OF CARE

Type and Number of Institutions[a]	Number of Inmates	Inmates Released or Sent to Other Institutions	Deaths	Inmates Remaining into 1853	Mortality Rate	Annual Cost in Rubles
Orphanages (22)	1,824	272	564	988	31.0	91,261
Homes (7) and sections in other institutions (12) for illegitimate children	3,309	564	733	2,012	22.2	34,720
Schools for children of government employees (16)[b]	918	36	5	877	.5	92,650
Schools to train doctors' assistants (5)[c]	193	33	2	158	1.0	13,880
Classes of children of "free" parents supported by prikazy in institutions administered by other agencies	579	—	—	—	—	144,172
Homes (34) and special sections in other institutions (16) for the mentally ill	2,554	780	407	1,367	16.0	126,029
Hospitals (542)	211,200	177,747	17,749	15,704	8.4	2,173,138
Almshouses (123), homes for veterans (10), and workhouses for sturdy beggars (2)	10,277	—	1,025	9,252	10.0	409,580
Homes (35) and correctional sections in other institutions (3)	5,152	3,252	98	1,802	1.9	107,239
TOTALS	235,953[d]	—	—	—	—	3,192,669

[a] 146, pp. 257–72. The sum spent for noninstitutional relief is not shown separately because it amounted to only 1,986 rubles, and averaged 17 kopeks per day per recipient.

[b] These were mostly orphans whose fathers had given long and outstanding service. Those who finished the course of instruction, if outstanding scholars, were given an opportunity for further education; if average, they had to work in government offices for eight years.

[c] Mostly orphans of lower middle class parents (meshchiane) and other free classes.

[d] Of all inmates, 2,353 paid for their keep, or payments were made on their behalf by relatives.

tween 20 and 68 kopeks, while only about three kopeks were spent on illegitimate children. The primary interest in relation to orphans and illegitimate children was to keep them alive as cheaply as possible until they reached majority; no thought was given to educating them.

Prikazy activity declined steadily after 1852; they had failed to rally public support. By 1864 most institutions under their administration were thoroughly disorganized; their dilapidated physical plants and the unsavory and even cruel practices of many of their personnel had earned them a bad reputation. *Prikazy* jurisdiction was too general and their impact often indirect (when they acted merely as fiscal agents for private donors).

The creation of *zemstvos* (rural self-governing bodies) on district and provincial levels in 1864, and the organization of municipalities into local self-governing entities under elected Dumas in 1870, ushered in a new era in social welfare.[23] *Prikazy* were to be disbanded; their functions and resources were to be assumed by *zemstvo* agencies, including responsibility for all matters pertaining to welfare.[24] By 1917, *zemstvos* were operating in 43 of Russia's 101 provinces; in 14 provinces poor relief was handled much as it had been a hundred years earlier—by *prikazy* or directly by the central government. The remaining 44 provinces were apparently without organized public assistance programs.

Most of the money the *zemstvos* used for public assistance came from interest on capital turned over by the *prikazy* and from donations—the *zemstvos* being reluctant to assign any of their own revenues, derived from limited taxes on real estate and business enterprises, for such purposes. The meager sums allotted varied considerably. In 1901 district *zemstvo* allocations for poor relief ranged from nothing at all to less than 5 per cent of their budget; provincial *zemstvos* allocated an average of 2 per cent—a proportion that declined steadily from 1890 to 1914 and remained the smallest budget item throughout.[25] Almshouses were the largest single welfare expense; by 1912 they existed in all but three provincial *zemstvos,* but the situation was less satisfactory on the district level. Although these institutions were supposed to care for all without regard to social class, discrimination was widespread; even when admitted, those from lower classes received far shabbier treatment than the privileged. With time, almshouses became dumping grounds for anyone who could not be exiled or left to beg: children, nursing mothers, the old, and the crippled lived side by side with thieves, degenerates, and the diseased. In a few almshouses there were rehabilitation programs that consisted of sporadic attempts to provide work and conduct Bible readings; in most, even these feeble measures were lacking. The *zemstvos'* efforts to control begging met with little success.

Only 11 provincial *zemstvos* maintained orphanages in 1912; in the others the children were sent to almshouses, private orphanages, or foster homes. Infant mortality in these institutions was as high as 80.2 per cent in 1912. In rural areas facilities were so inadequate that orphans were more or less left to themselves. In most orphanages, diseased and mentally deficient children were kept with normal, healthy ones; adoption was infrequent. In 1912, only two *zemstvos* had special correctional institutions for children; in the rest, they were incarcerated in adult jails.

The nature and extent of *zemstvo* welfare activities in 1912 are indicated in Table 2. The figures in this table and those in Table 1 (describing *prikazy* activity in 1852) should be compared with caution, since the categories may be differently defined. It should be noted, however, that welfare expenditures (excluding the sums spent for hospitals and the mentally ill in 1852) increased almost fivefold over sixty years, the last forty-eight years being under the *zemstvos*. Since part of this gain probably occurred in comparable programs, it seems reasonable to assume that the *zemstvos* gave new impetus to community efforts to aid the needy and helpless. *Zemstvos* also spent considerable sums on services allied to public assistance; in 1900, for example, when 1.5 million rubles were spent on direct assistance, two million rubles were expended on related benefits, including scholarships for needy students and hospital care for indigents. *Zemstvo* expenditures seem especially generous

TABLE 2

EXPENDITURES ON PUBLIC ASSISTANCE BY 40 PROVINCIAL ZEMSTVOS, BY
TYPE OF AID, 1912

Type of Aid	Thousands of Rubles	Percentage of Total
Almshouses	926.1)	
Orphanages	1,666.0)	63.8%
Children's correctional institutions	122.7)	
Subsidies and dues to charitable organizations	666.4)	
Subsistence payments to charitable	)	
associations for support of	)	17.5
zemstvo inmates	78.3)	
Direct (noninstitutional) relief	488.4)	11.4
Aid to families of army personnel		
(lower ranks)	40.7)	
Other expenditures	268.9)	7.3
TOTALS	4,257.5	100.0

Source: *439*, p. 109.

when compared with spending in the 14 provinces under *prikazy* or state supervision.

Zemstvo accomplishments are less impressive, however, when examined in relation to the existing need. More than 1.5 million persons in *zemstvo* provinces were in abject poverty at the end of the nineteenth century. Each required at least 200 rubles a year for even modest care, which would have necessitated a total expenditure of 300 million rubles, rather than the roughly nine million actually spent on poor relief and related activities. Some *zemstvos* simply ignored the poverty stricken, either because of pressure from the numerically dominant upper class representatives on their administrative boards, or because members could not agree on policy. Some believed that measures aimed at preventing poverty should have priority—a position that, however laudable, failed to consider that this would have required radical modification of the entire social order, which few of them would countenance. Still others felt that allocating resources to meet a hopeless situation was pointless. This halfhearted attention to poor relief explains the decline in expenditures near the end of the nineteenth century, despite an increase in need.

Municipalities accomplished relatively less than the *zemstvos* in the field of public assistance; their lack of resources was more acute, while their responsibilities were more extensive—including police and correctional work. In 1900, 755 cities spent only three million rubles on poor relief; 54 per cent of this amount was expended by just 38 of these cities, mostly industrial centers and provincial capitals. Seventy-three per cent of the cities spent either nothing or less than 1,000 rubles on their poor in that year. The major part of municipal funds supported institutions that housed the old, the infirm, the handicapped, the disabled, and the incurably ill. Most institutions for adults restricted admission to those from the social class that donated funds for their maintenance. Only sporadic handouts were available for vagrants and beggars, most of whom were subject to harsh treatment at the hands of the police—furthering the widespread belief that welfare was somehow connected with cruelty and repression. Administration under *zemstvo* and municipal auspices reinforced the principle of local participation in welfare matters introduced by Catherine. At the same time, the inadequacies of this participation were always apparent.*

Table 3 summarizes the available statistics concerning Russia's philanthropic institutions in 1899. Although 91 per cent served adults, the 9 per cent designated for children served larger numbers—probably because most of these children lived outside the institutions. Poverty was

---

* This fact probably contributes to the suspicion with which some sectors of the Soviet government still regard local autonomy, initiative, and innovative ideas.

TABLE 3

RUSSIAN PHILANTHROPIC INSTITUTIONS IN 1899, BY LOCATION, TYPE,
AUSPICES, RECIPIENTS UNDER CARE, AND CAPITAL

Institutional Category	Number	Per Cent
Location by Regions of Empire		
European Russia	10,934	73.60%
Baltic provinces	1,359	9.15
Poland	914	6.15
Caucasus	274	1.84
Finland	849	5.72
Siberia	383	2.58
Central Asia	141	.95
TOTALS	14,854	100.00
Location by Type of Community		
Principal cities and provincial capitals	5,720	35.50
District cities and communes	9,584	64.50
TOTALS	15,304	100.00
Type		
Children's institutions (880,000 children under care)[a]		
Education	933	6.28
Medical	48	.32
Welfare	358	2.41
TOTALS	1,339	9.01
Institutions for adults (670,000 adults under care)[a]	13,515	90.99
TOTALS	14,854	100.00
Auspices		
Public (assisting 800,000)	10,054	67.69
Private (assisting 750,000)	4,800	32.31
TOTALS	14,854	100.00
Capital (in millions of rubles)		
Private (controlled by voluntary organizations)	22	5.43
Public (controlled by the state)	383	94.57
TOTALS	405	100.00

Source: 98, Vol. 6, "Blagotvoritel'nost' " (Charity), p. 19.
[a] Numbers under care are my estimates.

interpreted differently for different social classes; it is likely that almost
70 per cent of these institutions cared for people from the upper classes
who had fallen on hard times. In 1898 welfare institutions spent 48.6
million rubles; by 1910 expenditures had risen to 50.5 million, of which

only a quarter came from *zemstvo,* municipal, and "social class" taxes. Thus, while less than a third of the institutions operated under voluntary auspices, private donations financed about three-quarters of the entire welfare effort, and assisted almost half of the recipients.

Mutual Aid and Social Insurance

Although mutual aid was practiced on a small scale by artels in the eighteenth century, mutual aid societies did not appear until the nineteenth; by 1900 there were approximately 300 such organizations. The original purpose of the workers who joined was to secure themselves and their families against the consequences of illness, disability, unemployment, and death. Gradually, however, the societies began to consider matters and engage in activities beyond the scope of their original intent, such as establishing schools and libraries, pressing for a shorter working day, regulating relations with management, petitioning the government concerning working conditions, and setting up strike funds.[26] The transformation of mutual aid societies into trade unions—often repressed by the police—was advanced by the spread of the mutual aid movement among the proletariat of the expanding industries (especially among the metallurgical, textile, and typographical workers); the government did not legalize labor unions on a large scale until after the 1905 Revolution. From 1906 to 1907 unions spent slightly more than one ruble per member for mutual aid—clearly too little to reach more than a few of those in need.[27]

The earliest proposal for social insurance had been made in 1833 by Bunge, the Finance Minister, but although the industrial working class numbered approximately one million by 1881, a law on the subject did not become operative until 1893. This first law provided some protection against work-connected illnesses, injuries, and death for workers in mining, the railroads, and the Navy Department. It created "brotherhoods" (*tovarishchestvos*) whose revenue was derived largely from an equal tax on employers and workers. The administrative organs were composed of representatives from employers, labor, and the state. Both pensions and temporary benefits were exceedingly low, and administration was complicated by many difficulties. By 1910 the brotherhoods had only 22,000 members.[28]

Widespread strikes in 1902 prompted passage of an accident and death compensation law in 1903 that covered more workers and, subsequently, all government employees.[29] Its main contribution was that it placed responsibility on the employer for accidents occurring during working hours. It did not, however, introduce compulsory insurance, and it was weak from many other points of view: employers frequently could not or would not pay claims, benefits were denied on grounds of negligence by the workers, and administration was entirely in the hands of employers and officials.

As for financial assistance during illness not connected with work, no compulsory provision existed until 1912. However, there were four kinds of voluntary arrangements: funds into which contributions were made by both employers and workers, commercial insurance purchased by employers, collective agreements that included sickness benefits at the expense of the employer, and funds accumulated from fines on workers.[30] Great variations in voluntary coverage existed between provinces, with the highest percentage of participation in those where collective agreements were made following the 1905-6 strikes. Medical care, in contrast to sickness benefits, was regulated by the 1866 law that required manufacturers to set up factory hospitals. Both the law and its administration received much deserved criticism; forty years after its passage, no medical care was available for workers in 62 per cent of the factories covered, and less than 8 per cent had hospitals. The quality of care was extremely low in most of these facilities.

Under the pressure of the 1905 Revolution, the government moved forward with reforms initiated in earlier years, but as reaction set in, progress was slowed.[31] It was not until 1908 that specific proposals were presented to the Duma; they finally became the Health and Accident Act of June 23, 1912.[32] This law covered workers in manufacturing, mining, and foundries, and on vessels on inland waters, streetcars, and auxiliary railroads. Severe exclusions, however, limited its application to only 23 per cent of the 13 million in the work force. Benefits were available for work-connected accidents, illness, maternity, and death; coverage for accidents was financed by employers, while the remaining contingencies were covered by contributions by both employers and workers.

Benefits for work-connected accidents were handled at the lowest level by the brotherhoods, controlled entirely by employers. The next higher echelon was a provincial authority (*prisutstvie*) composed of worker, employer, and government representatives, which supervised the operation of individual societies and carried out overall policy. The highest organ was the Central Social Insurance Council, also made up of worker, employer, and government representatives, which determined policy and conducted hearings on appeal from the *prisutstvie*. Further appeals could be taken to a court—the final arbiter. For sickness, maternity, and death benefits, the administrative machinery was the sickness fund (*kassa*) maintained by both workers and employers. There was no single central-government agency to operate the whole insurance scheme: the lawmakers felt that such an agency would be unable to adapt itself to the variety of local conditions in industrial establishments, and would make active worker participation impossible.

On the whole, the new law was extremely unpopular among the masses of workers: it fell short of their expectations in coverage and in the amount and duration of sick benefits.* Worker contributions made up three-fifths of the sickness funds—a step backward for those groups whose benefits had been financed by employers prior to 1912.[33] The primary value of the 1912 law was that through the funds it recognized the right of workers to participate in organizing programs concerning their welfare. This was a victory over those experts, employers, and officials who had maintained that the intellectual level of the Russian worker was too low to permit such participation. By January 1916, 2,250 sickness funds covering almost 1.8 million workers were paying benefits; another 650 funds, to serve 394,000 workers, were being organized.[34]

Laws of 1912 and 1914 extended existing provisions for disabled veterans and introduced a system for helping survivors of both conscripts and volunteers. Pension amounts depended to some extent on the degree and cause of disability and length of service, but the major factor was rank: officers received up to 6,000 rubles per year, noncommissioned officers up to 216 rubles; dependents received proportional amounts. In contrast, disabled and needy enlisted men received 36 rubles per year; their survivors, nothing.[35] Three voluntary Committees were interested in the military: the Aleksandrov, the Alekseev, and the Romanov. Supported by private individuals and government subsidies, they paid pensions, usually to officers and higher ranks, and assisted their orphans. In addition, the ministries of War and Agriculture were supposed to help veterans and their families. They were also to provide vocational rehabilitation, but actually only a few courses in clerical work were made available.[36]

In 1917 the sorely pressed Provisional Government gave little attention to social welfare. It passed a new labor law limiting night work for women and adolescents, but it was seriously curtailed by the proviso that it could be disregarded if it prejudiced execution of the war.[37] Three laws concerning social insurance were enacted that extended and improved coverage and broadened worker participation in provincial in-

---

* Dansky states that in 1912 the sum spent for sickness benefits and medical care for factory workers amounted to about 40 million rubles annually. By comparison, in Germany, the equivalent of 225 million rubles was spent annually for these purposes. These expenditures represented 3.50 rubles per person in the population in Germany, but only 36 kopeks in Russia—about one-tenth of the German expenditure (76, pp. 29–36).

surance administrations, but employers continued to wield important influence as members of control commissions.[38] The Bolsheviks, as might
be expected, found these new provisions wanting on every count.[39]

On the Eve of the Revolution

In progressing slowly from church-inspired charity to public responsibility for welfare, and in permitting privately supported charity as an
expression of community concern, Russia resembled other European
countries—but was far behind them. Catherine's *prikazy,* created in 1775,
typified the ambivalence with which the government accepted responsibility for welfare institutions—a responsibility clearly enunciated in England, for example, by the Act of 1536.

The unfortunate state of the welfare system was symptomatic of conditions on the larger social scene. Russia was relatively isolated from
Western Europe until the eighteenth century. By then the middle classes
were about to enter the European political scene (the French Revolution was in the making), but Russia was still a vast feudal domain. This
backwardness persisted into the nineteenth and early twentieth centuries. Germany passed its first obligatory law on social insurance against
illness in 1883; Russia's did not appear until 1912. The last tsarist statute
to deal with illegitimate children (June 3, 1902) improved their lot
somewhat, but its regulations on paternal responsibility, the children's
right to inherit, and their legal status placed them in a more unfavorable
economic and social position than did the laws in effect in Italy, France,
or Germany.

Frequently, efforts to prevent or treat social problems were defeated
by interests benefiting from them. Other efforts failed because of the
overwhelming pressure of oppressive social conditions, ignorance, and
superstition. Efforts to combat illegitimacy, for example, failed because
unmarried mothers were usually peasant girls who had been forced by
poverty to come to the cities to work in factories or as domestic servants
—easy prey for their male employers or other servants.[40] Young men
and women in factories lived crowded together in dismal barracks, and
many youths, forced to postpone marriage because of compulsory military service, engaged in illicit liaisons. When nurseries were opened to
permit mothers to go to work-relief projects, there was considerable resistance: many superstitious peasant women asserted that the nurseries
were the work of antichrist, and that eventually the children would be
conscripted or sent to "islands beyond the sea" to teach the children
there to speak.[41]

Welfare work in the public sector was hampered by outmoded and
"fossilized" administration and by the failure of the law to specify

sources of funds, delimit the respective competencies of local and provincial authorities, or create any machinery for coordination, fair hearings, or public accountability. Public assistance was handled by a series of independent departments, bureaus, and offices, making long-term planning almost impossible. The central government, which contributed no regular funds for local welfare, evidently made policy and supervised its application in a formal manner that had little meaning for day-to-day administration. Local public authorities and individual private charities were left to their own discretion to decide whom to help, how, and how much.

Voluntary charitable organizations created a diversified network of institutions and served relatively large numbers, but even though they dominated the welfare field, they were disorganized, slow to recognize need, lacking in adequate resources, unresponsive to progressive thinking, and complacent about low standards and harmful practices. They, too, were behind the times. No attempt was made to coordinate privately supported charities until 1909 (and then the attempt was only halfhearted);[42] by comparison, British organizations, to avoid conflicts and gaps in services, had formed the London Charity Organization Society in 1869.

The possibility of a change in the concept of public responsibility itself—from "charity" given the "deserving" out of pity, to a contractual relationship in which society obligates itself to assist the needy individual if he meets eligibility requirements—was completely ignored in tsarist Russia. The notion that the individual might have a right to assistance simply was not seriously considered. Most help was provided in kind, usually as institutional care and sometimes as food, clothing, and medical care for the poor in their own homes. Money was rarely given, although properly used it can be more conducive to self-respect and self-improvement than donations in kind. The persistent lack of adequate resources affected both public and voluntary welfare, as well as social insurance benefits; the resulting hardships, however, fell unevenly on different social groups, since funds were donated by class. Thus, an 1895 survey found that those few merchants who were poor enjoyed the highest level of aid; the petite bourgeoisie, more numerous and less wealthy than the merchants, received only a quarter as much; the still more numerous artisans, only an eighth. Peasants, 87.6 per cent of the population, received distressingly little public assistance, institutional or direct. In some provinces, poverty-stricken peasants were quartered among commune members for a week at a time. In others, the indigent were expected to beg because the village societies could give only meager help. Medical care was too expensive for most commune societies,[43] yet the peasants undoubtedly needed it more than other classes: the 1897 census, for example, revealed that the rate of blindness among peasants was 60 per cent higher than among nobles.

The gap between need and care affected about 6.5 million persons at the end of the tsarist era; assistance was so negligible and sporadic that it could not possibly prevent the ruin of a working class or peasant family faced with sickness, unemployment, or natural calamity. Welfare aid in Russia was never more than a palliative, and was rendered even more ineffective by the ravages of World War I. Although many of the welfare administrators were persons of high principle and genuine humanitarianism, the system as a whole was characterized by rigidity, apathy, condescension, and lack of professionalism. In many other countries, the twentieth century led to a heightened social awareness and to a desire to develop new approaches to the problems of caring for the poor, eliminating unemployment, and improving working conditions and wages; all this was "foreign to the Russian government."[44] It persisted in its belief that begging was bred by parasitism and laziness, and that poverty could best be eradicated by giving the police full power. It refused to recognize that poverty and despair are social phenomena, that individual want and helplessness are symptoms of a disease that is caused by and in turn infects the whole society.

Those who are really convinced that they have made progress in science would not demand freedom for the new views to continue side by side with the old, but the substitution of the new views for the old.

—Lenin

2

Soviet Psychosocial Theories, 1917–55

While all aspects of society are interdependent, and thus affect social welfare, certain of them exercise a more direct and profound influence on social welfare than others. One fundamental determinant is the society's view of man as a psychosocial being. Especially important are its theories concerning the way changes in behavior take place and the methods likely to produce desired change; its attitude concerning the character and function of the family, especially as this affects the treatment of children; and its policies with regard to income maintenance, particularly as these indicate the value attached by the society to the satisfaction of economic needs. It is in terms of these various factors that the following analysis will be presented.

The Soviet View of Man

The theoreticians of the Soviet regime claimed long before the Revolution that the transformation of society from capitalism to communism would involve creating what later writers called "a new Soviet man," who would be "capable not only of building communism, but of living in a communist society."[1] Communism, it was maintained, could not become a reality without a fundamental change in the consciousness of the people, in their views, their nature, and their customs.[2] Time served to strengthen this conviction. In 1917, however, the Soviet theoreticians had not yet fully developed their own concept of man as a psychosocial being. Rather, at that time Russian psychology was still essentially consistent with European psychology, although a number of pre-Revolutionary thinkers—Lomonosov, Radishchev, Herzen, Belinsky, Dobrolyubov, Chernyshevsky, and, most important, Sechenov—had developed a materialist, "natural science" psychology. As for Russian psychiatry, in contrast to developments in Europe in the nineteenth century, it took a strictly materialistic turn, and was established on a purely somatic and neurological basis, with little attention being paid to neuroses.[3]

Since 1917, according to Soviet scholars, psychology in the Soviet Union has passed through three distinct stages. The first was from 1917 to 1936, at which time "bourgeois" psychological theories, with their "erroneous" notions about the nature of consciousness, heredity, and environment, were found to be inconsistent with the doctrines of the new Soviet state; the second was from 1936 to 1948, when Soviet scientists revived the earlier "natural science psychology," recasting it within the mold of dialectical materialism; and the third was from 1948 to 1965, when Lysenko's theories of the inheritance of acquired characteristics enjoyed official support.

After the Revolution, Soviet psychologists struggled to adapt the various developments in Western psychological thought to the theories of Marx and Engels, while at the same time attempting to cope with the psychological problems created by a society in transition toward socialism.[4] They stressed the unity between the interests of society and the interests of the individual under socialism, and emphasized the potential of human nature for change. Since this nature manifested itself in different ways in different situations, it was argued that the way to change it was "not by direct attempts to modify individuals, but by altering the social order so that the desired traits ... may manifest themselves." This view that change was primarily determined by environmental factors was related to two central points of Marxist doctrine: the dialectical principle of continual change and the historical-materialist principle of the social nature of man. Man was regarded as a "meeting place in which biological and sociological factors work out their interrelationship." It was held that both desirable and undesirable behavior were socially determined, and that since the new regime was breaking up the old order to make way for the new, "Soviet" way of life, undesirable behavior would eventually vanish, its disappearance facilitated by the fact that man's motives are innately good.

But in 1930 dissatisfaction with these explanations began to gain momentum. As the "Soviet" way failed to make men behave in the desired fashion, it became necessary to hold individuals rather than the system responsible—to abandon the view of man as a passive "shell of his psychological self," and see him instead as conscious, independent, disciplined, in control of and responsible for his behavior, and able to change his environment through creativity. This change in philosophy was closely related to a drive to increase family stability, as well as to a policy of holding recidivists responsible for their antisocial acts. It was also related to a growing resentment against pedologists, who were accused of regarding school failure as a function of biological and social factors external to the school about which little could be done—of underestimating the value of active efforts to mold the child and overestimating the environment as a determinant of personality. The pessimism and fatalism that often resulted were condemned as reactionary.

A 1936 resolution of the Party castigated the pedologists for labeling an excessive number of children defective when, in fact, they were only educationally neglected or undisciplined. The resolution abolished the profession of pedology and initiated a basic change in earlier theories concerning mental retardation.[5] The subsequent refinements in theory, based on research and experimentation, are well summarized in the following statement, which deals with the question of how the presence of mental retardation is to be ascertained:

> [The question can be answered only by a] complex clinical-psychological and pedagogical study. Such a study must include a neurological and psychopathological analysis of the child that will yield a general picture of the genesis of the peculiarities of development that are being observed and a determination of their nature; into it must also enter a physiological study, particularly a study of the electric activity of the brain and of higher nervous activity; and finally, an important place in it must be occupied by a psychological-pedagogical study that makes possible an evaluation of the child's mental activity.[6]

This approach led to the conviction that in working with retarded children it was necessary to base treatment on their "tons of health" rather than on their "ounces of disease."*

Western psychology in general was condemned; only the Leninist theory of reflexology, it was claimed, could furnish the philosophic base needed for the fruitful development of psychological theory and prac-

---

* A systematic study of abnormal children was begun toward the end of the 1920's by L. S. Vygotsky in the Experimental-Defectological Institute that in 1943 became the Institute of Defectology of the RSFSR. In studying the abnormal child, Vygotsky insisted, a clear distinction must be made between his "primary" inadequacies, which are the results of organic defects, and the "secondary and tertiary" departures from normality that are often determined by social factors. Vygotsky and his co-workers showed that these "secondary and tertiary" characteristics can be made amenable to treatment. He believed that the leading role in this process should be played by education, and stressed the need to study the abnormal child in an educational setting (*380*, pp. 13–15).

tice.[7] The teachings of Pavlov, which stressed the physiological and rational in mental phenomena and thus were consistent with Marxist materialism and the concept of man's responsibility for his behavior, became more and more influential.* Freud, who up to 1930 had been praised because he assigned primacy to experience rather than to inherited factors, was violently rejected because, it was claimed, he was oriented toward the past, and put too much emphasis on purely psychological, irrational processes and too little on conscious processes and man's relationship to society. It was maintained that Soviet welfare personnel found psychoanalysis, with its "preoccupation with sex phenomena," futile in treatment. Lysenko, despite official support, exerted little real influence on Soviet psychology. Those psychologists who attempted to use his ideas found them to be of little or no value. By 1965 he had been totally rejected.

The psychological theories that emerged in 1936 were researched, refined, and strengthened during the next twenty years. As one authority puts it, Soviet psychology "studies the teachings of Marx and Engels and Lenin; it uses dialectical materialism as its foundation; it practices criticism and self-criticism; it fights against bourgeois survivals and for the proletariat; it is a true science and on its way toward fulfilling Makarenko's† motto: 'Man must be changed.' "[8] By 1955 the Soviets had created a distinct, "Soviet" system of psychology. This psychology is relatively unempirical and thoroughly "applied." It is based on materialism, defined as "all the theories which start from the assumption that the psychic factor has no independent existence, but is only a property of matter."[9] Psychic development is the development of the brain. Consciousness, the highest form of psychic life, emerges as a result of the interaction of the brain with an objective reality. Psychological processes have their own unique properties and laws, which cannot be reduced to the laws of neural activity. Man is not dominated by instincts or the subconscious, but rather by his reason, which reflects the world clearly and correctly. The "unconscious" is not denied, but is assigned a subordinate position in the explanation of human behavior.[10] When, as a consequence of illness or of conditions such as neuroses, a human being's relationships acquire a nonharmonious character, they nevertheless re-

---

* Zilboorg points out that "the work of Pavlov was purely physiological, and for a long time Pavlov failed to deal with the possible psychological implications of his experiments. He never actually worked on human beings, and he never subjected the variety of emotional subjective states of human beings to experimental evaluation" (509, p. 727).

† Makarenko (1888–1939) was a teacher who attained prominence in work with homeless and delinquent children in the 1930's. In the opinion of Soviet psychologists, he was the supreme master in designing programs of education and upbringing appropriate to a socialist society.

main conscious; hence, a change in attitude that can lead to recovery can be developed at the conscious level.[11]

Social relations are the most important among the factors that influence man. These relations are determined by the material conditions of a society—its geography and climate, its population, and, above all, its mode of producing food, clothing, shelter, and the other necessities of life. A child can feel secure within his environment only when he has established correct relationships with the people around him and when he has met the demands made upon him by society. Social needs, which are felt very early (and *not* biologically determined instincts), are the basis for his psychological development.* New needs emerge at each age level; they are directed toward the attainment of goals presented by society. The attainment of these goals secures for the child a positive social evaluation and a clearly defined place among the children and adults around him. "Communist society," writes Miasishchev, "is based on the principle 'From each according to his abilities, to each according to his needs.' For psychology, the most important aspect of this principle is that society not only demands according to abilities, but develops and nurtures abilities; in the same way, it not only satisfies needs, but forms and nurtures them."[12] Personality (*lichnost'*) is formed in a given system of social relationships; it is a result of interaction between nature and nurture, in which what comes from within and what flows in from without are inseparable.[13]

The principle according to which man develops is not simply adaptation, however. Nor is development primarily determined by inborn abilities: only certain anatomical and physiological characteristics can be inborn. Abilities develop in response to the requirements of specific activities; therefore, they are not a function of genetic endowment. They represent on an individual level the achievements of the socio-historical process—the experience of preceding generations of mankind.[14] Any advance in thought, any breaking free of the conditions of the present, is possible only on the basis of mastery of this prior experience.

Man is not a passive object of the influences of his surroundings, but is an active participant in creating the conditions of his life. This is in line with the teachings of Marx and Engels, as one commentator makes clear:

> While "men are products of circumstances and upbringing and ... therefore changed men are products of other circumstances and changed upbringing," it must never be forgotten that "circumstances are changed pre-

---

* Marx had insisted that personality is the result of a complex of social relations rather than the product of instincts and drives.

cisely by men and that the educator himself must be educated." ... It is
basic to the whole Marxian concept of society that man changes history
and is thereby himself changed, and that, in this sense, all history is really
nothing but a continual transformation of human nature.[15]

It follows that the present or former conditions of life do not irrevocably
determine psychic development. Man is "free" to influence this development. (Freedom according to the Marxist view consists of achieving scientific comprehension of the causes of natural and historical movement,
and of cooperating consciously with the operation of these causes—in
short, freedom resides in the control over ourselves and over external
nature that is founded on the knowledge of natural necessity.)[16]

From the social welfare point of view, this concept of man encourages
optimism.* If human nature is malleable, and if psychic stress is caused
by stresses in the environment, such stress can be lessened or eliminated
by changes in the environment. Since the conscious rather than the "unconscious" dominates the development of the psyche, the major techniques for molding and changing personality must be rational—persuad-
ing, sharpening awareness, strengthening reasoning powers—with the
ultimate aim being the subjecting of all behavior to the control of reason. Since consciousness and personality are formed and expressed in
activities, therapeutic programs are concerned primarily with the proper
organization of the individual's life and activities.[17] The welfare worker
must take a firm hand in determining the individual's decisions and in
changing or manipulating the environment, if this is called for, in order
to bring about his greater involvement in purposeful activities. The establishment of more harmonious relationships among people, the objective of social welfare programs in a socialist society, is facilitated by the
nature of such a society: all persons are members of one or more well-
organized groups during all periods of their lives.

It follows that in the great majority of social welfare situations, the
relationship between the welfare worker and the individual receiving
help is not carefully assessed. It is assumed that a constructive relationship will result almost automatically if the worker demonstrates genuine
interest, respect, sympathy, and kindness toward the individual being
helped—in short, if he practices "socialist humanism." Hence, in dealing with their clients, welfare personnel adopt a rational commonsense
attitude concerned primarily with rationally learned behavior. They do

* In 1919 social welfare responsibilities were defined as "the support of persons who had
lost their ability to work during military service, as well as the victims of counter-revolu-
tion, fires, floods, famine, epidemics, war, and abnormal social relationships bred by the
capitalist system—homelessness, begging, prostitution, physical and moral defects"—in
short, "returning to productive life everyone who has lost his way" (512, p. 22).

not probe into "deeper" causes, that is, into the emotional quality of interpersonal relationships. Even those Soviet welfare personnel who insist that "education and rearing will be more successful the deeper the teacher gets into the psychic life of the ... child, [and] the better he understands what the child is living through and the motives behind his behavior,"[18] are talking about a more skillful analysis of conscious, rational behavior, rather than of the emotional factors underlying this behavior.

The more sophisticated methods of using and assessing relationships are reserved for psychotherapy. According to Miasishchev, the two basic forms of psychotherapeutic influence are suggestion and persuasion, and the decisive element in each is the patient's attitude toward his physician. A patient develops feelings of respect, trust, and affection toward the physician only gradually, insofar as the physician enables him to comprehend, in an undistorted perspective, the complex, obscure, and confusing circumstances of his life, both past and present.[19] Lebedinsky points out that it is quite important "that the patient become thoroughly convinced of the physician's willingness to listen attentively, to appreciate his plight, and to do everything possible for him."[20] The physician then uses the relationship to "do all he can to persuade the patient to adopt a proper attitude toward his illness, to reassure him, and to mobilize the healthy elements of his mind for the struggle against the disease."[21]

Thus, Soviet psychotherapy relies heavily on suggestion, persuasion, and reeducation. It employs ego-strengthening measures, mobilizes those elements of the personality that are unimpaired, and diverts energy into constructive channels that lead to more purposeful social activity. This explains why in Soviet social welfare practice many problems that in the United States are thought to require psychiatric treatment are approached via pedagogy, training, and/or modification of the environment. However, the rigid early Soviet views about psychiatric treatment have been modified by subsequent research. For example, experiments have revealed that the same activity can develop different qualities of character, depending on the motives underlying the activity. Desirable qualities develop only when activities are based upon socially useful motives—a tacit admission that something intervenes between the stimulus from the environment and the person's reflex response.[22]

Since 1958, research in the psychology of education and the psychology of upbringing, separate until then, has been synthesized "in order to ... help overcome the separation that exists between the study of personality and the study of psychic processes...."[23] This synthesis was apparently prompted by the growing recognition that scholastic achievement is impeded by "incorrect" upbringing, and that there must be an effort on the part of the teacher to shape the personality so that the student will develop the proper attitude toward study—as well as toward "life."[24] The former exclusive centering of attention on education (*obuchenie*) and neglect of upbringing (*vospitanie*) was found to be a mistake: a child is a human being, not merely a learning entity.*

These developments have led to the realization that the teacher is a major influence on the child, not only as an imparter of knowledge but also as an example. Nevertheless, there has been no discussion of the need for self-awareness on the teacher's part that would appear to be required by these findings. Nor has there been any less stress on the methods, derived from Pavlov's teachings, of "reinforcing" habit formation. In the case of children, these "reinforcements" may include "the evaluation of the child's activity by adults, by his peers, his own satisfaction from his work, joy at overcoming a difficulty, awareness of unfolding abilities, [or] pleasure from injecting something new, something of his very own into his work."[25] In the case of adolescents, since it is felt that both the protest against social norms and the conflicts with others that characterize their behavior are the result of an incorrect upbringing,[26] the same "reinforcements" are used.

Welfare procedures are thought to be facilitated by the "social" nature of consciousness in all people who have normal brains. A "Soviet" man is supposed to be characterized by the subordination of his own interests to those of society, as well as by the presence of lofty motivation, many-sided interests, and unshakable ideals—side by side with a capacity for purposeful action that will lead to the creation of a communist society, and a sense of discipline that rises above "bourgeois" individualism and sentimentality. This means an ever-increasing subordination of personal goals to social ones. The unity of personal and social goals gives the concept of personal happiness a social dimension; only behavior that serves society permits the full expression of personal interests, the full satisfaction of material and cultural needs, and the highest development of physical and spiritual potential.[27]

Even though communist ethics do not require forsaking one's personal interests, but rather suggest combining them with the common interests, the ideal man remains one who devotes his energies, in collaboration with others, to the cause of building communism. There is a pronounced

---

* It is much easier, Soviet educators have found, to set up a first-rate system of education than a good system of upbringing. This is so not only because they have had many decades of experience with the former, but also because education is more "concrete" than upbringing.

tendency to play down or eliminate individual differences rather than to emphasize them.[28] As Cantril puts it, "The emphasis is on the restraint, the harnessing, and the directing of human feelings rather than on the desire of the individual to express himself, to have creative experience, and to make choices."[29] A huge institutional machinery—adult education, the schools, the youth organizations, the trade unions, supported by the entire galaxy of the mass media—is used to generate social pressure toward conformity. If this is not successful, fear, shame, and material self-interest are brought into play.

Deviations in the development of personality, it is believed, are caused by the internalization of what is a distorted relationship between society and the individual. An individual either does not have a proper understanding of the ideals underlying the demands made by society, or he lacks the ability to relate his own intentions, desires, and acts to the common purpose. In a socialist society, it is maintained, there is an uninterrupted rise in the standard of living and a complete elimination of poverty and exploitation; in such a society the basic causes for deviant behavior are absent. Deviant behavior occurs only because the influence of the dying order has not yet been fully extirpated from the consciousness of all persons. This long and complex process is slowed by ideas continuing to penetrate the socialist society from the capitalist world.[30]

In formulating a view of man, at first there was a strong tendency in the Soviet Union to underestimate the difficulties of social control. It was more or less assumed that once a socialist society came into being, the prevailing social conditions would eliminate problems of human behavior. When this did not happen, the regime thought it best to intervene not only in directing such activities as industrialization and collectivization, but also in the shaping of "Soviet man": making sure that his motives, consciousness, and behavior were appropriate to the new socialist society. This entailed developing methods that would prevent or change undesirable behavior. In this matter, that is, in applying psychological concepts to actual situations, the outstanding figure was Makarenko. His principal ideas—elaborated, refined, and adapted by numerous researchers and practitioners—are basic to present-day Soviet social welfare theory.

Three particularly effective methods, to be discussed in subsequent chapters, have been derived from this theory. They are (1) an integrated casework-group work method that addresses itself simultaneously to the collective (*kollektiv*) and the individual, (2) community participation (*obshchestvennost'*), defined as the effort of every individual on behalf of the total community, and (3) work therapy (*trud*).* As already noted, psychotherapy, which is in many respects similar to social casework as practiced by trained social workers in the United States, has been reserved for medical personnel and for those working under their direction. It was reestablished as an ideologically and scientifically acceptable form of treatment in 1950 when it was pointed out that since psychotherapy uses words, it is consistent with Pavlov's theory of the second signal system in man, in which verbal stimuli serve as a substitute for physical stimuli in the conditioned-reflex arc.[31] Psychoanalysis based on Freudian concepts was ruled out as inimical to welfare objectives, however.

* The findings of American scholars seem to indicate that to a large extent the same three methods are used with mental patients (*105*, p. 292; *107*, p. 89).

3

The Family and Child Welfare, 1917–55

The Soviet regime's position concerning the character and function of the family was clearly worked out prior to its assumption of power. However, there were eventually several violent changes in this position—all the way from efforts to hasten the "withering away" of the "bourgeois" family (until the mid-1930's) to attempts to *strengthen* the family's social role. At the close of the period under discussion, there was still a pronounced ambivalence in the government's attitude toward the family, resulting primarily from its concern with the falling birthrate (from 31.3 in 1940 to 25.3 in 1958) and its dissatisfaction with the way the younger generation was being reared. This essentially negative attitude was unjustified, many parents felt, and failed to assess realistically economic and social factors that hindered the family from carrying out its socializing function.

Early Legislation, 1917–25

Careful analysis supports the view that responsible Soviet policy-makers never planned to abolish marriage and the family as such. Rather, their attack immediately after the Revolution was directed against the formal institution of marriage and against the family as an economic and legal unit as these were to be found in the traditional father-dominated Russian family, which was "founded on the open and unconcealed domestic slavery of the wife" (Engels) and "a formidable stronghold of all the turpitudes of the old regime" (Bukharin). Breaking up the old family would clear the way for the new "Soviet" family, a primary group bound solely by the free will of its members.[1] The first steps taken were the secularization of marriage, the liberalization of divorce, and the emancipation of women and children.

Following the Marxist precept that there is a direct relation between the position of women in society and their status in the family, the emancipation of the fair sex proceeded at once on several fronts. Within weeks of the Revolution, Lenin signed a decree on the dissolution of marriage.[2] It provided that a marriage could be dissolved upon the appeal of either of the parties. No statement of grounds was required. Insisting on the equality of the sexes, subsequent legislation made both spouses responsible for the other's support if either should become needy because of disability or (added in 1926) inability to find work. Women's right to determine their own destiny was furthered by a 1920 law permitting abortion, provided it was performed in a state hospital by an approved physician. At the same time, laws were passed giving women employment rights equal to those of men, as well as allowing special privileges for pregnant women, nursing mothers, and mothers with many children.[3]

The new regime's hostility toward the old family, which it felt was incapable of providing the kind of upbringing appropriate for a socialist society, was especially marked in its precipitate campaign to emancipate children. The first Party conference on education stopped short of demanding that all children be raised in state institutions only because of the practical consideration that "the overwhelming majority of children would *for a time* [emphasis mine] remain divided between the school and the family."[4] In reaction to the failure of many adoptive homes to provide good care in tsarist times, the regime outlawed adoption. In explaining this action Goikhbarg said: "Our [state institutions of] guardianship ... must show parents that the social care of children gives far better results than the private, individual, inexpert, and irrational care by individual parents who are 'loving' but, in the matter of bringing up children, ignorant."[5] In 1918 a *Family Code* was enacted that enunciated the parental duty to care for and educate children, but failed to specify the responsibilities that this duty entailed or to invest parents with sufficient authority to meet such responsibilities. Parents were absolved from this duty if they were destitute and unable to work; in such cases the children were obligated to maintain their parents if the latter were not eligible for support from public funds.

Although the protection of the law was not extended to illicit relations, a radical change was made in the legal status of illegitimate children. The law of December 18, 1917, eliminated all distinctions between legitimate and illegitimate children and proclaimed that blood and not marriage determined responsibility for the care of children. Parents' duties to their children were the same whether the children were born in or out of wedlock. Simple procedures were established for determining the legal father. If the man named as the father by the mother did not contest her declaration, his silence was taken as acknowledgment of paternity. In contested cases the court could not demand proof from the mother: the man named by her was declared to be the father if the relation of the parties made her claim probable. The "father" could not free himself from responsibility by establishing that the mother had had sexual relations with several men at the time of conception. In such cases all the men involved were made responsible and had to contribute to the support of the child.[6]

The lot of delinquent children was also improved by the Soviet regime. In January 1918, commissions were created within the Ministry of Education to deal with offenders under sixteen years of age. Measures taken by these commissions were varied, depending on the circumstances of each case, and ranged from mere discussions with the children, and returning them to the care of parents, relatives, or "upbringers-investigators," to foster care (*patronat*) or guardianship, or placement in jobs, schools, or institutions. Whatever the measure, however, it had a "medico-pedagogical" character, punishment being ruled out. Despite this progressive approach, many commission members regarded delinquent youngsters as "morally defective"—clearly a carry-over from the tsarist era.[7] (Adolescents between sixteen and eighteen were under court jurisdiction. They could be placed on probation or sent to a children's home, but if recidivists, they were sent to a labor colony.)

Early statutes forbade the employment of children under fifteen, and allowed those between fifteen and eighteen to work only six daytime hours. By 1920, however, these laws were revised to hasten reconstruction of the country's ruined economy. The beginning age for employment was lowered to fourteen; children between fourteen and sixteen could work four daytime hours, while those sixteen to eighteen continued to be limited to six hours. The 1922 *Labor Code* retained these regulations, but added that persons under sixteen could be employed only in exceptional cases, with the permission of a labor inspector. Besides night work, it ruled out overtime and heavy, harmful, and underground work for those under eighteen, and required that they be paid for eight hours for working six. Implementation of these regulations proved difficult, however: production processes in the factories were such that many adult workers depended on their young assistants for the completion of tasks. Most important, many youngsters were orphans or supported families.

Hence, labor inspectors recognized many "exceptional" cases, even permitting some overtime work by adolescents and occasional employment of children under fourteen in agriculture and as assistants to rural craftsmen. Equally difficult to implement were the regulations governing pay practices.[8]

The violence of the Soviet regime's attack on the "bourgeois" family led many students, revolutionaries, and intellectuals in the urban centers to adopt an amoral attitude toward sexual behavior. During the chaotic days of war communism, illicit sexual liaisons and the breakup of unstable marriages combined to produce confusion, and in many instances had a profoundly destructive impact: the old family patterns were shattered, while the new, hoped-for patterns—with the coming together of men and women motivated only by love and mutual interest and with no need for state regulation—did not emerge. On the contrary, many abandoned the ideal of the monogamous family, believing that they were encouraged to do so by the Soviet leadership.

The new laws, while they improved the legal status of women and children, failed to provide adequate social and economic guarantees. Many women lost the benefits of "bourgeois" family life without acquiring either a new "Soviet" family or economic independence. The undermining of family stability only added to the precariousness of home life for the ever-increasing number of children who were already suffering from the miseries bred by World War I, the civil war, the famine of 1921–23, the collapse of the standard of living, the serious and persistent unemployment, the unwillingness of relatives to care for orphans when food and work were scarce, and the general social disorganization that characterized the country into the 1930's—a disorganization of such breadth and profundity as to be scarcely imaginable to Westerners.

In the child welfare field, administrative reorganization to implement the new laws was extensive. All private charitable societies were transformed into government agencies, the old asylums were reorganized into children's homes under the Ministry of Education, and most of the old personnel were replaced. A new type of agency, the "socio-legal bureau," was established in 1919 as a result of the realization that the prevention and treatment of disease are inextricably related to social conditions. The bureaus helped mothers with social and legal problems that prevented their full utilization of medical services.[9] By the end of 1923 socio-legal bureaus were considered a necessary part of any adequately staffed medical center.

The problems of the handicapped and the retarded were not neglected during this period. The first all-Russian conference on the physically and mentally defective was held in 1920 and was addressed by A. V. Lunacharsky, the famous Commissar of Education, as well as by Maxim Gorky. The conference recommended the taking of a census of abnormal children, the development of a network of special facilities, and compulsory education. Questions of defectology were also examined at general pedagogical conferences and at a 1924 meeting concerned with the sociolegal protection of minors. Unfortunately, lack of coordination, serious economic difficulties, and inexperienced and unqualified staff defeated efforts to plan, and lowered the quality of care in the homes for children both defective and "normal." Progress was made impossible by an avalanche of homeless and deserted children (*bezprizornye*), who became the most serious child welfare problem of the country immediately after the Revolution and for the next fifteen years. The homes were so crowded with these new arrivals that they had to operate on a chronic emergency basis.

The *bezprizornye* had numbered more than two million prior to 1917. Now to their ranks were added the children caught up in the process of rapid social change set in motion by the Revolution—the youngsters swept into the cities from rural areas, for whom work could not be found and schooling could not be arranged, whose "social assistance" was too meager to sustain life, who were fleeing from starvation, whose families had either disappeared or disintegrated, who did not know where to turn or what to do. The problem reached its peak in 1922–23, after the great famine, when Krupskaya (Lenin's wife) reported that there were seven million children on the homeless register.[10]

At first, responsibility for "eradicating" homelessness was divided among four power-hungry ministries—Justice, Social Welfare, Health, and Education—with the result that there were dozens of commissions, innumerable decrees and regulations, hundreds of meetings and projects, but no appreciable progress.[11] In 1921 the task was assigned to the Ministry of Education under the guidance of an interdepartmental Children's Commission whose first chairman was the famous revolutionary Felix Dzerzhinsky.* But the Ministry was continually handicapped by a paucity of resources. In spite of its strenuous efforts and substantial aid from foreign sources,† countless numbers of children died, and many others were left stunted, sickly, debilitated, or dull.[12] (Even among children living with their own families there was an alarming rise in

---

* During the struggle for power, two voluntary agencies and one semi-official agency— the League for Saving Children, Friend of Children, and the Council for the Defense of Children—were abolished, although they had done most of the constructive work (*45*, pp. 4–9; *102*, pp. 3–228; *461*, pp. 3–48; *459*, pp. 3–64).

† The American Relief Administration fed more than four million children; another group, supported by twelve governments and 48 Red Cross societies and headed by Fridtjof Nansen, gave sustenance to 250,000 youngsters.

physical and emotional illnesses in all parts of the country because of the "socio-biological peculiarities of that epoch.")[13]

During the period 1917–25 the principle was established that every adult has a duty to work and every child to study, on the one hand, and a right to care by the government when he is unable to work or to attend school, on the other. Charity, pity, and handouts were rejected.

Domestic Relations, 1926–34

Measures designed to destroy the "bourgeois" features of the old family were intensified during the New Economic Policy (NEP) period (1921–28), and continued into the early 1930's. On October 22, 1926, an RSFSR code on domestic relations was enacted. Followed in the main by all the other Soviet republics, it permitted divorce simply by application to the Department of Registering Acts of Civil Status (ZAGS), thereby eliminating the need for court procedures and introducing the era of the so-called "postcard" divorce, in which either spouse had complete freedom to secure a divorce without providing any reasons. However, the most radical departure of the new code was the granting of equal recognition to registered and unregistered marriages.

It is not possible to estimate with any degree of accuracy the number of children affected by divorce during this period because, among other things, reliable statistics on the number of divorces are not available. Fragmentary data, however, indicate an alarming rise in the divorce rate. In Moscow, for example, the number of divorces in 1927 was 450 per cent higher than in 1926; in Leningrad, 300 per cent higher.[14] While the divorce rates in Moscow and Leningrad were undoubtedly higher than in smaller cities and rural areas, they show clearly that the trend was upward, and that the number of children affected was rising.

That many children responded to the weakening of the family relationships, and the resultant lack of effective discipline, with antisocial behavior is abundantly clear. Of the children examined by juvenile delinquency commissions in Moscow in 1925, 34 per cent had been living with their families (as distinct from those who had been living in institutions or among the homeless children), but had not been properly supervised by their parents. By 1928 this percentage had risen to 72.5 per cent. In 1925, only 38 per cent had been living with both parents (as distinct from those who lived with only one parent or were full orphans), but in 1927, *half* had been living with both parents.[15] By 1929 the commissions had come to the conclusion that there were proportionately fewer homeless children and proportionately more unsupervised children (*beznadzornye*) becoming juvenile delinquents. Illegitimate children were a special problem. Experience had shown that it was disorienting to them to have several men designated as their fathers; in 1926 it was decreed that the court had to recognize one man as the father of each child. If the man wished to challenge the court's decision, he had a year to do so, but during the interval he had to provide support.

The insistence upon identifying both married and unmarried parents and obtaining support from them for their children stems partly from the fact that most of the 1918–26 legislation concerned with child welfare was essentially inoperative. It was not until the latter year that a program on behalf of homeless children was undertaken in earnest,[16] and a variety of resources mobilized to help them.[17] Previously, primary reliance had been placed on "homes" in which children under 12 received sustenance and elementary education, while those over 12 received occupational training.

If we accept Krupskaya's statement that the homeless register (which was not a complete count) listed seven million children in 1923, along with the government's maximum claims concerning the number offered care in the "homes," then it is clear that these institutions did not begin to meet the need. At their peak in 1922 they accommodated only 600,000 children. From then on the number of homes declined because of dwindling resources.[18] In addition, the homes lacked experienced and qualified personnel. The "upbringers" were a motley group, made up of the mean and kind, the wise and stupid, and those who worked only for the ration card and a place to stay. Paid hardly enough to sustain themselves, and sometimes going without pay for months, they were unable to handle the *bezprizornye,* many of whom knew more about life than their mentors. In response to their situation, some staff members became sadistic; others left. (One home had 62 different directors in two years.) Another difficulty was that the bright, normal, and healthy children were herded together with the psychopathic, the severely retarded, and the handicapped. Furthermore, almost none of the homes could satisfy even the most elementary needs of the children. The result was that while good upbringing was achieved in a few of the homes, in most failure was complete and cruel.[19]

This situation persisted into the 1930's. In 1931 Semashko, the Commissar of Health, characterized the homes as "completely unbearable."[20] Fortunately, several factors reduced the number of homeless children to manageable proportions by about 1932. These factors were compulsory seven-year education, growing availability of employment for those 15 years and older, improved welfare facilities, a rise in the standard of living, and a reestablishment of family authority that began to gain momentum at that time. The agonizing experience with the *bezpri-*

zornye did not go unanalyzed, however.[21] Many thoughtful and genuinely concerned people, especially Makarenko and Krupskaya, learned a great deal about the causes of homelessness and the kinds of children who become its victims. They also had the opportunity to test various methods of helping them.

The foster home program, which in 1921 had provided for nearly 100,000 children, was caring for less than 7,500 in 1927. This may be explained by the widespread *de facto* adoption of foster children—a phenomenon contributing to the legal reinstatement of adoption in 1926. Another form of protection for the homeless child—"dependency"—was created in 1928. This offered less protection than adoption, but more than guardianship, for the child taken as a dependent was guaranteed care and education so long as he was a minor or was unable to work, even if the person who took him wanted to end the relationship. The child labor regulations continued to be enforced, but this soon became unnecessary because of the extensive unemployment that set in soon after the Revolution and rose steadily until almost the end of the 1920's, destroying work opportunities, especially for the young.* Later, however, there was a growing demand for labor, generated by the first five-year plan, which was inaugurated in 1928; it finally wiped out almost all but frictional unemployment.

In the midst of these more widespread concerns, the handicapped and retarded children were not forgotten. For the former, this period was marked by the development of specialized schools and preparations for a program of universal compulsory education; for the latter, by a concerned effort to determine which among them were capable of benefiting from instruction in the regular schools and which would require special instruction.

Restoration of Family Stability, 1935-40

By the middle of the 1930's, it had become clear that the new attitudes toward sex and love had broken down the sense of family responsibility. As late as 1932 the primary concern of health and welfare personnel was abandoned infants. Institutions for these children were always overcrowded. The social unrest generated by forced industrialization and collectivization—"a situation of unparalleled disorganization"—left a large number of children homeless or unsupervised, and added to "the general inability of parents to maintain effective control over their children,"[22]

---

* The number of unemployed adolescents increased both absolutely and in proportion to the labor force during this period. By 1928, more than 16 per cent of the unemployed registered at labor exchanges were minors (*23*, p. 154).

as well as to material want and the collapse of moral standards. In 1937 there were some one million persons in the USSR under court order to pay maintenance costs for their offspring; 100,000 had evaded payment.* Several million children were without a home environment provided by two parents.

Tightening up all along the line was initiated in 1935. A law of April 7, 1935, made a child over the age of 12 (not, as earlier, over 16) liable under the regular provisions of the criminal code if he committed a serious crime. A law of May 31, 1935, introduced criminal penalties for neglectful parents and guardians: they were made responsible for the delinquent behavior of their children and held liable to fine. In addition, the Ministry of Education was required to advise social organizations, such as trade unions, at the parents' places of work of any absence of parental supervision over a child, and if parents did not mend their ways, to initiate proceedings for depriving them of custody. On April 1, 1936, a law on foster care was passed that was designed to induce persons with homes to open them to foster children on a paid, temporary basis. It required a study of the foster family and supervision after placement; the foster parent could be held criminally responsible if the child was left without supervision or support while in the foster parent's charge.

A new *All-Union Code of Family Law* (which replaced the separate laws of the several republics) of June 27, 1936, marked a turning point in the Soviet attitude toward the family. It inaugurated a campaign on the part of the authorities to stabilize family life by restoring its former legal and economic as well as spiritual bonds. In divorce proceedings both parties were now required to appear personally at ZAGS and have the fact of the divorce entered in their passports. Fees, formerly nominal, were raised, increasing sharply with each new divorce. Abortions were forbidden unless there was peril to the life or health of the mother or danger of transmission of serious sickness. *De facto* marriages were recognized as legal,[23] and support payments for children were fixed in relation to the income of the parent. A penalty of two years' imprisonment was imposed for nonpayment.

To assist parents in carrying out their responsibilities, the 1936 law made grants available to mothers of large families, irrespective of marital status, beginning with the seventh child. The network of socio-legal

---

* An article in *Izvestiia* of April 10, 1935, noted the insignificance of alimony payments: in 20 per cent of the cases they did not exceed 20 rubles per month. But even these small sums were not regularly paid: only 39.8 per cent of the fathers who were workers paid, and only 45.1 per cent of those who were employees. (Cited in *329*, p. 27. The 1937 data are from *135*, p. 428.)

bureaus was expanded, playground capacity was increased, and the number of nurseries and kindergartens rose significantly.[24] Nevertheless, these measures could only partially counteract the social disorganization of this period. Homeless children remained a problem until the outbreak of World War II, continuing to swell the ranks of juvenile delinquents, who became the primary child welfare problem in the late 1930's. Added to the homeless were the unsupervised—the children left to their own devices because both parents worked, there were no responsible relatives to look after them, and there was not enough room for them in schools, kindergartens, or playgrounds.

Receiving and distribution centers, isolation homes for difficult children, and labor colonies under NKVD, as well as "homes of a normal type" administered by educational authorities, were the core of the child welfare program in the 1930's.[25] In 1940, special "children's rooms" were added in each militia district station, where misbehaving and insolent children and delinquent adolescents were kept until sent home or to a detention facility.[26] After 1940 more attention was devoted to studying the characteristics and needs of delinquents with a view to separating the "hardcore" group from those who could benefit by education in schools with a "special regimen."[27] The physically handicapped and the mentally retarded were placed in institutions separate from "normal" children, and special curricula were organized for them, the number of specialized facilities was increased, and research into learning problems was initiated.

The changes in law brought about a realignment of functions and a new division of responsibility among the four ministries concerned with child welfare. The Ministry of Education was assigned the care of "normal" children who were totally dependent, as well as of those who had no homes of their own but received maintenance payments from their parents and of "defective" children who needed special education; the Ministry of Health was made responsible for children in need of long periods of medical care; the fifteen republic Ministries of Social Welfare were placed in charge of the permanent invalids and the severely retarded; and the Ministry of Internal Affairs was assigned the "hardened" delinquents.

Thus, by the outbreak of World War II, the Soviet Union had made distinct progress toward strengthening and diversifying its child welfare programs. Some help, primarily of an economic nature, was available to children in their own homes; guardianship, adoption, foster care, and institutional care were available to others—the latter continuing to be the major form of assistance both for orphans and for those whose families neglected them or could not provide for them adequately.

World War II and After, 1941–55

World War II interrupted the development of the child welfare services that was beginning to take place after the turmoil of the post-Revolutionary years. All resources were mobilized to cope with a new wave
of devastation and disorganization as the country plunged into an all-out
fight for survival. Children who had reached the age of 12 years were
needed to work in industry and agriculture; a fairly large number left
school to help in the war effort. The network of special schools was
sharply reduced, and socio-legal bureaus concerned themselves primarily
with assisting families of military personnel.

As a result of the destruction of families, homeless children appeared
in numbers not seen since the civil war of some 20 years earlier, and there
was a sharp rise in juvenile delinquency.[28] Emergency measures to cope
with the situation were taken; adoption, foster care, and the "taking
in" of dependent children were encouraged.* But once more the greatest
reliance had to be placed on institutional care: institutions replaced families not only for orphans, but also for children whose parents were at the
front, in the ranks of partisans, or working in relocated factories, as well
as for youngsters who had lost contact with their parents altogether.[29]
After the war, those children whose parents were alive and could be
found were returned to their families. For those who had to remain in
institutions, living conditions were poor for a long time.† Substitute
family care again played a relatively minor role, and the wartime experience with it was left largely unanalyzed.[30]

The war had other profoundly adverse effects on family life, especially
by creating an unbalanced sex ratio and by increasing what Soviet writers
called "moral aberrations." The 1959 census showed that there were 20.8
million more women than men in the population, this preponderance
existing primarily in the group over 32 years of age. During the war
many people entered into extramarital relationships; the result was that

---

* Adoption was extensive: during the years 1941–45, 200,000 children were adopted in
the RSFSR alone. Foster care, too, took on a mass character: in 1944 large numbers of
war orphans were transferred from institutions to foster families. The homes provided
under both these arrangements were often one-parent homes; that is, the parents were
women, single or widows, with or without their own children. Because of war conditions
and of the mass character of placements, study of foster care and adoptive homes became
a mere formality, and follow-up for the most part was lacking or only sporadic and superficial (*416*, p. 4; *410*, pp. 421–23).

† For example, a 1949 report on the children's homes in the Kazakhstan republic notes
that the average expenditure for care was less than seven rubles per year per child. The
report insisted that something had to be done about the terrible overcrowding and the
shortage of sinks, drinking glasses, and spoons, as well as that more personnel had to be
hired so that older children could study instead of taking care of the younger ones (*276*,
pp. 6–58).

in the hectic readjustment period that followed there was a high divorce rate and many illegitimate children. So anxious was the government to strengthen marriage bonds and produce strong family units that it issued a fourth *Code of Family Law* on July 8, 1944, that impaired considerably the position of the illegitimate child that had prevailed up to that time. It abolished the unmarried mother's right to appeal to the court for the purpose of establishing paternity and obtaining support. No longer could the father's surname be given to an illegitimate child: his birth certificate had a line drawn through the space for the name of the father. Instead, he was given the mother's surname. No longer could he inherit on equal terms with children of a registered marriage. Thus, while the concept of illegitimacy had not been officially reintroduced, the policy of equal treatment of legitimate and illegitimate children had been abandoned.*

The loss of support from the father was made up to some extent by monthly payments to unmarried mothers. These were paid from the birth of each child until he reached age 12. But the sums granted were smaller than the average sum earlier given as alimony, and alimony had been paid until the child reached majority. Subsequent experience revealed two serious weaknesses in the 1944 law: all unmarried mothers were treated the same, whether or not they were promiscuous, and "unregistered" children were deprived of the right to have a legal father even when the father was single. As a Soviet educator put it, the 1944 law was intended to restrain unscrupulous women, but its end result was to encourage unscrupulous men.

The 1944 code not only abolished the unregistered marriage, but also brought about a fundamental change in the approach to divorce: for the first time since the Revolution, the law established a judicial process for divorce and introduced procedures aimed at reconciling the parties.†️ The intent was clear: marriage was once more to be a lifelong union. Abortions remained outlawed until 1955, when they were legalized once

---

* Many of the scholars who are now critical of the 1944 law defended it when it was passed. For example, in October 1947 Sverdlov wrote: "By liberating the unmarried mother from the often difficult situation in which she found herself in connection with the establishment of paternity and the recovery of alimony, and extending assistance to her for the rearing of her child, the state has at the same time created a more normal situation for the child, by no longer placing the latter in dependence upon the possibly accidental outcome of a paternity case" (*415*, p. 501).

† The government's anxiety to strengthen the family was undoubtedly motivated by its desire to avoid a repetition of the disorders of the 1920's and 1930's. The leaders realized that the revolution in personal values and the development of child care resources essential for implementing Marxist ideas on marriage and the family simply had not taken place. They reminded the proponents of free love that Lenin had branded the "glass of water" theory—the notion that in a communist society the satisfaction of sexual desires should be as simple and unimportant as drinking a glass of water—as "un-Marxist" and "antisocial" (*507*, pp. 56-60, 68-70).

more, provided they were performed in hospitals by qualified physicians.[31]

Government policy emphasized that the rearing of children is a sacred parental duty. Under socialism, more than in any other type of society, it said, the support and upbringing of children become a way of serving one's country, of carrying out one's duty to the people. To assist the parents in fulfilling their duty, family allowances, which had been introduced on a limited scale in 1936, were considerably extended in 1944, with some financial help becoming available upon the birth of the third child.[32] The number of nurseries, kindergartens, summer playgrounds, and camps was increased. Child labor laws, inoperative during the war, were revived and later strengthened.*

These aids to parents underscored the government's expectation that they would carry out their child-rearing duties as *partners* of the state, inculcating those qualities and traits that should underlie the behavior of every citizen of the Soviet Union. No longer was there to be a division of labor, with the family making a man out of the child, and the school an educated citizen ready to struggle for communist ideals. In this partnership the state not only provided educational, welfare, health, and recreational facilities for children, but also assisted parents with advice from trained personnel. A journal whose major purpose was to "help parents in every possible way in the task of rearing and educating children and youth"—*Sem'ia i Shkola* (*The Family and the School*)—began publication in January 1946, under the aegis of the RSFSR Academy of Pedagogical Sciences.

That it was not easy for the parties to the partnership to fulfill their responsibilities in the postwar years is clear from many sources.[33] But the difficulties involved were viewed differently by the two parties. From the point of view of the family, the difficulties were due primarily to social and economic conditions over which the families had no control, as well as to inadequacies in the aids that were available. The state, on the other hand, while it admitted these inadequacies, blamed parents for "errors" in child rearing that stemmed from "incorrect" attitudes, rather than from living conditions. It maintained that many parents were not providing a family upbringing "saturated by the same high sense of purpose, ideological and political content, the same high moral standards that constitute the content of societal communist upbringing."[34] As a result, they were contributing greatly to the existence of juvenile delin-

---

* At present, adolescents who are 15 years old are permitted to work four hours a day, and those between 16 and 18, six hours a day. No overtime or night work is allowed. The older group is given a full month's vacation each year and special facilities for study.

quency, sexual promiscuity, and other social problems;* in general there was a lack of discipline, which was responsible for a variety of problems in learning and conduct.[35] As one commentator put it:

> When some, in surprise, ask why in our socialist society one still meets people infected with the poison of parasitism and greed, thieves and takers of bribes, flatterers and killers, [and] why among them there are quite a few young people who grew up under socialism and who have never even laid eyes on capitalism, to this one must answer directly and without excuses: because in our society there are still families and parents who exhibit an irresponsible attitude toward the business of child-rearing and thus to the future of their children, who manage even under socialism to endow their children with parasitic, bourgeois habits, as a rule not even realizing the tremendous harm they are inflicting both on society and on themselves.[36]

Apparently, the changes relating to the family that had been introduced by the Soviet regime after 1917 did not fully achieve the desired results. At the beginning of its rule, the new regime considered the family a battleground in which bourgeois ideology would fight for its existence. After nearly forty years of struggle, a Soviet authority on the family commented: "The overwhelming majority of Soviet families are the embodiment of truly human relationships based on the lofty principles of socialist morality. At the same time it is exactly in the sphere of family relationships, family life, that the survivals of the past in the minds of the people are fairly strong."[37] It is not surprising, therefore, that by 1956 the partnership between the family and the state in raising the young became weighted in the direction of the latter: the leading role was transferred to the school, that is, to a small group of trainers who carried out faithfully the state program of instruction *and* upbringing. Reliance on parents remained conditional: if their "unremitting efforts" did not conform to the standards set by the Party and the school, they were to be rebuked and even rejected by society.

---

* In connection with one of these problems—sexual promiscuity—it was officially acknowledged in 1960 that in Soviet "pedagogical and psychological literature questions of [sex] are eschewed [so that] many parents... [are]completely helpless" (9, p. 423). A recent writer points out that "questions concerning the intimate life of the family only now are beginning to be illumined in our artistic literature. We simply do not have any special pedagogical literature devoted to this important theme" (*193*, p. 45).

4

Income Maintenance Policy and Programs, 1917–55

The position of the Soviet regime at its very beginning with regard to income maintenance faithfully reflected the program of the Russian Democratic Labor Party worked out during the period 1895–1912. The Soviets took a firm stand in favor of the "institutional" approach to social welfare, thereby rejecting the "residual" concept that was dominant before the Revolution. They did not think of welfare assistance as a sporadic activity to be brought into play only in cases of social breakdown, when the "normal" market economy and/or family solicitude proved inadequate. Rather, they regarded welfare as an ongoing, comprehensive social institution whose major function was to *prevent* social breakdown, but which made help available as a right to those who were qualified if a breakdown occurred.

Soviet theoreticians argued that the residual concept, which they associated with the detested means test and the humiliation of charity, was appropriate only for a capitalist society, which cares nothing about eliminating social risks that have disastrous consequences for the working class. The struggle to institutionalize social welfare, they maintained, is one of several forms of the class struggle; gains in protection against social risks are concessions wrested from the bourgeoisie by the revolutionary proletariat. Institutionalization of social welfare can come to full fruition, they insisted, only when the proletariat triumphs and a socialist order is created. Then welfare benefits and services become additions to wages, increasing as productivity rises and as the new society moves toward communism.[1]

This position entailed discarding the deeply embedded notion that economic insecurity is essential for efficiency and material advance. Rather, said Soviet welfare planners, a high level of economic security and a clear concern on the part of the state for the welfare of its citizens are essential for maximum production. While aware of the necessity for precautions against malingering, they believed that such antisocial behavior would disappear with the advent of the "new communist man," who would place the interests of society above his own. As a rule, welfare benefits were to be in the form of money payments, in order to permit the recipient the greatest possible freedom in fulfilling his individual needs and desires. At the same time, benefits "in kind"—such as residence in a home for the aged—were to be available for those who could not remain in the community. Major reliance for maintaining income was to be placed on a state social insurance system (*gosudarstvennoe sotsial'noe strakhovanie*) that would be based on four fundamental principles: (1) coverage of *all* risks—death, disability, sickness, old age, pregnancy and childbirth, and unemployment; (2) coverage of *everyone* working for hire and members of his family; (3) benefits equal to *total* earnings, financed entirely by employers and government; and (4) administration of all forms of social insurance by unified organs of a *territorial* type, in which the insured exercise complete control.[2]

In subsequent decades, beset by a myriad of economic and administrative difficulties, the Soviets were far from consistent in adhering to these policies and principles. There were four well-defined periods during which different policies were followed: 1917 to 1921, 1921 through 1928, 1929 through 1955, and the post-1955 era. In time, four types of income-maintenance programs became available: social insurance for wage and salaried workers; allowances for all the children in the population; mutual aid—self-help arrangements for farm workers, to which the government did not contribute (changed to a system of social insurance in January 1965); and public assistance for those in dire need who were ineligible for social insurance, unable to work, and without responsible relatives who could or would help them.[3]

1917–21: The Period of War Communism

A basic tenet of the Soviet government in 1917 was that productive labor rather than need determined the right to economic support. Its first provision against want, introduced five days after its assumption of power, was social insurance for hired workers, who were divided into wage earners (*rabochie*) and salaried employees (*sluzhashchie*). This insurance, which protected them against most major risks, was financed by the employing establishments, and provided benefits based upon former earnings. The only contingencies that remained uncovered were old age, non-work-connected disability, and the loss of a breadwinner from non-work-connected causes.[4] Handicraftsmen, artisans, and peasants who owned land were considered to be self-employed and were excluded. A year later, however, despite those who warned of the "sharp necessity of concerning ourselves with today and with the transition period which promises to be quite long,"[5] the principle of insuring hired workers only was abandoned. Social assistance was extended to "all toilers who do not exploit others," irrespective of the nature of their employment. In this way, the zealots in the Party hoped to outstrip the capitalist countries, almost overnight, in their slow progress from outworn systems of poor relief to modern social insurance provisions built on the proposition that security from want is a fundamental right.

A series of decrees implementing this principle culminated in the general act of October 31, 1918, which extended coverage to all persons supporting themselves by their own labor, including artisans, handicraftsmen, and landless peasants. The act added insurance for non-work-connected disability and continued to place the entire financial burden on employers; benefits were based upon "norms for minimum subsistence." The pre-Revolutionary social insurance administrative structure was radically changed: the funds (*kassy*) were retained, but their functions were expanded so that they became the local administrative organs for all types of social insurance. Supervising the funds were social insurance management boards attached to the Commissariats of Labor in the republics and at Moscow.

In practice, the new arrangements created numerous and often insurmountable difficulties. The insurance for peasants, artisans, and home workers never materialized, and even for wage earners and salaried employees it was impossible to implement the social insurance laws to any significant extent. With industry nationalized, the government became the sole employer and thus the sole contributor to social insurance. Labor service was imposed on all employables, placing them at the disposal of the state; as a result, they acquired the right to be maintained by the state when unemployed. (Often, however, the "nonproletarian elements" among the employables, no matter how clear their right to benefits, were denied them.) In short, everyone who received support got it from the state, either in wages or in "benefits."[6] This system resulted in heavy burdens on the employing establishments, which were forced to pay contributions amounting to as much as 21 to 28 per cent of their payrolls. Because of these inordinate rates, as well as inefficient administration, in some cases less than 30 per cent of the amount due was collected. Obviously, the sweeping objectives enunciated in the fervor of the Revolution could not be reached; the government found it impossible to meet even minimum obligations. Although in 1920 the Commissariat of Social Welfare distributed money and supplies in kind to more than ten million persons,[7] this help was so sporadic and meager that it probably alleviated only the most acute suffering.

1921-28: The Period of the New Economic Policy

With the introduction of the New Economic Policy, there was a drastic reorganization of the income maintenance system. Some private enterprise was permitted, and there was a return to the 1917 position that eligibility for social insurance should be based upon productive labor rather than need. A distinction was made between wage workers and "independent" workers. The latter were deemed unsuitable for inclusion in a social insurance system because they were not "hired" and there was no "giver of work." By means of a series of theoretical twists and turns, this questionable distinction eventually became dogma, and the principle of equality of social insurance for all classes of workers was given up. "Independent workers"—peasants, artisans, home workers, and members of artels and producers' associations (including invalids' cooperatives)—were covered by a separate system based on mutual aid.[8] The arguments against inclusion of the largest group—the peasants— among the hired workers were especially weak. Wrote Miliutin:

> To the extent that for the proletariat it is essential to guarantee *earnings*, to the same extent [it is essential to guarantee] *income* for the peasant. This, of course, does not mean that the peasantry does not need social insurance. Many of its forms even now may be organized on the same general principles as the social insurance of the proletariat. [This includes] insurance against death, widowhood and orphanhood, work-connected injury, old age, disability, and provision of medical aid. . . . To speak seriously about voluntary insurance is [ludicrous]. . . . At the same time, if now a sharp deviation is made from the class character of social insurance, then in the future it will become a purely bourgeois institution of a general insurance type. This consideration is the only serious objection against uniting . . . the social insurance of workers and peasants.[9]

Even after collectivization, the exclusion of peasants from social insurance coverage continued, on the grounds that peasants were self-employed persons. Thus, the population was divided into three groups: those covered by the state-financed system of social insurance; those whose income security was to be achieved through mutual aid, that is, by their own initiative and resources; and those ineligible for either of these forms of assistance. Medical care and children's allowances were available to all, however.

Social Insurance. Attempts to translate social insurance principles into practice led to serious difficulties. In theory, eligibility for social insurance had nothing to do with need; in practice, insurance benefits were frequently denied to workers who had any kind of income or resources— a practice, it was pointed out, that "under no circumstances fits into a social insurance concept if it is to be interpreted in its true sense."[10] But the new state, wracked by poverty and want, was unwilling to pay benefits to eligible workers who had savings, even though this reintroduced the despised charity approach; eligibility was based upon "the absence of security rather than the right to security."[11]

A consistent theory of what social insurance is supposed to accomplish was lacking. Some said that the objective of social insurance is to replace earnings when a worker becomes disabled or unemployed—to guarantee the standard of living he has struggled to attain. Others branded this view as bourgeois; in a socialist society, they maintained, the objective is to guarantee a common level of well-being; hence, inequalities in earnings should not be reflected in inequalities of insurance provisions for individuals or families—as is true under capitalism.[12] No one appeared concerned with the broad economic implications of socialist social insurance policy, especially its influence upon productivity.

The system of social insurance was expanded in 1927, when old-age pensions for textile workers were introduced. Prior to this time the aged had been protected to some extent: those either totally or partially disabled for work by old age were classified as invalids. Six categories were recognized, ranging from the totally disabled (Group I), who required constant attendance, to the partially disabled (Group VI), who suffered less than a 15 per cent loss in earnings. Up to 1925 pensions were paid only to the first three groups, but in that year benefits were granted to the last three in cases of industrial accidents or occupational diseases. As for the amounts paid, the government was only partially successful in its effort to provide a decent minimum: in 1928 pensions paid to Group II invalids averaged only slightly more than 15 rubles per month, while working invalids earned an average of 54 rubles per month.[13]

Thus, in spite of the tremendous difficulties that beset the country during the 1920's, progress was made toward implementing three of the four principles enunciated as basic to a sound social insurance system by Lenin and his followers: protection was provided against all of the major threats to income, the system was financed by employers and the state, and the insured had a decisive voice in the system's administration. But most of those who received benefits got an amount less than equal to their previous earnings—an indication both of the weakness of the economy and of the desire of the regime to distribute the available resources to as many people as possible.

The 1921 decision to adhere to the "productive-labor" rather than to the "minimum subsistence" approach may be explained in two ways. On the one hand, it was a necessary decision for a state seeking to survive in a period of utter chaos, when the demands upon welfare programs exceeded the capacity of the government to meet them. On the other hand, it was one of the outcomes of the struggle between those who wished to adhere to the socialist precept "To each according to the quantity and quality of his work," until such time as the transition to a communist society had been made, and the enthusiasts who wished to act on the communist precept "To each according to his needs," without waiting for the millennium. The losers claimed that their more radical approach was rejected not because it was theoretically unsound, but because the young Soviet state, beset by enormous economic and other difficulties, could not muster the resources required to implement it.[14]

Mutual Aid. Mutual aid societies for peasants (*Krestiianskie Obshchestva Vzaimopomoshchi—KOV*) were organized in 1921 to provide relief in cash or in kind and to organize community assistance for victims of bad harvests, fires, or other natural or social calamities. They were to make certain that the interests of hired hands and small peasant households were protected against the "kulaks." Membership was voluntary, but no doubt there was severe pressure to join. However, Miliutin said that "it would be the height of folly to drive the peasants into the committees at the point of bayonets."[15] He counseled persuasion.

Collectivization transformed the societies into mutual aid organs for collective farms; under a 1931 law, a society serving either one or several farms might be established by a two-thirds majority of the peasants. It was to be directed by elective officers and supervised by the village soviets and the social welfare authorities. Finances were to be derived from several sources: (1) members' contributions, proportionate to individual earnings and fixed annually by a general meeting at not more than 2 per cent of those earnings; (2) payments from the common funds, not to exceed 2 per cent of the value of a farm's total output; (3) sums received from the social welfare authorities; and (4) fines levied by the state courts. The societies were required to assist widows and orphans, as well as members incapable of working because of old age, disability, sickness, or maternity, and to improve living conditions by organizing health and welfare services. They also were to make loans to members in case of serious misfortunes and for basic improvements such as the construction and repair of buildings.[16]

Exactly what proportion of earnings the benefits from most collective farm societies represented it is not possible to say. There are indications that the benefits were lower than those paid by the state social insurance system to workers and employees, and that they were shorter in duration. There was no centralized budgeting; rather, individual collective farms managed their own funds. This means that the less successful collective farms had less available for benefits than the more prosperous ones; unfortunately, it was likely that the former included proportionally more members who needed assistance. Also, it appears that the same principle of differentiation that operated in the social insurance system was applied by the collective farm societies: the greater a person's earnings, the greater the benefits for which he was eligible. The societies' efforts to alleviate poverty were ineffective because in general their link with the "masses" was weak, their leadership passive, their funds often expended in a haphazard way, and their resources extremely meager.[17]

Artisans and handicraftsmen, also excluded from state social insurance coverage, were encouraged to organize mutual aid societies.* But it appears that not many of them were interested. (It was later claimed that this was also the case with former landlords and capitalists, kulaks, speculators, and other nonproletarian elements.)[18] In the absence of a central supervisory organ, each society that was organized was a law unto itself, and many spent their funds on things that had nothing to do with aid. The situation was complicated by the amorphous character of the groups of "self-employed," which included people of many different social origins and backgrounds. The mutual aid movement continued to languish until 1929, when an act establishing mutual aid societies in producers' cooperatives was promulgated. It required the payment of benefits similar to those in the state social insurance system. (Exceptions to the general apathy were the producers' cooperatives designed to provide employment for invalids. In existence since the end of 1921, they were supervised by social welfare organs and developed mutual aid programs fairly rapidly.)

Eventually it became apparent to the Soviet authorities that social insurance benefits were inadequate to meet the minimum needs of even the industrial workers who were covered by social insurance, and they were encouraged to form mutual aid societies in order to ease their lot in times of severe need. Each society was registered with a trade union. A 1928 act gave local union officials some discretion in determining eligibility for mutual aid benefits; in general, however, they were directed

---

* In 1927 a small group of handicraftsmen instituted a mutual aid society along religious lines. They were allowed to continue, with welfare authorities looking the other way (*Voprosy Sotsial'nogo Obespecheniia*, No. 4, February 15, 1927, p. 1).

to use such aid to reward workers who achieved high rates of productivity (*udarniki*).

Public Assistance. From the very inception of the new regime, needy people who were ineligible for social insurance, disabled for work, and without responsible relatives able to support them were in principle eligible for public assistance. The "responsible relatives" requirement was tied into regulations governing family relationships. In the 1918 *Code of Laws Relating to Acts of Civil Status,* the duty of parents to maintain their children, as well as the duty of children to support their parents, was limited to those instances where one or the other was destitute and unable to work. This duty of support was recognized only insofar as the children "were not provided for from public or state funds" and the parents did not receive old-age pensions or other forms of social security. The 1926 *Code on Domestic Relations* omitted the qualifying clause making the duty of family support dependent upon the absence of public or government support. Said Gsovski, "The state evidently did not visualize a social security system as a substitute for support by next of kin." As for the wife who needed alimony because of inability to work, the husband was required to pay, but only what was absolutely necessary, in accordance with the principle of the equality of the sexes.

During 1918–21, when aid was based upon "norms for minimum subsistence," the eligible needy were indistinguishable from the others helped by the government. But from 1921 on, an effort was made to differentiate them from those covered by social insurance. They were categorized as war invalids, dependents of those killed or wounded at the front, and "others" (*prochie*)—a catchall category for those who had fallen on hard times because of natural and social calamities not directly related to the war. The obligation to assist the "others" from public funds was first acknowledged in a 1926 decree.[19] However, from the outset, the war invalids and the dependents of military personnel were distinguished from the "others" and were given the preferential status of "regular" social welfare clients, whose needs were met through a special pension system. The "others" got what was left, so to speak.

The assistance provided for the "others" was based upon evaluations by social welfare personnel. It consisted mainly of handouts to the most desperately needy, the amounts depending upon the funds at the disposal of local welfare departments. In 1927 a number of provinces with especially acute problems of homelessness and begging attempted to do something about them, but their efforts were unsystematic and sporadic.[20] In 1928, welfare personnel all over the country declared that they were unable to deal with homelessness and begging because the resources available to them for emergency grants (*edinovremennye poso-biia*) were woefully inadequate: they made possible monthly grants of only five rubles per recipient at a time when the average monthly wage of a manual worker was 63 rubles. Furthermore, almost half of those who needed assistance got nothing at all. The plight of the rural population was especially acute; they were aided only in the most extreme circumstances. Welfare institutions were filled to capacity with poverty-stricken people, even though many of these facilities lacked the most elementary amenities and were structurally unsafe.[21] During this period local welfare offices were continually faced with the problem of what to do with people who were excluded from the state insurance system and for whom the peasant mutual aid societies had no resources.

1928–55: The Period of the Five-Year Plans

Social Insurance. The forced industrialization drive inaugurated in 1928 as part of the first five-year plan enormously increased the number of workers and employees. In 1928, exclusive of prisoners, they numbered 10.8 million; by 1940 their number had risen to 31.2 million; in the postwar era it rose from 27.3 million in 1945 to 47.3 million in 1954.[22] Hence, developments in social insurance for this group assumed a greater importance in the total welfare system than they had in the pre-planning period. These developments were aimed primarily at increasing labor efficiency and maximizing output, as was required by the successive five-year plans and World War II. The high point was reached in 1936–37. Article 120 of the 1936 Constitution declared that "citizens of the USSR have the right to material security in old age as well as in the event of sickness and loss of capacity to work. This right is ensured by the wide development of social insurance of workers and employees at the expense of the state, free medical aid, and the provision of a wide network of health resorts for the use of the toilers." Additional benefits were specified in provisions in the Constitution concerned with the equality of rights of women. In 1937 all employed persons became eligible for old-age pensions.

However, in order to further the industrialization drive, social insurance benefits were paid only to those who could not possibly be integrated into productive life. By the end of 1929, differences concerning the objectives of social insurance were brusquely resolved; the overriding purpose was declared to be the increase of labor productivity. Egalitarianism (*uravnilovka*), the reverse of differentiation, was denounced by Stalin as a heresy in 1931. This resulted in less stringent eligibility requirements and a more advantageous benefit formula for "superior" workers, trade union members, and those in "leading" industries and unhealthy occupations. In 1932, those who suffered only a minor loss of working capacity were made ineligible for pensions by the substitution of a three-tiered classification of disabilities for the earlier six groups.

In October 1930 temporary unemployment benefits were abolished, even though they had been available to only a few of the unemployed—those without any income whatsoever. At that time, unemployment was at its lowest point.[23] To what extent this was due to the demand for labor generated by the first five-year plan, on the one hand, and to the great increase in the population of the corrective labor camps in 1930, on the other, it is difficult to say. That both these factors influenced the employment situation is undeniable. Unemployment insurance has never been reintroduced. Presumably the trade unions have been able to find employment promptly for any unemployed, able-bodied man or woman, though not necessarily in his own trade or at his place of residence. For those needing to acquire certain skills, training is provided free, along with a living allowance. Anyone incapable of work has to be medically certified and is then classified as sick or disabled.

The 1931 social insurance program represented a "break from the past." No longer was it limited to the mere providing of material security; rather, its concern was with "broader" objectives—strengthening labor discipline, encouraging socialist competition, and increasing productivity. Hence, funds for pensions and sick benefits were cut, both absolutely and relatively, while funds for "in kind" and "socialized" forms of benefits—medical care, prophylaxis, children's homes, institutions for invalids, special diets—were increased. In 1931, 40 per cent of the budget was allocated for such benefits; in 1932, half; and in 1933, almost two-thirds.[24] The sharp curtailments in cash benefits—part of an overall plan to reduce consumption and income in order to achieve the goal of rapid industrialization—seriously undermined the program of social insurance for the aged and the disabled.

Complaints about exceedingly low pensions were heard throughout the 1930's. The pension act of December 28, 1938, improved the situation somewhat by increasing the pension payments, but the effect was only temporary, since there was a sharp rise in price and wage levels after 1938. Its long-term effect on pensioners was disastrous, because it reduced the maximum amounts payable to less than 50 per cent of former earnings. The effect of the 1938 law on paid maternity leave was to shorten it, and to require a longer uninterrupted period of employment for eligibility. The law also imposed penalties on persons who quit their jobs voluntarily or who were fired for violations of labor discipline, by lowering or denying them their benefits. It cut the sick benefit rates in half and doubled the employment period required for the maximum rate.

This situation was further exacerbated after World War II, when huge differences between the pensions received by privileged groups and those received by ordinary pensioners were permitted; the former in some instances received benefits 14 times as high as the latter. Pension maximums established in 1932 continued in force until 1956, although there had been a tremendous rise in wages. This meant that pension rates had declined drastically in relation to earnings, and that aged and infirm people were frequently forced to live a life of hardship and neglect. The Soviet novelist Yuri Bondarev sketched the plight of a Group II invalid in 1945 in these words: "Pensions—the size of a sparrow's beak. It is more expensive to sneeze."[25]

Provisions for the "Self-Employed." There were no substantive changes during this period in the concept of mutual aid for the "self-employed." Mutual aid arrangements in producers' cooperatives, legalized in 1929, were made obligatory in 1933, with financing from artel profits, that is, without deductions from the earnings of members themselves. Urged on by zealots, cooperatives engaged in frequent "cleanings" throughout the 1930's to eliminate the socially undesirable. "Let us clean the pensioner ranks of enemies and hangers-on!" became a frequently heard cry. This led to harrowing situations for many disabled, sick, and helpless people.[26]

Peasants' mutual aid societies also were beset by problems, besieged as they were by people branded by the authorities as "parasites" and "do-nothings," when in fact they were poverty-stricken and fearful individuals who did not know where to turn. The primary function of social welfare organizations in the villages, it was insisted, was to participate in the class struggle to achieve collectivization and liquidate the kulaks; they were to do so by placing all their activities under the control of the "mass of poor farm-hands."[27] It is not difficult to imagine the harsh and prejudiced treatment received by those who were not part of the "mass."

The notion that mutual aid should be used only for the "self-employed" was discarded, however, when this suited the purposes of the regime: in 1931 mutual aid societies of a "special type" were authorized in 12 heavy industries and in railway transport. Financed entirely by the government and supervised directly by factory committees, these societies soon became indistinguishable from the social insurance organs.[28] Trade union mutual aid funds, sizable enough to have a significant impact, also were set up to help workers in "basic" sectors of the economy; these provided various forms of assistance in addition to social insurance benefits. In 1931 such funds amounted to 75 million rubles; by 1938 they had risen to 104 million rubles. These funds, it is interesting to note, were subsidized from the social insurance budget.*

But people who were not "essential" to the economy did not get any subsidies for their self-help efforts. A 1930 instruction from the commissariats of social welfare and health to their regional and district organs said the following:

> In order to assist declassed elements—[who are now] beggars, adult homeless, and women engaged in prostitution or on the verge of it—during their sojourn in work houses and treatment centers in which they live not as hired personnel but as persons being reeducated to acquire work habits, the organs of social welfare and health must concern themselves with accumulating funds for helping these people when they are temporarily unable to work.... Inasmuch as these people are not covered by social insurance, the funds must be obtained from deductions of a set percentage (not more than 10 per cent) from the earnings of *these people* [emphasis mine].[29]

Public Assistance. Despite the meagerness of social insurance benefits during the period 1930–55, the policy of not using public assistance funds to supplement incomes was continued: such financial support was to be provided by social organizations, however unrealistic the expectation for help from this source. Nor was there any change for the better in the circumstances of the "others," for whom public assistance was the sole means of support. To be eligible for such assistance, each applicant was required to prove destitution by a statement certified by either the management of the building in which he lived, the local militia, or the local soviet. Assistance was in the form of flat monthly grants (*ezemesiachnye posobiia*) financed from local funds, rather than from the national budget for social insurance. These grants differed in amount according to the locality in which the poor person lived. In cities, the "others" received the same amounts as severely disabled war veterans, but without allowances for family members. In rural communities, a set monthly amount was stipulated, considerably less than what veterans received. Those among the "others" who were totally helpless were placed in institutions with the veterans.[30] "Single-time," nonrepeating grants were used for emergencies.†

---

* In 1951, the factory "Krasnyi Proletarii" (Red Proletarian) reported that with the sums it received from the trade union budget for mutual aid it had created a half-million ruble revolving fund from which, in 1950, 400,000 rubles had been diverted to repayable and nonrepayable loans (*405*, pp. 93–94).

† For example, a 1943 regulation provided that families of military personnel who were receiving monthly grants be given "single-time" grants—in money, produce, firewood, clothing, repair of living quarters—if especially acute need for any of these was ascertained (*116*, pp. 11–12).

In fact, however, local soviets in many communities simply did not appropriate funds for helping the "others." Their desperate situation was only sporadically relieved by special allocations from the People's Commissariat of Social Welfare.* In rural areas, institutions erected by the more affluent collective farms were often the only form of public assistance available, and they were open only to the old or disabled indigent.

Family Allowances. As noted earlier, mothers' subsidies were introduced by a law of June 27, 1936, for families with seven or more children. According to this law, at the birth of the seventh child the mother was paid a lump sum of 2,000 rubles, and then 2,000 rubles a year (in monthly payments) for the four succeeding years. The same amounts were paid for the eighth, ninth, and tenth children. At the birth of the eleventh child, a lump sum of 5,000 rubles was paid, with monthly payments for four years thereafter totalling 3,000 rubles a year.

This system of allowances for children was considerably liberalized by the law of July 8, 1944, and until 1965 it remained the only provision available to *all* children, whether their mothers were workers, employees, or collective farm members, married or unmarried. Allowances were financed from general revenues and consisted of three types: lump-sum payments to a mother upon the birth of a third child and each subsequent child, the amount increasing with succeeding children; monthly payments to a mother after the birth of a fourth child and all subsequent children, starting in the month when the child reaches the age of one and continuing until the month before he is five, the amount increasing with succeeding children; and monthly payments to an *unmarried* mother, payable from each child's birth until he reaches age twelve, the amount increasing with each additional child. The payments to an unwed mother did not cease upon the mother's marriage unless the children were adopted by the husband. The sums involved for married mothers were as follows: upon the birth of a third child, a lump sum of 400 rubles was paid; beginning with the fourth child, a lump sum of 1,300 rubles was paid at birth, in addition to monthly payments for four years totalling 960 rubles a year; after the fourth child the benefit rates increased to a maximum lump-sum payment of 5,000 rubles for the eleventh and each succeeding child, with monthly payments for four

* For example, funds earmarked for war veterans were sometimes used to relieve the blind in such communities—"as an exception and only in the presence of acute distress" (*VSO*, No. 4/100, 1930, p. 15). In 1932, the grants to adult blind who were attending schools were raised to the level of pensions for the most severely disabled war invalids. These higher grants were possible only because funds from local soviets were doubled by allocations from the Commissariat of Social Welfare and from the All-Russian Society for the Blind (*Sotsial'noe Obespechenie*, No. 7–8, 1932, p. 61; 26, pp. 207–10).

years totalling 3,600 rubles a year. (To fully appreciate these amounts, it should be borne in mind that in 1944 the minimum monthly salary of an industrial worker was 250 rubles.)[31] Unmarried mothers could not get allowances for children for whom they were receiving pensions or support payments, whose fathers had acknowledged paternity, who had been adopted, or who were living in households maintained by both parents, even though the marriage had not been registered.

Probably the reason that monthly payments did not begin at the birth of a child is that the lump-sum payment presumably took care of the extra expenses during the child's first year of life. The only benefit available for the first two children of married mothers was a small cash allowance for families with low earnings, intended to meet the cost of a layette and of the infant's food during the first nine months. This, too, was financed from general revenues.[32] Without any explanation, however, both lump-sum and monthly allowances were cut in half by the law of November 27, 1947, and the cut has never been restored.

It is possible that if the Soviet industrialization drive had not been so all-enveloping, unrelenting, and rapid, Soviet income-maintenance policy might have been more successful in meeting immediate welfare needs. Given the circumstances and the scarcity of resources, however, it is not surprising that such needs were regarded as secondary. But this does not mean that the worst effects of assigning a low priority to welfare needs—exclusion of large segments of the population from income protection, provision of inadequate benefits, discrimination against the most helpless—were inevitable consequences of the drive to advance the country. The fact that programs emphasizing human development—especially medical services, education, and children's allowances—were maintained despite the scarcity of resources indicates that political and ideological considerations were not forgotten.

5

Highlights of the Post-1955 Decade

In the post-Stalin era a less politicized approach to social problems has been possible, leading to a more genuine implementation of socialist humanism and a bold search for causes of problems whose very existence was often denied before. Juvenile delinquency, crime, begging, drug peddling, alcoholism, child neglect, lack of motivation to engage in socially productive activity (*bezdel' nichestvo*)—all have been targets of a great deal of attention, indignation, and concern.[1] Deviant behavior has been subjected to searching analyses, and sex education has gained outspoken adherents. In February 1956 sociology was established as a separate discipline, and since then, supported by sizable research funds, it has developed rapidly, producing more high-quality social science work than has appeared in the Soviet Union since the 1920's.[2]

Although claims are constantly being made that social ills are diminishing, with percentage reductions between earlier and later years cited to prove it, it is difficult not to question these optimistic pronouncements. Skepticism is justified both by the continuous flood of discussion already referred to and by observations in the field. For example, it is not rare to see drunken rowdies herded out of restaurants, drunken men and women collected from sidewalks, vicious drunken brawls broken up, drunken men and boys being led home by their wives, mothers, or girl friends, women accosted by drunken males on streets, in elevators, and in queues—in Moscow, Leningrad, Kiev, or Tashkent. Even if it is true that alcoholism is not as widespread in the Soviet Union as it was in pre-Revolutionary Russia, that does not mean that steady progress is being made. Soviet welfare professionals are continually asking for stricter laws and additional facilities for dealing with drunkenness.*

As for juvenile delinquency, a Soviet crime expert pointed out in 1961 that "statistical data showing a drop in juvenile delinquency are to a certain extent affected by the fact that in recent years educational measures have been applied more and more extensively in working with minors, supplanting penal measures. In view of this, not all offenses committed by juveniles are included in our criminal statistics."[3] One recent report[4] describes a teenage battle in Red Square that left one dead and seventeen wounded, giving "new urgency to appeals for better police protection in the face of increasing juvenile delinquency."†

The Post-1955 Soviet View of Man

The Soviets still adhere to the position that all mental processes are based upon physiological processes in the brain. However, Luria has postulated a third source of mental development in addition to nature and nurture: acquisition of experience through language. This capacity does not exist in animals, and is the most distinctive characteristic of human beings.[5]

It is now recognized that Pavlov's principles are not adequate for explaining human behavior and must be expanded and revised.[6] Miasishchev, a leading Soviet psychotherapist, maintains that social relationships determine an individual's character and behavior, both healthy and neurotic, and emphasizes the role of social stress in behavioral disorders.[7] But his conception of man's interaction with his environment is much less neuro-deterministic and less historically oriented than earlier theories. By 1960 an important Soviet book could include the following statement by a well-known Soviet psychologist:

> The ardent desire of Soviet psychologists to oppose the domination of consciousness to the "unconscious" of Freud and other exponents of "depth psychology"—to show that man is not merely a puppet dancing to the will of certain dark forces, but is rather the master of his behavior, with his deeds and actions being based upon consciously posed problems and consciously made decisions—is altogether understandable.

---

* An all-union conference on the "Question of the Struggle Against Alcoholism" was held in February 1959 (*183*, pp. 23–40). The most recently established research section of the Bekhterev Institute in Leningrad is concerned with alcoholism.

† The most recently opened research section in the Psychology Institute in Moscow is concerned with the psychology of juvenile delinquency. However, it had only one staff member from 1963 to 1967, when a second one was added.

But in the struggle against the domination of the "unconscious," consciousness has come to be regarded as the demiurge of personality. It has been thought that all that was necessary to develop personality was to reason with the child, to develop his consciousness. It is not possible to accept this exaggeration of the role of consciousness. In our researches we are constantly confronted with phenomena lying outside the child's consciousness, which cannot be ignored either by psychologists or by teachers. For example, in studying motivation in the learning process of children, we have established that the primary motives for learning ... are as a rule not consciously perceived by the child.

Similarly, in researches concerning the formation of the child's moral character we are constantly confronted by the fact that the child's actions are often determined by feelings and habits that have developed from social relationships independently of his consciousness and sometimes even contrary to his consciousness.[8]

But neither this unusually honest statement nor the renewed interest in psychotherapy means an acceptance of the teachings of Freud or of the method of psychoanalysis. Freud is accused of disregarding the social nature of affects by viewing them as the results of repressions of biologically determined drives, and psychoanalysis is condemned "as one of the most reactionary manifestations of modern bourgeois ideology: in emphasizing the individual factors in unhappiness and psychic problems it distracts the people's attention from those contradictions which are the basis of class struggle."[9] The most that is admitted is that "a failure to appreciate the significance of the Pavlovian concepts of excitation and inhibition" has led Soviet psychology to deny or misunderstand the role of the unconscious in psychic life.[10] Unconscious motivation is to be interpreted in terms of Pavlov's view of conscious behavior as higher nervous activity.

Deviant Behavior. Although the claim is made that under socialism no class struggle is possible, it is acknowledged that there are contradictions in the development of socialist society and "that even under the conditions of communism, with all its harmony, human life will be only relatively harmonious, inasmuch as perfect relations between phenomena are an impossibility."[11] Certain contradictions cause personal and social conflicts, and these conflicts need to be studied in order to determine their causes if they are to be resolved. During the period under discussion, such study has led to a modification of the traditional Soviet theory of deviant behavior as the result of an incisive examination of the interaction between the environment and the individual.[12] The point is stressed that survivals of the past persist because changes in consciousness lag behind economic changes, because the capitalist world is still strong and thus exerts an influence upon Soviet society, and because there are weaknesses in the socialist economy that hinder the transformation of all the people into "new Soviet men." These survivals are dangerous: they plague people raised under capitalist conditions who, unable to shake off the old psychological concepts, pass them on to the next generation. It is argued that particular attention must be paid to the four environments that play especially powerful roles in forming the personality—the family, the school, the collective on the job or in the social organization, and the immediate home environment.

With regard to the family, the traditional charges that children are improperly brought up and that parents do not set a good example, are not strict enough, and spoil and make egotists of their children are repeated, this time on the basis of certain findings about delinquent youngsters. The criticisms of schools also are not new: they are criticized for failing to develop love for labor and a proper outlook on life, for sacrificing the development of the individual to competition for scholastic success, for ignoring parents, for concealing mistakes and yielding to the pressures of influential fathers and mothers. The various collectives are again attacked for their indifference and neglect in situations that clearly demand their intervention, as well as for failing to create an atmosphere intolerant to delinquent behavior. As for home environments, the well-known facts about overcrowding, poor housing, inadequate recreational facilities, lack of good eating places where people can relax in comfort, and shortages of nurseries and kindergartens are presented without the usual rationalizations. It is maintained that all four environments are adversely affected by weaknesses in the economic-technical base of socialism, which result in pronounced inequalities in the distribution of goods, differences in rewards for intellectual as opposed to physical labor, and failure to take realistic account of the material interests of the workers.

From this point Soviet theoreticians have proceeded to consider the subjective, psychological factors that create antisocial views and motives. They have raised questions about the "depth and persistence of the antisocial nature of the personality" found in different categories and types of criminals.[13] In studying antisocial people, they have said, account must be taken of "peculiarities of the individual personality—temperament, character, willpower, and emotional traits."[14] They have then specified several objective, external circumstances that generate antisocial views and motives: arrogant conduct of many leaders and bureaucrats toward those under them, groundless repressions of individual citizens, unequal treatment of people guilty of similar antisocial conduct. Particular note has been taken of the activities of the militia, courts, lawyers, and prosecutors. For years they had made no effort to rehabilitate criminals, resorting instead to punishment and deprivation of liberty. They did this even in cases of minor infractions, when the guilty persons might have been reformed readily without isolation from society. Children were sent to labor colonies on the flimsiest of pretexts; those who committed minor crimes were thrown together with confirmed delinquents, the older with the younger. The general point has been made that it is an oversimplification of the problem to assume that antisocial behavior can be corrected by propaganda.

From this account it may appear that the traditionalists are no longer placing the entire responsibility for deviant behavior on a political and social structure that was done away with fifty years ago. But the concession that there are contradictions and weaknesses in socialist society that lead to deviant behavior is couched in terms that are not immediately helpful to personnel involved in the treatment of individual offenders. One is reminded of a 1929 report that listed the main causes of juvenile delinquency as poverty, lack of culture (*nekul'turnost'*), unemployment, movement of population from villages to urban centers, bad housing, alcoholism, family dissension, neglect of children, and ignorance about correct child-rearing practices.[15] Nor does this concession explain recently announced Soviet findings that juvenile delinquency is highest in the middle-income group, and that bad housing conditions are of little or no significance—findings that seem to point to mental, rather than economic and material, factors as the most decisive in creating delinquents.[16]

Those seeking a deeper understanding of the causes of crime perceive them in the interaction between environmental factors and particular types of individuals. They recognize that similar circumstances have different effects upon different individuals, that the

> conditions in which a person may find himself do not mechanically influence his thinking and behavior. ... One person finding himself in unfavorable conditions, experiencing family difficulties, can emerge from the situation with credit, acting in conformity with the rules of socialist society and Soviet laws, in line with communist morality; but another person contaminated with survivals of the past, finding himself in the same conditions, may commit an amoral act or even a crime.[17]

This view, generated by a more perceptive interpretation of family influences, confers great significance on interpersonal relations. Loss of parents and improper upbringing are considered in terms of their influence upon the way in which a given individual deals with the conditions of his life. The point is stressed that the treatment of a particular individual must be based upon an understanding of his personality. While assignment of preeminent importance to the role of the child-parent relationship in shaping the psyche is eschewed, a tendency to take this role more and more into account—along with the influence of "objective" environmental factors—is emerging. This tendency is still being resisted by the traditionalists, however.*

Sex Education. Recently, a number of booklets have been published that deal with the anatomy, physiology, and hygiene of sex organs, sexual perversions and their harmful effects, venereal disease, contraceptives, and the undesirability and danger of abortion (especially in first pregnancies).[18] The position is taken that the major responsibility for conveying scientifically based sex information, as well as for providing instruction in the moral principles relevant to sexual behavior, must be assumed by parents, teachers, and physicians. Silence or the ignoring of sexual tensions in boys and girls is considered inexcusable. Sexual feelings in the growing adolescent must not be crushed, but rather directed into constructive channels. Sex education does not conflict with ethical norms; on the contrary, it is essential for strengthening them and for achieving a healthy daily life. Such education must not neglect the close relation between sex and love: Makarenko said that the child who has not learned to love his parents, his brothers and sisters, his school, and his country, and who has become a confirmed egotist, will be more likely to become sexually promiscuous and less able to take part in creating a rich family life. Among the broad principles concerning sex that ought to be inculcated are the following: motherhood is the greatest happiness and the sacred duty of every woman; complete sexual fulfillment can be achieved only when full physical and intellectual maturity have been reached; sexual abstinence, often required by the realities of modern life, is good for the organism; alcohol must be avoided as a poison that often shortens or ruins the wondrous time of true love. Furthermore, in socialist society sexual love and spiritual love are inseparable—hence, sexual activity should begin with marriage. Questions of love and family life cannot be regarded as strictly personal, because they affect the total society, just as sexual promiscuity is dangerous not only for the individual but also for the entire social order.

Field findings indicate that Soviet welfare workers are no longer shying away from frank discussions about problems involving sex—as they were apt to do in earlier years. Even those who hold that sexual develop-

---

* New thinking is hindered by the extreme paucity of materials on the psychology of deviant behavior. The only authors to whom Soviet researchers refer are Sakharov and Pronina—authors whom they consider to be too general, dogmatic, and superficial to be helpful to anyone who has to deal with live delinquents. The journals *Sovetskoe Gosudarstvennoe Pravo* and *Sovetskaia Iustitsiia* occasionally have helpful material.

ment in adolescents is not as powerful a force as "bourgeois" psychologists make it out to be concede that it cannot be ignored. Some express the belief that when a child is absorbed in constructive activity, when he is happy and relates well to the various collectives in which he moves, sex problems will not erupt: the child will be "normal." None, however, can define normality in this context. They simply stress the need to use up the youngster's life energies in study and physical activity so completely that none will be left for what they consider undesirable sexual interests and experiments. An extension of this approach is the emphasis on "comradely, work-together" relationships, on sharing ideals and goals, while at the same time steering away from the sexual domain. In other words, friendship—yes, sex—no. Some oppose sex education in schools, feeling that it will arouse too much excitement and curiosity. Many are frankly at a loss, and hope that in the discharge of their responsibilities they will not be faced with clients with sex problems.

On the other hand, many advocate the inclusion of sex education in school curricula—not only scientific information about the reproductive process, but instruction that makes it clear that in sexual matters each person has certain rights that must not be violated. Mutual consent is essential, and the sex act must be an expression of love. They insist that if adolescents are to be persuaded to abstain from sexual relationships before marriage, work with them must begin long before biological maturity is reached. Preparing the adolescent for sex and love must emphasize the development of strong willpower. Love is a deeply intimate relationship between two people, and it is important that both have strength of character.[19]

The Family and Child Welfare

During the post-1955 period, the dual nature of Soviet policy toward the family has become more pronounced. On the one hand, scholars like Kharchev, Soloviev, Sverdlov, and Tadevosian affirm the enduring role of the family as the basic social unit of society, emphasizing its central contribution in bringing up the future generation, and insisting that under communism the family will be more essential than ever. In their view, socialization of domestic work and broadened government participation in the rearing of children will enrich the personality and strengthen the monogamous ties between the sexes. This, in turn, will hasten the dissolution of the family as a union for economic purposes, but will reinforce it as a spiritual and moral union—more necessary for communism than for any other social system. On the other hand, the program of the Party envisages the development of a ramified network of children's institutions that will make it possible for more and more families (and in the 1980's for every family) to keep children and adolescents free of charge at children's establishments if they so desire.[20] This is interpreted by academician S. Strumilin to mean that under communism all children, from the day of birth to the stage of maturity, will live outside the family, while the parents will only visit them. He predicts that "each Soviet citizen, as he leaves the lying-in hospital, will receive a travel ticket into the nursery, from it into a 24-hour-a-day kindergarten, then into a boarding school, and then into independent life, either in industry or in further study in line with his chosen specialty."[21]

All agree that the "remnants" of the unequal position of women in domestic life must be totally eliminated. That these remnants are still substantial is obvious. Adhering to "old-fashioned" ideas, many Russian men still try to assert control over their wives, especially when the latter are submissive and uncomplaining about abuse and overwork. Even when wives hold full-time jobs, they do most of the housework single-handedly. When they do not work outside the home, they spend between ten and twelve hours a day on housework, with no help from other members of the family, in addition to caring for the neighbors' small children and for invalids.[22] While the time women spend on cultural activities has been increasing, it is appreciably less than the time similarly spent by men. Thus, the equality of women and men in the family has not yet been realized.* As Semashko wrote in 1946, "Equality of the sexes cannot be really effective if it is merely declared in law, and is not backed by the creation of conditions that enable women to avail themselves of their equality."[23]

Family life is adversely affected by other factors as well. Housing conditions are still miserable in the extreme. In a period of enormous population transfers, the Soviet housing effort has been quite inadequate and produced conditions of overcrowding far worse than any known during the industrial revolution in Europe.[24] Field findings indicate the accuracy of this recent description:

> The typical picture is . . . of an apartment, which in the West would be the exclusive domain of one family, being shared by as many families as there are rooms, with joint use of the bathroom (seldom indeed is there more than one) and kitchen. . . . If one has a room in a reasonably pleasant building the situation can be manageable. But some people inevitably find themselves in slum areas, where conditions are very bad.[25]

---

* A woman welfare official in Fergana, Uzbek Republic, insists that the position of women is not as good as claimed. She says that they are still servants to the men in the home, and that there is not a man, however stupid, who does not think that his wife ought to serve him. In addition, religion and superstition, particularly among Moslem women, remain great problems.

What this does to people and their relationships is not difficult to imagine.* The majority try to escape the confined, shut-in atmosphere of their overcrowded rooms by joining the huge throngs on the streets and in the parks; some go to theaters, concert halls, libraries, museums. But those who cannot escape readily—the old, the infirm, the overworked mothers, and the very young—are victims of the hardships and irritations that are inevitable. The situation is particularly unbearable for those experiencing marital troubles who must continue to live together because they cannot obtain separate quarters. Frequently, children witness the sexual activities of adults; this is particularly unfortunate when the adults are not aware of the possible effects upon the children.

Evidence on divorce is also revealing of the difficulties involved in maintaining a stable family life. In spite of the fact that getting a divorce in the USSR is complicated and expensive, many people get divorced. Statistics in the Demographic Yearbook of the United Nations show that the reported national annual divorce rate doubled from 0.6 per 1,000 inhabitants in 1955 to 1.6 in 1965. In general, the urban rate tends to be at least twice as high as the rural rate. These rates are considered high by Soviet authorities, and the fact that they have risen is causing alarm. It is pointed out that the 1965 rate is more than double that in France and England (0.7 in both these countries), although considerably lower than that in the United States (2.4 in 1964).

The extent of marital discord is not fully revealed by these statistics, however. Housing shortages, already mentioned, force some couples to remain together even though their marriage is beyond repair. Unregistered marriages are still quite common, so separations often take place without court procedure. Sverdlov describes another situation that keeps down the number of official divorces:

> In legal practice there are frequently cases where the substance of the situation clearly demands divorce, but standing in the way is the fact that if divorce is granted, the wife may find herself in a very difficult position: in the course of long years of devoting her strength to the family, housework, and children, she has not worked outside the family, has no professional skills, is not receiving a pension, and is not able to earn anything. The necessity of refusing her alimony on the basis of an abstract concept of ability to work deprives the court of the freedom to render reasonable and just decisions in such cases.

---

* An important Party official reported that his father was "a simple school teacher before the Revolution, and the family had five rooms. Now, fifty years later, my wife and I and our two children have one room—and I am not a simple school teacher. When we come home from work, tired and short-tempered, there is no privacy, no escape."

Current regulations have led to evasions in the form of *de facto* divorces and unregistered remarriages, rather than to greater family stability among persons who are legally married. This has created problems for unmarried mothers: quite a few of them are *de facto* married to the fathers of their children, but these men have not legally divorced their former wives because of the publicity and expense that would be involved. To remedy this situation, one proposal has been urged that has gained fairly widespread support: the total abandonment of the court form of marriage dissolution—in short, the reestablishment of the method that existed prior to 1944. It is argued that breakup of marriages does not depend on what the law specifies about divorce, but rather on social, economic, and personal factors. Other proposals call for modifications, rather than the complete abandonment, of court procedures. Supporters of these proposals maintain that the removal of all barriers to divorce would revive promiscuity and an irresponsible attitude toward the family. The moderate group is apparently winning out. The draft for a new law does not contemplate a return to the divorce practices of the twenties. The changes that are proposed—lowering divorce fees, confining jurisdiction to people's courts, reducing delay, and doing away with publication procedures—are apparently directed at discouraging excessive haste, eliminating red tape, and reducing the number of evasions.

The lack of appreciable advance toward the Marxian ideal of the relationship between men and women is vividly illustrated by the current debate on what to do about illegitimacy. The press frequently describes cases of unmarried mothers who, in the reporter's opinion, have been mistreated but who cannot get help either from courts or from welfare agencies—help, that is, that would go beyond the small allowance for the child.[26] The substance of one proposed remedy is a return to the pre-1944 position, accompanied by a requirement that future spouses become engaged or enter into some other form of "social revelation" concerning the premarital relationship between them. This is an effort to avoid the technical problems of tracking down and identifying unwilling fathers. An opposing view argues for the status quo, accompanied by more adequate institutional facilities for children and more generous governmental aid to unmarried mothers who wish to keep their children. There are official proposals that birth certificates no longer show a line drawn through the entry "Father." There would be an opportunity for voluntary admission of paternity, and in certain cases, for determining paternity through the courts. Apparently the main concern of the lawmakers is to secure economic support for the child from his parents, whether or not he lives with them. They obviously are not anticipating a transition in the foreseeable future from the regulation of relations between men and women by law to a purely moral system based on matured socialist consciousness and socialist democracy.

As noted in a previous chapter, the school has been moving steadily toward a dominant position in the family-school partnership in rearing the young. By 1955, dissatisfaction with the family's performance in this undertaking, voiced more or less vigorously throughout the Soviet regime's existence, seemed to come to a head. The Party attempted to give the school complete control for a period long enough to mold the child into the kind of person the regime desired. At the Twentieth Party Congress in 1956, Khrushchev announced the decision to develop boarding schools (*internats*) as a new departure in Soviet policy, to the end of solving "on a higher level the problems of the preparation of thoroughly developed, educated builders of communism." While the boarding school was charged with improving curriculum and instruction, with providing answers to many of the educational problems that the ordinary elementary and secondary schools had been unable to solve, its primary purpose was to achieve control over the early formation of basic attitudes and values. In these boarding schools it would be easier to supervise the development of all major facets of the personality: not only would they involve the child in a correctly organized and many-sided program of educational activities, but they would also be families to children from age seven until they graduated from secondary school. Enthusiasts predicted that eventually all children, "normal" and "defective," would be educated in boarding schools, with the consent of their parents.[27]

To make the scheme more palatable to parents, the Soviet regime stressed that its purpose was to increase the moral and material help to families in raising children. Parental authority and supervision would remain a major factor in correct rearing, and experience and direct help from parents would be widely applied. It was claimed that, as a result, the moral influence of parents would be not only totally preserved, but reinforced. Parents were promised that they would be allowed to visit at any time, as well as have their children visit home on Sundays (if the distance involved was not too great, as it was in many instances), and spend their summers at home. With regard to the summers, however, since the children would also be attending Pioneer camps, a month would be all the time that they would have at home. The Pioneers, as well as other youth organizations, would continue the "social control through institutional management" that would prevail in the schools during the academic year.[28]

In spite of the determined effort to popularize *internats,* the project met resistance as it became obvious to sizable numbers of parents that they were under censure for having failed to do an acceptable job of raising their children for communism. This, plus the fact that boarding schools are expensive, forced a redirection of policy. Even at the Twentieth Party Congress, Khrushchev had indicated that children of "lone" mothers and those "for whose upbringing the necessary conditions in the family are absent" would have priority in being admitted to boarding schools. Thus, from the outset these schools were conceived both as an ideal educational facility from the point of view of the regime, and as institutions for child protection and for the prevention and treatment of undesirable behavior. By 1958 educational authorities began emphasizing the second function as the more important one. *Internats,* they said, were for children from homes that were not on a high cultural level—for example, homes where drunkenness and fighting were common. In individual cases, boarding schools were permitted to accept children who had no parents and, in accordance with decisions of local and district soviets, children from large poor families. By 1961, however, boarding schools, although greatly expanded, were no longer considered practical for handling the majority of children. By that time they had become a facility primarily for underprivileged, difficult, predelinquent and mildly delinquent children. A 1958 report stated: "The group of children is the same . . . in all *internats*—illegitimate, orphans, children of mothers with many children and of invalids."[29] In 1961, in the Leningrad Boarding School No. 36, 325 of 422 children had a mother only; 15, a father only; and 16 were full orphans. Only 66 had both parents, many of whom, however, were leading "abnormal" lives. In Boarding School No. 9, about 100 children out of the 330 attending had parents who were under care in psychiatric clinics. Writing in 1964, Kharchev concluded on the basis of these and similar data that "it is characteristic that a significant part of the contingent currently filling existing boarding schools is made up of children coming from incomplete or 'socially unsuccessful' (*neblagopoluchnye*) families—and often the two are synonymous."*

* Welfare workers would not dream of sending their own children to boarding schools. An example is a young woman who visited welfare institutions who had come to Moscow from Krasnoyarsk for further training. Since her husband was working and could not care for their eight-year-old daughter, the child was sent to her maternal grandmother far away from Krasnoyarsk: her parents would not think of putting her in a boarding school even for a few months, although there were several in the city. Another example is the director of a school for deaf children who rejected the demand of the Party that she transfer to another region, because this would have meant placing her child in a boarding school. When her superior, amazed, asked why she would not consider such a school, she said: "I simply cannot bring myself to do this."

Partly as a response to these developments, the extended-day school approach, a modification of the boarding school idea, was revived. An extended-day type school had been opened in Moscow and Leningrad on an experimental basis in 1955 and was then recommended for the entire Russian Republic beginning in the academic year 1956–57. But because of the enthusiasm for boarding schools, the extended-day idea did not take. It was not until the boarding school program began to falter that the extended-day proposal was taken up in earnest in a decree of February 15, 1960. Since then, extended-day schools have been developing at a greater rate than boarding schools, and it is claimed that an increasing number of parents are expressing a desire to place their children in them.[30] This type of an *internat,* open from 8 A.M. to 8 P.M., although it removes the child for long periods of time from parental influence, does not have such obvious condemnatory connotations for the parents as does the boarding school. Furthermore, it is not as expensive as boarding schools, needing less capital outlay. The care of a child in a nursery or kindergarten costs 300–400 rubles per year; in an elementary school, 89 rubles per year; in an extended-day school, 150 rubles; in a boarding school, 900 rubles.[31] That extended-day schools are also designed primarily for underprivileged, difficult, and predelinquent children is indicated by field findings.*

Income Maintenance Programs

Although by 1950 the economy had almost completely recovered from World War II, the economic situation of millions of pensioners remained desperate; no changes in social insurance provisions for workers and employees were made until 1956. In that year, the social insurance system was thoroughly revised—so thoroughly, in fact, that Soviet welfare personnel now refer to the pension law of July 1956 as the beginning of a new era. From the welfare point of view, the most beneficial features of this law were the substantial increase in the level of benefits, the extension of coverage, and the elimination of gross inequalities of the past. These improvements were achieved within the framework of the basic principles that had been developed in the preceding years, i.e., that the major purposes of social insurance are the encouragement of greater labor productivity and the discouragement of labor mobility. What the 1956 act achieved was a degree of harmony,

---

* Boarding schools, extended-day schools, and "homes" are currently grouped and discussed together in official reports—an indication that they are thought of as fulfilling similar functions. They are spoken of as the institutions that permit the most perfect preparation for true builders of communism, while at the same time opening a way for "tearing the child out of a destructive parental milieu." (The quotation is from an interview with Sverdlov in January 1965.)

absent before that time, between the welfare needs of the population and the economic needs of the regime.

However, the situation of collective farmers remained unaltered until 1964, when a social insurance system for them was created that came into effect in January 1965. This quarter of the Soviet population was finally extricated from the unequal, ineffective, and largely inadequate system of mutual aid benefits to which it had been subjected for 48 years. On the other hand, no modifications have been introduced in the system of family allowances. Nor has there been any significant change in the functions of public assistance. This residual line of defense against economic want remains available only for the aged and totally disabled who cannot qualify for social insurance benefits and who have no source of income or relatives legally liable for their support. The types of aid provided by public assistance also remain the same.

PART TWO

CURRENT PRACTICE

All men tend to become the thing they oppose.
—French proverb

6

Organization and Personnel

The basic administrative pattern for social services in the Soviet Union, evolved in the 1930's, has remained virtually unchanged. The four directly involved state organs are the Ministries of Welfare, Education, and Health, and the All-Union Central Committee of Trade Unions. If the primary need of a person seeking help is health care, he is referred to the Ministry of Health; if the best way to solve his difficulties is through training and upbringing, he is sent to the Ministry of Education; if he requires custodial care or long-term economic assistance, he turns to the Ministry of Social Welfare;* if he is a member of the labor force and his need is for assistance—economic and social—arising out of temporary illness, or for rest and recreation, he applies to the trade union at his employing establishment. However, of the four organs, only the Republic Ministries of Social Welfare devote their entire activity to social services; for the other three, the welfare function is only an auxiliary one. Therefore, the discussion that follows will center on the Ministries of Social Welfare; their relationships with the other three ministries will receive brief attention, primarily to clarify arrangements for achieving coordination.

* The Russian word *obespechenie* has been variously translated into English as social assistance, social aid, social security, social maintenance, social guarantee, and social welfare. None of these expresses the meaning of the word exactly, but "social welfare" is used here because it seems to convey more adequately than the others both the spirit in which social services are offered in the Soviet Union and the range of their functions.

Republic Ministries of Social Welfare—Development and Growth

Created at the beginning of the new regime, a republic welfare division was first called the People's Commissariat of Philanthropy (*Narkomat Prizreniia*)—an awkward combination of the "new" with a carryover from tsarist times. This name was quickly abandoned as inappropriate for a socialist society, and on April 30, 1918, was changed to People's Commissariat of Social Welfare (*Narkomat Sotsial' nogo Obespecheniia*). In 1946, "ministry" was substituted for "commissariat" throughout the entire governmental structure.

During the turbulent years of the first post-Revolutionary decade and the first five-year plan, the Commissariat's status was repeatedly and unceremoniously changed from that of an independent agency with republic-wide jurisdiction to that of a minor bureau in the Commissariat of Labor. At present, the highest positions in the social welfare hierarchy are at the republic level. Their connection with the Union administration is through the State Committee of the USSR Soviet of Ministers on Questions of Labor and Wages and Salaries (*Gosudarstvennyi Komitet Soveta Ministrov SSSR po Voprosam Truda i Zarabotnoi Platy*)—specifically, the bureau of state pensions within this committee.[1] In contrast, the Ministry of Health operates at two levels—the Union and the republic—in the performance of all its functions, and the Ministry of Education has a Union ministry for higher and specialized secondary education and republic ministries for elementary and general secondary education. The conclusion is inescapable that there is no all-Union ministry of social welfare because welfare is not yet considered as important as health, education, or labor. This puts social welfare ministries at a disadvantage: compared with the Health and Education ministries, in particular, they have less prestige and resources and their personnel are less skilled. Because they stand lower in the bureaucratic hierarchy, the fifteen Republic Ministries of Social Welfare do not find it easy to obtain cooperation for interdisciplinary endeavors.

Throughout Soviet history, social welfare has been thought of as two-dimensional: "broad" and "narrow." In the broad sense, it is a network of state programs directed toward securing the material and cultural well-being of those who cannot adequately provide for themselves. In the narrow sense, it is specific welfare activities.[2] In the confusion of the immediate post-Revolutionary period there were frequent shifts in emphasis from one dimension to the other, e.g., from concern for "labor invalids" only to attempts to assist all who had been forced out of productive life for any reason whatever. These shifts were dictated by political and economic exigencies rather than by a consistent philosophy of social welfare.

As a result, the first few months' existence of the RSFSR Commissariat, for example, were almost grotesque. Its first commissar, Alexandra Kollontay, found that she was responsible "for relief of various sorts, for people in all parts of the country." The most troublesome were the war veterans. "They formed themselves into an association and elected delegates who every day appeared at the Commissariat of Social Welfare pleading for help, hysterically at times. Often the anteroom of the Commissariat took on the appearance of a mental clinic, when the delegates of the war invalids' association broke down with disappointment and despair."[3] In 1921 the Soviet of People's Commissars decided to close down the Commissariat altogether because they felt it was unable to render even minimal aid and was using up administrative funds to no good purpose. Lenin, who was absent when the decision was made, protested it, and the Commissariat remained open.[4] But as late as January 1926, one official expressed the hope that "the growth of socialist economy ... [will move] social welfare ... from the dead stop at which it has stood up to this time."[5]

The effort to define the appropriate area for welfare activity was not easy. In addition, welfare administration was riddled with apathy, indifference, and inefficiency, was isolated from the community, and had only indirect control over key services. These problems were compounded by constantly changing clientele and by changes in the "norms" of assistance, depending upon the state of the economy. Social welfare was not popular with local soviets, who often ignored it or cut its budget. Finally, the first five-year plan brought in its wake a new host of difficulties. Welfare administrators had to abandon former attitudes and create the conviction that work is a potent rehabilitative tool—a position to which previously only lip service had been given. The changeover was not a smooth one; the proverbial swing of the pendulum took place, and the emphasis on work was overdone.[6]

In 1937, the functions of welfare organs were appreciably increased: the administration of old-age pensions and pensions for disabled workers and employees was transferred from the All-Union Central Committee of Trade Unions to welfare organs.* At the same time, welfare organs inherited the Medico-Labor Expert Commissions (*Vrachebno-Trudovye Ekspertnye Komisii—VTEK*), which had been moved to the Ministry of Labor from the Ministry of Health on May 8, 1932. This oc-

---

* Since 1937, the All-Union Central Committee of Trade Unions and its local branches, the "local plant soviets" (*fabrichno-zavodskie mestnye komitety*), have disbursed social insurance benefits only to those still in the labor force, that is, to working pensioners and to those disabled by temporary illness, pregnancy, maternity, and short-term conditions arising out of work-connected injury or disease. They have also handled funds for sanatoria and rest homes, cultural centers, pioneer camps, and layettes and burials.

TABLE 4

Social Services Provided, Persons Served, and Sums Spent by Fourteen Republic Ministries of Social Welfare in 1963

Republic	Number of Regional and District Departments	Number of Regional and District VTEKs	Number of Nonworking Pensioners	Amount Spent on Nonworking Pensioners (thousands of rubles)	Number of Mothers Receiving Grants	Amount Spent on Grants to Mothers (thousands of rubles)	Number of Inmates in Institutions for Aged and Disabled	Amount Spent on Inmates in Institutions (thousands of rubles)	Number of Trainees in Sheltered Workshops	Amount Spent on Trainees (thousands of rubles)	Amount Spent on Prostheses (thousands of rubles)
Russia	1,729	1,807	14,096,981	4,537,302.0	870,300	218,079.0	130,876	99,220.0	5,442	5,750.0	20,256.0
Ukraine	468	457	3,625,005	1,172,820.0	588,468	45,817.0	35,700	22,593.0	750	591.0	6,618.0
Belorussia	104	84	629,000	155,000.0	178,500	13,575.0	10,000	6,000.0	70	20.0	1,261.0
Kazakhstan	179	285	800,000	250,000.0	488,000	45,600.0	5,735	3,938.4	310	216.5	—
Azerbaidzhan	55	80	242,257	78,033.0	246,703	25,631.0	1,125	822.3	303	96.9	313.0
Latvia	32	23	231,098	71,913.0	25,013	1,829.0	7,670	4,267.1	—	—	313.3
Armenia	—	—	149,129	50,450.0	83,427	8,220.0	850	483.0	—	—	193.0
Estonia	22	20	134,000	42,940.0	18,360	1,110.0	4,400	2,749.0	89	62.2	121.0
Turkmenia	30	50	79,775	2,112.0	47,710	3,364.0	835	554.8	—	—	256.0
Uzbekistan	95	101	435,139	127,800.0	522,690	52,727.0	2,830	1,604.4	565	274.8	1,182.0
Grusiia	66	71	338,357	87,230.0	86,000	7,348.0	810	573.0	300	150.0	351.5
Lithuania	52	43	153,000	39,335.0	51,720	4,700.0	5,600	3,665.0	200	123.0	123.0
Kirgiziia	35	49	127,545	39,519.1	113,879	12,128.6	1,393	947.9	—	—	268.0
Tadzhikistan	40	28	75,564	16,275.0	162,500	12,186.0	1,140	703.2	110	82.8	223.0
Totals	2,907	3,098	21,116,593	6,670,729.0	3,483,270	452,314.6	208,964	148,121.1	8,139	7,367.2	31,478.8

Source: 125, pp. 4-12 and 4-9, respectively. Data for the Republic of Moldavia are not available.
All ruble values are given in terms of the "old" Soviet currency used before the monetary revaluation of January 1961.

curred not because the welfare organs had become administratively effective, but rather because of the unions' disappointing performance in handling social insurance. It should be noted that the unions' task had been complicated by pension legislation that was complex, unsystematic, encumbered with provisions no longer in force, and confused by differences in interpretation. The unions had simply become bogged down in this morass; it was beyond the comprehension of the "toilers," they said.[7]

During World War II, welfare ministries concentrated on helping the military and their families. After the war, some changes were introduced to achieve a more precise division of functions with allied agencies. But these modifications have not been sudden and unpredictable, as were those made during the first 30 years. The pension act of 1956 finally cleared away the encrusted debris of a vast number of statutes, decisions, and regulations whose complexity and inconsistency had led to endless errors that resulted in justified complaints from beneficiaries. As a result, in the past decade it has been somewhat easier to transform policies into programs.

Republic Ministries of Social Welfare—Structure and Operations

While developments in the fifteen Republic Ministries of Social Welfare have not been identical or simultaneous, all have been modeled on procedures in the RSFSR Ministry.* By now similarities far outweigh the differences in modes of operation. Collectively, the ministries serve an area of 22,400,000 square kilometers, with a population of almost 230 million persons, of whom about half live in cities and half in the countryside. For administrative purposes each republic is divided into regions (*oblast'* or *krai*) and each region into districts (*raiony*) and municipalities (*goroda*). (This parallels the governmental structure.) Sometimes, districts and municipalities are divided into sectors (*uchastki*).

Table 4 presents data on welfare services in fourteen republics in 1963. The total number of recipients indicated in this table is 24,816,966. To these must be added 1,966,000 unmarried mothers who received allowances for their illegitimate children, and a small number of severely retarded and grossly handicapped children and non-ambulatory adults. This increases the number of social welfare clients in 1963 to about 26.8 million. If the more than seven million children in families of "many children," the 2.3 million illegitimate children for whom their mothers

---

* However, the RSFSR Ministry devotes more attention and resources than the others to research and publication. For a number of years, it has supported a "scientific council," which was described in 1965 as a consultative research organ. In addition, it publishes *Social Welfare* (*Sotsial'noe Obespechenie*), a monthly journal that is both authoritative and widely read.

receive allowances, the approximately two million public assistance recipients,* and an estimate of the entire client group for Moldavia are included, the grand total comes to about 38.5 million people. In addition, republic ministries supervise the All-Russian Societies for the Blind and Deaf (*Vsesoiuznoe Obshchestvo Slepykh—VOS* and *Vsesoiuznoe Obshchestvo Glukhikh—VOG*), which in 1963 had 370,395 members in 14 republics and were operating 649 training-producing establishments for the blind and deaf. Altogether, then, the activities of social welfare organs touched the lives of almost 39 million people in 1963, or about 17 per cent of the population.

Expenditures amounted to 7.3 billion rubles. If to this sum are added the expenditures for public assistance, allowances to unmarried mothers, and sums spent for the care of severely retarded and grossly handicapped children, the total comes to more than 7.5 billion rubles. The services involved in disbursing these sums do not exhaust the responsibilities of social welfare personnel, however. In addition, their functions include arranging training for invalids in settings other than sheltered workshops, finding suitable employment for the entire invalid group, meeting "daily life" needs of pensioners, making grants to public assistance recipients, running the prostheses-manufacturing establishments, disbursing funds for certificates to retired pensioners for rest home or sanatorium care and for the purchase of medicines and transportation, paying for burials, and supervising a variety of social organizations—peasant mutual aid societies, pensioners' groups, invalids' mutual aid funds—that assist in carrying out the government's objectives in the field of social welfare. In 1963 this work was carried out by fewer than 3,000 regional and local departments of social welfare, which at that time employed about 125,000 welfare workers, and by fewer than 3,100 Medico-Labor Expert Commissions—the key units in vocational rehabilitation for the permanently disabled.

The work of Republic Ministries of Social Welfare was greatly increased in January 1965 when they were assigned a key role in the administration of pensions for members of collective farms. By 1966 more than eight million farmers were receiving benefits.

Chart 1 shows the lines of authority connecting a republic ministry with the government organs to which it is responsible as well as with those subordinate to it. It will be noted that the Republic Minister of Social Welfare takes his directives from and is accountable to both the Republic's Soviet of Ministers and the Bureau of Pensions, which is an all-Union organ. Social welfare departments below the republic level

---

* This estimate is based on a 1962 statement to the effect that since 1958 in the RSFSR "the number receiving regular monthly grants increased by 700,000" (*513*, p. 3).

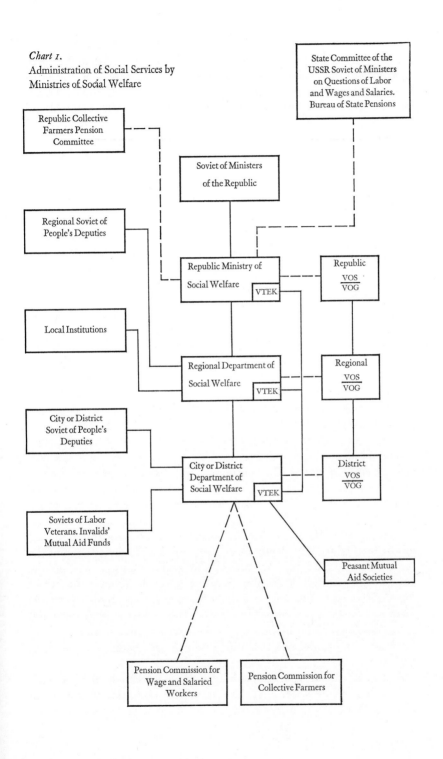

Chart 1.
Administration of Social Services by
Ministries of Social Welfare

State Committee of the
USSR Soviet of Ministers
on Questions of Labor
and Wages and Salaries.
Bureau of State Pensions

Republic Collective
Farmers Pension
Committee

Soviet of Ministers
of the Republic

Regional Soviet of
People's Deputies

Republic Ministry of
Social Welfare
VTEK

Republic
VOS
VOG

Local Institutions

Regional Department of
Social Welfare
VTEK

Regional
VOS
VOG

City or District
Soviet of People's
Deputies

City or District
Department of
Social Welfare
VTEK

District
VOS
VOG

Soviets of Labor
Veterans. Invalids'
Mutual Aid Funds

Peasant Mutual
Aid Societies

Pension Commission for
Wage and Salaried
Workers

Pension Commission for
Collective Farmers

are similarly related to two governmental bodies: the next higher division in the social welfare system itself and the governmental unit at its level of competence, that is, the regional, district, or city soviet. This is because welfare activities are financed by funds from the national and republic budgets as well as local budgets. Benefits for retired old-age and disabled pensioners (and their survivors) from among workers and employees are financed from funds of the social insurance system, contributed by employing establishments, which are transferred to the ministries for this purpose. Benefits for old-age and disabled pensioners (and their survivors) from among collective farmers are paid out of central funds to which the farms and the state contribute; these are also transferred to the ministries for disbursement. Pensions to former members of the military and their families and grants to mothers of many children and to unmarried mothers come from the Union budget. Institutions are financed out of republic budgets, and public assistance out of district budgets.

City-wide and regional organizational divisions supervise and control district offices. At the district level, the personnel usually consist of a director and his assistant, a chief inspector and a senior accountant, supported by a number of subordinate inspectors and some clerical help. A given office's territory is divided into "microcosms" in which case loads are undifferentiated, with an inspector and a clerk in charge of each. This arrangement is preferred to the type where each worker is responsible for only one aspect of the total complex of functions because it avoids, as one administrator put it, "forcing the same pensioner, with several problems, to 'spread them out' in front of different workers."[8]

Medico-Labor Expert Commissions (VTEKs) are made up of three physicians—an internist, a surgeon, and a neuropathologist—and two nonmedical members, i.e., a trade union representative and a staff member from the local welfare department. Instructions for determining eligibility for welfare and lists of occupational diseases are composed jointly by the Ministry of Health and the unions. The latter appoint the commissions' union representatives; the health ministry sets up the panels from which VTEK physicians are selected. About a quarter of the VTEKs now function on a daily basis, with the physician experts forming a permanent group. The local VTEKs are responsible for initial determinations; those highest in the hierarchy review complaints and integrate into practice new scientific findings and advanced methods of expertise.[9]

A disabled person is sent to a VTEK by physicians in the country's regular health care system. At the time of referral, a careful evaluation of the individual's remaining work capacity, if any, is undertaken by the VTEK. The VTEK determines not only the degree of loss of work ability and the reasons for this loss, but also the possibilities of compensating for lost functions. The objective is to define as precisely as possible what kind of work an individual is able to do and what kind of working conditions he requires.* In this way, expert commissions are closely related, procedurally and jurisdictionally, to the local organs of health through which the individual receives his medical treatment, and to the local trade unions and employment enterprises. The reason for placing work with the disabled under a single agency—the Ministry of Welfare —is to achieve integration of the services deemed essential to the rehabilitation process.

The central welfare organs, with policy-making and supervisory powers, make their influence felt throughout the administrative hierarchy not only by requiring reports and conducting spot studies and inspections, but also through their control over budgets. The question arises whether this centralization does not discourage local initiative and prevent the flexibility that is necessary in helping people when they suddenly become helpless or overwhelmed.

A partial answer to this question is that day-to-day administration of programs is the responsibility of the district departments of social welfare, and that substantial powers of review and control are exercised by a variety of local groups. For example, within the newly introduced system of social insurance for collective farmers, the point at which an application for a pension is initiated is the collective farm pension committee (*soviet pensionirovaniia kolkhoznikov*), chosen by the total membership and approved by the farm administration for two years. These committees prepare the necessary documents and make recommendations concerning eligibility, which are then reviewed by the local welfare department.

The next higher links in the chain of command are the district, regional, and republic committees. These are made up of representatives of collective farms, soviets, departments, Ministries of Social Welfare, and state fiscal units. All serve for two years except the republic committee, which remains in power for four years. The district committee makes final determinations on pension requests, and sends approved applications to the local welfare department for payment, later checking to make sure that the payment was made as directed. Regional committees assist with complicated cases, republic committees determine policy.

---

* Disabled persons' cases are subject to periodic reexamination to consider any changes in their condition—Group I invalids every two years, and Groups II and III invalids every year.

Thus, the Soviet welfare system is characterized by centralization of policy-making and financial planning, on the one hand, and extensive decentralization of administration, on the other.

This administrative decentralization has enhanced appreciably the role of republic and local authorities and furthered democratized decision-making in social welfare. Opportunities for flexibility have been increased. Local union committees and pension commissions are familiar with the individuals they are dealing with and with their communities. And although local expenditures must follow the budget worked out jointly with higher-ups, local pressure can have considerable influence at the point at which welfare affects the people most directly. Activity by voluntary social welfare agencies is also subject to local pressure. In response to such pressure local leaders sometimes act without waiting for directives from above, for which they are occasionally recognized and rewarded. Thus, the social welfare structure at the local level, in close association with various citizens' groups, may serve as a shield against the sweeping powers of the central committees. However, the occasional wielding of the big stick by these committees is not necessarily injurious to the individual recipient: it may protect him from local inefficiency and prejudice.

Insight into the degree of democratization of the social welfare process may be gained from examining the fair hearings machinery. For wage and salaried workers who are applying for old age and survivors pensions, appeals from the action of pension commissions are to the "deputies of working people," that is, to the local soviets or their executive committees. Complaints cannot be taken to courts. If the person who appeals is not satisfied with the decision of the local soviet, he may proceed to the Republic Ministry of Social Welfare or, as is more often the case in larger cities, to the city-wide soviet and from thence to the Ministry. The Ministry reviews but does not have the power to reverse the Pension Commission's decisions. If the Ministry finds that the commission's decision is based upon an erroneous interpretation of the law, it can request the department of social welfare in the locality where the appeal originated to resubmit the case to the commission, appending the Ministry's recommendations. Some Soviet authorities find that this procedure is not "orderly" and deplore the fact that unions have no decisive voice in appeals.[10] (If a trade union member of a pension commission disagrees with the others on the commission, all that he can do is seek a reversal by having his position considered at a higher level of the trade union hierarchy, which can then appeal to the appropriate local and regional soviets.)

Collective farmers who are applying for old-age and survivors pensions may submit oral and written requests to the district, regional, and republic pension committees within their system of social insurance, as well as directly to their local departments of social welfare and the soviets. But all end up in the regional committee, whose decision is final. Again, however, welfare organs can make recommendations and ask that a case be reconsidered.

Disabled persons from the wage and salaried group have three channels for lodging complaints: their trade unions, the social welfare organs, and the VTEKs at all levels. Eventually, almost all complaints end up with the Republic VTEKs, which review them in detail, sometimes giving the invalid a complete new medical examination. This time-consuming and expensive process is said to be justified by the recent decrease in complaints—a decrease that is considered a reliable indicator of qualitative improvement in VTEK work.[11] There is evidence that in recent years complaints from welfare clients have received increasingly careful and objective consideration. Social welfare literature now abounds with discussions of the subject, in contrast to previous years when complaints and the need to pay attention to them were rarely mentioned.

As might be expected, welfare operations are not free of problems. There are jealousies, "empire building," and vested interests. Some union officials, for example, believe that the Ministry of Social Welfare is doing a poor job of pension administration and that this function should be returned to the unions—a belief not shared by the Ministry, which points to "weaknesses and errors" that continue to mar the unions' own performance in its segment of the insurance field.[12] Controversy about the best home for the Medico-Labor Expert Commissions—the Ministry of Social Welfare or the Ministry of Health—is still going on, with the unions favoring transfer to the latter, a position held by only a few in the Welfare ministry.[13]

Cooperative arrangements with unions, employing establishments, and a host of other agencies that are required for the smooth operation of welfare programs are not easy to achieve. Nor do things always go well within the Welfare ministries themselves. There are delays, gaps, and inconsistency in interpreting complicated or disputed points.[14] Many "errors" are made, and review teams have to "control" everything. There is red tape and an inordinate amount of paper work.[15] The organizations under Welfare supervision are often accused of formalism, favoritism, bureaucratic attitudes, and contempt for rank and file members;[16] in addition, administrators are cited for callousness and dishonesty.

Existence of problems should not obscure the fact that there has been a slow but undeniable gain in the stability and stature of Republic Ministries of Social Welfare. This gain is evident in greater willingness to entrust new, complex, and important functions to them; readier acceptance of their activities by the community; a higher standing vis-à-vis other government agencies; and a more generous support of research and training—quite a contrast to their turbulent earlier history, when functions were brusquely taken away, workers belittled and underpaid, and the whole operation generally treated with scorn. Involved in a "humanitarian business" that to many may not appear to contribute substantially to the productive forces of the country, social welfare departments have nevertheless grown in prestige and influence.

At the close of 1963, fourteen Republic Ministers of Social Welfare—ten women and four men—responded to a request for suggestions for improving administration in the welfare field.[17] Their suggestions included the following: wider use of machines to save staff time and ensure greater accuracy; an up-to-date compilation of laws and regulations in a manageable size and format, translated into the languages spoken in the several republics; regular scheduling of all-Union conferences and scientific meetings, to which representatives from allied disciplines and professions would be invited; greater efforts to achieve a uniform interpretation and application of welfare legislation in the different republics; and the creation of an organ that would coordinate social welfare activities for the country as a whole. This last proposal, made by the Tadzhik minister, appears to envisage an All-Union Ministry of Social Welfare. Presumably it would be equal in stature to the Ministries of Health and Education, and would assure direct influence at the highest levels of government. Such a suggestion seems to reflect a striving for higher status for social welfare agencies and their staffs—as well as for the people whom they serve.

Personnel

Social work as a profession does not exist in the Soviet Union. Welfare functions are performed by a multitude of people with different backgrounds and types of preparation. Among them, the major groups are social insurance delegates directed by unions; welfare workers employed by the fifteen Republic Ministries of Social Welfare; physicians and nurses in public health; and teachers, children's inspectors, and upbringers (*vospitateli*) in the educational system. The latter group is guided by theory and research developed and conducted by psychologists—themselves a part of the educational system who, however, are not clinicians and consequently do not practice. The activities of these major groups and the training they receive are the next matters for consideration.

Social Insurance Delegates. From the standpoint of numbers, the social insurance delegates outrank all other welfare personnel.[18] These delegates, about half of them women, are trade union activists elected to their office by open vote of the trade and professional groups in the industries and agencies in which they work. They first appeared on the scene in 1930; by 1964 they numbered an impressive 1.2 million and represented four-fifths of all the trade and professional groups. They act in accordance with regulations set forth by the All-Union Central Committee of Trade Unions and are accountable to the union social insurance committee in their place of employment.*

While the responsibility of an insurance delegate embraces everything that can be subsumed under "constant comradely concern" for the well-being of members in his group, his major task is to help sick employees and workers. This means making home visits to those who have not come to work (sometimes this exposes malingerers) and doing what seems required in each particular situation, e.g., calling the doctor, fetching medicines, shopping, arranging special diets and proper child care. If a worker has been placed in a hospital, the delegate will visit him there. He will request material assistance from the plant insurance committee for him, if it is needed, will make sure that a special diet is followed if this is specified by the attending physician, and will see if a member needs rest home or sanatorium care. In addition, he participates in social insurance determinations for those in the labor force, checks work records, assists in assembling documents needed to apply for pensions, makes payments to working pensioners, helps retired workers who wish to continue in employment find suitable jobs, and represents their unions in the VTEKs and pension commissions.

These are the delegate's official duties. But the exigencies of life force him to intervene in situations not covered by official instructions: maintain contact with nonworking pensioners to make sure that their material and medical needs are being met and to encourage them to take part in recreation and volunteer activities; ease the lot of invalids by bringing news and gifts; get in touch with relatives and arrange guardianship for those who are incompetent; counsel drunkards and delinquents, and help victims of the disruption and misery that they create; give advice to spouses embittered by marital conflict; settle intra- and inter-family disputes; recognize and refer cases of mental illness; make suggestions about vocational and employment problems; help widows, unmarried mothers, and the mothers of many children—in short, do a myriad of things to enable human beings to function productively.[19] That is the

---

* These delegates are not to be confused with union officials who work as such on a full-time basis and are paid accordingly, or with union representatives on pension and Medico-Labor Expert Commissions who receive full wages while carrying out commission functions.

major objective—to maintain productivity at a high enough level to fulfill, and preferably to overfulfill, the *Plan* (goals and norms set by the
government to increase production of goods and services).

Delegates are supposed to perform their tasks outside of working
hours; however, it is permissible for a worker to talk to a delegate about
a problem briefly during working hours. Delegates receive no pay, but
the union's insurance budget provides for prizes of varying amounts,
given as a mark of appreciation for good work. Delegates must be responsive, attentive, and sensitive; they must be "true comrades," genuinely concerned about the welfare of their fellow workers and sympathetic to their needs. They are expected to know how to deal with different individuals and to give the right kind of help at the right time.
"The person before everything else!" is their motto—the person not
only as a producer but as a member of his family and community, so
that "we may *work and live* like good communists." Delegates are often
called "the eyes and hands of the collective" and "lovers of people," for
to be a good delegate is to love and care for people, to protect them from
sickness, to help any who find themselves in trouble.[20]

In 1965, the country's trade union budget of 10.5 billion rubles allocated 1.8 million for "training of personnel and social insurance education." Currently, a few delegates are granted paid leave to attend a two-
month course in social security at a Leningrad institute run by the
RSFSR Ministry of Social Welfare. Most, however, depend on short
courses and seminars organized by local unions and on conferences and
meetings at which experiences are discussed and analyzed. This type of
training has increased in recent years, but virtually all of it is directed
toward giving the delegates the technical proficiency necessary for administering social insurance.

Delegates who are genuinely involved in helping their comrades are
apparently motivated by the satisfaction they derive from seeing that
they can do things for people, that they are among the "builders of the
new society." But not all delegates are so involved—some because they
are not told what is expected of them and do not know what to do,
others because they are not interested. On occasion, these self-styled
lovers of the people are received with suspicion, and their clumsy efforts
at comradely help are resented or ridiculed. The training currently provided frequently fails to prepare even "sensitive" and hard-working
delegates for the duties officially assigned to them. Particularly unfortunate is the fact that no organized training is provided to equip delegates for dealing with human predicaments that point to deep-seated
maladjustments of a psychological nature that often lead to what Soviet
authorities call "social anomalies."

Welfare Ministry Personnel. Personnel in the fifteen Republic Ministries of Social Welfare constitute a distinct group, numbering perhaps 150,000.* Today's welfare workers are the products of a stormy evolution that has left visible scars. Major problems have been their inadequate educational preparation, high turnover, low occupational status, and, on occasion, open corruption. From the outset, social welfare operations (*sobesovshchina*) in their totality have been considered an unproductive activity, with a staff characterized by ignorance of reality, lack of know-how, unwillingness to cut through red tape, and failure to cooperate constructively with allied agencies.[21]

It was not until 1935, when Stalin proclaimed that "cadres determine everything," that serious thought was given to educational leaves and in-service training and to the encouragement of constructive self-criticism. Although concern with producing and retaining qualified personnel has been a prime consideration since then, progress has not been easy.[22] Staffs are still composed of people with different training from different fields, at times very far removed from social welfare.[23] There is dissatisfaction with the training that is available. Writing in 1957, one worker said:

> It isn't that in general there is no place for us to study. No. There exist in our republic institutes, technicums, and schools of varying "profiles," both regular and correspondence courses. But what is to be done if a person has decided to devote himself to welfare work? Such special educational facilities do not exist in our system.
>
> People will object to this by saying that there are law schools and institutes; go ahead and study! But [these schools] prepare court investigators and not welfare workers. What we would like is, without leaving our jobs, to have access to special training, precisely for our work, to raise our qualifications in order not to fall behind in life.[24]

Four years later, in January 1961, the Minister of Social Welfare of the RSFSR wrote: "The training of personnel, improving their qualifications, and raising their professional and political level—this is our major task for the coming year." Currently, the literature is still full of discussions about how to hire, train, and retain qualified personnel.

The main obstacles will not be unfamiliar to American welfare workers. There is still the problem of status. Even the physical aspect of the welfare operation indicates the relatively low esteem in which social welfare activity has been held. "Sometimes the conditions [in which

---

* This estimate is based upon data which show that in 1960 three republics—RSFSR, Ukraine, and Uzbekistan—employed 107,000 workers and that the ratio of workers to clients is quite similar throughout the country (*SO*, No. 1, January 1961, pp. 3–6; and *453*, pp. 81, 83).

welfare workers at the bottom of the hierarchy] have to work constitute a crying denial of the most elementary sensitivity toward pensioners—sick, aged people, often without limbs," complained the editors of *Sotsial'noe Obespechenie*. "For some unknown reason, in a great many cities," they continued, "to welfare are assigned the most unattractive, dilapidated, and, above all, crowded quarters, where even the inspectors sit shoulder to shoulder, and as for pensioners—there is no place for them to sit."[25] One pensioner-activist explained:

> [During] the six months [following the passage of the 1956 pension law], the role and the prestige of local welfare departments have grown considerably. Before this it was not rare to hear people speak of welfare with contempt: said they, " 'Social welfare,' what is it? It isn't industry or agriculture; it isn't a department of education or health." Welfare usually found shelter in the worst buildings, and if it asked for something better, the answer was: "Look who comes to you."[26]

That improvement in housing has been slow is obvious to anyone who has seen Soviet welfare offices. In 1965, the Uzbek Republic Ministry, for example, was housed in a building so dilapidated as to appear unsafe, to say nothing of its many broken windows stuffed with newspapers. Within the framework of a system that places overwhelming value on "productive" work, it has been difficult to assign high priority to the labors of personnel to whom the Soviet government has entrusted the care of those who often cannot look after themselves. That contempt for clients exists even among welfare workers, who unconsciously brand their own activity as unimportant, is revealed in a statement made by a regional director in June 1961. "In district offices, bureaucratism is most often exhibited by staff who either forget or do not understand that welfare in our socialist society has nothing in common with charity. The welfare worker ... is not doing the client a favor, is not showing him kindness—rather, he is helping the client realize his constitutional rights as a citizen."[27] Welfare workers' low place in the occupational ladder is reflected in the fact that their salaries usually lag behind those of teachers and health workers, although their case loads are heavy. All this results in a high turnover.

The absence of a recognized profession with competence specific to the welfare field is another major problem. Anybody can be a welfare worker. Because of a preoccupation with fulfilling legal provisions, the qualifications that have come to be valued most are law and economics degrees for inspectors, specialized medical training for doctors handling disability determinations, and training in finance for bookkeepers. An increasing proportion of new workers come with these qualifications, but the majority still have only a general secondary education or less.

In 1958, for example, the total number of welfare workers with law degrees was 900—out of a total of perhaps 100,000.[28] In 1966 the personnel in the RSFSR social welfare ministry was supposed to include 3,610 attorneys and 11,318 workers with special secondary education. In fact, the totals in these two categories were 539 and 344, respectively. Furthermore, in many regions in-service training was not available or was irregular, and what was available was frequently of low quality.[29]

For a selected number of workers in key positions, arrangements can be made for them to take the necessary courses in law, economics, and finance by correspondence, supplemented by paid leaves to attend a thirty-day summer session to prepare for and take examinations. For others, in-service training is made available. These efforts are supplemented by "training letters" and materials in professional journals. In-service training instructors are, for the most part, practitioners with degrees in law, economics, and bookkeeping who emphasize correct procedures for eligibility determination.

Socialist Humanism. The increase in special training, reinforced by greater organizational stability, has raised appreciably the competence of welfare personnel to determine eligibility. However, the feeling that this type of competence alone is not sufficient to meet the job demands has been slowly gathering momentum. The need for personnel to possess other skills became evident in 1945 when the major attention of welfare workers was claimed by war invalids. Top priority directive with reference to them was "not to cut everyone's hair in the same style," but to know each individual and his special needs.[30] This stress on an individual approach spread from war invalids to other clients. Especially since 1955, there has been a willingness to adjust procedures to clients, to some extent at least, instead of expecting clients to adjust to administrative demands. It has been stressed that "sensitivity, attention to 'petty things,' which for clients are not at all petty, is the clear-cut responsibility of every welfare worker." Formalism and bureaucracy have been condemned: a worker is not to give a cut-and-dried answer to the client to the effect that he is either entitled or not entitled to something or other, without bothering to explain why this is so or offering to help if the client is bewildered or crushed.[31] Workers have begun to visit clients' homes and their places of employment to learn what their needs are, to "become convinced of their urgency and reality." Welfare personnel are instructed to display a genuine concern, to study complaints carefully, rectify mistakes promptly, make explanations clearly and patiently.

This has led to the belief that welfare workers are "good" people who know that the way clients are helped is important in making the process constructive. As one lecturer pointed out:

Soft chairs, however numerous, will not create a desirable atmosphere during the reception process if the inspector is gloomy, irritable, and grumbling, if his very appearance and tone reflect the fact that he wishes to get rid of the client as soon as possible. The inspector should not let the client understand that he does not trust him, or phrase questions in an insulting manner. The inspector must not talk to the client while looking in another direction or digging among his papers: this may save time, but shows a lack of attention and respect for the client. Obviously, the worker must not address the client familiarly or fail to offer him a chair.[32]

A similarly insightful attitude seems to be evident in instructions to the VTEK:

It is always necessary to make sure that the invalid's visit to the VTEK is not burdensome and unpleasant for him. During these visits the invalid must always find a genuine concern for his health, his fate, his life plans. It is essential that the conduct of VTEK personnel should create confidence. Of extreme importance is the need for the expert physicians, at the invalid's or the sick person's very first visit, to create a warm relationship with him. If this obtains, the actions and decisions of the experts take on a psychotherapeutic significance which can, more forcefully than anything else, inspire the invalid or the sick person with confidence in his strengths, create a perspective for getting well and returning to work. The physician must be a friend to the invalid and the ailing, an adviser and consultant. . . . The entire activity of the expert physician, its content and form, must be saturated with the spirit of socialist humanism.[33]

Like social insurance delegates, welfare workers are being asked to infuse with service the technical operations of income maintenance provision, both for people whose needs fall within a "normal" or socially acceptable range and for the "socially anomalous"—unmarried mothers, alcoholics, defectives, and the like. But while training for technical proficiency is by now quite well organized and widely available, the only advance in the service realm is the recent stress on "culture." That respect for human dignity, good manners, and recognition of the right to economic aid are essential in administering welfare programs is well known; that in modern society these features do not add up to "service" is equally recognized. However, the need for what Soviet administrators call "deeper" training is not being seriously discussed.

Further insight into the attitudes and problems of some welfare workers is afforded by a summary of a discussion with an administrator:

This regional director of social welfare had been on the job for less than two months; she was assigned the job by the Party, and took it because it is the duty of every communist to do what the Party asks. But she does not like the job. She is 42 years old and has 18 years of experience teaching in secondary schools—history and literature. Changing jobs did not adversely affect her material circumstances, but she cannot get used to the "difficult contingent of clients" she must serve, considers them hopeless in terms of growth and change, and is not particularly interested in their long tales of past deeds and experiences and in helping them live out their lives in comfort and dignity. Also, she said, it is most depressing for her to find that among her staff of 30 workers, there is not a single one with higher education. She feels that she cannot talk with them about anything except the technicalities of the job. She is aware that there is some jealousy and dissatisfaction over the fact that she was forced on them as director and that people on the staff with years of experience in welfare work were passed over. She criticized vociferously the fact that there was only one inspector in charge of arranging employment for invalids in her entire region. Obviously, she said, he is too overburdened to do an effective job. She was indignant that agency structure does not allow the assignment of a regional staff person to supervise the seven invalids' and retarded children's homes in the region. This means that her office has no control over what goes on in these homes. She was quite upset by the large number of complaints. She said that the controllers who come from the republic office are only interested in correct eligibility determination and care nothing about socialist humanism, an individual approach, or the best interests of the clients. She found them formal and rigid. She asserted that her staff is in welfare work either because they like it—something she simply could not understand—or because they cannot find better jobs. She does not think she will last on her job.

This regional head literally hung on me, being visibly hungry to talk to someone whom she considered educated and humanitarian (this she told me in no uncertain terms), even though not a communist. Further conversations revealed that she is bitter, divorced, and worried about her 20-year-old son. Later, her superior explained that she is not considered a good Party member, that she had done a poor job of teaching and was transferred to her present job because they did not know what to do with her, and that they were disappointed with her because she had been given opportunities to become a leader and had failed.

Indigenous Nonprofessionals. In spite of lip service to the "withering of the state" theory, welfare organs did relatively little toward developing and using indigenous nonprofessional personnel in a consistent fashion during the first 40 years of their existence. Apparently, they had their hands full with problems of regular staff and were unable or unwilling to take on the task of integrating an amorphous segment of "activists" into their much-buffeted and much-maligned structure. It was not until they became swamped with demands generated by the 1956 pension law that they resorted to the indigenous group.

Since then volunteer inspectors (*vneshtatnye inspektora*) have been used in many cities (they are almost unknown in rural communities) as helpers to paid welfare personnel, being "attached" to the latter and under their supervision. They are not paid, but do enjoy a semi-official status that lifts them above the client mass. These indigenous volunteers are said to be especially helpful to regular staff in public assistance cases, in providing services to pensioners, and in the handling of complaints.[34] Currently, there may be as many as 60,000 active volunteers—a sizable adjunct to the country's 150,000 welfare workers. The work of indigenous nonprofessionals is not always a clear gain for the welfare department, however. It is almost impossible to spread their activities evenly to cover the entire client load; they must be taught if they are to do more good than harm; to be worthwhile their work must be carefully planned. All this takes time and effort on the part of the regular staff.[35] A more fundamental difficulty has cropped up in recent years: the Soviets of Labor Veterans, a volunteer parent organization, has been accused of wanting to "supervise" instead of "work," and to undertake activities deemed "inappropriate" because they are at cross-purposes with what is wanted by government, Party, and trade union organs.[36] This explains, in part, why there has been no increase in indigenous personnel since 1958.

The All-Russian Societies for the Blind and the Deaf. In the early days these societies' staffs consisted for the most part of indigenous nonprofessional volunteers. In-service training organized for them aimed at raising their political and cultural level. But as the training-producing establishments under the societies' control expanded, the need for translators for the deaf and specialists in setting up and maintaining appropriate work situations for both groups of these handicapped became acute. The societies began to employ more paid workers, and increased allocations for training.[37] To date, however, the number of qualified paid workers remains insufficient, so that the paid group continues to rely heavily on volunteers to carry out its plans and directives, especially in localities far removed from the centers.

Medical Personnel. Basic to the social service activities of medical personnel is the concept of "patronage," which in Russia has always extended to many areas of life and implies a comradely, protective relationship. This orientation leads to a willingness of Soviet medical workers to go more than halfway to reach a patient and, together with the fact that women constitute a large majority of this group, explains the emotionally supportive rapport that frequently develops—especially with the less sophisticated patients and those bowed down by age, pain, or grief. Emphasis on prevention and on a team approach to treatment that characterize Soviet medical services are natural concomitants, it is claimed, of collective philosophy. Pediatricians and nurses are expected to work closely with other specialists in the medical setting and with persons on the outside who have a role to play—parents, teachers, managers of employing establishments, and members of social organizations.

Educational Personnel. In the Soviet Union teachers perform child welfare services as well as teaching functions, and parents frequently turn to them for advice on child behavior and child guidance, and occasionally for counsel with their own personal problems. Hence, educational personnel in nurseries, kindergartens, elementary and secondary schools, and children's institutions contribute importantly to the provision of social services for children.

The conviction that a child's progress in school depends significantly on how his parents play their roles is widespread among Soviet educators —as is the feeling that discussions with parents in the school setting are often too general and are carried on without due consideration for the differences in cultural and educational levels of parents and without an adequate understanding of the patterns of upbringing in the home. Hence, home visits by teachers are fairly common. In the home, the teacher is expected to acquaint herself with the child's general life situation, and especially with the nature of the interaction between him and his family as it is reflected in upbringing and disciplinary practices, attitudes toward the child, and his responses. The teacher must strive to develop a relationship based on mutual respect and confidence, and only as a last resort bring to bear the authority of the educational system.

Many teachers find it difficult to fulfill these expectations because of large classes; others have not completed their secondary education—although this is a requirement—and do not know how to handle some of the problems their pupils present; and a few, according to Soviet writers, are drunkards, money-grabbers, and degenerates. In some areas of the country, primarily the Central Asiatic and outlying republics, teachers do not engage in child welfare services. It should also be noted that as a child gets older, and especially in the secondary schools, visits by teachers to the homes become extremely rare: the relationship between the school and the home grows more formal and more strictly confined to educational demands made on the student.

Certain teachers—usually those with at least a secondary education, considerable experience in working with children, and demonstrated ability to involve the community in serving children—are selected to work as children's inspectors.[38] These inspectors deal with nonattendance and other behavior problems, investigate complaints of neglect and abuse, and make arrangements for those who cannot remain in their own homes. The inspector's management of a given situation may take one of three directions in cases in which the rights of children are jeopardized: he may embark on an educational campaign for parents and other responsible persons, bringing in, when necessary, the pressures of a series of relevant collectives; he may initiate action to deprive the parents of custody because there is no reasonable possibility that they will ever offer the child a suitable environment; or he may act as a third party in quarrels between separated or divorced parents.

Upbringers in Institutions for Normal Children. Upbringers concentrate on the physical and moral aspects of child-rearing and on psychological conflicts. They are concerned with "living" as contrasted with "learning." For the most part, upbringers are teachers. Some have benefited by in-service training or special institutes that stressed the psychological aspects of growth and development.

A sizable portion of the huge Soviet literature on institutional care is devoted to detailing the qualities that a true upbringer must possess. First and foremost is genuine love of children, since nothing good can come from the most persistent efforts if love is lacking. Further, the upbringer must be imbued with openmindedness and sensitivity; only then can he appreciate the needs and problems of the children. He must be able to establish the closest and most intimate relationships with his charges without, however, permitting familiarity. He must be strict, but not petty or pedantic. The upbringer who wishes to attain lasting results must develop his character, his willpower, and his knowledge so that he will be a good example for the children, for whether he knows it or not, he will profoundly influence them.[39] All this presupposes that he has fully absorbed the knowledge, insight, and understanding derived from his study of psychology.

He must also know how to utilize the strengths of the collective—the collective formed by the children themselves within the institution, as well as their collectives as members of the Young Communist League (*Komsomol*) and the pioneer organizations; in addition, he must connect institutional life meaningfully with the community. The upbringer must be skilled in utilizing interests and abilities that he uncovers in his charges, and in broadening the sphere of their interests.

That many upbringers fall far short of the ideal is widely recognized, and the difficulty of finding qualified teachers willing to undertake the arduous upbringing task is not an infrequent theme in the literature.

Reasons for these shortcomings are several. Soviet administrators and researchers do not know how to select the right kind of people for up-bringing work. They have not worked out manageable criteria that could be uniformly applied, even though some are beginning to realize the importance of eliminating guesswork and vague generalizations in selection. No significant work has been done on how to evaluate the potential unbringer's personality. In the better institutions, judgments are based on whether or not an upbringer is "good to the children," since the belief is widespread that being good *to* children is good *for* children, and that the children's feelings about the upbringer are the best measure of this goodness.

Another problem is that there is no agreement about what kind of training the upbringer ought to receive and what his skills should be. Some believe that no special training is needed, and that what is required is skill in organizing games and teaching children table manners.[40] Others believe that upbringers ought to get qualitatively different training from regular teachers—for example, in using the interview as something more than a friendly conversation—and that they must be skilled in "charting the personalities of their charges" in terms that demonstrate a mastery of psychology.

A third difficulty is that the overwhelming proportion of upbringers—as well as of other types of welfare personnel—are women. The possible undesirable effects of this "matriarchy" on children in institutions are obvious; its extension to a wider sphere is a matter for serious concern. As one educator pointed out in 1964:

> At present a serious problem is the insufficiency of male influence on boys in and out of school. Among teachers and pioneer leaders the majority are women. In the family the rearing of children is primarily the job of the mother, and often this is true not so much because the father is occupied but because of the strength of undesirable traditions that persist in the family—"the father works, at home he must rest."[41]

A fourth problem is that upbringing work attracts the less qualified teachers. Thus, of every 1,000 women employed in educational settings, 189 have higher education and 594, secondary and incomplete secondary education. But of every 1,000 women who work in children's institutions, the respective numbers are 39 and 609.[42] This tends to create in the institutions a hard-core, "vested interests" group of those who resist change and new thinking. The struggle that has to be waged by some staff members to make a "newer" point of view prevail is clearly observable in many settings.

Defectologists. It is universally agreed that for raising and educating children who suffer from mental and physical handicaps, the teachers and upbringers should have special training—should be "defectologists." Although as yet progress toward this goal has been spotty, it has been accelerated in the present decade. Currently, special training is offered in Moscow, Leningrad, Kiev, Minsk, and Sverdlovsk; it has progressed from a general defectological preparation to specialization, starting in 1959, in deafness, mental retardation, blindness, and speech defects. This special training follows secondary education and continues for five years, being one to two years longer than the regular teacher-training course. In order to attract able young people, stipends are 50 per cent higher than those paid to regular teachers, and salaries of defectologists are 25 per cent higher than those of regular teachers. It is claimed that the interdisciplinary character of the training program makes it possible for defectologists to work effectively with a variety of specialists involved in serving handicapped children.*

Since 1960, when this aspect of their work was found to be woefully inadequate,[43] defectologists have had to pay more serious attention to vocational training for their charges—in addition to teaching specific academic subjects and working with parents in order to interpret to them the meaning of their children's handicaps. The latest thinking also stresses the use of psychotherapy:

> Not only psychoneurologists must know how to employ methods of psycho-therapeutic influence on abnormal children, but defectologists as well. Psychotherapeutic methods must be the basis for organizing any institution for abnormal children (organization of routine, relationships between the teacher and the children, the character of the rewards-punishments system). The role of psychotherapy is especially great in the individual approach to each child.[44]

Recognition of the benefits to be derived from a therapeutic community approach is likewise evident.†

---

* The following knowledge areas are included: general political, general pedagogical (including some age-centered psychology), subject specialty, medical (fundamentals of normal and pathological physiology, neuropathology, psychopathology, clinical retardation, clinical knowledge of diseases of organs of hearing and speech), special pedagogical, special methodological. Besides this, future defectologists receive training in physical education, drawing, and hand work. Theoretical preparation is coordinated with practical training (90, pp. 42–44; 514, p. 26).

† However, the concept of a therapeutic community is discussed only in connection with defective children. In 1960 two eminent defectologists noted the importance of "special preparation of nurses, attendants, and the entire service staff in institutions for [severely] retarded children. These personnel in many instances determine the quality of work in these institutions, since they are in constant contact with the children" (95, p. 11).

The following summary of an unscheduled conversation the author had conveys an unofficial view of Soviet educational personnel. The speaker is a specialist in pre-school education who has achieved considerable eminence in her field, and is now traveling throughout the Soviet Union as a consultant and organizer to arouse interest and help communities set up adequate facilities.

The influence of the Stalin repressions is by no means over, she said. Many people in education are still frightened and will not speak out or agree to innovations even though these are badly needed. A lot of what is done is lip service only, "for show," and has no real substance. If you look a little beneath the surface, you find that the "show" aspects are for a few children, while the great majority are still receiving services of poor quality. It is extremely difficult to obtain resources for some educational efforts, especially those that enhance life but do not result in something specifically productive, as, for example, for aesthetic aspects of pre-school education. In Moscow and some of the other larger cities the situation is incomparably better than on the periphery. In the outlying districts, teachers often become almost desperate and have to fight or cajole to secure resources.

The higher-ups in education—in the Academy of Pedagogical Sciences and its affiliates—are quite far removed from reality. They are so taken up with their experimental and base schools that they do not know what is actually going on. In practical situations it is often impossible to achieve the goals they set up; but failure is interpreted as personal rather than being seen for what it really is. Much that is published is a repetition and embroidery of what Krupskaya and Ushinsky had said better. As for Makarenko, she does not share in the general idolatry of him, because he worked in special circumstances, and she thinks it is a mistake to apply his teachings across the board.

She thinks that pedagogues and defectologists are poorly trained. In her experience with speech therapists, for example, she found them quite ineffectual. She said that some young teachers resent guidance by experienced, older teachers. In her view, the family is irreplaceable. For this reason she is critical of parents who, once a child reaches school age (or even earlier, if they can get him into a nursery or kindergarten) wish to divest themselves of responsibility for his rearing. On the whole, she thinks that there is too much emphasis on the rational, knowledge-oriented aspects in Soviet education, and too little on upbringing, by which she said she meant the heart as distinct from the mind, character as distinct from skill. The result is one-sided and does not produce rounded, fine people, she thinks.

She believes that it is impossible to achieve anything of lasting importance without traditions. In Soviet society it is most difficult to establish traditions because of the frequent changes from one approach to another and from one program to another without analysis, follow-through, or evaluation. She cited the British as outstanding in respect to creating traditions and building on them. That this intelligent and refreshing woman occupies a position of importance bodes well for improvement in services to children.

Only one generalization appears valid with regard to Soviet welfare personnel: as a group, psychologists, physicians, defectologists, and teachers are more sophisticated and more professional than the others. But within each specialty wide variations in attitudes, in knowledge, and in skills are apparent. Some stand out as intelligent, well-informed, willing to discuss the matter at hand rationally, without resort to bombastic claims. Usually, these are the people who concede frankly that ideals and reality in their country are far apart, and sometimes even hint that they are ambivalent about the ideals. Many are excited about their work and interested in innovations—even if these come from a "capitalist" country. They rose in spite of hardships and seem to be people who are not afraid to speak up for their clients, who know their clients well and respect them, and who do not spare themselves in giving the best possible service. Warm and sensitive, they do more than the rules require, thereby commanding the kind of respect that is accorded to skilled professionals who also are impressive human beings. "Socialist humanism" is especially apparent among indigenous nonprofessionals. For the most part, they are retired men and women, many with backgrounds of revolutionary work, who have experienced both the "old" and the "new," and unquestionably prefer the latter. Most are dignified, poised, and good-humored, at once creating a relaxed and congenial atmosphere. Quite a number in all groups are alive and searching, keen on a genuine exchange. With them "short" interviews turned into day-long discussions. This is especially true of research workers, who frequently have a broad intellectual orientation and wide knowledge and culture. A few are truly able people—with open and inquiring minds, eager to experiment, to learn and to share, endlessly dedicated—to say nothing of being excellent conversationalists.

In sharp contrast, some are arrogant, suspicious, hostile, intolerant of anything that does not fit with their preconceived notions about "capitalist" society. Usually these are people whose knowledge about social welfare in the United States is woefully inadequate and inaccurate: in many instances, the information is withheld from them by those in the higher echelons. In relation to clients, some show only a superficial concern, are rigid, cold, and condescending. Among administrators, some lack perspective and breadth, are insecure and overbearing, shut off questions with which their subordinates are fairly bursting, and are given to propounding the official line and to answering in vague and irrelevant generalities—thereby often embarrassing their own staffs. Some are strict disciplinarians, interested only in getting the clients to do what is required. Even among many of the researchers, knowledge of Western thought is disappointingly limited, and their eagerness to prove that Soviet knowledge and practice are superior to what is known and done in the West, childish. Few are secure enough not to be defensive about gaps and inadequacies, and some are unable to accept admittedly justified criticism—even when it is couched in friendly and constructive terms. As might be expected, some are almost visibly maladjusted people who cannot tolerate anything that challenges their status and achievements.*

One feature characterizes the outlook of practically all welfare workers: they are markedly goal-oriented, and their goals appear to be quite immediate, clearly posed, and understood within a sharply limited frame of reference. Almost no one talks about improving social functioning or providing the means for happy and well-adjusted lives. Pensions, grants and benefits, medical care, custodial care, jobs are seen as desirable in themselves and are not judged in terms of their potential for enriching social and personal life. With regard to children, what most welfare personnel are interested in is how to teach the required subjects so that the youngsters will pass, how to keep them healthy, disciplined, and attuned to societal values that are clearly spelled out and about which there can be no dispute. Few wonder whether all this adds up to a happy life for the child. It is more or less assumed that if character is properly formed, the child will be happy. By energetically striving toward what they consider well-defined, specific, and realizable goals, welfare personnel feel that they are contributing to building communism and to strengthening the Soviet state.

* One psychologist, in a monograph on adolescents, quoted from two of Margaret Mead's books that were published in 1928 and 1942 because, he said, although coming from a "bourgeois" scientist, Mead's findings supported his own conclusions. When asked whether he had read Mead's later works, published in 1951 and 1955, in which, among other things, she was quite critical of Soviet child-rearing practices, the psychologist became infuriated and declared violently that he had not read them and would not read them for, he said, "I spit on her!" These later works are in the Lenin Library.

7

Treatment Methods: Collective-Individual

The Soviet psychological theories that emerged after 1936 led inevitably to a heavy reliance on the *collective* (defined by the Large Soviet Encyclopaedia as "a joining of people who are linked together by common work, general interest, and goals"). Makarenko and his followers saw the collectives—the family, the school, co-workers, political or social organizations, and, finally, the whole of Soviet society—as the most powerful factors in molding the individual.* According to their thinking, no collective should be isolated from the others; on the contrary, each should be integrated with the others, should be guided by the same principles, should seek the same objectives, and should exhibit the same basic characteristics. The ideal is a group-centered society dedicated to developing the individual in such a way that he will want to stay within each group, and feel, think, and act in conformity with it.

At the same time, Makarenko and the more perceptive and flexible

The discussion in Chapters 7 and 8 is based in part on some of my previous writings: *240, 244.*

* The major formulator of the collective philosophy was Makarenko. His teachings began to attract attention in the latter part of the 1930's; during the next twenty years, he attained undisputed preeminence in his field. He is still frequently quoted (see, for example, *27*, pp. 4–5; *12*, p. 16; *114, passim*), and conferences are devoted to discussions of his ideas (see *14*). Other thinkers often referred to are K. D. Ushinsky and Krupskaya. The latter was especially concerned that the pressures exerted by the social group should not destroy the child's individuality, but rather aid in developing his unique personality.

among the Soviet welfare workers who follow his theories insist that the collective philosophy presupposes the genuine individuality of each person—an awareness of his differences from others and of the peculiar ways in which the conditions of his life have affected him. However, the individual can achieve maximum potential only *through, by,* and *for* the collective; it is the collective's values that he must use for judging his behavior and establishing his life goals. Identification with the group protects him from maladjustments such as withdrawal or rebellion, and opens the way for genuine growth and self-fulfillment. A normally developing individual will not seek escape from the collective.

Soviet theoreticians contend that an appreciation of each person's individuality requires not only the gathering of biographical and medical data, but more important, an understanding of his interests, what he values in friends, what work means to him, how he responds to group demands, how he behaves toward those in authority, and how he handles his own and the collective's possessions. The welfare worker arrives at this understanding by carefully observing the individual's behavior in different situations and by distinguishing what is really essential to his character from the accidental or temporary. Sometimes an apparently insignificant act, a casually uttered word, or a minor temper outburst, scarcely noticeable to the untrained, can become for the sensitive observer the key to understanding the inner world of the individual. However, Soviet authorities urge that caution be exercised when attempting to distinguish traits attributable to inherited factors from traits shaped by the influences of the environment. They point out that even young children, by the time they come to the attention of welfare personnel, exhibit firmly established personalities in which the inherited and the acquired are inextricably interwoven. The welfare worker must avoid basing his treatment on superficial characteristics, and must seek to include in his evaluation both the positive and negative aspects of an individual's personality.[1]

Collectives are nurturing to the individual only when correctly organized. They must have a clear-cut social purpose; the demands they make on individuals must be reasonable, taking into account weaknesses as well as strengths; they must make sure that individual feelings are protected and that respect is shown to the individual, so that group disapproval can be used to spur incentive; they must impose a "constructive" discipline, a discipline based upon the individual's recognition that his own interests and those of society are the same; they must be willing to try new methods to overcome difficulties;[2] and finally, in order to prevent alienation, they must be integrally connected with the society. Sustained by the authority of both the welfare worker and the group, the individual's obligation to adhere to the decisions of the collective becomes almost a necessity. This combination of forces is the basis of the influence exerted by welfare personnel—an influence that is effective only if each member of the collective participates actively in the making of group decisions.[3]

Given a correctly organized collective, group criticism and self-criticism—procedures widely employed in Soviet society as mechanisms of social control—will have a beneficial effect, and the collective will not be regarded by the individual as cold or distant because of its impartiality. On the contrary, the individual will feel that he can always count on the collective to help him, no matter what his problem or in what situation he finds himself. If, for example, his family rejects him, he will see that this "first collective" is only part of society, and that the overwhelming number of his fellow citizens are ready to welcome and help him.* This frees him from fear of sharing his problems with others, and thus from becoming excessively concerned with himself. He is then better able to carry out his obligations to society.[4]

The Soviet welfare worker acts on the assumption that "the specific conditions of personality formation and the principal features of the relationships that arise are entirely determined by the influences of collectives," and that therefore societal norms exert a greater influence on the personality "if they are supported by the collectives."[5] Thus, a child's progress in learning will be determined as much (if not more) by the aid he receives from his fellow pupils and the guidance he obtains in his family as by his ability to absorb what the teacher says.[6] Soviet doctors emphasize "the importance of work done in groups—on the theory that the group [is] a most important social entity in re-motivating and re-socializing the patient."[7] Failure to treat the individual as a member of the collective at all times weakens both the individual and the collective, it is said. For example, a major obstacle to changing a child's behavior can be created if a teacher separates her work with him from her work with the entire group, concentrating on his particular interests rather than seeing them as inseparable from the common interest. Even if she helps him to learn better, she will not make of him "an activist in social development"—a conscious, purposive member of Soviet society.

---

* A prominent psychologist, when asked if the solicitude shown by the government and the Party for the people's welfare does not foster dependency, or at least a tendency to slough off responsibilities, answered that, for the most part, present arrangements are designed to prevent dependency, and that much of what the state does for people is done out of necessity rather than because of an unduly paternalistic solicitude. As an example, she noted that many mothers must work and therefore kindergartens (of which there are not enough) must be available. Besides, she remarked, some people would become dependent even if the state did nothing.

Findings in the field leave little doubt that the therapeutic potential of the collective is widely understood by welfare personnel. They know that the stronger the individual's identification with the group, the greater the influence of the group upon him; that the greater the number of the individual's needs satisfied by the group, the stronger his propensity to identify with it; and that the greater the uniformity of group opinion and the larger the segment of the environment controlled by the group, the greater the influence it will exert on the individual.[8] But this knowledge is applied with different degrees of sophistication. Some workers hew to Makarenko's teachings almost blindly. If failures occur, they say it is because a collective was not created and manipulated skillfully, and because Makarenko's ideas were not used "creatively." Others are striving to introduce some flexibility and to use the collective with greater regard for specific circumstances.

Considerable differences of opinion exist about what is required to create a beneficial collective that will not exceed its proper functions. For example, many educators feel that groups are often permitted to make judgments that are too harsh and to exert pressure that is oppressive. Others caution against collectives that enforce a stultifying uniformity. One prominent teacher of deaf children writes:

> It is essential to avoid the kind of boarding school life where the child during the whole day carries out various tasks because he *must*: he must get up on time, he must do gymnastics, he must take a walk before breakfast, he must eat breakfast, he must attend classes, he must do his duty as monitor, he must participate in social work. The pedagogical process built on the principle of "must" stifles initiative and can easily lead to a breakdown in behavior that conceals an unconscious protest.[9]

Some professionals believe that the creation of sound collectives is an undertaking requiring skill, and should be entrusted only to personnel trained in the behavioral sciences,[10] while others maintain that lay persons, without professional guidance, can create them by themselves. There also appears to be a split between those who regard all collectives as capable of dealing with both material and psychological needs, and those who would allow only professionally guided collectives to handle the latter function. This latter group also maintains that rigid and excessive reliance on the group may do more harm than good. For example, the achievement of true individuality may mean that some children will require more than the average amount of attention from the welfare worker. The other children may feel that this is not "objective" treatment and shows favoritism.

In contrast to Soviet theory, which emphasizes the role of the collective, American theory emphasizes the role of the individual. However, there has been an effort in both countries, especially in the past decade, to develop an integrated theory that will combine the best features of both approaches. Described below are four cases, selected from the best examples of Soviet practice, which are representative of this new approach, that is, a more discriminating use of collectives and a greater emphasis on individual treatment.

Case 1. Andrei: 9 years old, 2nd grade. Therapist: Teacher[11]

Andrei, who was repeating the second grade, was brought to school by his grandmother. "I have suffered from him during the past few years," she said; "when he was small, he obeyed and was loving, but now he is impossible: he is rude, mischievous, disobedient, refuses to study. Please be strict with him."

During the first two schooldays I repeatedly tried to draw A. into classroom activity, but without success. On the third day he ran away. I notified the parents and asked them to come to school. A day later the boy was again brought to school by his grandmother, who declared that his father and mother were busy and could not come. They asked that I be stricter with A. The boy remained for the day and then ran away again.

I visited the family and discovered that the father, a skilled worker, is almost always at work, and that the mother, also a specialist, is busy from morning till night. The upbringing of the boy is left to the grandmother, who is helped by a domestic worker, Zoya, whose influence on the boy is generally a harmful one. For example, she constructs a house of blocks, and then tells the boy to knock it down. She fills his head with tales of witches and water and forest spirits. All this was told to me by the grandmother, who insists that she devotes all her own energies to raising the boy: she feeds him herself, washes him, puts on his shoes, dresses him, takes him to films and puppet shows, refuses him nothing.

I asked if the parents know about A.'s behavior, and if so, how they reacted to it. "I don't tell them everything," the grandmother replied. "I feel sorry for the boy. Some things they know. . . . But what is the good of it? They are almost never home, especially the father. And the mother, too, like a guest—comes, eats, and goes away again until late at night. And when she happens to have a free evening, she laughs at the boy's mischief, and kisses him, and then he behaves worse."

I left a note for the parents, insisting that one of them come to school. On the next day, the mother came during her lunch hour. I tried to persuade her of the necessity to change the abnormal conditions in which her son was being raised. My remarks made no impression on her, and she declared: "There is no need for you to be concerned. A. is a good boy, healthy, gay; when he is older he will realize the value of study and will study well. Right now he is still too young, and there is no point in forcing him. If he has to repeat a grade, that's not so bad." She then smiled pleasantly and said that she was in a hurry to return to work.

I invited the father to school, and explained to him the causes for his son's failure. He became very upset about his failure to concern himself with the upbringing of his son. We set a date for a family conference, which would include himself, his wife, the grandmother, and the domestic worker. At this conference it was unanimously agreed that a different approach to A. was required. (The father again expressed regret about neglecting the upbringing of his son.) The boy was called in and told that henceforth he must conduct himself in a manner appropriate for a second grader; he must dress himself, see that his clothes and shoes are clean, put away his things, and, most important, attend school and do his lessons conscientiously. We discussed the "Rules for Students" and how best to help the boy follow them.

A. was very surprised to see us all so seriously concerned about him. His mother and grandmother were amazed at the degree of the father's concern, and my insistence upon improvement in the boy's behavior at home and at school forced them to think carefully about the way they had been rearing him. A.'s father demanded that they cease amusing the boy with silly nonsense, and that they stop doing for him what was within his own capacity.

The father and I agreed to keep each other informed about the boy's behavior. In the beginning the father talked with the boy almost every day to see how he was doing with his studies and household duties. I helped the boy make friends with his classmates and included him in the collective's socially useful tasks: monitoring, keeping the classroom clean, caring for the flowers, and so forth. I visited the family often to see if the mother and grandmother were fulfilling their part of the agreement. It took a great deal of work, but through the joint efforts of the school and the family we eventually achieved results. A. started to attend school regularly, acquired needed self-discipline, studied conscientiously, and was passed into the next grade.

In Andrei's case, note that the teacher concentrates on securing only the information that will help her understand the boy's immediate problem—his lack of interest in school. In seeking this information, as well as in using her experience, she takes the initiative and is active and persistent. The objective she sets for herself is limited and well-defined, and to achieve it she relies exclusively on rational means: discussion, explanation, exhortation, persuasion. She succeeds in changing the parents' behavior toward their son by using the authority of the school system and her own expertise. She sets in motion a direct, easily understood program that the family has helped to formulate, and persists until the desired goal is reached.

Case 2. Yosif: 15 years old, 4th grade. Therapist: Teacher[12]

I familiarized myself with Yosif's background prior to the beginning of the school term. My attention was drawn to him by the following description submitted by a former teacher: "Y. has spent two years in each class. He can learn, but is terribly lazy. He reads, writes, and solves problems as his fancy moves him, but ignores things that must be learned. He pays no attention during lessons, occupies himself with irrelevant things, fidgets. He rarely does his homework, and what he does is always done badly. Often he runs away from lessons; his mother brings him to school through one door, and he runs out the other. He missed 157 lessons without an excuse. His parents are only superficially interested in his school work. They make no demands on him and disagree about his upbringing. Often Y. beats up his classmates. He is rude to adults. He is extremely slovenly."

This description raised many questions in my mind. To answer them I decided first to observe the boy's behavior in school. At first I found Y. to be a healthy boy, with no signs of mental retardation. However, further observation revealed that he had limited knowledge and poor study habits. The saddest discovery was that this 15-year-old boy had set no objectives for himself and lived without purpose. It was difficult to include Y. in the collective or in the pioneer group not only because he had a weakly developed feeling of collectivism, but also because he was four or five years older than his classmates.

When Y. came to school on the first day very sloppily dressed, I noted it, but did not say anything to him. Prior to the beginning of the lessons, I introduced two new students to the class and said that it was necessary to treat them as good comrades. The pioneer leader asked permission to speak and declared: "We shall be friends with them if they study well, so that there will be no failures in our class either in study or discipline." On the first day Y. behaved well, but he did not exhibit any great interest in study. At the end of the day's lessons, I discussed the "Rules for Students" with the class. We talked in detail about the fifth rule: "Come to school clean, combed, and neatly dressed." We then held elections for the "sanitary commission." Somebody proposed Y. as a candidate. I supported the proposal, and Y. was elected unanimously. He declared with joy that he would try to do a good job as a member of the commission.

On the next day, before the beginning of lessons, the commission members checked the hands, ears, collars, and handkerchiefs of the students. Y.'s hair was combed and his shirt ironed, but he was not as active during the inspection as the other members because his hands were dirty. When the results of the inspection were discussed, a student pointed out that Y.'s haircut violated school regulations. I told the school nurse about Y.'s behavior. Following our conference, the nurse discussed the significance of cleanliness with the members of the sanitary commission, and checked to see how the commission was doing its work. One day she attended the class inspection. She praised the commission, and Y. beamed with joy. He had acquired habits of personal hygiene in the process of performing a socially useful task under the guidance of the collective.

I began working on the problem of Y.'s failure to pay attention during lessons by asking the pioneer leader and Y. to help me straighten up the bookcase. Y. eagerly consented and worked conscientiously. We talked about books, and it became clear that Y. liked to read and had read quite a bit. I asked the boy what he wanted to be. He answered that he did not know because he was stupid. Asked why he thought he was stupid, he replied that everyone, including his teachers and his parents, had told him so, and that his inability to pass the fourth grade proved it. I insisted that this was not true, that if he studied well he could become a first-rate student, and that I wanted to discuss the matter with his parents.

When I asked Y. when would be the best time for me to visit his parents, he suggested that I ask them to come to the school. He did not want me to go to his home, but I wanted to see what his family life was like, and on my next free day I called upon his parents. Y.'s mother, with anguish in her voice, asked what kind of trouble he was in. She said that they were used to having teachers call, and that I was the eighth teacher Y. had had. She then began describing Y.'s upbringing in detail. Before entering school, she said, he had been wonderful, but after starting school he became a different child. It was as if the school had transformed him—made him stupid. He became disobedient and ill-mannered both at home and at school. All attempts to persuade him to change his behavior, including physical beatings, accomplished nothing. She suggested that perhaps he was born stupid, but insisted that he at least finish the fourth grade.

It became apparent that during Y.'s preschool years he had been badly spoiled. He had not been taught the skills needed for participating in a school collective, nor had his will to overcome difficulties been developed. Afraid of work, he began to avoid his lessons, and soon acquired the reputation of being stupid.

During my conversation with Y.'s mother, his father listened attentively, but only toward the end did he comment: "It would be good to straighten out the boy so that he can at least finish elementary school." At this moment Y. entered the room. I felt that it was essential that I destroy the notion in the minds of the parents and of the boy himself that he could not study, and substitute for it a faith in his potentialities. Using Makarenko's tactic of surprise, I said to the parents: "Your son can and will study well in the same way as the other good students. We have both agreed on this and shall put forth our best efforts, but you must help us in every way you can."

Y.'s mother continued to talk for a long time about the boy. She indicated that they previously had given up hope, but that now she felt something might come of him after all. She agreed to pay closer attention to the boy's appearance, see that he had a place to do his homework, and assign him errands that would be helpful to the whole family. I insisted that both parents stop beating Y. and screaming at him, and that no matter what he did or how he behaved, they were to control themselves and substitute tenderness and caresses for curses and blows.

In Y.'s case it was clear that both the school and the home had been at fault. For seven years he had been told he was stupid, lazy, and rude. This angered him, and his protest took the form of rudeness toward good students, deliberate breaking of the "Rules for Students," and hostility toward his teachers and other adults. To develop new patterns of behavior, I decided to apply

Makarenko's pedagogical principle of practice in correct acts. But first it was necessary to instill in Y. some confidence in himself.

Soon after my visit to his home, Y. and I had a long talk about his future. The boy declared that he wanted to get a job and be independent of his parents. He said that he had been trying to do this for a long time, but that nobody would give him a job. "They say, 'You are of school age; you must study.' But I don't know how to study." I told him firmly that he was able to study in the same way as other students. We agreed that he would try to do his lessons every day, and that I would help him finish fourth grade, after which he could get a job and enroll in an evening class for young working people. In this way a meaningful goal was established.

To achieve this goal I had to arouse in Y. an interest in learning, as well as help him to develop a habit of systematic study. Guided by Makarenko, I tried to give him as many happy experiences as possible in connection with the overcoming of his difficulties. I worked slowly to arouse his interest in learning, and then to accustom him to a firm routine and regular work habits.

Y. enjoyed and was fairly good at reading. On one occasion he did very well in reviewing a book for his classmates that I had recommended; I praised him in the presence of the other students, which made him very happy. I began to draw his attention to books that I thought would be both interesting and useful to him. These helped to develop his moral standards, as well as to increase his participation in the collective and motivate him to work and study. Cautiously and trying to avoid being obvious, I gave Y. social assignments—work that was for the good of the whole collective—and helped him carry them out, praising even his smallest successes and stressing that he would be able to do better in the future if he tried. He was put in charge of the class loan library, was sent to buy theater tickets for the whole class. These activities gave the boy a sense of satisfaction and nurtured a feeling of self-confidence. He developed the drive to carry out each assignment conscientiously. The class began to recognize his contribution and to treat him as a deserving member of the collective—a good comrade.

During the first quarter Y. was not late a single time and did not miss a single lesson. He gained confidence in his abilities and increased his capacity to learn, but there remained serious gaps in his training. The most difficult to fill proved to be his lack of knowledge of Russian and arithmetic. It was necessary to obtain the assistance of the class collective. I worked with Y. individually, called upon him to recite in class, and praised him, which gave him great pleasure, but this was not enough. It was imperative to resort to the collective. Y. was ashamed to receive help from children younger than he. A solution was found when the pioneers decided to organize "mutual aid" for all students who needed to do better in Russian and arithmetic. This cooperation in study created a constructive setting for learning and strengthened the collective, developing in the children a feeling of responsibility for their classmates. It was a good influence on Y. Gradually he became friendly with his classmates; absorbed by the group activities, he began to act in accordance with the interests of the group.

I decided to find out how Y. was behaving at home, and on my free day I visited his family. His parents greeted me happily and told me that their son had changed completely; he studied, read, and tried hard. In turn, said the mother, they were trying to do everything we had agreed upon. She had not come to school because the boy forbade her to. He insisted that he was a big boy and did not need his mother to watch over him. The parents were glad that their son had finally settled down and become responsible.

After lengthy cooperative work between the school and the family, Y. became a well-behaved student and finished fourth grade with all 4's and 5's. [The Russian grading system is from 2 to 5 in ascending order of excellence.]

In Yosif's case, the teacher works with two collectives: the family and the school. In the process, a sound relationship develops between the boy and the teacher. Note, however, that the teacher takes this relationship for granted. She does not know what role it is playing in her efforts to help the boy, and therefore cannot use it as a therapeutic tool. On the contrary, she deliberately limits herself to rational means and to dealing with the boy on a "conscious" level. With Yosif's parents, the teacher's exercise of authority is tempered by her finding that they suffer keenly over their son's failures and by her belief that their errors in upbringing stem in part from their low educational and cultural level. This contrasts with Andrei's teacher's critical attitude toward his parents, whom she considered at fault and insensitive. At school, Yosif's teacher sets in motion the progression advocated by Makarenko. First, she makes demands upon the boy, then has her demands supported by the other children, and, finally, has the boy make demands upon himself within the standards set for the whole collective. She is successful with Yosif not only because she herself accords him respect while making reasonable demands upon him, but also because she sees that the collectives of his classmates and of his family act in the same way. She gives encouragement, trust, and rewards, expresses confidence in his abilities, and is consistently patient and supportive. The goal she establishes is limited and well-defined and, most important, understood and desired by Yosif. She moves toward it cautiously, but in a systematic way, with her major steps taken only after careful thought.

Case 3. Oleg: 9 years old, 1st grade in a boarding school. Therapist: Psychologist[18]

Prior to boarding school, Oleg attended a regular school, where he failed to be promoted to the second grade. Even though he was studying the class material for a second time when we began to work with him, he was doing badly. The boy usually looked angry or morose; he almost never smiled. Often (sometimes several times a day) he had fights with other children; during the fights he became frenzied. These fights were brought on by the most insignificant incidents: someone accidentally pushed him, or made a joke about him, or took one of his possessions. Some fights occurred without any visible reason.

During classes O. fidgeted, talked, or annoyed his comrades. Not infrequently he would leave his seat without the teacher's permission and promenade around the classroom. Neither the teacher nor the upbringer could stop him. Outside of class he conducted himself in much the same way. He fought in the dining room over his place in line, in the bedroom over his turn to go to the bathroom. If he wanted a game or a book when it was being used by another child, he grabbed it away from him; he would never share his own belongings with anyone.

O. never admitted that he was at fault; he always blamed one of the other children. He was stubborn, and insisted upon doing everything his own way. For example, if during a lesson he desired to read or do something else, under no circumstances would he do the work at hand, no matter how much he was coaxed. His stubbornness became especially pronounced after punishment. (His behavior was inconsistent: there were occasionally days when he behaved fairly well.) With upbringers and teachers he was withdrawn and uncommunicative. The teacher who taught O. prior to his entering boarding school sent an unfavorable report, which ended with the statement: "Nothing good can possibly come of O. He is a psychopath, lacks ability, is perhaps even mentally retarded, and is altogether undisciplined." A neuropathologist who had observed O. for a year reported that O. had had a brain concussion when he was six years old, and had spent a month in the hospital. Noting that at present there were no neuropathological deviations, he nevertheless concluded: "Neurotic development, mental retardation of unclear etiology."

In order to gain a better understanding of O., we studied his mental development. Our initial observations made us doubt the diagnosis of mental retardation. O. was able to recount past events well; he was well-oriented to his surroundings. We found that in terms of general knowledge he was not behind the good students in his class; in fact, in some respects he was superior to them. We decided not to be satisfied with these data, however, and to check to see if there were deficiencies in O.'s intellectual activity that would account for his poor performance in school. We found that he could understand material more complex than that which is usually presented to children in his class and recount it well. His knowledge of nature, society, and work processes was equal to that of the best students in his class. These data forced us to doubt even further that he was mentally retarded. In order to settle the question once and for all, we carried out an experiment designed to reveal how quickly he learned—the most important criterion in diagnosing mental retardation. Summarizing all our data, we concluded that O. was not mentally retarded.

Perhaps what hindered the boy from doing well in school was a poor attitude toward study. To see if this was the case, we observed how he worked in class and during the preparation of his homework; we also had discussions with him. He clearly had a very positive attitude toward study, a finding confirmed by a statement made by the boy's father: "Last year things did not go well for O. in school. He was very upset by this, cried, strived to do better at any cost. But for some reason he did not succeed."

We then turned our attention to the nature of the boy's failure. To our surprise, we found that his writing was adequate, that he read well, that he could solve the arithmetic problems included in the first grade curriculum. Given these facts, it was difficult to understand why he received low grades, often did not know how to answer the teacher's questions, and came to class with his homework either poorly done or not at all. We decided to seek an explanation of the boy's peculiar behavior in his interpersonal relationships.

Studying O.'s relationships with his comrades, we saw that the conflicts that arose during class had an immediate effect upon his work. For a long time after a conflict, he did not calm down: he was agitated, muttered to himself, etc. As a result, he missed out on the lesson, did not hear the teacher's explanations or the questions put to him, and generally neglected his work, with the consequence that he did not have enough time to complete the assignment. Often he came to class still angry because of an earlier conflict and again could not get interested in the lesson. In addition, he frequently felt mistreated by the upbringers, a feeling that lasted several hours and was expressed in sullenness—for which he was often made to leave the classroom. This also slowed his scholastic progress. When he was calm and listened to the teacher's explanations attentively, he carried out his assignments well and rapidly. But he was rarely calm. It was essential to discover the reasons for the continual conflicts between O. and those around him, and for his lack of self-control, stubbornness, anger, and the other peculiarities of his behavior that hindered him from studying well and made him so difficult to deal with.

We found that O.'s reaction to conflict, as a rule, was not appropriate; that is, he overreacted. For example, he would beat up a comrade merely because the comrade touched him. However, in most cases, O. was not the initiator of the conflict. Hence the idea that he was a hating and vengeful child was altogether incorrect. Actually, he was the victim of his own heightened emotions. For example, at first everybody thought that O. was at fault in his treatment of his neighbor in the dining room and his neighbor in the classroom. But close observation revealed that both these children made fun of O. precisely because he reacted quickly and excitedly. Unobserved by others, these children tormented him by joking about him, touching him, taking away his books and pencils.

The next thing to be determined was whether O.'s peculiarities had become permanently established forms of behavior. This required, on the one hand, finding out what events precipitated the appearance of these peculiarities, and on the other, discovering what O. was experiencing within himself at the time and what his attitude toward himself was.

According to data received from the family, O.'s early development was normal. He was a docile child, ate and slept well, began to talk and walk on time, was well-behaved. However, when he was six years old, his mother deserted the family. (Prior to the desertion she had paid little attention to O. and his younger brother, being preoccupied with work, amusements, and personal affairs.) The father, an invalid (missing one hand), worked as a punch press operator. He was attached to his two sons, took them to the movies, the zoo, etc. After his wife left he refused to put the children in a "home," and took care of them himself. But between his job and all the household chores he had little time for O. Thus the boy grew up almost without supervision.

The desertion by his mother had a great significance for O. It had a destructive influence on him, as it would on any child. However, it was complicated by another circumstance. It was soon after his mother's desertion that O. suffered his brain concussion, after which he began to be irritable and excitable. In his interpersonal relations he began to show lack of self-control. He frequently got into fights and quarrels, and while there was someone to take the part of the other children, O. was alone and defenseless without his mother and father.

According to relatives and neighbors, O. was blamed and punished by the parents of children he hurt, as well as by acquaintances and relatives. Because he was growing up without a mother, everyone considered it his duty to "raise" O. He could not complain to anyone except his father, who was away at work all day. (The boy lived with his grandmother and aunt, but with neither of them could he establish a relationship that could compensate even in part for the absence of his mother. His relatives had their own families, and paid little attention to O.) O. felt that he was unjustly treated, and that he was alone and defenseless. He became stubborn and responded negatively to any punishment and to critical remarks by adults. In his relationships with children he became suspicious, watchful, and strived to defend himself —no matter what. Thus, even prior to entering school he had established a definite pattern of relating to peers and adults that made him extremely difficult to deal with in the collective.

Entering school did not eliminate O.'s difficulties: it exacerbated them. In school he continued the same pattern of relating to children—frequent fights and conflicts. The possibility of such conflicts increased because he was forced to associate with others constantly. When a fight took place in the yard of his apartment, O. could go home, but at school he had to remain until the end of the school day. The teacher, failing to take into account the boy's peculiarities, reacted sharply to his behavior and punished him often. These punishments increased O.'s irritability and excitability. They not only did not diminish the number of conflicts he had with other children, but even led to conflicts with the teacher. All this hindered the boy from studying and led to poor grades. The problem was further aggravated by the boy's frequent dismissal from class; this meant that he missed important lessons. At home nobody could help him. Poor grades led O. to behave badly at lessons. He became involved in irrelevancies, talked, argued; his scholastic position deteriorated further. The teacher who taught him during that period reported that he stopped obeying her altogether, and did what he wanted when he wanted. His behavior at home also worsened, complaints from neighbors increased, and the boy was punished oftener.

O.'s disturbance increased when his father, to whom he was attached, began to punish him. His father was the only human being with whom the boy was tender, close, affable. Now this contact too was destroyed. Gradually O. began to withdraw. By the middle of his first year at school, he was seeking to escape from the other children. His teacher reported: "O. tried to remain apart. He was not interested in the activities of his comrades." He became morose; his face expressed anger and hate.

Briefly, the dynamics of O.'s behavior were as follows: The departure of his mother, coinciding with the neuropsychic trauma following his brain concussion, led to a gradual breakdown in his interpersonal relationships. Conflicts and quarrels generated emotional disturbances, which were deepened by lack of success in school. All this brought about a defense reaction that expressed itself, on the one hand, in withdrawal and stubbornness, and on the other, in aggressiveness and pugnacity. Gradually these traits were transformed into rage, moroseness, suspicion, and general ill-will toward others. Entry into boarding school only worsened the boy's emotional state by tearing him away from those close to him and forcing him to associate with others constantly.

In order to begin pedagogical work with O., it was necessary for us to gain an understanding of how he himself regarded his behavior, his scholastic potential, and his interpersonal relationships. Most important, we had to find out whether or not O. desired to change his position in the collective and was suffering from its negative evaluation of him. Over a period of time, we observed him, had a number of discussions with him, and requested that he address himself to a variety of problems. It became clear that in non-academic activities—sports, games, monitoring duties, artistic endeavors—O. considered himself less capable than other children, but was quite calm about this incapacity, and did not strive to equal the others. In contrast, in the academic area he considered himself as capable as the best students in his class—an evaluation that corresponded with his real potential. Failures in academic work were the main causes of emotional disturbances in the boy: he endeavored to do well academically, and when he failed, he became very upset. It became clear that O. was unhappy about his interpersonal relationships, and that he suffered from his schoolmates' negative evaluation of him, when he burst into tears and declared that his life was a very unhappy one because he was a poor student and behaved badly.

We attempted to solve the problem of O.'s emotional outbursts through several interrelated measures. First, it was necessary to overcome the hostility of the boy toward adults, specifically toward upbringers. This required giving him the attention and kindness and showing the concern and trust that he was deprived of when he lost his mother. Because of the conflicts that had arisen in the boarding school, the participation of an outsider—someone who would be able to win the boy's trust and love—was enlisted. In this case the outsider was a male psychologist. In addition, it was necessary to change the feelings of O.'s upbringers and teachers toward him. This required acquainting them with the special situation of the boy, and making it clear that the difficulties in his behavior were the result of his emotional state. Because O. felt punishments were unjust, and evidence of dislike of him, it was necessary to eliminate them as a pedagogical measure in his case. Punishments deeply traumatized him. If O. strived to study and behave well, it was decided that the fact that he could not control himself and was excitable was not something that he should be punished for. This decision turned out to be a wise one and led to good results rather quickly.

The psychologist's first efforts with O. were met with hostility. But after the boy began to feel the positive intentions of the psychologist, and was told that in the psychologist's laboratory he would be able to play with good toys, he cooperated—though he was still suspicious. At the laboratory, O. became aware of the psychologist's genuine interest in him. Soon he began to come on his own initiative, but he refused to discuss his behavior or school work. Although at first O. was morose and withdrawn, after a week the psychologist was able to evoke an answering smile, and gradually, in the presence of the psychologist, the morose and angry look began to disappear. In the laboratory, O. became happier, livelier, talkative; after ten days, he responded to the psychologist's kindness with a caress.

O.'s relations with the upbringers also changed. The cessation of punishments at once eliminated his feeling of being unjustly treated, and he began to accept criticisms willingly. After a month the upbringers noted that O. had become more cheerful. "It turns out that he knows how to smile," declared one of the upbringers. Concurrently, measures were taken to improve the disturbed relationships between O. and the other children. First, his school routine was individualized to afford rest, to give the boy an opportunity to spend some time alone, and to provide for greater variety in his school activities. These measures lessened the strain on the boy's nervous system. Second, O. was taught to control himself, and to analyze his behavior. The reasons for his conflicts were explained to him, and he was shown that often he himself was to blame. He came to understand that his comrades sometimes teased him only because he reacted so stormily. Third, he was given additional help with his school work. Since every bad grade led to a breakdown in behavior and dismissal from class, it was decided not to give O. any bad grades for a time. If he did his assignment badly, he was allowed to do it over. If he did not hear the teacher's explanations or did not understand something, he was given additional explanations and help. In case of conflicts in class, he was given a chance to calm down, after which he was allowed to return to work.

These three measures improved O.'s emotional state, but certain of his habits and traits of character were still well-entrenched. Even in a calm state, he was greedy, impatient, and given to lying. To eliminate these faults, we decided to utilize the principle of self-education. Discussions revealed that O. recognized his failings quite well. This made it possible to set before him an objective: overcome these failings. When this overall objective was accepted by the boy, we divided it into a series of specific goals. Only a few goals were set at a time; after these were achieved, new ones were set. The first goal was an improvement in O.'s behavior during lessons, then in the bedroom, then in line, and, finally, in the dining room. O. eagerly cooperated, noting daily (in a notebook issued to him especially for this purpose) whether or not he had achieved the established goal. His behavior was systematically examined and analyzed to determine why it was or was not successful, and how he must behave in the future.

The boy's behavior consistently changed for the better. His conflicts with comrades gradually came to an end, he became much better disciplined, he ceased being negative and stubborn. There were occasional breakdowns, but only in those instances when upbringers disregarded the prescribed pedagogical measures. (This happened most often when substitute teachers were in charge.) Gradually, the breakdowns ceased altogether—even in reaction to severe punishment. The boy's scholastic performance improved greatly: from the end of the third quarter of the first grade and during the entire second grade, he received 4's and 5's in all subjects except writing. After two months of work with O., he stopped withdrawing, began to associate with comrades, and willingly participated in class activities. The boy's internal change was reflected in his external appearance: he began to smile often, and appeared cheerful and friendly. In his family, too, sharp improvements were noted.

At the end of treatment, which lasted five months, O. presented the following picture: He had passed into the second grade with 4's and 5's; he was intellectually well-developed; he read a great deal and understood well what he read; he was friendly and well-behaved with comrades; he had almost completely ceased quarreling and fighting. He was still slightly excitable and lacking in self-control, particularly when fatigued or when he found himself in especially difficult circumstances. When he did not do well in his school work, he would occasionally ignore a request, get angry, or become stubborn. But all this happened rarely.

Thus, by using an appropriate, individualized approach, it was possible to train O. to study properly and behave himself in the collective, as well as develop other positive traits of character. However, O. apparently had some defect in his nervous system that caused a permanent instability in him—a fact that his upbringers had always to keep in mind.

In Oleg's case, the psychologist works with a boarding school collective. She gathers data from a variety of sources: the boy's father, relatives, neighbors, a former teacher, a neuropathologist, and his current upbringers, teachers, and classmates. She uses a variety of means to arrive at a diagnosis: analysis of background data, observation of the boy in different situations, numerous tests, periodic discussions with the boy. With patience and care she scrutinizes the explanations advanced for the boy's destructive behavior—including the neuropathologist's diagnosis of retardation—until she establishes what she deems to be the true etiology. In this case, in contrast to the two previous cases, the therapist consciously creates a situation that encourages the boy to enter into a constructive relationship with a man, in order to help him break out of the circle of traumatizing relationships that engulfs him. But this relationship is used as a therapeutic tool for only a short period of time, and is not relied upon for a major change in the boy's behavior. The therapist is aware of the undesirable pressure on Oleg from his constant association with the collective, and introduces measures to mitigate it. Unlike the other therapists, she does not have a circumscribed goal for her client. While the short-term objective is to help him achieve his scholastic potential, there is also a long-range goal of equipping him to cope successfully with the difficulties that may crop up in the future. She does not view her accomplishments with Oleg with the finality that seems evident in the first two cases; rather, she considers the task of developing positive traits of character in him as only begun.

Case 4. Valya: 15 years old, 8th grade. Therapist: Psychologist[14]

Valya had developed many negative traits: she was suspicious, distrustful, jealous, hostile, rude, and aggressive. By the time work with V. was initiated, she had lost all her friends and was always becoming involved in quarrels with her classmates, occasionally coming to blows. Below are some descriptions of V. by her classmates:

(1) "Nothing in class genuinely excites her. When we discuss something, she shouts, argues with everyone. She is terribly fond of shouting, of being a commander. But when we decide to do something, she refuses, saying she has no time. She imagines things—for example, that people are badly disposed toward her. Her attitude toward people is altogether bad. She lies about even insignificant matters."

(2) "V. is not liked in class. She keeps herself apart, does not carry out a single assignment, wrecks everything, always gets angry. She is very rude, shouts at everyone, doesn't let anyone say a word. If she is criticized, she is altogether impossible. Most important, she butts into everything; this is very irritating."

(3) "She has no trust in anyone. It always seems to her that she is being abused, that everyone wants to find fault with her, to treat her worse than anyone else."

With teachers, also, V. had become rude, distrustful, and suspicious. They complained that she was doing badly in many subjects. One teacher insisted that V.'s behavior had become unacceptable, that she not only behaved badly herself, but disrupted the entire class. At home V. was always quarreling with her mother and the neighbors and fighting with her brother; as for her father, she simply ignored him. "She has changed greatly," her mother said. "Only last year she was no problem: she was doing well in school, obeying me. She gave me nothing but joy. But she has become reserved, sullen. She does not talk about anything. Her character has become hard. My heart bleeds for her."

To determine what had led to the sudden appearance of these negative traits in V., we collected material about her progress in earlier grades. We learned that she had been considered a good pupil, although her report cards showed that during the first three quarters of each year she had a number of 3's and only in the fourth quarter earned 4's and 5's. V. had been regarded as a good student because she was industrious, neat, disciplined, and at the same time clever, with varied abilities; she carried out all kinds of social assignments, always led in reading poems at the morning assemblies, danced, etc. She was friendly with her comrades, participated with pleasure in pioneer work, helped backward children—all this further strengthened the opinion that she was a good student. Up to the fifth grade, in conversations with V.'s mother, the teachers had always praised V.

In her family, V. had been the favorite since early childhood. Her relatives were proud of her success in school, in general considered her a remarkable child, and praised her to outsiders. This attitude toward V. contrasted sharply with her parents' feelings toward her brother, who was a poor and undisciplined student. They tended to make an example of V., and often described her in an extravagant manner.

Through the beginning of the sixth grade no basic changes in V. took place, although she began to study more assiduously. Her position as a good student continued. Her relations with her classmates remained good, although on occasion she adopted a commanding tone. V. had a high opinion of herself; at the beginning of sixth grade she described herself as follows: "Very able, smart....I understand everything, I can do everything well. ...Whatever I want to do, I can do....If I weren't lazy, I would have straight 5's." She considered herself better and smarter than the others in the class and strove to be an oustanding student. She began to study six to eight hours a day, but her achievement was not commensurate with her efforts: she got 3's and occasionally 2's. Her poor showing became more and more obvious both to the class and to V. herself. However, because of her excessive self-esteem, V. saw the reasons for her failures not in herself but in the teachers, in increasingly difficult school assignments, and, finally, in the malice of her comrades.

The Russian teacher spoke repeatedly of V.'s deteriorating work—in class, at meetings with her parents, and in conversations with the girl. But V. and her mother suspected the teacher of bias against the girl and of incorrectly evaluating her performance; they regarded her criticisms as groundless and unfair. The mother did not hide her attitude toward the teacher from the family or from V. All the members of the family felt sorry for V. and looked upon her as a "victim." The fact that in the sixth grade V. did poor work not only in Russian but in other subjects as well was not taken into account. V. became tense in her relations with her comrades. While she valued the opinion of the collective and was chagrined if difficulties arose between her and her classmates, she acted incorrectly toward the collective. She accused her classmates and teachers of treating her badly. In the middle of the year she had a serious quarrel with her best friend, accusing her of disloyalty and jealousy. This quarrel caused her great pain.

Toward the middle of the school year, V.'s behavior at home began to change. Her mother noticed that she became more irritable and reserved, and stopped talking about school and her friends. She studied as much as before, but was nervous and tense. Her mother attributed her behavior to general fatigue. V.'s mother stopped visiting the school because she was displeased with the teacher and because V. concealed the dates of the parents' meetings from her. As a result, at the end of the school year she was surprised greatly by the 3's on her daughter's report card.

In the seventh grade there was a pronounced deterioration in V.'s work. By this time nobody in class considered her a good student, which caused her keen suffering. She still considered herself more able and intelligent than the other students, and saw her failures as only temporary, explaining them by her laziness, fault-finding teachers, and everyone "getting off the track." Her relations with her teachers and classmates got worse. She refused to accept the slightest criticism, argued with everyone about everything. She lost her authority in class, but under no circumstances would she yield. She interfered in everything, gave advice to everyone. Striving to be the center of attention, she told lies in which her comrades often caught her. Blaming her classroom supervisor for her failures, she became the leader of a group that opposed her in class. Since the classroom supervisor was strict and the class was afraid of her, V. considered it heroic to speak to her insolently. V.'s behavior was admired by some of the students, but the class as a whole condemned her. The girl felt this and became even more anxious; in school she often had breakdowns. At home, when no one was around, she cried, but was rude and forward when others were present.

V. could no longer hide the deterioration in her work in school from her mother. Her mother finally learned that not only was V. doing badly in her school work, but also that she was misbehaving. For the mother this was a serious blow, forcing her to adjust completely. V. had been her hope, her pride. All this brought about a sudden change in her attitude toward V. She showered the girl with reproaches and criticism. The girl's position in the family changed radically: where before she had been the favorite, now at every opportunity her mother belittled her, depriving her even of deserved praise. She expressed her feelings about her daughter's failures to acquaintances and neighbors in the girl's presence. V. retaliated with insolence and defiance; conflicts flared up often. V.'s relations with her parents became especially strained when the question of her future arose. Previously the girl had planned to complete ten grades; her mother had encouraged her and had even dreamed that her daughter might become a physician. Now she announced to the girl that after the seventh grade she was to enter a technical school, since she was "incapable of studying in an institute." V. insisted that she would finish ten grades and study to be a doctor. In spite of the mother's objections, the girl won out and went on to eighth grade, but only on the condition that she would be a good student. To study well became, in V.'s words, "a question of life or death."

In the eighth grade, thanks to superhuman efforts, everything went well during the first few days, and V. received good grades. But a week later she received three 3's and a 2. At this time a group of her classmates began to prepare for entry into the Komsomol. V. wished to be included, but she was held back by her poor grades. In order to improve them, she began to study during all her free time, but her marks failed to improve. V. began to behave badly again. At a class meeting, the collective demanded that she change her attitude toward her teachers and comrades and raise her poor grades. V. refused help and behaved insolently at the meeting.

V. concealed both her academic failures and her unsatisfactory relations with the collective from her mother. On one occasion she was asked to leave the class, and the supervisor requested that her mother come to the school. This created a furor at home. V. promised to improve, but the improvement that followed was only temporary. She retreated into herself, isolating herself from both the school collective and her family. V. was not accepted into the Komsomol, and her conduct was discussed for a second time in class. She again refused help. The class supervisor asked to see V.'s mother again, but V. concealed the request from her mother. At home and at school she was nervous, cried, and resented the slightest criticism. She avoided the class supervisor and lied to her teacher, making up reasons for her mother's inability to come to school. She tried to take advantage of any excuse to miss classes; finally, she decided to transfer to another school. She had reached the breaking point, and eventually she broke down.

We had no reason for supposing that V.'s difficulties in school were due to low intelligence. Hence, we sought the causes in her attitude toward study and her study methods. After observing the girl doing homework, checking what she had learned, and talking with her mother, we concluded that though V. tried to study well and spent a lot of time on lesson preparation, she neither liked to study nor knew how to study. Her motivation for study stemmed from her need for self-assertion rather than from a genuine interest in knowledge, which meant that she had to force herself.

We could now state a hypothesis concerning V.'s general situation. In the lower grades she had been considered a good student, often undeservedly. Since a child's self-image and self-evaluation are a reflection of the objective position he occupies in life and of the evaluations made by those around him, V. had formed a high opinion of herself and her potential. Up to the sixth grade this inner position did not clash with her objective position. Upon her entry into secondary school, however, the demands on V. became greater. The methods of study and the attitude toward knowledge that enabled her (although with difficulty) to maintain her position as a good student in the lower grades could no longer assure her this position. If an adolescent has arrived at a clearly defined self-concept, a change in his position in the collective and its evaluation of him will not be reflected in his self-evaluation at once; there is a lag, especially if the change is a negative one. In V.'s case this kind of situation arose first in the sixth grade, then deepened in the seventh. It is characteristic of adolescents to strive to establish themselves in the collective: to win respect and to obtain authority. V. strove to be an outstanding—not just a good—student, at all costs. This was essential to the maintenance of her self-concept. Thus, the divergence between her self-evaluation and the evaluation of her by others, between her ambitions and her potentialities, between her inner evaluation and her objective position led to sharp emotional disturbances, exacerbated by her failures in school.

We believed that the existence, in the girl's eyes, of a hopeless situation was an auspicious moment for beginning our work with her, since she was now prepared to accept help. To eliminate the disharmony between the objective situation and V.'s evaluation, we worked out the following plan:

(1) We would teach her correct methods of study. This would make it possible for her to stop the decline in her scholastic progress.

(2) We would change her self-evaluation and self-concept by teaching her to see her own limitations and by helping her to perceive the abilities of her comrades.

(3) We would improve her relationships with those around her.

We injected ourselves into the girl's situation at the point of sharpest conflict. One day when she refused to go to school, feigning illness, we had serious discussions with V., her mother, and her brother. We explained to V. why things had turned out so badly for her at school and at home, and we succeeded in convincing her that it was possible for her to find a way out of her painful situation, to finish school, and to go on to further study. The conversation went well, V.'s spirits rose, and she decided to accept our help. In our conversation with V.'s mother, we stressed the girl's good points, showed the mother her mistakes in raising the girl, and tried to convince her of the necessity to change her attitude toward V. We asked the brother to help his sister with her mathematics and physics. As a result, the tense atmosphere in the family was relaxed somewhat, and the conditions necessary for further work created.

Work with V. consisted of conversations with her and of teaching her the correct ways of mastering school material. At the outset we found that we could not convince her that she was studying incorrectly. The most effective method of changing her mind was to test her after she thought she had learned the material, and then point out her mistakes. In addition, the girl saw that when she continued to prepare her lessons as before, her grades did not improve. Once V. understood the reason for her failures, she was ready to accept our advice. This became the turning point after which work with the girl started to yield constructive results. However, V.'s changed self-evaluation brought on a certain lack of confidence, a feeling of uselessness, and even a lack of desire to study. After a time, an improvement in her work in school became obvious, but as soon as she came up against difficulties or experienced failures, her lack of confidence would reappear.

We found that V. was more frank with us than anyone else. In school, in cooperation with V.'s teachers, we tried to include her in the life of her class, to give her opportunities for socially useful work, and to encourage her to participate in after-school study in mathematics and physics. V. finished the school year without 2's and passed the examinations with 4's and

5's. This led to a change in the girl's behavior in school and in her relationships with her comrades and teachers. She began to notice that in school everyone was showing her good will, genuinely wanted to help her, was happy at her successes. She became more trusting, less suspicious, less easily hurt. She began to behave correctly, and her work was praised by her comrades and by her class supervisor. When praised, V. literally bloomed.

At the end of the third quarter, the class selected a group of seven that included the best students; they were socially active and enjoyed a position of authority in the class. V. was very proud that she was among the "seven." Her attitude toward the children in this group was good; she considered them the smartest in the class and was not hurt when they criticized her. However, toward some other classmates, specifically those whom she considered to be "second-rate people," she was indifferent and even rude.

During the whole period of rehabilitation, V.'s spirits and behavior in many respects depended on her successes and failures in school, both scholastic and social. Often her negative traits reappeared in instances when she had to admit her mistakes, when she received a grade that seemed too low, or when she had to acknowledge a comrade's superiority. V.'s relationship with her mother and father continued to be tense for a long time. The mother, who had been deeply disappointed by V.'s poor showing and behavior in school, for a long time refused to notice the girl's successes. Sometimes without reason she insulted V. and deprived her of pleasures and recreation, punishing her not so much for present as for past behavior. Quarrels arose over trifles, and dramatic scenes occurred at each poor grade, "poor" grades including not only 2's but also 3's earned with great difficulty. On occasion we succeeded in convincing the mother of the injustice of her treatment of V., but she was inconsistent and sooner or later lapsed into her usual behavior. Nevertheless, very slowly, V.'s relationships within the family began to improve. The conflict in the family was decisively removed at the end of the school year when V. finished without 2's and passed all her examinations with 4's and 5's.

In the ninth grade we no longer worked systematically with V., but in difficult situations, such as when she was appointed a pioneer leader, she still sought our advice and help. Her work and relationships in school improved with every month. At the end of the second quarter, she was accepted into the Komsomol. Thus, in the ninth grade the divergence between V.'s inner evaluation and her objective situation in school and in the family was almost eliminated. A discrepancy remained in only one area—scholastic achievement; she did not become an outstanding student. The diminishing of this gap laid the basis for eliminating her negative behavior and strengthening her positive personality traits. The first traits to be eliminated—coarseness, lying, stubbornness, competitiveness—were those that had come into the open in the seventh and eighth grades. The more deeply rooted traits that had developed in the elementary grades did not disappear: the overestimation of her abilities, her desire to command, her ambition, her condescending attitude toward other students. The presence in V. of this combination of traits constituted a potential for new conflicts. Thus, although V.'s behavior improved, the fundamental reshaping of her personality that would lead her to change her feelings about herself remains to be done.

In Valya's case, the psychologist works with two collectives: the family and the school. A substantial amount of data is gathered, including the evaluations of Valya's classmates and her self-analyses. Diagnostic procedures include tutoring the girl in several subjects and offering guidance, particularly with regard to her role as pioneer leader. Here the thoroughness with which the psychologist subjects her hypothesis to critical testing is impressive. As in the other cases, a constructive relationship is established, but is sparingly used. The therapist is careful to avoid over-permissiveness and relies primarily on rational procedures and on keeping Valya's eye on the goal of improved scholastic achievement. Note also that the therapist is not concerned with trying to help Valya's mother, who is herself beset by problems. The mother is told how she can facilitate the work with the girl, but the psychologist does nothing further. The father is ignored altogether; apparently he is seen as having little to contribute. In Valya's case, the school collective fails to take into account the girl's "peculiarities." It is a pressuring, judging group, demanding that the girl behave in line with its views on purposeful activity. Without the intervention of the therapist, this collective might have become so punitive as to damage the girl irreparably. The therapist in this case realized that she had achieved only limited goals with Valya, and that the work of reshaping her personality had not even begun.

General Remarks. That the therapists in the four cases presented here were socialist humanitarians in the best sense of this concept is important. They genuinely wanted to help, but were not sentimental. They worked hard at helping, but demanded equally serious efforts from their clients. They kept their clients from becoming dependent by involving them actively in the measures that were undertaken and by relating consistently to the demands of reality. They all showed a strong belief in the capacity of their clients to overcome obstacles—those of their own making and those that stemmed from the conditions of their lives.

Diagnosis in these cases centered on those physical, social, and ideational factors in the environment that were within the range of the child's comprehension. Some attention was paid to other factors that had an impact upon the child, but of which he was unaware. However, the therapists delved only lightly into this wider circle of environmental factors. Consequently, treatment primarily emphasized giving the child an understanding of his situation and involving him in experiences that would prove rehabilitative and developmental.

This approach seems to provide the most direct attack on the child's difficulties, while avoiding frustrations for all concerned. Factors hindering desirable behavior seem to be eliminated quickly. On the other hand, the failure to give the child a better insight into his feelings and previous relationship patterns may close off for him important dimensions of personality development. He may be inadequately prepared to handle future problems because the affective processes that underlie his actions remain unexposed and unaltered. Thus, reliance on rational types of treatment can yield beneficial results, but a superficial understanding of the role of the therapist-client relationship and the failure to use it appropriately may lead to a one-sided perception of the situation. (For example, though the therapist used the technique of helping Valya to study correctly in order to ameliorate the girl's situation, it is possible that she was motivated to study by the good relationship she developed with the therapist, so that if some other technique had been used, a similar easing of tensions would have resulted.) In all four cases, an authoritarian stance is taken, though in varying degrees. This may help set realistic limits and demands, and thus support the efforts on both sides, but to a certain extent it imposes treatment from above, rather than starting from where the child is, and thus prevents the therapist in some measure from preparing the child psychologically for accepting help as well as for meeting the demands of the collective.

8

Treatment Methods:
Community Participation and Work Therapy

Community participation is an extension of the collective principle from the small to the large group, a group less intimately involved in the daily life of the person being helped and more formal in its structure, which can exert a quasi-official pressure because of its links to the state, and can secure compliance through force if necessary.

In the early years, the Soviets restricted community participation to politically reliable groups; eventually, participation by a widening circle was encouraged. An educational campaign has been waged urging every citizen to become an "activist"—a volunteer concerned with furthering the welfare of all.* Extensive community participation in welfare matters has had the beneficial effect of broadening the base from which welfare services are administered; it has brought them closer to the people, lightened the weight of bureaucracy, and, to some extent, influenced policy.

---

* Currently, almost three-quarters of the urban population claim that they engage in "social activity." Pensioners seem to be the least active in this context: nevertheless, 40.5 per cent of them are socially active (*129,* p. 3, Table 4). What this activity consists of, however, is unknown. Undoubtedly, for many people it is merely an innocuous expenditure of short periods of time. The 27 per cent of the urban population who are not active are probably people who have grown tired of stereotyped slogans, of demands so severe that they often force neglect of other activities in which they are more interested, and of the Party doing things in its own way in the end. No information is available for the rural population, but it may be confidently assumed that it is much less active in this sense than city people.

There are several reasons behind the effort to extend community participation. Since privately supported agencies are not permitted, the state is obliged to carry the entire burden of meeting human needs. This burden is considerably lightened by involving large sections of the population in activity directed toward the handling of social problems. Such activity has been familiar to some segments of the people from tsarist times, and hence is easily popularized. Furthermore, it is consistent with the Marxist theory of "the withering of the state," a process during which government functions are transferred gradually to social organizations.

Some forms of Soviet community participation are similar in function to those in American society, while others are radically different. Among agencies and groups familiar to Americans are the Red Cross* and Red Crescent, lay committees for children's institutions, and Parents' Associations.[1] Others carry out functions not handled by similar organizations in the United States. Trade unions, for example, play an important role in the provision of child welfare and family services, including services to unmarried mothers.[2] Still others are unique to Soviet society. "Veterans of labor," for example, are old-age pensioners engaged in helping others like themselves who may be sick or alone, or who may need legal aid.[3] "Soviets of cooperation" are active in hospitals, dispensaries, and other medical institutions. Composed for the most part of trade unionists in the district served by a given medical facility, they help with nonmedical welfare tasks and check to see that food, linen, and other items meet established standards.[4] "House committees" not only manage buildings but also look after their tenants, dealing with suggestions and complaints, organizing play areas for children, visiting the sick.

Other important forms of community participation are Children's Commissions, People's Patrols, Comrades' Courts, Parents' Committees, and Patrons' Committees. Children's Commissions, working in accordance with 1961 regulations, are an arm of the local soviet.[5] They are composed of teachers, lawyers, doctors, welfare workers, and Party, Young Communist League, and trade union leaders—all people who hold regular jobs elsewhere and participate in commission work because of their "social consciousness." Their duties include locating children and adolescents who need help, finding jobs for those who should be working, helping parents and parent substitutes to raise children properly, placing children in institutions when necessary, and securing child support payments. They also make recommendations to law en-

---

* In 1957 the Soviet Red Cross, which is officially sponsored, had 24 million members in 318,000 branches (*400*, p. 619).

forcement agencies with regard to persons who incite juveniles to commit antisocial acts. The commissions can censure parents or refer them to Comrades' Courts, impose fines, require reimbursement for losses caused by children not to exceed 20 rubles, and petition courts to deprive parents of their parental rights. The commissions are also expected to maintain reception centers, labor colonies, and medical and educational institutions in which children within their jurisdiction can be placed.

Since the 1950's community participation has been playing an increasingly important role in the administration of justice, through the auxiliary police called People's Patrols (*Narodnye Druzhiny*) and the Comrades' Courts (*Tovarishcheskie Sudy*). These patrols and courts have a dual—what Berman calls a "parental"—function: "They bring the will of the collective to bear on miscreants, and at the same time educate the participants in what Soviet writers call 'popular self-government.'"[6] The patrols are especially active in the field of juvenile delinquency, while the courts are concerned with anything that reduces productivity, as well as with people who try to escape doing socially useful work, who lead "parasitic" lives, who fail to raise their children correctly, or who are "amoral" or alcoholic.

In certain situations community participation involves direct assistance to individuals who are unable to cope unaided with their problems. Since the individual and the collective are considered indissoluble and "responsibly interdependent," the problems, desires, and hopes of every member become the legitimate business of the group, and the latter is held responsible for the welfare and behavior of each member. The view that what an individual does is strictly his own business, unless he chooses to share it with someone else, is rejected as unhealthy. Hence, the community frequently intervenes where there are marital difficulties, whether or not the couple directly involved seek this help. Factory administrations and trade union committees concern themselves not only with providing summer camps for the children of the employees but also with aiding widows who are losing control over their adolescent sons or unmarried mothers who are rearing their youngsters singlehandedly. They may also intervene in the affairs of a young man who, because of the unreasonable objections of his old-fashioned mother, is unable to marry the girl he loves—even though he opposes such intervention. Factory committees are expected to call to account parents whose children fail to attend school regularly, and a Young Communist League branch was reprehended for neglecting one of its members to the point where she expressed a desire to become a nun—although she sought to be left alone.[7]

These actions are considered to be legitimate intrusions into the private lives of individuals: "The community will rightly be interested in how a person behaves, will punish delinquents, will ask a person where he obtained the funds with which he built his summer home. But this has nothing in common with crude interference in the personal lives of good citizens, with furtive peeping through keyholes."[8]

No records dealing with the process of organizing the community for participation exist in Soviet literature. Soviet welfare personnel see no need for a scientific analysis of this process, being certain that it involves merely being good communists and organizers. However, there are numerous descriptions of the activities undertaken through community participation. A few will serve to illumine this method.

The functions of Parents' Committees—"a tested means for organizing and strengthening friendship between the family and the school"[9] —are specified by decree. These groups, closely supervised by school personnel, are composed of parents who have been successful in raising their own children. Their terms are staggered and extend over a period of eight to nine years, lengthy uninterrupted participation being considered desirable because it permits the parents to become thoroughly acquainted with the teachers and children and assures a continuity of interest. The committees are subdivided into subcommittees with specific responsibilities: instructional-upbringing, cultural, sanitation-health, housekeeping, etc. The instructional-upbringing group concerns itself with children who are not doing well in school. It studies each child's home life, and then decides how best to help the family with the child. This delving into the life of a family and giving advice requires a great deal of tact. The following provides a description of some correct and incorrect procedures:

In one school, before visiting the families of pupils who did not do well during the first quarter, the chairman explained to the committee members that they should talk to the parents in a positive manner. At first they should tell the parents about their child's strengths, and then advise them in a friendly way how to work with the child at home, how to organize his daily routine and his homework. When parents feel the genuine desire of the committee members to help them, they will trust them; then it will be possible to suggest to the family how to help the child to overcome his negative attitude toward study.... In another school the chairman did not give any such preliminary instructions. Some members of the committee immediately started blaming the parents for poor upbringing practices. They had no words of praise for the child, no sympathy for the parents. Naturally, this visit ended in conflict. It was very difficult for the class supervisors to settle this conflict and to reestablish normal relations between the school and the family.[10]

Discussions with families often lead to the institution of measures to meet the needs of particular children. For some children who belong to families in which all the adults work, "extended-day" school sections are organized; others are "attached" to families of classmates whose mothers do not work outside the home. If parents are overburdened with social duties, the committees contact directors of employing establishments, trade unions, and Party units and obtain relief for them. If parents are recalcitrant, the committees appeal to the various collectives of which the parents are members to apply pressure.

The formation of Parents' Committees in boarding schools is often an arduous task, because parents whose children are placed in these institutions tend to divest themselves of responsibility for the children. The following is an account of how these difficulties were overcome in one instance.

> Parents began to come to the school one by one—to help those children who were slow in learning to take care of their clothes. Teachers and upbringers shared with them their ideas about parental cooperation. They pointed out that the participation of the parents was improving the class atmosphere. Toward the middle of the school year, a basic change in the relationships with the parents took place. Parents of almost all of the children began to take a lively interest in the youngsters, not only their own, but all those in the school. Many parents helped conduct excursions, hikes, trips to theaters and exhibits. The individual potentials of the parents were taken into consideration, and the more tactful and gracious were asked to help with investigating the home lives of certain pupils. They carried out this work very conscientiously, and cooperated with the parents in inculcating proper work habits in the children.
>
> Class meetings with parents were prepared for by the whole class. All the children were eager to exhibit their work and to take part in writing for the wall "newspaper," in stage performances, and in other types of artistic activity. Such meetings aided in solving a whole complex of problems. Essentially, they were a display of the students' collective to their fathers and mothers, which stimulated the children to engage in new socially useful activity. Parents gained a clear conception of the things that influenced the collective and how best they might cooperate with it.[11]

Patrons' Committees for children's institutions came into prominence immediately after World War II. They consist of representatives from industrial and agricultural enterprises, the Party, the Young Communist League, and other social organizations, as well as individuals cited for outstanding contributions to society. Their primary purpose is to coordinate the activity of various community groups on behalf of orphans. In their early days, they were particularly concerned with recreational activities. Consider, for example, this account of the work of a Patrons' Committee of an orphans' home located near the complex of factories called "Trekhgornaiia Manufactura":

> Not a single holiday, not a single important event in the life of our country goes by without a visit from the patrons to their small friends. Especially gala occasions are the joint birthdays celebrated monthly. Patrons and Party, Komsomol, and trade union activists visit the home on these occasions, bringing presents. The factory's trade union committee allots money for a birthday pie and for entertainers. A New Year tree celebration is organized annually at the home, and some of the youngsters attend such a celebration in the great ballroom of the Trade Union House.[12]

As the postwar crisis ended, the Patrons' Committees were urged to take an interest in all aspects of institutional life—the children's scholastic performance, their "ideological-political" level, and their health and work habits. In addition, they were asked to give individual attention to each child, and especially to those who were finding it difficult to take their place in the group.[13] At present the better functioning Patrons' Committees, like the Parents' Committees, are divided into subcommittees, each concentrating on a specific area such as education-upbringing, "culture," housekeeping-labor, or health and physical education. A program, formulated jointly with the director of the particular home being served, is drawn up. Experience has shown the need for care in the selection of members, for checking on their performance, and for developing clear lines of authority and accountability. Institution personnel help patrons to understand the inner world of each child, to know what his interests and peculiarities are, how to be sensitive to his desire for independence, to respect his personality. According to the report of one director:

> The patrons bring much joy into the life of the home. They organize radio, photo, drama, choreography, and orchestra groups, arrange monthly lectures on political and scientific subjects, and assume special responsibility for individual children.... They concern themselves with the children's successes and failures in study and behavior. They insist that the delinquent children correct their mistakes and catch up; they take those who deserve encouragement to the movies, to the theater, for walks, and occasionally to visit their own families. Birthdays are always marked by celebrations and gifts. Frequently the children are invited by the patrons to concerts, sports events, or movies—either in small groups or as a whole collective.... This spurs them to study better, to conduct themselves properly, to carry out honestly the duties assigned to them by the collective. They are eager to earn the praise and encouragement of their patron-friends.[14]

Comrades' Courts are composed of ordinary citizens elected annually by residents of a given neighborhood or by workers in an industrial plant or collective farm. Their punitive powers, limited to a ten-ruble fine up to 1965, have since been increased to fines of 50 rubles.[15] Their jurisdiction has been extended to cover the following types of behavior: acts that do not break laws, but violate the prevailing Soviet standards of morality, and minor crimes, including petty theft, rowdiness, black market speculation, and other misdemeanors. Berman states that "they issue mostly reprimands and warnings. However, they may also recommend eviction from an apartment or disciplinary action (including demotion but not discharge) by factory management.... Such a recommendation ... is a serious matter."[16] Increasingly, investigation of a delinquent person's behavior includes what he does outside the work establishment—in the family, among friends, in social organizations. This, it is claimed, permits Comrades' Courts to carry out their work more successfully.[17] In accordance with the philosophy of the collective, the positive approach is stressed: the ideal is for the Court to exert its influence not through punishment and compulsion, but rather by means of a skillfully conducted discussion with the culprit in the presence of his comrades that will persuade him that his conduct is unworthy of a Soviet man. The following example is a good illustration of a Comrades' Court in action:

> Into the Kalinin House of Culture came the sisters, the brides-to-be, the wives of those who worship "the green snake" (alcohol). The "heroes" themselves came as well—heroes of family scandals and street brawls. There was to be a discussion of the terrible material and moral damage alcoholism inflicts upon the family.
>
> Everyone made speeches against alcoholism, including the "heroes." Many of them repented, acknowledged the harm done by alcoholism, and cried, saying that they could not overcome the charms of "the green snake." However, there was one chronic alcoholic who said that he saw a sort of youthful bravado in alcoholism. This was a deaf blacksmith who systematically drinks and beats up his wife and child.... Everyone in the hall condemned and rejected him. When everyone who had wanted to speak finished, the verdict for the alcoholics was read: "We suggest, as a measure of social reproach and judgment, that photographs of the drunkards in all their repulsive appearances be exhibited on special boards ... that can be readily seen in factory shops and dormitories. If this measure does not lead them to reform, then the drunkards will be answerable to society, and, if necessary, to the People's Court."[18]

Testimonials to the good that has been accomplished by Comrades' Courts abound. Their effectiveness is attributed to the fact that they are composed of persons who know the defendant well, who suffer directly from his misbehavior, who know his living conditions, who understand the problems he faces. It is held that being found "guilty" by this kind of group is feared more than condemnation by a regular court, which is composed of people who are far removed from the daily life of the culprit and to whose judgment, therefore, he does not respond with as deep a feeling.[19]

However, there are frequent criticisms of community participation as a treatment method. Often the community is indifferent. A husband beats his wife unmercifully, but nobody intervenes, considering it simply a family matter; a mother has a son who is a drunkard and beats her, but the administration of the establishment where he works does not want to interfere; village leaders make no effort to find out where two young hoodlums get the money for their drunken sprees. The history of an eight-year-old boy, Petya, reads in part:

> Petya's mother, a factory worker, raised him and two younger children without their father. She was so totally occupied with the problems of providing material support for the family that she devoted no attention to her son's intellectual and emotional development—to providing books, pictures, toys to stimulate the child's curiosity. There was only one room for five people, with screaming, noise, and quarrels between the mother and the grandmother to which the boy reacted with pain.[20]

Community participation did nothing to help this mother—an especially reprehensible failure because the collective in her factory had been represented in trade union literature as an example for all to emulate. Helpful community participation was also conspicuously absent in the case of Oleg (see pp. 115–22 above), whose handicapped father strove desperately to keep his home together.

Often, instead of being intolerant of deviant behavior, the community creates obstacles that hinder proper handling of delinquents and criminals. An individual's bad behavior is often concealed in testimonials sent to legal authorities; families and communities do not report drunkards because of excessive kindness toward them.[21] The community participation method is often prying, petty, and annoying—instead of being supportive and educational;[22] often it is futile and powerless. Examples:

> The Penza Komsomol committees were reported to be doing a poor job of caring for children without parents. "They do not know how or where the children are living and who their guardians are. For example, education agencies in Kuznetsk placed a little girl in the care of old people after her mother died. The aged people gave the girl a room in which there

were neither chairs, a table, nor a bed. One year she did not even attend school."[23]

Or—one mother told the court that during ten years of married life her husband systematically beat her and threatened to kill her. The community tried to influence the husband, but got nowhere.[24]

Or—no matter how many times the collective farm members talked with S., criticizing him for his alcoholism and debauchery, nothing helped.[25]

Decisions of Comrades' Courts are frequently ignored, and sometimes complaints are lodged with the judged person's social organization or local soviet against the courts themselves, when they "misapply" the law. People's Patrols, too, are castigated for being brutal or exceeding their authority.[26]

Among social welfare personnel, there is considerable defensiveness and skepticism about what the community participation method can do to help people with their problems and prevent undesirable behavior.* On the other hand, there are positive reactions to this method when it is limited to specific tasks, does not interfere with professional responsibilities, and is used with sensitivity and genuine concern. Thus, officials in the RSFSR Ministry of Social Welfare see community participation as appropriate in fringe administrative functions, under supervision of the professional staff. The director of a large Moscow clinic, for example, felt that the lay committee attached to it should render social assistance when needed—clean patients' homes, do the shopping, see that the children attend school. But she made it quite clear that she would not tolerate interference from this committee in her sphere of responsibility, in which she included everything of a medical nature.

There is no doubt that community participation as a treatment method has not reached the level of development attained by "collective-individual" work. It has not been analyzed or researched. It remains a conglomeration of disconnected activities, operating haphazardly. Successes and failures are explained by the presence or absence of "good communists" to direct it. The theoretical base for community participation—the con-

---

* Community participation is often ineffective because areas of responsibility are not clearly defined. For example, it is not clear whose job it is to find employment for people who have served sentences in penal institutions: the community acting as a collective or a given state agency. The legal position of the People's Patrols has not been defined in some republics. Nothing is said about what to do with people who will not appear before Comrades' Courts. There are no uniform instructions about what to do when an injured party disagrees with the opinion of the Comrades' Court and insists that the case be taken to a regular court. There are no rules about who initiates the probation process and who represents the community in this process. It is not clear whether observation of a probationer includes watching his behavior only when he is at work or during leisure hours as well (*422*, pp. 36–38, 72, 87–88, 106, 108).

cept of the "withering of the state"—has not been empirically tested; it is an *a priori* assumption that has little relevance to a method used for dealing with real people and their problems. Hence, it has not generated a transmittable body of knowledge or a basis for a systematic training program for its practitioners.

There exist both similarities and differences between the method of community participation as used in the Soviet Union and the method of community organization as used by American social welfare personnel. In the United States, social workers regard community organization as a process by which a community identifies its needs or objectives, ranks them, develops the confidence and will to work to achieve them, finds the resources to deal with them, and takes action with respect to them; in so doing it extends and develops cooperative attitudes and practices in the community. There are three basic elements in such community organization: (1) that which aims at the achievement of a specific objective or reform; (2) that concerned with general planning; and (3) that concerned with the development of a process for reform. This third element is thought to be the most significant; it requires the achievement of self-determination, cooperative efforts among various groups, and the development of the capacity to solve community problems.

This view of a community-oriented treatment method would probably be acceptable to Soviet welfare personnel; in some measure their practice involves all three of the elements described. Structurally, however, the Soviet system is quite different from the American. For example, because no community-wide, voluntary social planning agencies exist, the planning function is monopolized by governmental agencies. Community participation in this area is likely to be of little importance. Government domination also means that community action is limited to undertakings that do not alter major policies and that community participation usually consists of carrying out government plans, rather than achieving self-determination or developing a capacity for solving community problems.

Work Therapy

Idealization of work has permeated the Soviet scene since the communist regime came to power—an inevitable development that has its roots in the working class orientation of Marxism-Leninism and has been continually nurtured by the regime in its drive to industrialize and raise productivity despite manpower shortages brought on by huge losses in two world wars, a civil war, and a revolution, as well as by disease and famine. Engels wrote: "Labor is the *sine qua non* in all human life; it is such to the extent that we must, in a certain sense, say: labor has made man." The Soviet view is that through labor human society has formed, human speech has developed, and the structure and functions of the human body and of its highest organ—the brain—have evolved. Since work is the basic means for developing physical and intellectual abilities in man, for shaping his moral character and strengthening his will, it is considered a natural necessity, and its role in human growth and regeneration is stressed.[27]

Social and psychological pressures have been brought to bear to support this idealization throughout every facet of Soviet life, including social welfare.* The latter is consistently rewarding industriousness and punishing laziness. No failure on the part of parents is as reprehensible as raising a child who refuses or does not know how to work. "One need have no fear that a Soviet court will grant alimony to a healthy person who is able to work, but who places himself in the position of needing assistance by virtue of an amoral ambition to live at the expense of his spouse."[28] And a person who is unable to work because of a drunken brawl, for example, is deprived of his sickness benefits if he has no dependents. An unmarried mother's indiscretion is regarded much more tolerantly by the society if she is a good worker.†

Constantly emphasized is the idea that love and respect for socially useful work help the child to grow in a harmonious and well-rounded manner because they minimize the possibility of his becoming self-centered, on the one hand, and facilitate creativity, independence, initiative, and a critical attitude toward himself and the world in which he lives, on the other. Further, as the child, through work, develops ever more significant ties with his environment, he becomes a truly active member of the collective, building on this constructive relationship to attain his full potential.[29] It is stressed that the child learns not only by indoctrination, but also by doing: much of what he learns is acquired indirectly. Hence, appropriate physical labor for children, both normal

---

* In 1921, in setting down guidelines for rehabilitating prostitutes, Kollontay enunciated a famous dictum that has become symbolic of the entire effort: "What is subject to censure is not that the woman sells her body to many, but that she is not . . . doing useful work for the collectivity" (*185*, pp. 11–12). Prostitutes were placed in correctional labor institutions where a firm work regime, educational activities, and socialist competition, combined with medical treatment, were used to rehabilitate them. Once a former prostitute took her place on the production line, she gained the status of a good citizen (*368*, pp. 109, 112; *104*, p. 195; *65*, pp. 81–113; *112*, pp. 15–174; *61*, pp. 64–69).

† This theme was the basis of the plot of a widely acclaimed film made in 1960— "Prostaia Istoriia" (Simple Affair). The moral was that, because of their hunger for love, women must be forgiven for illicit relationships, provided they are good workers and do not destroy another family.

and defective, is desirable as soon as they can undertake it. The only question is how should this labor be organized, how is the upbringer to make sure that engaging in it will develop in the child a love of labor that will remain with him throughout his life.[30] Much research is devoted to answering this question in connection with work in the school; detailed studies are also made to determine what kinds of work children should be asked to do in the home.[31] The best way to maintain the physical and mental health of elderly people, it is claimed, is through work: data are marshalled to show that a majority of the people who live beyond 80 are persons who worked until late in life. An active working life at an advanced age is recommended as an effective medicine against aging for most people.[32]

This attitude toward work leads to the view that moral qualities, including a sense of discipline, are developed best through intellectual and physical labor. For example, it is thought that no amount of explaining the importance of being organized and disciplined will produce the same results as correct structuring of work activities, combined with consistent and reasonable work demands and regular checking to see that assigned work has been done.[33] Socially useful work is the major tool in the complex process of creating a genuine collective.

Because of the powerful effect it has on the human psyche, it is believed that work can be used therapeutically to prevent psychic disturbances and to cure them if they occur. Work not only distracts the individual from dwelling on morbid experiences, but also brings the healthy elements of his mind into play, prevents him from withdrawing into himself, and keeps him firmly in contact with reality. Work strengthens the ties that each person must have with his environment, clears the way for his participation in the many collectives in which he plays a role, enriches his life with new knowledge, widens his interests, and increases his skills. All this enhances the value of the individual to the group, to society; he gains a satisfying sense of his own part in the overall contribution of his collective to the nation's progress. Thus, the therapeutic effects of work are reinforced by the unity of personal and social interests.

To achieve the desired goals, work therapy must be correctly structured, which requires skill, understanding, and an appreciation of the many factors involved. Special attention must be paid to make sure (1) that the person being helped feels the deep connection between his work and the purposes of the collective, (2) that the particular work he does takes into account his skills, preferences, and needs; (3) that the work is useful—not make-work; (4) that the usefulness of the work is clearly apparent to him; (5) that motivation to achieve higher purposes and acquire greater skills is built into the work through expectations that are within his capacity to fulfill; and (6) that striving to achieve does not deteriorate into a destructive competition for personal gain, but is directed to advancing the welfare of the group and, indirectly, the society. These requirements reflect the Soviet emphasis on the rational rather than the instinctual elements in behavior, the theory of the unity of consciousness and activity, and the optimism concerning the educational effects of work. It should be noted that the concept of work as a therapeutic tool is reinforced by the practical value it has for the person being helped: he knows that once he has acquired certain occupational skills, a job will be found for him—although the job sometimes may be located in an out-of-the-way place, or the work boring or poorly paid.

As with community participation, no case studies focused specifically on work therapy can be found, although such therapy was used throughout all of the cases included in the preceding chapter. Field findings indicate that the efficacy of work therapy is so completely accepted that its theoretical base is not even questioned: the efforts of welfare personnel are concentrated on applying the method in such a way as to maximize its impact. Work therapy has been applied more often by welfare personnel than any other kind of therapy—including physiotherapy, psychotherapy, and "active" therapy (therapy based in the main on chemical, electrical, and surgical methods). Work therapy requires determining the extent to which a client can be productive, in what occupations he can work, and how to help him reintegrate himself into the collective through labor. This applies to the "victims of social relationships" as well as to those whose productivity has been impaired by biological factors.

Work is also recommended for "normal" children living at home. Parents are urged to assign well-defined household tasks as ongoing responsibilities: if these tasks are assigned at random and are merely parts of the regular activities of adults, the child is bound to resist them. The child ought to begin regular home duties early so that needed habits and skills are firmly established and work becomes easy and simple. In institutions for normal children, work is used to develop initiative, responsible attitudes, and supportive relationships. While the value of acquiring skills and habits that can come only from actual doing is recognized, this is not the major objective. Rather, it is hoped that the child will acquire traits essential for fulfilling successfully the role of a worker in an industrialized society: discipline, punctuality, accuracy, diligence—all based upon a clear understanding of the place of work in human life.[34] Example:

Valya was coarse, brusque, and lacking in self-restraint when she came to us. We assigned her the task of helping the upbringer who was working with the small children. While she was rearing the little ones, demanding good behavior from them, V. began to grow rapidly herself. It was necessary for her to read to the little ones; she prepared for this and began to love reading herself, while before she never opened a book. It was necessary for her to talk with the little ones; she collected materials, read the papers, magazines. The little ones loved her, caressed her, called her "our Valya." The girl was transformed, became softer, happier, more cheerful. Children began to respect V., and elected her to the Soviet of the Brigade.[35]

Or—

Lyuba was sloppy. To the suggestions of adults she replied with coarse expressions; in the collective, nobody respected her. She was given the task of keeping the sports outfits for the girls in her group in order. Her duties included issuing the sports outfits on the day preceding sports activity— pants, sweaters, shoes—and on the day following sports practice collecting the outfits and examining them to see that everything was in order. At first L. was not too successful with these duties: she forgot to issue or to collect the outfits, it was necessary to remind her constantly, to help her. Several times she had to be criticized in the group and through notices on the bulletin board. But gradually she learned to be responsible; she became demanding toward herself and toward others. The children elected her to take charge of housekeeping for the group.[36]

Work is also considered therapeutic in the upbringing of sick, weak, and physically and mentally handicapped children. For this reason, the RSFSR Institute of Defectology includes helping each child to become productive in socially useful work as an appropriate treatment objective for the handicapped. A child can be happy only if he is productive, it is maintained. Hence, among the pedagogical problems that are persistently investigated, perhaps the most important is how to teach self-care and work skills. Greater attention is paid to this question than the psychology of learning, methodology in teaching academic subjects, and curriculum content. An expert in work with the blind writes:

One of the most important concerns in dealing with a blind person during the first period of the loss of sight ought to be placement in work that is within his power and is interesting for him.... Our observations have shown that when the blind are drawn into socially useful work that interests them, their feelings about themselves are visibly improved. They are carried away by joy, energy, satisfaction with the results of their work; their belief in their possibilities is strengthened; gradually, the pathological effects on the nervous system are reduced—the effects brought on by the loss of sight and the reaction of the personality to blindness.[37]

Patients in the Central Research Institute for Prostheses in Moscow —most of them horribly mutilated by diseases and accidents—are either currently employed, have jobs to which they will report upon release, or are studying in order to qualify for jobs. The emphasis in treatment is on self-care and vocational rehabilitation for adults, and on self-care and schoolwork for children. In spite of a gloomy and overcrowded building, the patients appear hopeful and reasonably cheerful, which the staff attributes mainly to the fact that work is available, that study and retraining are open to everyone, and that everything is done to involve—not compel—patients in one or the other. Instances of patients not interested in work—even among the most severely handicapped— are few.

While welfare personnel accept without question the effectiveness of work therapy in changing behavior, there are difficulties in the use of this method, stemming primarily from two factors: failure on the part of large segments of the population to internalize the Soviet regime's idealization of work (although lip service may be paid) and a narrow concept of work education that results in training the student for specific skills that are useful for a temporary period, but often leaves him helpless in the face of new job demands.

Says Kent Geiger: "Most Soviet citizens feel little reluctance to "take it easy," and certainly the absence of a strong valuation on work as an end in itself helps explain typical patterns of deviant behavior in Soviet occupational life, viz., bureaucratism, careerism, and parasitism, as well as suggesting why the leaders feel it necessary to provide different forms of incentives and conduct campaigns for the mobilization of labor."[38] Frederick Herzberg found that job satisfaction increases with job skill in both the Soviet Union and the United States, but that American workers are more satisfied with their jobs than their Russian counterparts. More Americans than Russians rate "meaningful work" above wages, he discovered.[39] Material self-interest, which, in spite of endless rationalizations, is still equivalent to personal acquisitiveness, is relied on heavily by the Soviets to increase productivity.*

---

* An official from the Uzbek Ministry of Social Welfare told me that when his son finished secondary school, he refused to continue his education, to the great sorrow of his parents. Instead, he got a job. After working for two years, however, he decided to go on to an institute after all. The father remarked that, unknown to the son, he had had a great deal to do with this decision. "For two years I kept telling the boy that if he obtained a higher degree, he would earn more money and he would be able to tell others what to do instead of taking orders from others." On another occasion I was having dinner with a very gracious, intelligent man, proud of being quite high in Party circles. As usual, we had to wait a long time to be served. My companion remarked: "If the waitress were paid on the basis of how many people she served rather than on a straight salary basis, we would get good service!"

Insistence on connecting education with "life" through work has tended to narrow the former rather than broaden the latter. The resulting emphasis on technical training, unintegrated into a liberal arts philosophy, is causing problems. Says one authority on special education:

> There are many weaknesses in the education and upbringing of blind children. The most serious among them is the lack of necessary connection between general education, technical training, and work. In many schools, education on the job still has the character of trade training, is limited by narrow specialization, and does not give the students general technical knowledge and practical skills in line with the demands of life and the demands of developing industry. The absence of a clear connection between general education and work training is not conducive to a deep mastery of knowledge and to a many-sided development of the student.[40]

Similar problems plague training for the deaf. On the one hand, job training adapted to the limitations of deaf people is not worked out: the deaf are expected to do the same work as non-handicapped workers; on the other, teaching methods are outmoded, with the result that trainees are unable to compete even in a limited sense with persons who have normal hearing. Hence, though work therapy is often "successful" in relation to an immediate and limited objective, there is no assurance that it will prepare the individual to handle problems that he may face in the future.

The failure to apply scientific procedures to the study of human behavior raises doubts concerning the reliability and efficacy of all three major Soviet treatment methods. This failure is illustrated vividly by the fact that the Soviet welfare field has yet to produce an evaluative, comparative, or follow-up study—either as a separate effort or as part of a larger work—that has any scientific respectability. Some welfare personnel do not seem to be concerned about this. For example, the sizable literature on children's homes abounds with glowing accounts of how well the children turn out. Without exception, these judgments are arrived at either through correspondence with former charges who write enthusiastically about what they are doing, or through conversations with previous residents who visit the institution when special occasions are being celebrated. Adjustment is invariably considered good if the person in question is doing well on his job or in school, and no concern is shown about his more intimate relationships.[41] In the enormous literature on special education there is a similar lack, although some researchers in this area realize that such studies are important. Costly mistakes can then be avoided. So far, however, few are calling for a significant change in the attitude toward research, so that prospects for the near future, at least, do not appear promising.[42]

The reasons for this state of affairs can be summarized as follows: During the Stalin era, such studies were discouraged or forbidden; since the "thaw," no significant research has been undertaken (except by sociologists) because many scholars feel that the effort and expense required would outweigh its usefulness: life moves so swiftly, they say, that by the time an elaborate study is completed, its findings are out of date. In addition, field findings suggest that there is a lack of technical know-how needed for mounting such studies: little evidence exists, for example, that Soviet welfare personnel understand the control group as an evaluative device. The weakness of this aspect of their work is rationalized by some Soviet social researchers into a strength: it helps them avoid dealing with the veritable mountains of findings, including statistics, that in bourgeois countries are often hindrances to action, they claim.

9

Family and Child Welfare Services

The Soviet Union has never developed any formal, professionally staffed system of marriage counseling or any kind of psychiatric approach to family problems. The only agency available for counseling husbands and wives is the divorce court. Divorce procedure requires both parties to be summoned before a People's Court in which the judge must "establish the motives for notice of dissolution of marriage and take measures to reconcile husband and wife" by pointing out to them the social importance of the conjugal bond, especially if there are children.* No data are published on how many divorce applications end in reconciliations. Should efforts at reconciliation fail, the petitioner has the right to file for divorce with the next higher court. Only in that court may the divorce be granted. Since divorce proceedings are cumbersome and costly, the cases that reach courts are probably those in which the rift is deep and clearly irreconcilable. Field findings indicate that judges usually grant a divorce if, after ritualistically attempting to patch things up, both parties agree, so that couples are rarely reconciled.[1] In addition, since there are no services to support resumed relationships, some of the reconciliations achieved by the courts do not last.

---

* In 1968 Soviet divorce laws were liberalized to allow childless couples to separate through simple proceedings at a registry office. Court reconciliation procedures are still required when the couple has children or if the divorce is contested.

That many Soviet spouses are in need of help with interpersonal and practical problems arising from their marital status is suggested by divorce statistics, by the literature, and by field findings. Teachers who visit the homes of problem children report alcoholism, desertion, moral disintegration, and indifference.[2] Wrote Kharchev in 1964, "At present, along with open fatherlessness, there exists hidden fatherlessness, which is personified by fathers who, although living in the family, take no part in the rearing of their children." A 1960 book that reports on eleven intellectually gifted children shows that only five had both a father and a mother at home, well and active: five had broken families, and one an invalided father.[3] A 1958 investigation in one village revealed that women were the heads of 44.5 per cent of the families.[4]

The absence of professional social services to spouses as *people* is in sharp contrast to the profusion of services available to them as *parents*.[5] Though the attainment of communism calls for the eventual transfer of family functions to society, the placement of all children in a state-manipulated upbringing environment is impossible, and considered by many undesirable, in the foreseeable future. The family, it is conceded even by those who would reduce its function to a strictly biological one, will remain influential in personality formation, and it is crucial therefore that it be a good family. The current thinking of those who may be described as the "pro-family" exponents can be best presented, perhaps, in the words of Kharchev:

> What is the . . . necessity for family upbringing? Above all . . . [such] upbringing is more emotional than any other kind. . . . Constituting of itself a small group, a kind of "microcosm," the family is most skilled at meeting the demand for a gradual adaptation of the child to social life and to the broadening of his outlook and experience by appropriate stages. . . . In contrast to intellectual development, which continues throughout life, the development of character, willpower, feelings takes place basically in childhood and youth. This means that the emotional pattern that is established in the family determines the future psychological development of a person to a much greater extent than the intellectual pattern [determines] the future content of his intellect.[6]

These views are widely shared by practitioners. Hence, major effort is currently devoted to helping the family do its job "correctly" by rectifying "mistakes" while the child is still part of it—rather than removing the child from its influence.*

---

* Policies to help parents keep their children at home continue to be developed. Some officials are urging the payment of social insurance benefits to mothers who stay at home in order to care for their children, to compensate them for the loss of earnings that they would receive if they worked outside the home.

Among the pre-Revolutionary welfare concepts that have been taken over by the Soviet regime is the belief that "normal" children must be separated from "defective" children—the physically handicapped and the mentally retarded. After the Revolution, there emerged two distinct systems of education and rearing: one for the normal, the other for the defective. The defective are further divided into those who can benefit by instruction and those who cannot benefit at all or only to a limited extent. The uneducable are placed in institutions managed by the fifteen Republic Ministries of Social Welfare; the educable are instructed in special schools operated by the Ministry of Education. Normal and defective children have almost no contact with each other during the first 16 years of their lives. While recommendations are occasionally made that closer contact between them be encouraged in order, especially, to provide a more effective moral upbringing for the defective, there is no visible movement in this direction. Integration of services is seldom discussed: rigidity, hostility, and derision are exhibited at its very mention. Many defective children live at home when attending school, but a larger proportion of them than of normal children live in institutions.[7] Institutional living is preferred by the majority of defectologists.

Services for Normal Children Living at Home

These services are provided or supervised by the Ministries of Welfare, Health, and Education.

Services under the Ministries of Social Welfare. In principle, workers in the family allowances program are expected to satisfy the social needs of the mothers and children involved: find suitable work for the mothers, improve their living conditions, help adolescents find work and enroll them in evening schools, place small children in nurseries, kindergartens, or, when necessary, institutions, and assist neglected, abused, and unsupervised children. However, most local offices do not furnish any of these services, claiming that mothers who have social problems can get the necessary help at their places of employment or in their social organizations.*

Services under the Ministries of Health. Child welfare services are often provided by medical and "socio-legal" personnel in women's and children's clinics. Within these clinics, a physician-"patronage" nurse team is responsible for about 800 children whom it serves from before their birth to age 16. The training of a "patronage" nurse is identical to that of a medical nurse: the difference in title reflects the focus of the

---

* So little importance is attached to this aspect of the duties of welfare personnel that in the 11 years since administration of family allowances was transferred to the Ministries of Social Welfare (prior to 1956 they were administered by the Treasury) only two articles have appeared about them in *Sotsial'noe Obespechenie*.

former on the home and of the latter on work in the clinic. If the team finds that a child's development is hindered by social problems facing the mother, it may refer her to an attorney in the socio-legal bureau located in the clinic. Such bureaus are usually found only in the larger medical establishments; smaller ones can combine administratively to set them up, but for the most part they have not done so. Consequently, socio-legal bureaus are spottily distributed, with few in the smaller and rural communities.

The purpose of the socio-legal bureau is to explain to women the rights of mothers and children and to help with problems relating to living conditions, employment, and marital relationships.[8] Their services are free. The bureaus are child- and home-centered; that is, the child's welfare is the primary consideration, and his own home, unless it is quite unsuitable, is considered the best place for him, with the home of relatives next best. This applies to the children of both married and unmarried mothers. It is considered essential not to rely on methods of help such as placing a child in an institution, for example, simply because this takes less work than keeping him at home. Complex custody settlements are avoided, if possible, because they often result in psychological traumas for both parents and children. Socio-legal bureaus may give financial aid in emergency cases. They cooperate closely with other agencies, and in complicated situations they may consult physicians, psychiatrists, teachers, and interested individuals from social organizations.

Psychiatrists, neuropathologists, and medical and patronage nurses are also employed in special outpatient psychoneurological dispensaries for children only. They help "nervous" (emotionally disturbed) children and adolescents who need not be committed to inpatient institutions (they may live at home, in boarding schools, or spend part of their time in day-sanatoriums and the rest at home or in school), and are also responsible for following up those discharged from inpatient institutions. In addition, the dispensary physicians participate, together with others concerned, in determining whether or not a child is defective and should be sent to a special school.[9]

"Nervous" children who need inpatient care are divided into two groups: those whose problems stem from external conditions and those who are suffering from an internal problem. The latter are treated in medical facilities under the Ministry of Health; some of the former are treated in special residential schools under the Ministry of Education. In both, the treatment includes discussions with parents and other responsible adults to help them understand the children's "peculiarities." It is claimed that most children who enter residential schools become well enough within one academic year to return to a regular school.

Usually they also return home, but if the home is unsuitable, they are placed in a boarding school.

There has been an increase in the number of nervous children whose defects arise from external social conditions. But it is maintained that this is not an increase in incidence: it is due to more complete case studies and better treatment facilities accessible to larger segments of the population. There are plans for an increased number of residential schools to deal with this problem. Currently, such facilities are unevenly distributed: in 1965 Moscow had five residential schools, while the entire Uzbek Republic had none.*

Services under the Ministries of Education. School personnel most directly involved in child welfare services are the classroom teachers and the children's inspectors. Classroom teachers work with parents to handle both preschool and school difficulties of their students.[10] This cooperation is considerably facilitated by the fact that the same teacher remains with the children for four years, moving up with them from the first to the fourth grade, so that she learns to know them and their parents well. As shown in cases 1 and 2 in Chapter 7, teachers hold individual conferences with parents and with family groups, in school and at home. In these contacts, they try to limit their activity to the purposes of the school, but there are instances when parents who have personal problems seek and receive help from them. Reports one teacher:

> I react to every development in the child's family—try to help with advice, at times even interfere in the life of the family, or, more correctly, in the conduct of the members of the family. This takes great tact. For example, the mother of S. is living in an unregistered marriage with his father. On a home visit, I found only the father in. He told me that he is suffering deeply from the refusal of the wife to register their marriage, that he takes it very hard that there is a blank in the boy's birth certificate in the place reserved for the father's name. Once, when the mother came for her son, I started talking with her about this—carefully and softly, for fear the woman would refuse to listen. We discussed the matter for more than half an hour, and she gave me her word that she would get the marriage registered.[11]

Children's inspectors are teachers whose special assignment is to deal with socially disorganized families and to protect neglected, abused, and dependent children. Cases come to their attention from schools, other agencies, social organizations, relatives, neighbors, and interested individuals. Inspectors investigate each child's living conditions to ascertain the reasons for his difficulties. They then take the measures required,

---

* See Appendix A for a description of a clinical facility for nervous children, as well as a case study.

keeping in mind that parents are to be deprived of custody and the child to be removed from the home only in extreme situations—only when supportive help in modifying the environment fails to create a suitable milieu.

Findings from the field and from the literature indicate that services offered by school personnel to children in their own homes differ considerably, both in quantity and quality. Many parents, especially in outlying areas, receive no help at all with their problems; in many instances school personnel are not sufficiently skilled to understand the children's problems or to bring about the necessary changes. Inspectors are overloaded and usually unable to devote needed time to their many responsibilities; quite often, their efforts are limited to mere admonitions and warnings.

Since 1961, day-care nurseries and kindergartens have been within the jurisdiction of the Ministries of Education. (Prior to that date, nurseries were run by the Ministry of Health.) Nurseries sometimes accept babies only one day old and care for them to age three; then they enter kindergarten, where they remain until age seven. In these preschool facilities, there are three types of care arrangements: one is for a period of nine hours—equal to the mother's working hours plus time for shopping; one is for a longer period, for children whose mothers live some distance from the facility; and one is an all-day service, for mothers whose jobs require them to travel or to work at night, and who can take the child home only on Sundays and holidays.

The staff in many nurseries is sufficiently large to allow two staff members (or even more) for every five children. There are pediatricians, nurses, teachers, and nursemaids. If the nursery is a large one, the director is likely to be a pediatrician; smaller crèches are run by doctors' assistants (*fel'dshers*) or nurses. In some nurseries, when children are moved from one group to another, the staff moves with them in order to avoid any emotional upsets for the children. Fees for nursery and kindergarten care are determined on the basis of family income, number of children in the family, length of stay, and whether the facility is urban or rural. Charges are reduced by 50 per cent for widows of military personnel whose death was service-connected, for unmarried mothers if their monthly earnings are less than 60 rubles, and for mothers of four children—no matter what their earnings. No payment at all is required for orphaned children living with guardians or relatives. It is estimated that, overall, parents pay about 20 per cent of the cost of this care.

Soviet authorities believe that day-care services are popular, especially with working mothers, because they allow them to participate actively

TABLE 5

NUMBER OF PLACES IN PERMANENT NURSERIES AND KINDERGARTENS
BY SELECTED YEARS, 1913–1963

(*Thousands*)

Year	In Nurseries	In Kindergartens
1913	.55	4.
1928	62.1	130.
1940	859.5	1,172.
1945	832.8	1,471.
1956	966.1	1,882.
1957	1,048.	2,060.
1959	1,208.	2,671.
1960	1,260.	3,115.
1963	1,491.	4,813.

Sources: *442*, p. 349; *443*, pp. 157, 203; *444*, p. 511.

in economic, cultural, and social life and at the same time fulfill the duties of motherhood. The mothers also realize that the preschool facilities create the conditions needed for the correct physical and psychological development of children.* Close contact with the children's families is maintained by home visits and by inviting parents to the facility, the main object being to teach parents correct methods of upbringing. In 1956, the policy of separating facilities for those under age three from those between three and seven was abandoned in order to simplify matters for mothers having children of different ages. Also it is thought that bringing up a child in the same establishment during the first seven years of his life guards him from psychic injury that may be caused by a transfer from one group of children to another, and from a familiar circle of teachers and nurses to a new one.

The Soviet government has been steadily increasing the network of preschool facilities (see Table 5). In addition to permanent facilities, there are seasonal nurseries in agricultural areas to care for children while their mothers are working in the fields. In 1960 these and summer playgrounds were available for about 3 million children. Thus, in that year 7.4 million preschool-age children received day-care in permanent and seasonal facilities—almost 23 per cent of the 33.4 million such children reported in the 1959 census. In some republics the situation is less satisfactory than in others: in Armenia, for example, according to

---

* Perhaps some mothers have other reasons. One nursery I visited, with its whitewashed walls and immaculately clean beds and floors, stood out in stark contrast to the quarter in which it was located, with its mud huts, its lack of sewage facilities, its pumps in the middle of unpaved streets.

a 1962 report, in the past ten years plans for building nurseries and kindergartens have been fulfilled only 27–50 per cent.[12] For the pre-schoolers for whom facilities are not available, group day-care is sometimes organized by house committees, some children are looked after by grandmothers, and some by servants, if their families are wealthy enough to employ them.

The number of children who spend part of the summer in the country—in pioneer camps, sanatoria, excursion hostels, or country homes—has also been rising: it reached almost 8 million in 1960. Camps and some of the other summer facilities are administered by trade unions and financed from social insurance funds and contributions by industrial establishments: parents pay about one-third of the cost. The camp season is organized into three four-week periods, with about half the children staying throughout the summer.[13] While these are impressive figures, it should be noted that in 1959 the children to age 16 numbered nearly 63.5 million, so that the 8 million who enjoyed summer outings, even when augmented by the 730,000 who were enrolled in city day-camps, represented less than 14 per cent of the total.

Extended-day schools and groups made their appearance in 1956; four years later, they were extended by decree throughout the entire country. "Extended-day" means that the child does not go home after school, but remains until the parents call for him or until they telephone to say that he may come home, usually after 6 P.M. During the extra time, the children are fed, do their homework, and take part in supervised recreation. Social, economic, and pedagogical conditions stimulated the growth of these schools. In many Soviet families both parents work long hours, so that if the child comes home immediately after school, he is alone; institutional care is expensive; boarding schools do not offer the emotional richness of normal family life; and for the most part, families do not have at their disposal the variety of pedagogical devices that the school can offer the child.

Extended-day schools are designed to deal with problems associated with broken homes, lack of supervision, and inadequate parental guidance: poor scholastic performance, dropping out of school, and delinquency. They rely not only on individualized, skilled instruction, but also on upbringing practices that will restructure the child's personality. Hence, both teachers and upbringers are employed. Of basic importance in their operations are small classes (not more than 25 children for one teacher and one upbringer working as a team) and the participation of the most highly qualified teachers and upbringers, which means that higher salaries must be paid to them than to regular school personnel. This makes them more costly than mass schools. In addition, in some instances, there is initial resistance on the part of parents who object to the lengthy travel to and from school that extended-day arrangements may involve, and to the curtailing of free time for the youngsters.

Services for Normal Children Not Living at Home

These services are for children who have lost their parents or whose parents are unable or unsuitable to care for them. This includes children who have been removed from parental custody; whose mothers, whether married or unmarried, prefer not to make a home for them; whose parents are incarcerated; who are orphans with no suitable relatives to take them in; who are abandoned; who need short-term care because of a temporarily disorganized situation in the family; or whose parents are burdened with such large families that they request institutional placement for some of their children. The Ministry of Education, responsible for furnishing these services, discharges its assignment in one of four ways: guardianship (*opekunstvo*) for children under 15 and trusteeship (*popechitel'stvo*) for those between 15 and 18; permanent or long-term foster family care (*patronat*); adoption (*usynovlenie*); and institutional placement.[14] In cases of children under three, educational authorities collaborate closely with the Ministry of Health; occasionally, the Ministry of Social Welfare may be involved as well. All of these ministries act as representatives of local soviets who delegate the responsibility for child protection to them.

Guardianship and Trusteeship. Guardianship is arranged for each child who lacks adequate parental care and is not living in a children's institution. Compulsory in cases of the death of both parents, guardianship may be instituted while the parents are alive—when they cannot give care because of ill health, absence on long trips required by their work, or mental illness, or when they are legally deprived of custody. The guardian and the ward must live together, since this is the only way to achieve family upbringing, but the guardian may place the ward in an institution for temporary periods, if permission for this is granted. Both relatives and nonrelatives may become guardians, although the former are preferred and are used in most instances, including older brothers and sisters. In the selection of a guardian, careful account is taken of his personal characteristics. A guardian is not paid for his services: he is expected to support the child at his own expense[15] or to use whatever wealth the child himself may have (grants for children of unmarried mothers, pensions, support payments). The guardian cannot dispose of the child's property without the approval of the Ministry of Education. (Guardianship and trusteeship arrangements for defective children are identical with those for normal ones.)

Foster Family Care. It will be recalled that foster family care was used quite extensively by the Soviet regime during "emergencies"—the post-Revolutionary period and during and after World War II—to deal with homeless children. It was never thought of as a temporary method for handling children, until their own parents became able to provide a suitable home for them. Foster family care is still used only as a permanent or a long-term arrangement and only in those instances when a child has no means of support and the person who takes him in does not have sufficient resources of his own to raise the child. If at some time after placement in a foster home, a child acquires support funds that amount to more than the foster care grant, the foster care agreement is terminated, and the foster parent is appointed the child's guardian.[16] Although they have neither experimented with temporary foster family care nor studied the experience of countries who have, Soviet authorities continue to feel that it is trauma-producing, loyalty-dividing, and frustrating for all concerned. Only when the child's natural parents are completely out of the picture, they believe, can the child and the foster parents form meaningful relationships. When the parents are alive but are incapable or unwilling to provide the kind of upbringing the society desires, only an institution can help the child to become the right kind of person. By now, what little *patronat* there is applies primarily to orphans, and the hope is to eliminate it altogether.

This attitude may be a carry-over from tsarist experience, reinforced by frustrations accumulated during the Soviet era. Today, the housing shortage, the low sanitary standards in many homes, and the continuing absorption of women into the labor force would make it difficult to find temporary foster homes on any scale. However, there are currently 10 million able-bodied women devoting themselves entirely to housework—a potential pool of foster mothers that may be sufficient during the present period in Soviet history. Perhaps the unwillingness of Soviet welfare personnel to explore the possibilities of temporary foster family care arises from a conviction that to raise a child who has experienced parental neglect or inadequacy is too difficult a task to be entrusted to anyone except trained communist upbringers. There is little doubt in their minds that institutional care is more amenable to planning, eliminates the necessity of undoing what poorly selected foster parents have done, and places control squarely in the hands of the regime.* As for the

* In discussions of the potential of temporary foster family care, many Soviet child welfare workers manifest a lively interest and grasp the idea quite easily and quickly. Others are hostile to it, maintaining that such foster care is a "capitalist" invention, developed because it is cheaper than institutional care. Still others simply cannot understand the concept; they think of foster family care as permanent and as a method useful only in

preference for guardianship over permanent foster family care, the reason for it was stated quite frankly by a number of welfare workers: guardianship offers the same service to the child and does not cost the state anything, whereas foster family care is fairly expensive.

Adoption. Only children under 18 may be adopted, and only if the consent of any living parent or guardian has been obtained. Such consent is not required if parents have been deprived of custody or have failed to keep in touch with their institutionalized child for a period of at least one year, and cannot be located. In that case, the administration of the institution must consent, and the child himself if he is ten years old. If the adopter is married, the consent of his spouse must be obtained. Certain persons are not permitted to adopt: those who are themselves under guardianship, those whose interests conflict with the interests of the ward, the mentally ill, those deprived of their rights as citizens, and those who have not reached majority.* Differences in race, nationality, or religion are not bars to adoption, and single women can adopt if they have experience working with children, as do teachers and pediatricians, for example.

Approval by the local soviet, based on a finding that adoption is in the best interests of the child, must be given before the adoption is final. The adopter must guarantee proper care of the child's health, as well as proper education, moral upbringing, and preparation for a working life. Adoption severs all legal ties with the natural parents, in order to protect the child from intrusion on his adoptive relationship. Once adoption is completed, the child is referred to as if he were born in wedlock to his adoptive parents. Adopted children and their descendants have the same personal and property rights and duties to the adopter as do the adopter's natural children. However, this legal tie applies only to the adopted child and the adopter: it does not extend to the relationships between the adopted child and members of the adopter's family. Criticizing this feature of the law, one Soviet scholar states that it is justifiable "only when the determining role in adoption is played by property interests, interests of inheritance, when broad rights of the adopted child in the family of the adopter can bring about material loss to the heirs"—in short, in a capitalist state and not in a socialist one.[17] An adopted child cannot inherit from his natural parents.

---

great national emergencies. No discussion of foster family care appears in the literature. Since 1946, *Sem'ia i Shkola* has published only three short letters from readers who have been foster parents.

* "Majority" is interpreted differently in different republics. In Grusiia and Belorussia, the adopter cannot be younger than 20 years, and in the latter, must be at least ten years older than the adopted; in Azerbaidzhan, the adopter must be at least 18 years older than the adopted.

If after adoption it develops that the new status is harmful to the child, a court can set aside the relationship.[18]

According to Soviet authorities, current applications to adopt exceed the number of available children. There is no problem finding homes for children under three, for whom the demand is greatest; it is more difficult to find homes for older children. Handicapped children are not offered for adoption; it is felt this would be unfair to the adopter. Policy with regard to siblings is to place them in the same family: it is believed that the support and love that siblings can give each other when experiencing loss of their own parents or starting life with new parents is valuable. Exceptions are made, however, if the siblings are very young. The children adopted include orphans, stepchildren, those for whom adoption constitutes a legalization of already established relationships, a few illegitimate children (it is claimed that unmarried mothers rarely wish to give up their youngsters), and a few children who are legally free because their parents have lost custody. Soviet personnel believe that it is not possible to determine what a child will be like before age five months; hence, very young children are placed only in the most exceptional circumstances. Age does not matter in stepparent adoptions, which are granted almost automatically.

Practically all of the children who are adopted are first placed in institutions. Their medical and developmental history and social background are studied, and their characteristics observed by upbringers. If adoptive parents wish additional information, the child they are interested in is observed more closely. All available information is given to the prospective parents. The majority of applicants for adoption are people who, for one reason or another, cannot have their own children. The next largest group are those whose own children are either away from home or who have perhaps only one child left, making the family seem incomplete. Among the latter, adoption usually involves older children, and is preceded by guardianship. Some adoptive parents are single women, or people who somehow get involved in adoption by chance or because of unusual circumstances. The investigation of an applicant for adoption includes a study of the composition of his family; the employment, income, health, and education of its members; the sanitary conditions in the home; the quality of the relationships among family members; and the motives the prospective parent has for seeking a child. Authorities who make the study are urged to become knowledgeable about the daily life of the family, find out how the parents care for their own children, what their cultural level is, whether there are any persons in the family who may exert a harmful influence. If the prospective parent is employed, a report must be received from his place of employment that includes the opinion of his co-workers.[19] Additional information is sought from neighbors and from others who know the family.

Prospective parents apply at the Ministries of Health and Education and, if deemed suitable, are directed to appropriate institutions. Parents have quite a bit to say about which child they will take. Efforts at "matching" children and parents are minimal; age limits are not rigidly set: some Soviet workers feel that occasionally 60-year-old women should be allowed to adopt infants. An attempt is made to maintain contact with the adoptive family for a year after placement in order to facilitate adjustment, but this is not easy, because most parents do not want neighbors to know that their child is adopted and seek to move to a new district. Few adoptions are annulled: if the home relationship is unsatisfactory, adoptive parents are expected to place the child in an institution and pay for his support—an important consideration in holding down annulments.

Although Soviet welfare workers invariably refer to adoption in the most laudatory terms, there is no doubt that adoption applicants are given scant assistance by the agencies involved. Children's inspectors, overloaded with duties, devote little time to helping applicants find a child, to suggesting criteria to guide them in selecting a child, to making sure that they are suitable parents for a particular child, or to assisting with problems that may arise after the child arrives in the home. Generally, parents are left to search through institutions and enter into negotiations on their own. It is difficult to reconcile the community's supposed approval of parents who adopt with the frequent requests from these parents for help in moving to a different community. No follow-up studies have been undertaken; hence, welfare personnel do not know how adopted children turn out. As a matter of fact, the literature—so prolific about the child-rearing functions of natural parents—is almost completely silent about adoptive parents: for example, for nearly 20 years the monthly journal *Sem'ia i Shkola* published not a single article on the subject. Eight references to adoption appeared during these years, but five were in letters from readers and three were one-page statements by a legal expert about the rights and responsibilities of adoptive parents.[20] The impression conveyed is that adoptive parents need services but are not getting them.

Statistics on adoption are not published (and perhaps not even gathered), but it is doubtful that many adoptions are consummated. This may be partly because few children are available for adoption, but this is not the whole story. With institutions bursting with children, many of whose parents might not oppose relinquishing their rights, more youngsters could be adopted if the state backed up its declarations about the desirability of home life by improving adoption procedures. (There are indications that even present procedures are not consistently followed.)*

Again, findings from the field indicate that guardianship, foster family care, and adoption services differ considerably, both in quantity and quality, between regions and between urban and rural communities. For example, in outlying republics such services are practically unknown.

Institutional Care for Normal Children

In contrast to the lack of worthwhile literature on substitute family care, the literature on institutional care is enormous. It ranges from novel-like accounts that appeal to the emotions to dry reports of conferences and in-service training institutes.[21] A new journal, *Shkola-Internat* (Boarding School), began publication in 1961. It is obvious that placement in institutions is the preferred method of caring for children outside their own homes, and that a great deal of effort and thought is being devoted to its development and improvement. According to findings in the field, currently operating institutions include the following: homes for children up to age three, under the Ministry of Health; and homes for three-to-seven year olds, homes and boarding schools for the seven-to-eighteen age group, two boarding schools for children from one to fourteen, and special homes for children seven to fifteen who are musically gifted—all under the Ministries of Education.[22]

Planning for the future is taking two forms: for children of preschool age, homes of 100–150 capacity will continue; for children of school age, homes will be transformed into boarding schools, each serving 300 to 600 children. The trend toward "giant" institutions is gaining momentum, even though large collectives may have a crushing effect on individual children, because the greater financial resources of large institutions make it easier to provide the expensive equipment needed for training in technical skills. As for the transformation to boarding schools, in spite of delays caused by vested interests and traditions, it is by now fairly complete. Both homes and boarding schools are now serving orphans, children of large and poverty-stricken families, youngsters from broken families, and families with other difficulties (unmarried mothers, mentally or physically incapacitated parents, or rejecting stepparents, for example). Normally, "good" parents do not think of sending their children to boarding schools (except in isolated and sparsely populated regions where schools are too far away for daily commuting), nor are children sent from "bad" families when the parents are from among the privileged groups. For the most part, institution children come from

* See Appendix B for the case history of an adopted boy.

deprived circumstances; for many, life has been hard, and almost none have received a correct upbringing. Occasionally, juvenile delinquents are sent to the homes and boarding schools. Usually parents themselves petition the local children's commission for permission to place a child in an institution. If approved, adjustments in fees, similar to those for day-care, are made.[23] Sometimes petitions come from school personnel, relatives, housing committees, neighbors, or other interested persons—if parents should but do not act.

The staffs of boarding schools and of homes that have been converted into boarding schools consist of teachers and upbringers; in untransformed homes, there are only the upbringers who work cooperatively with the teachers in the mass schools their charges attend. Upbringers make it clear to each child in the institution that there are rules of behavior that must be obeyed, and they explain to him precisely why these rules are necessary. Each child must see that the rules are for the children —not the children for the rules. Helpful methods for internalizing collective values are traditions such as "patronage" of younger children by their older comrades; making sure that children elected to self-governing bodies express the "right" values; criticism and self-criticism; membership in youth organizations. Upbringers believe that a positive atmosphere is created by stressing trust and confidence in the children's strengths and potentialities, by requiring uniform treatment by all adults of each child, and by using punishment as an expression of collective disapproval—not as a way to stigmatize the child or make him fearful. The upbringer's concern and responsibility often extend beyond the institution, when he continues a supportive relationship with those for whom the transition to the less sheltered life in the world may be difficult. In some instances, young people are permitted to live at the institution even after they begin outside jobs.

Upbringers in institutions do not live in, but there is a live-in staff, and at least one nurse is on duty at all times. Most institutions have isolation wards and a physician who visits every day, but major medical treatment is given at district clinics. Children are supposed to stay with the same upbringer from grades one through eight to assure continuity of relationship; in fact, this continuity is often broken when the upbringer quits her job. In the institutions, children exhibit the usual gamut of problems: many who have experienced cruelty and disorganized and meager existences need to be physically strengthened and given special attention; some who have never lived in a group setting find the adjustment far from simple; some lack even rudimentary skill in self-care; some suffer keenly from the separation from their families and tend to withdraw or to become aggressive; some are retarded, and efforts to help them do well enough scholastically to avoid being sent to a special school are not always successful. One of the upbringers' major worries is how much and how well the children learn. They will not hesitate to "skin them three times" (*tri shkury sderut*) to get them to pass.*

By 1965 initial enthusiasm about boarding schools had cooled and criticisms became frequent. According to Soviet personnel, one of the major weaknesses is that most institution directors are concerned only with the percentage of children who pass into the next higher grade and pay little attention to upbringing. Upbringing interests them only from one crisis to another. They ignore the principle of Soviet psychology that correct upbringing determines the moral character of the future "Soviet man," and creates a firm base for high scholastic achievement: strictly educational measures can have only temporary results at best.

The institutions are too isolated from life, from family and friends. Efforts to connect them with life are, in many instances, sporadic and unsuccessful. Parents do not always keep in touch, and children do not always go home on weekends and in the summer. This means that mistakes on the part of the upbringers in an institution are not likely to be compensated for by outside influences. To make matters worse, it is almost impossible to find the needed number of qualified upbringers. Hence, many institution children are undisciplined, indifferent to the welfare of the collective, and devoid of a sense of responsibility.

It is difficult to resist the pressure for conformity in the large institutions that militates against the expression of individuality and the creation of a "family" milieu—the only type of environment in which a many-sided development of the child is possible. Upbringers try to counteract this pressure by dividing the children into relatively small groups with common interests, in order to establish a more intimate atmosphere.† But this is not easy. The difficulties are compounded by overcrowding and by lack of space where the children can be by themselves. In their free time, when they are not outside, the youngsters have no place to go.

Current opinion among the more thoughtful upbringers is that boarding school policies are dictated more by practical circumstances than by their inherent desirability. They seem to agree with Kharchev that "family and social upbringing are closely interrelated, complement each other, and within certain limits can substitute for each other, but in their totality they do not equal each other. That is why total substitution of one for

---

* See Appendix C for a description of a boarding school for musically gifted children.

† From institutions that allow children of different age groups to spend some of their time together it has been learned that such companionship leads to the development of "brother" and "sister" relationships. This led Kharchev to conclude that when children are reared outside the family, they require an "imitation" family.

the other always results in serious losses for the child, the family, and society."[24]

Services for Defective Children

Services for Educable Defective Children. Educational arrangements for this group are shown in Chart 2. No statistics are published on the country's total number of defective children or on the number attending the schools shown in the chart. With regard to the preschool group, it is freely admitted that the facilities now available accommodate only a part of them,* relatively fewer than similar facilities for normal youngsters.[25] But it is claimed that the number of compulsory special schools is now sufficient for the entire contingent of defective children of school age. (Those who cannot attend school are given individual instruction at home.) Regulations require that classes for the blind, deaf, and those with impaired vision and hearing be limited to 12 pupils, classes in schools for the retarded to 16, and classes for those with speech defects to 10. These standards are not uniformly maintained, however: in the schools for the retarded, for example, most upbringers are responsible for about 22 children.

The growth of special education has been marked by (1) program differentiation resulting from better understanding of handicapping conditions, (2) heavy reliance on boarding schools and, if these are not available, on extended-day groups in order to keep children under special tutelage as much as possible, and (3) insistence on occupational training as part of the basic curriculum for each child. At present, the handicapped are taught not only the "traditional" trades—carpentry, shoemaking, locksmithing, sewing, basketweaving, and brushmaking—but also radio and electrical appliance assembling, lathe work, and certain forms of construction work. Selection of the trades to be taught is determined not only by the students' handicaps but also by the resources of the individual school and by the community's need for particular skills. The graduates of special schools who continue their education attend "training-producing" enterprises operated by the All-Russian Societies for the Blind and the Deaf, or the other types of facilities for vocational training shown in Chart 2.

Services for Noneducable Defective Children. These children may be placed in one of three kinds of institutions: homes for the physically

---

* This may be due in part to disagreement among experts about the desirability of separate facilities for them. Some believe that mentally retarded preschool children should attend kindergartens together with normal children, unless their condition requires institutionalization; others insist that complete separation is more desirable. There is no such disagreement concerning the treatment of children with other types of defects, and (it is claimed) specialized facilities for them are rapidly being developed.

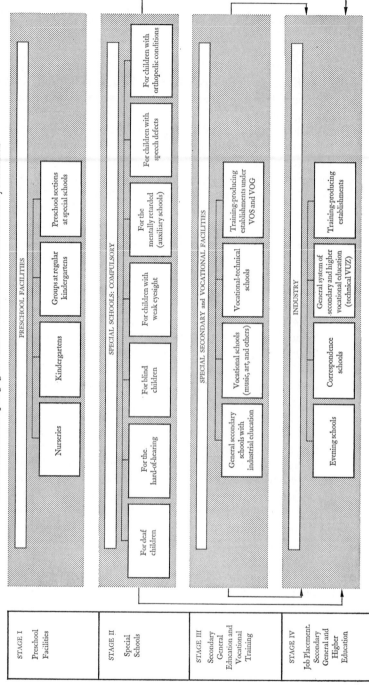

Chart 2. Education and Upbringing for Educable Defective Children Within the Ministry of Education

PRESCHOOL FACILITIES

SPECIAL SCHOOLS: COMPULSORY

SPECIAL SECONDARY and VOCATIONAL FACILITIES

INDUSTRY

Nurseries

Kindergartens

Groups at regular kindergartens

Preschool sections at special schools

For deaf children

For the hard-of-hearing

For blind children

For children with weak eyesight

For the mentally retarded (auxiliary schools)

For children with speech defects

For children with orthopedic conditions

General secondary schools with industrial education

Vocational schools (music, art, and others)

Vocational-technical schools

Training-producing establishments under VOS and VOG

Evening schools

Correspondence schools

General system of secondary and higher vocational education (technical VUZ)

Training-producing establishments

STAGE I
Preschool
Facilities

STAGE II
Special
Schools

STAGE III
Secondary
General
Education and
Vocational
Training

STAGE IV
Job Placement.
Secondary
General and
Higher
Education

handicapped, in which they may attend a regular eight-year school and receive vocational training in agriculture or in shop work; homes for imbeciles who are physically well, in which there is a four-year school as well as shop and agricultural training; and homes for idiots, in which the emphasis is on rudimentary tasks, mostly of a self-care nature. Payments by parents are pro-rated according to income or not required at all.

It is claimed by personnel in the Ministries of Social Welfare that the great majority of the graduates of these institutions are able to find jobs in state enterprises and on farms. Those who cannot are transferred to adult institutions. The program of education for the retarded apparently has been less successful than that for the physically handicapped. To some extent, this may be because the retarded have been relatively neglected by the authorities. The first all-Russian conference on the severely retarded did not take place until 1955; it was followed by a 1960 meeting at which improvements introduced during the intervening years were discussed. Most of the time, however, was spent pointing out that services were still substandard. It was noted, for example, that 50 per cent of the institutions did not have a physician on their staffs, and none had a psychiatrist. Upbringers were overloaded: each was responsible for an average of 23 children. It was recommended that the number be lowered to 16 and that a music teacher be added to the permanent staff of each institution. Leaders in the field are now advocating that job descriptions be prepared for the physicians and pedagogues to be employed in the institutions, and that thought be given to methodological aids and periodic conferences for personnel. Suggested administrative improvements are the removal of barriers to communication and co-operation between the Ministries of Social Welfare, Health, and Education and the elimination of obstacles that often delay placement of personnel in the institutional network and sometimes make it impossible. It is urged that facilities be more precisely differentiated in order to deal with retarded children who do not seem to fall within any recognized category. In addition, there is concern with overemphasis on custodial care and a lack of research into the relationship between social milieu and retardation.[26]

Whether or not a particular child is defective is decided by expert commissions (at city, district, or regional levels) that include representatives from the local school system, from special schools (if there are any in the community), and physicians—both general practitioners and specialists. When mental retardation is suspected, the specialist must be a psychiatrist. The commission bases its conclusions on materials compiled by parents, teachers, and physicians, as well as the findings of its own examination. If the child is defective and there is no special school in his area of residence, he is sent away to school. Each student's status must be reviewed annually by a pedagogical committee to determine if he is correctly placed; if he is not, he is transferred to another facility—in some instances a regular public school.[27] Recommendations concerning preschool children are made by medical personnel who have had contact with them and their parents from the time they were born.

In cases of deafness and blindness, precise measurements to guide expert commissions are readily available. In cases of mental retardation, however, if retardation is not detected prior to the age of seven, no determination is made until the child has spent a year in a regular school. Even then, the expert commission will not recommend transfer to a special school until it is satisfied that the regular school has taken all possible measures to improve the child's performance, without obtaining positive results,[28] and until child psychiatrists have concluded that inability to pursue regular studies is caused by mental deficiency of organic origin.

Many mistakes are made by expert commissions, the most common being the placing of too many children in the borderline category. The following is an attempt to provide some of the reasons for these mistakes:

> The artificial office atmosphere [in which the special commission operates] does not predispose the child to cooperate, does not stimulate him to show his potentialities, while the strangeness of the surroundings...distracts him. In addition, the material concerning the slow learner that is sent to the commission is frequently put together in a superficial manner: it does not provide complete information about the child—about the kind of difficulties he experiences while attempting to learn, how the teacher helps him to overcome these difficulties, what kind of individual assistance he is given, how he behaves himself, what his relationships within the collective are, how he reacts to the teacher's demands, the peculiarities of his speech, etc. In the pedagogical evaluation often only the negative characteristics of the child are described. There is no attempt to explain from what these negative qualities stem or how the teacher has tried to eliminate them.[29]

It can also be assumed that members of some commissions are not sufficiently skilled to conduct the thorough study that is required. This is probably especially true in remote regions. It has been found that when defectologists visit schools and help teachers analyze the poor performance of some pupils, the number of recommendations for special schools is lowered.

Success in work with the defective has always been measured academically—how many pass to the next grade, are outstanding students, go on to higher education—as well as by how many obtain jobs.[30] The 1958 law designed to strengthen the schools "by connecting them with life" was not enthusiastically received by all defectologists: there was disagreement about the weight that should be attached to the teaching of occupational skills in curricula for the handicapped. Some insisted that it ought to be the major element, "so that the student would lose no time after graduation in becoming efficiently productive"; others believed that it should be subordinate to general education, because handicapped children cannot be expected to be "productive."[31]

Within a few years, supporters of the 1958 law carried the day. Emphasis on work as a learning process was intensified, and the integration of work into general education was increased. The main objective now is to train pupils at the higher technical level demanded by industry, so that upon graduation they do not find themselves out of step with "life" —something that many experienced prior to 1958, it is held. The preoccupation with vocational training at first resulted in a curriculum that made handicapped children work harder and longer than normal children, and had a deleterious effect on general education by requiring children to begin the study of vocational subjects at age eleven. Both these problems have now been solved, it is insisted: the first by concentrating on general subjects in the lower grades, the second by allowing pupils to begin vocational training when they are more mature.[32]

The educational program for defective children appears to be equivalent to that for normal children as far as physical accommodations, medical care arrangements, and norms are concerned.* There is strict discipline everywhere. Parents' Committees are active in many schools. One day a week is usually set aside as a visiting day for parents, and most children are taken home on weekends if they do not live too far away. Staff members help parents to understand their child's defect, to plan with the school for his further education—in short, they work to strengthen the parents' interest in everything that concerns the child. There is a preference for purely institutional care, as opposed to having the children remain in their own homes while attending special schools, which is justified on two grounds: (1) there is a greater degree of socialization—the child grows up less egotistic, less spoiled, more appreciative of the needs of others, and (2) there is less of a burden on parents, which in many families would be intolerable—the parents work, transportation is difficult, the homes are crowded.†

There is no doubt that increasing attention and resources are being devoted to work with the handicapped, including research at several special institutes. Each of these institutes has experimental schools and carries out research projects on its own, as well as in association with personnel in other institutions of research. Scientific conferences and

---

* See Appendix D for a description of one of the country's best facilities for defective children.

† When the bussing of children to special facilities on a daily basis was proposed to those interested in the education of the handicapped—both professionals and lay persons—many seemed very interested. Some said that this is something they ought to look into seriously when their country becomes more affluent.

other types of meetings are held, and a large number of books and monographs are published. A journal, *Spetsial'naia Shkola* (Special School), is published by the Institute of Defectology of the RSFSR.

However, field observations raise a number of questions concerning present treatment of the handicapped in the Soviet Union. For example, in their eagerness to equip the handicapped with vocational skills, defectologists appear to neglect the aspects of education that make it possible for an individual to respond to changing work demands; hence, their preoccupation with training in specific skills may be defeating the very purpose they wish to attain. Also, it seems inconsistent to erect a wall between defective and normal children that the former are expected somehow to scale upon reaching adulthood. Many graduates of special schools experience difficulties in solving "life problems"—organizing their daily routine, spending their earnings sensibly, establishing proper relationships in their work collectives, maintaining acceptable standards of self-care.[33] Often they are easily swayed by "normal" people, and induced to commit petty thefts and other crimes. Some defectologists feel that if a retarded youngster lives with his family, rather than in a boarding school, he is less likely to be so helpless in handling the affairs of daily life. But in the words of one eminent Soviet defectologist, written in 1960, "The problem of family upbringing of children with physical or mental defects awaits solution."[34]

It appears that this solution is not being actively sought: on the whole, work with parents is the least important activity of those concerned with defective children. So much effort has gone into creating institutional facilities for the handicapped that relatively few defectologists are concerned with determining if they are in fact the best places for all handicapped children. Only a few conceive of the institutional system as perhaps merely a stage in the development of education and services for such children. Parents, on the other hand, frequently have very definite views concerning institutions. Some parents of deaf children, for example, refuse to let them leave the home to enter preschool facilities; others prefer to send their children to boarding schools because of the special training provided, though they suffer at the separation. Practical considerations play a major role: boarding schools are essential for children who live in outlying districts and for orphans and abandoned children (*odinochki*); it would be difficult or impossible for parents to make two trips daily to the school.

Services for Unmarried Mothers and Illegitimate Children

There are no special provisions for these mothers and children; that is, nothing is set up specifically for them rather than for all mothers and children. This is in keeping with the official position that the status of illegitimacy does not exist in the Soviet Union. Hence, there are no institutional or foster homes operated solely for unmarried mothers, nor are they dealt with by separate agencies manned by specially trained personnel. Medical care, paid pregnancy and maternity leaves, and laws protecting pregnant women from harmful employment are the same for all expectant mothers. If an unwed mother needs help with problems arising with regard to work, housing, education, relatives, her economic circumstances, or the securing of her legal rights, she can obtain it from a socio-legal adviser or a patronage nurse at the medical center to which she is urged to report regularly before and after the birth of her baby. Special attention may be given to her because of the difficulties connected with establishing paternity and the securing of support funds. Efforts are made to identify women pregnant out of wedlock as early as possible—as well as married pregnant women divorced or deserted during pregnancy—in order to prevent abortion or the abandonment of babies. However, because socio-legal bureaus do not exist in every community, many unmarried mothers do not get any counseling, or are left to the uncertain solicitude of community participation groups.

The unwed mother has the power to make all decisions regarding her child—whether to keep him with her, place him in an institution on a temporary or permanent basis, or give him up for adoption. In any counseling she may receive in the process of making her decision, the welfare of the child is stressed above all. Soviet informants claim that although many unmarried mothers resort to institutional care, many choose to keep and bring up their children themselves—a choice that is lauded by the authorities. Some who at first place their babies in institutions reclaim them after a short period.

In addition to legal and moral help given unwed mothers, they are given economic assistance. During the first year of her child's life, an unmarried mother cannot be laid off unless permission has been secured from a committee higher in the trade union hierarchy than the local committee in the establishment where she works; if the child is older than twelve months, she is given preference over others with equal qualifications when workers are being laid off. She receives a monthly allowance for her first child, whereas married mothers get no allowance until their fourth child is born; if she has three children out of wedlock, she receives the benefits to which all mothers of "many" children are entitled. The allowance for her child is more generous and continues for twelve years, whereas for a child born in wedlock it is discontinued at age five.[35] Should she wish to arrange nursery care for her child, she will pay less than other parents in equal economic circumstances; should she

marry a man other than the father of her child, the allowance will continue. If, however, an unwed mother wishes to keep her child but is
judged unfit, she is deprived of custody just as other parents are.

If an unwed mother places her child in a boarding school, she has the
right to take him out at any time and for as long as she wishes. During
the child's stay in such a school, the allowance for him is discontinued,
but the mother does not pay anything to the institution, as married
parents must. Nor can the institution demand removal of the child of
an unmarried mother, as it can of married parents whose circumstances
have improved. The desirability of maintaining contact with her child
is impressed upon the mother by the institution staff. The school's upbringer makes a study of the mother's situation and intentions, involves
the child's relatives on both the mother's and father's side (and the
father himself if this seems desirable), and makes every effort consistent
with the child's welfare to establish a home for him. If the mother finally
decides to give up her child, and this seems the best thing for the child,
she is permitted to do so. In such instances the institution may either
raise the child until his majority or arrange for adoption. There is no
reason to question Soviet claims that the number of illegitimate children
abandoned or killed by their mothers has been steadily diminishing,
dwindling in the past twenty years to almost none.

There has been a striking change in recent years in the community's
attitude toward unwed mothers. While in 1960–61 it was consistently
maintained that unmarried mothers experienced no shame or grief, that
society did not condemn them (except when they took a father away
from his legal family), and that they were just as happy as other women,
the situation was quite different by 1964–65. While unmarried mothers
and their children still get special economic benefits, they are unhappy
and ashamed. In 1960–61 it was claimed that all kinds of women were
found among the ranks of unmarried mothers; by 1964–65 it was im-
plied that there were no "good Soviet" girls among them. For example,
a patronage nurse who works in a middle-class neighborhood said that
among the families she is responsible for there are very, very few "immoral" unwed mothers. They are mostly students who live with their
own families, who simply did not get around to registering at ZAGS.
She emphasized that they register eventually, so that their state of unmarried motherhood is strictly a temporary one. It is the uneducated,
the unskilled, the handicapped, and the immoral mother who fails to
register.

There has also been a change in attitude toward the fathers of illegitimate children. Earlier, authorities were not at all interested in them,
because they were not obligated to contribute to the child's support. Now

there is pressure to force the father to give his name and support to his child, rather than allowing him to choose whether or not he will assume responsibility by adopting the child or marrying the mother.

The reasons for these changes in attitude are undoubtedly many and complex. Field findings suggest that one of the most important is the general hostility toward social welfare programs which, as is usually the case, is vented upon a socially weak group. This hostility appears to be compounded of both conscious and unconscious elements. On the conscious level, the community resents having to assume the economic and social burden of raising illegitimate children when it feels there is no longer any rational justification for illegitimacy—when, on the contrary, opportunities for personal fulfillment in approved ways are thought to be widely available. This burden seems all the heavier because there are still considerable economic hardships for sizable portions of the population, as well as constant pressure to raise productivity. On the unconscious level, opposition to the official morality exemplified by unmarried motherhood may be shared by many people who have internalized the official standards only partially. The guilt feelings generated may express themselves in a condemnation of the envied behavior.

In assessing the position of the illegitimate child in Soviet society, it appears that his economic status is somewhat worse than that of the child born in wedlock, because he receives no support from his father (unless the father voluntarily wishes to contribute) and cannot inherit from him. As a rule, this loss is only partially made up by the longer allowance period and the other economic privileges that the child or his mother, on his behalf, enjoys. Allowances are smaller than the average amount received as support from the father under court orders prior to 1944— hence, probably smaller than what legitimate children now receive through court orders. Also, allowances are paid only till age twelve, while support is required until the child reaches majority. On the other hand, his basic needs—for medical care, education, housing, recreation —are apparently met in the same way and to the same extent as the needs of all children.

Available data suggest that in the emotional and social spheres the child is not always shielded from a feeling of deprivation and desertion, and often suffers from social stigma. Given the Soviet glorification of the "communist family," it seems inevitable that sooner or later the Soviet child born out of wedlock begins to regret his fatherless state. He is invariably stigmatized when it is discovered that his father's name is not given on his birth certificate. The unfortunate effects upon the child are also evident in the scanty glimpses into the unmarried mother subculture that one gains from Soviet publications: the mothers hide the existence of the father from their children; often they do not seek support in order to avoid disgrace for themselves and their offspring;[86] many tell their children about their illegitimacy only after they have convinced them that the father was "bad." It is not likely that, as regards the child's emotional development, the situation is better for those illegitimate youngsters whose mothers have forced their fathers to continue support under Section 43 of the 1926 Family Code (still in operation), which provides that a person who has voluntarily taken upon himself the support of another person cannot relinquish it without substantial reasons. The fact that unwed mothers have priority in placing their children in boarding and extended-day schools, as well as other facts, in many cases means that they are doing a poor job of child-rearing.

There does not seem to be any doubt that in the Soviet Union many unmarried mothers need counseling and other services that they do not get, and that they are not the complete mistresses of their own and their children's destinies that the authorities would have the world believe they are.

Services for Juvenile Delinquents

Facilities for dealing with delinquents include children's rooms in militia wards;[87] reception and assignment centers for runaway and other children who must be detained until it is determined what should be done with them; children's commissions operating as an arm of local soviets; schools of special regimen (*shkoly osobogo rezhima*) administered by the Ministries of Education; labor colonies operated by the army under supervision of Organs of Social Protection (*Obshchestvennaia Okhrana*); and a variety of community participation groups, among which the most directly involved are the People's Patrols and Comrades' Courts.

The initial contact of the adolescent with the law is through the local militia, which includes a "children's worker"—a teacher or a lawyer, or someone with special interest in children. If the youngster is brought in for a minor offense, the children's worker obtains a minimum of identifying information, talks with him, and lets him go. If the youngster becomes a repeat offender, the children's worker calls together an informal committee of people from the community, and brings in the adolescent and his parents. This time the talk includes a warning that if no improvement takes place the case will have to go to the Children's Commission. If at this informal hearing it becomes clear that the parents are at fault, the children's worker may get in touch with the collective at their place of employment to exert pressure.

If all this fails, the children's worker will study the situation in depth for presentation to the Children's Commission. In making this study he will obtain evaluations from the school, health authorities, the house committee, and others who know the adolescent. He will visit the offender's home to see what the economic and cultural situation is, and to ascertain whether or not the parents are socially conscious and cooperative. The Commission, in addition to reviewing the report of the children's worker, will call in the child and his parents. One of two things may result: the child and his parents may receive a reprimand and be warned that if another incident occurs harsher action will be taken, or the child may be institutionalized.

Schools of special regimen are a result of the more permissive atmosphere of the post-1956 decade, which has brought about a liberalization of legal provisions governing juvenile crime.* There is now less of a reliance on punishment and hard labor in labor colonies and a more widespread use of educational measures, the previous approach having failed to prevent recidivism.† Organs of Social Protection were recently directed to continue to use labor colonies for those who commit serious crimes and are sentenced by courts, and to transfer to the Ministry of Education those facilities that now house the 11 to 18-year-olds who are "difficult to rear" (*trudnovospituemye*) or have a record of minor crimes. The Ministry of Education is to transform these facilities into schools of special regimen. The policies to be followed in these schools have not yet been finally set, but certain features seem to be emerging. Children will remain until they complete at least an elementary education; they will not be isolated from society altogether—parents and others will be encouraged to visit them and, as rewards for good behavior, they will be allowed to visit their families and spend vacations with them; their education will stress work within a collective; classes will be small, to obtain best results, and there will be two upbringers for each

---

* Until 1956, children under 14 could be charged with limited criminal responsibility for rape, assault, molesting, etc. From 14 on they were held fully responsible. Under the 1956 law, full responsibility does not begin until age 16. Those between 14 and 16 are criminally responsible only for murder, rape, armed assault, theft, premeditated physical injury, vandalism, and derailing of trains.

† A Soviet delegate to the Second United Nations Congress on the Prevention of Crime and the Treatment of Offenders, held in 1960, said that only about 50 per cent of the children released from Soviet labor colonies become useful citizens. In 1966 it was reported that 30 per cent of those released from such colonies become recidivists (*Sovetskaia Iustitssiia*, January 1966, p. 19). However, a number of accounts of those who have been regenerated in the colonies are available. (See, for example, 282 and 257. 257 is a novel that has enjoyed considerable popularity in the Soviet Union. It deals with the fictional offender's home life, his school, his peers, the criminal subculture, the agencies with which he was involved, the methods used in his reeducation, and the role played by the community.)

group of twenty; in each school there will be a diagnostic unit composed of teachers, psychologists, physicians, and consulting psychiatrists —in addition to the usual personnel.[38]

Decisions about the release of adolescents from these schools are made by the Children's Commission of the district in which the school is located. Upon release the youngster reports back to his home district commission and its children's worker for help with readjustment, which consists mainly of helping him to find a job—something that is not easy. The reasons for this are several. Jobs are unevenly distributed: in some commission districts there are many enterprises, and they can absorb a larger number of young people than the commissions send, but in others opportunities for youth employment are scarce.[39] In addition, some enterprises are reluctant to hire young workers, especially former delinquents, partly because of the special privileges granted by law to working minors.[40] (To deal with this problem, the government for the past several years has required all enterprises to hire a set number of adolescents each year.)[41] Also, directives from Children's Commissions are often ignored, and some commissions do their work poorly or not at all,* one reason being that members cannot always spare enough time from their regular jobs.[42]

As for People's Patrols, in 1960 there were 80,000 of them, with the number of participants reaching the impressive figure of more than 2.5 million—in itself a commentary on the crime and delinquency problem since, as the Soviet delegate to the 1960 United Nations Congress said, "There would be no need for voluntary services if there were no problems." These patrols are headed by Party members and are made up of workers, employees, farmers, students, and pensioners. They are supposed to persuade and educate; in fact, they often resort to the use of satirical newspapers, leaflets, and photographs of lawbreakers, ridiculing and exposing them. Patrol members take lawbreakers into custody, interrogate them, communicate with their families, their employers, their schools, and the police.[43] They are said to be constantly extending their sphere of activity: not only do they concern themselves with drunkenness, profiteering, and illicit distilling of vodka, but they also expose persons who lead parasitic lives and bring to light cases of child neglect.[44] Suggestions are being made that special patrols be created that will devote all their time to dealing with unsupervised children, working with them on a daily basis.

---

* A 1966 study revealed that of those juveniles who became recidivists within six months after release from labor colonies, 90 per cent received no help with their problems from the commissions (*Sovetskaia Iustitsiia*, January 1966, p. 19).

Soviet Child Welfare Services: An Estimate

The preceding discussion indicates that a Soviet definition of child welfare services would not differ essentially from the definition currently used in the United States. One U.S. definition reads as follows:

Child welfare services are those social services that supplement, or substitute for, parental care and supervision for the purpose of: protecting and promoting the welfare of children and youth; preventing neglect, abuse, and exploitation; helping overcome problems that result in dependence, neglect, or delinquency; and, when needed, providing adequate care for children and youth away from their own homes, such care to be given in foster family homes, adoptive homes, child-caring institutions, or other facilities.[45]

How many children in the Soviet Union are receiving such services? Because no published statistics are available, an estimate has been made (see Table 6).[46] Of the 82 million children under age 18 estimated to have been living in the Soviet Union in 1963, about 8.6 per cent appear to have been served by child welfare programs. This reflects both the need for such services and the concern of the government for the rising generation. More than 7.1 million children were apparently receiving help in

TABLE 6

ESTIMATED NUMBER OF CHILDREN, AGES 0–18, RECEIVING CHILD WELFARE SERVICES
IN THE SOVIET UNION, BY LOCATION OF CHILDREN, 1963

Location	Number of Children
1. In their own homes, but illegitimate, ages 0–12 (living with their mothers)	2,314,000
2. In substitute homes under guardianship, trusteeship, *patronat,* and adoption arrangements	1,940,800
3. In their own homes, but attending extended-day schools ..	1,352,100
4. In boarding schools for normal children	1,047,900
5. In "Children's Homes" for normal children	246,000
6. In schools (primarily boarding schools) for children with intellectual and physical defects	217,000
7. In institutions for severely retarded and grossly handicapped noneducable children	3,500
8. In residential treatment centers for "nervous" children	1,250
TOTAL	7,122,550
In own or substitute homes 5,606,900	
In institutions 1,515,650	

1963; of these an estimated 80 per cent were living in their own and substitute homes, and somewhat more than 20 per cent in institutions. This distribution bears a striking resemblance to the situation in the United States, where, of the children served by child welfare programs in 1962, 79 per cent were in their own and substitute homes and 18 per cent in institutions. (It should be noted that the United States institutional population included children in voluntary and public training schools for delinquents.) While the actual implementation of child welfare services may differ appreciably between the two countries, and while it is obvious that the Soviet groups listed in Table 6 are quite different from the groups served by child welfare programs in the United States, it is nevertheless significant that the pattern of location (home vs. institution) of the children being served is so similar in the two countries.

IO

Services for the Aged
and Vocational Rehabilitation

Services for the aged, disabled, and handicapped have continued to follow the pattern laid down in the early post-Revolutionary years; the only innovations have been shifts in emphasis. These services still include economic support in the form of pensions and benefits,* institutional placement, medical care (including prostheses), and training, retraining, and job placement for those able to work. Medical care is provided through the same system that serves the rest of the population; training, retraining, job placement, and the administration of vocational rehabilitation research institutes and prostheses-manufacturing establishments are the responsibility of the Republic Ministries of Social Welfare.

Services for the Aged, Disabled, and Handicapped in Their Own Homes

Ninety-eight per cent of the aged, disabled, and handicapped live at home on pensions, in some instances augmented by earnings from work or by other resources. For social services they depend on welfare workers and indigenous nonprofessionals from the Republic Ministries of Social Welfare and on their own collectives, the latter usually being trade union committees at their former places of employment or the All-Russian Societies for the Blind and the Deaf (VOS and VOG).

* Discussed in Chapter 11 below.

While there is no specific regulation governing this aspect of their duties, welfare workers from the ministries are expected to visit each pensioner about once a year. The trend toward "getting closer to the masses"—that is, visiting homes instead of concentrating on paper work and office interviews—is by now official policy. It is claimed that it has resulted in better services for clients and has made social welfare work more interesting and rewarding. Nevertheless, in most instances there is no once-a-year visit, particularly if the pensioner does not insist on it because he has a family, friends, or a genuinely helpful collective that assists him in his daily life and provides opportunities for meaningful community activity, such as instructing newcomers to factories and plants; serving on house committees or committees attached to children's institutions, medical facilities, or welfare departments;[1] inspecting operations in stores and restaurants; propagandizing for higher productivity; planting orchards and gardens; baby-sitting; or reading and telling stories to older children.[2] Many employing establishments confer permanent honorary rights of entry on pensioners, enabling them to enjoy social activities free of charge. Shop committees visit them and bring gifts and factory news. As for the aged who continue to work, for the most part they arrange to remain at their old jobs by putting in shorter hours. In many situations, however, pensioners who need services but are too timid or depressed to make this known may be ignored by welfare workers, as well as by everyone else. As the editors of *Sotsial'noe Obespechenie* said in January 1966: "If he [the pensioner] does not come to us, we do not go to him."

On the other hand, if the pensioner complains or insists, he may receive several visits a year. What is done for him, it is said, depends primarily on the character of his welfare worker. The "concerned" worker performs a variety of services: he may eject a roomer who was supposed to take care of an aged pensioner, but turned out to be unreliable and cruel; he may reconcile an aged person with the son and daughter-in-law with whom he is living; he may move an old person to more suitable quarters or help him obtain better furniture; he may work out a room exchange when a pensioner refuses to move because he wants to remain with the same doctor; or he may even clean an invalid's room and bring in firewood. Sometimes the welfare worker turns over the visiting duties to indigenous nonprofessional helpers. The main objective is to establish a link between the pensioner and a genuinely concerned collective that can be depended upon to do whatever is necessary on a continuing basis. If the welfare worker is not the "concerned" kind, or if he is overloaded, he may even turn over to volunteers service duties that require skills they do not possess, without giving them the supervision they need.

In whatever form social services are provided, it is expected that they will be offered in the spirit of socialist humanism. Welfare personnel are convinced that this is all that is needed, except in those relatively few instances when mental failure or deterioration makes medical intervention necessary. There is no clear recognition that some pensioners may require professional help in reconstructing their lives, resuming their family roles, and living through emotional upheavals. It is more or less assumed that somehow collectives will provide the necessary help—even though it is acknowledged that collectives may not act in time, may expect somebody else to act, or may act unwisely.

The Soviet government does not publish statistics about the disabled—"invalids"—separately: they are shown together with the retired aged as "pensioners."[3] That invalids always have been and still are a numerically large group is beyond doubt: to the ranks of the handicapped inherited from tsarist times were added those who survived the carnage of two world wars, the Revolution, the civil war, the famine of 1921–23, and the tortures and privations of Nazi occupation. These numbers were further swelled by victims of work accidents, a consequence of the rapid industrialization that drew millions of peasants and women who lacked familiarity with machines and mechanized processes into factories, and of the introduction of machinery into agriculture. If to work-connected disabilities are added disabilities from non-work-connected causes, then it is almost certain that there have always been several million invalids in the Soviet Union.*

Soviet vocational rehabilitation personnel employ several devices—"indicators"—to determine the pattern of invalidity as it changes over time. During the ten years 1956–65, with 1956 taken as 100, the *initial invalidity indicator*—the total number of persons who became invalids for the first time—declined to 38.6 in 1965, showing a steady decrease every year. The *intensity indicator*—the number of workers and employees who became invalids per each thousand insured—decreased to 34.6 in 1965. This was due to a rise in the standard of living, wider

---

* World War I left 1,750,000 disabled; the Revolution and the civil war—400,000 (*Sotsial'noe Obespechenie*, No. 7–8, July–August 1932, p. 22). A 1920 census that covered only the European part of the RSFSR, which contained roughly half of the country's population, reported almost 1.1 million persons who were blind, deaf, dumb, or lame, had paralyzed extremities, were missing hands or feet, or were hunchbacked; in addition there were more than 200,000 mentally ill, not including the mentally retarded (*440*, pp. 14, 16, 19, 20). In 1933, Soviet estimates placed the number of severely invalided—those in the first three of the six invalidity groups—at 3 million (*Sotsial'noe Obespechenie*, No. 7–8, July–August 1932, p. 25). The Soviet government has released no statistics on the number disabled during World War II. That the rate of work accidents was high in the postwar decade is indicated in a number of sources (*359*, pp. 35–37; *84*, p. 42; *167*, pp. 49–50).

availability of medical and prophylactic services, and improved work by the Medico-Labor Expert Commissions (VTEKs). But the decrease was uneven, and some localities even showed a sizable increase. In contrast to these declines, the *severity of invalidity indicator*—the division of new invalids among Groups I, II, and III, in descending degree of severity—showed a regressive tendency: the percentage of Group I invalids rose from 5.3 in 1956 to 8.5 in 1965 and the percentage for Group II rose from 41.7 to 53.1 per cent. Only for Group III, the least disabled, was there a decrease—from 53.0 per cent in 1956 to 38.1 per cent in 1965. The age of those disabled for the first time—the *age indicator*—appears to have been stabilized; however, the number of persons under age 29 disabled in 1965 was 23 per cent less than in 1956. It is claimed that there has been a steady rise in the *return to productive work indicator*—the proportion of invalids who improve sufficiently to be removed from the invalid category—from 2.7 to 8.0 per cent. Among these who are not removed from the invalid category, there has been some lessening in severity, but this has varied in different localities.[4]

Statistics concerning the causes of invalidity are available for 1958 (see Table 7). Five diseases—diseases of the cardiovascular system, tuberculosis, diseases of the nervous system, of bones and joints (other than tuberculosis), and of the digestive system—were responsible for half of the cases. During 1956–65, tuberculosis, mental diseases, and diseases of the eye declined as causes of invalidity. On the other hand, work-connected injuries, cardiovascular diseases, and malignant tumors persisted at the same level. The major causes at present appear to be heart conditions, diseases of the digestive system, psychoneurotic disturbances, and tuberculosis.[5]

Vocational Rehabilitation. The greatest difficulties in developing training facilities for the disabled arose in the early post-Revolutionary years, mainly because economic poverty and chaos precluded allocation of needed resources, and severe unemployment demoralized both the authorities and the disabled. Efforts to improve this situation lagged until the 1930's, when training was stepped up to meet the manpower demands of the first five-year plan. The Decree of July 19, 1930, directed the Republic Ministries of Social Welfare to strengthen assistance to invalids and their families "considerably" by providing remunerative work, for "this form of social assistance corresponds most closely to the purposes of the Soviet nation and yields a sizable improvement in the material conditions of invalids." The motto became "Not a pension, but a paycheck!" In subsequent years, the demand for increased training facilities did not abate; indeed, it was made more urgent by continued industrialization, collectivization, and World War II. While all persons

TABLE 7

CAUSES OF INVALIDITY, AGES OF INVALIDS, AND INVALIDITY GROUPS, 1958

Cause of Invalidity	Per Cent of Total	Percentage by Age Group		Percentage by Invalidity Group	
		Up to Age 29	From 30 to 45	Groups I and II	Group III
1. Tuberculosis (all forms)	12.1	21.8	14.1	16.0	9.0
2. Diseases of respiratory organs (other than TB)	5.9	2.8	4.8	5.1	6.6
3. Diseases of bones and joints (other than TB)	8.1	9.8	9.0	5.9	10.4
4. Work-connected injuries	5.0	9.0	5.9	4.5	5.5
5. Diseases of the nervous system ...	9.1	9.6	9.8	8.5	9.8
6. Psychic diseases	5.5	9.6	6.5	7.5	3.3
7. Diseases of the cardiovascular system	22.5	10.0	15.0	22.2	22.9
8. Diseases of the digestive system..	7.2	6.5	9.0	5.3	9.1
9. Industrial poisonings	1.2	0.7	1.9	0.4	2.0
10. Malignant tumors	6.4	2.2	6.5	11.3	1.4
11. Total or partial loss of sight	5.6	5.9	5.9	5.0	6.2
12. Other diseases	11.4	12.0	10.6	8.3	13.8

Source: *433*, p. 26.

needing vocational rehabilitation were entitled to be trained, the emphasis was on training for war veterans and workers in state establishments. Few farmers received training, and they were either forced by their handicaps to leave the labor force or were given farm work they were still able to do.

Apparently the activity of the Medico-Labor Expert Commissions with regard to disabled persons from the peasant class was relatively minor up to 1965. Directives to regional VTEKs became more frequent after a series of model acts for peasant mutual aid societies was promulgated in 1958. Expert Commissions were urged to include collective farmers in their work loads, to serve them "more energetically." However, they were warned that experience gained in handling insurance for workers and employees could not be applied directly to the rural sector; rather, new principles, criteria, and methods for dealing with peasant invalids had to be developed.[6] That this warning was not taken seriously in all cases seems evident from the fact that when social insurance for collective farmers was instituted in January 1965, many local commissions that had failed to issue special directives and establish special procedures found themselves overwhelmed by the invalids from this long-neglected contingent.

In the period after World War II, training for the workers and employees who became disabled was offered in three types of facilities: sheltered workshops administered by Republic Ministries of Social Welfare, training-producing enterprises run by the deaf and blind societies, and state enterprises in which the disabled person sustained his injury. Data on sheltered workshops for 1963 are given in Table 8. In examining this table it should be noted that in 1963 the average monthly wage for an industrial worker was about 85–90 rubles.

For the RSFSR, information is available concerning what the workshops were teaching in 1965. In that year the Ministry of Social Welfare was administering 53 workshops, of which 43 were "vocational-technical" and 10 were "secondary-technical" boarding and day schools. The former admit everyone between ages 16 and 40 with a fifth-grade education, train them about two years, and provide them with a modest amount of general education. They stress preparation for the less skilled occupations, such as repairing various machines, radios, and television sets; operating movie projectors, sewing, shoemaking, bookkeeping,

TABLE 8

Sheltered Workshops Administered by Republic Ministries of Social Welfare in 1963, with Number of Trainees, Annual Expenditures, and Amounts Spent per Trainee per Month, by Republics

Republic	Number of Sheltered Workshops	Number of Trainees	Annual Expenditure in Rubles	Amount Spent per Trainee per Month in Rubles
Russia	55	5,442	5,750,000	88.05
Ukraine	4	750	591,000	65.66
Belorussia	1	70	20,000	23.80
Kazakhstan	1	310	216,500	58.19
Azerbaidzhan	2	303	96,900	26.65
Latvia	—	—	—	—
Armenia	—	—	—	—
Estonia	1	89	62,200	58.32
Turkmenia	—	—	—	—
Uzbekistan	4	565	274,800	40.53
Grusiia	5	300	150,000	41.66
Lithuania	1	200	123,000	51.25
Kirgiziia	—	—	—	—
Tadzhikistan	1	110	82,800	62.72
Total	75	8,139	7,367,200	75.43 (average)

Source: *125*, pp. 4–12 and 4–9, respectively. Data for Moldavia not available.

bookbinding, landscaping, and technical laboratory work. "Secondary-technical" schools accept only people with secondary educations, train them four years, offer them a fairly extensive grounding in general education, and prepare them to be technologists, agronomists, zoo-technicians, mechanics, accountants, etc. The ministry has not yet succeeded in getting invalids admitted to higher professional and technical schools, but they can get into schools for working youth on the same basis as other applicants, if they pass the entrance examinations.

In all of the republics, it is the local welfare department that selects those to be trained, guided by VTEK recommendations. Actually, this usually means that if VTEK recommends an occupation for which social welfare training is offered, then the invalid is "selected" and sent to the appropriate school. Large cities have city-wide schools; smaller communities band together and set up interdistrict schools. After completing training, most invalids return to work in the communities of which they are residents, but some may be placed elsewhere. Invalids who attend day schools receive their full pension and a stipend during study. Those in boarding schools retain only a part of their pensions, because while training they are given room and board, clothing, and medical and cultural services.

It seems likely that at present between 75,000 and 85,000 invalids are retrained annually. (In 1965 the number retrained in the RSFSR was 60,000.) But welfare authorities are still concerned because invalids' needs for training are not being fully met. Apparently this is particularly true in rural areas. Many sheltered workshops are still ineffective because of old equipment and poorly qualified instructors. Training is sometimes disrupted by disciplinary problems and by absenteeism brought on by medical conditions incorrectly evaluated by VTEK.[7] Perhaps the major weakness is the failure to change the curriculum to enable invalids to acquire the new knowledge and skills essential for them to keep up with technological developments and retain the jobs they have worked so hard to secure.

Job Placement. Prior to 1960, employment for the disabled was provided by VOS and VOG enterprises and by invalids' cooperatives. The cooperative movement, born in 1921 out of the near-desperate situation of the great majority of the handicapped, was ignored in its early years by state organs, as well as weakened by dishonest administrators. It was not until 1927 that the system was accorded the benefits enjoyed by other producers' cooperatives, such as inclusion in the supply and credit plans of the related industries.[8] Administered by elected officers, the cooperatives' hierarchy was fitted into the country's political subdivisions, with the All-Russian Center of Invalids' Cooperatives at the top. Membership increased from 35,000 in 1927 to 500,000 in 1958, but this was still a minority of the working invalids.[9] As they gained in resources and prestige, the cooperatives pressed for better training, cultural and educational opportunities, and more adequate insurance benefits. From these efforts the disabled learned that they gained more by relying on themselves and working through their own collective to the limit of their capacities than by relying on governmental or societal help. Apparently the latter would come to their assistance only if they demonstrated their capacity to be productive. In April 1956, 4,000 of the largest specialized cooperative establishments were merged into state industry, and in October 1960 the merger absorbed all of them. The only establishments that were permitted to remain independent of the state were those under VOS and VOG. According to the authorities, the reasons for this absorption were that the cooperatives "paralleled" certain state enterprises (in a sense, competed with them), that their technical equipment was poor, and that their methods of operation were outmoded, so that from an economic point of view they were inefficient.

At the present time, invalids work in six types of facilities: in regular state enterprises, among nonhandicapped workers (this, it is claimed, is where the majority work); in state enterprises that have special sections for the handicapped—primarily those suffering from tuberculosis, hypertension, and cardiac conditions; in VOS enterprises that employ Group I and II blind; in VOG enterprises for Group I and II deaf (Group III blind and deaf work in state establishments); in "welfare" workshops (this is where the most "difficult" invalids are placed); and at home (raw materials are delivered to the homes and the finished products later picked up, payment being made on a piece-work basis). Invalids suffering from "nervous" conditions are seldom placed in jobs by welfare authorities: they are served by neuropsychiatric clinics, which, as part of therapy, operate sheltered workshops.

Soviet efforts to find employment for the disabled languished until 1930. In that year a decree was issued concerning the placement of invalids in jobs.[10] This law was strengthened and expanded by two decrees issued in May 1942 that obliged the Republic Ministries of Social Welfare to arrange for the training, retraining, and employment of war invalids, and forbade the dismissal of invalids from jobs without first consulting with welfare authorities and trade unions. These laws, amended in line with changing demands, have remained in force.[11] Data on the number of invalids actually placed at various times are fragmentary, but they convey the impression of a fairly steady rise.[12]

Since World War II, the placing of invalids has required considerable effort and, at times, coercion. Local soviets plan and control the placements. Each year they set the percentage of the labor force that is to come from invalid ranks, and classify the occupations open to them. Local welfare departments then select the specific enterprises to be used, the kinds of jobs they are to provide, and the number of invalids they are to employ. Checking to see that invalids are actually doing the jobs recommended by VTEK and under suitable conditions is done by three organs simultaneously: regular physicians, trade union committees, and VTEK. An invalid cannot be laid off a job without (1) a decision from VTEK that he ought not to continue on the job in question, (2) the consent of the local welfare department, and (3) the approval of the trade union. If VTEK recommends that he be employed in another job that is available in the same enterprise, transfer to this job is obligatory.

It has been difficult to make enterprises follow these regulations, but after the 1960 absorption of cooperatives violations became especially flagrant. In September 1961, a fairly stiff decree to deter violators was issued by the RSFSR Ministry of Social Welfare and copied by the other republics. Nevertheless, difficulties continued. In July 1964, another decree was issued, making it clear that many enterprises had paid no attention to the 1961 edict. Even though the production plan for an enterprise that employs a number of invalids takes into account the lower productivity of this contingent, the growing emphasis on profits makes it likely that some directors will be reluctant to employ the handicapped in the future.

Numerous current reports, by invalids themselves and by a variety of officials, expose "secret resistance" by enterprise directors, failure of welfare workers to take any action when they find such resistance,[13] and dismissal of invalids on flimsy grounds, such as an alleged need to reduce staff. Some enterprises simply refuse to employ invalids, and almost nothing is done about it. Investigations by local soviets and others often reveal that even when invalids are placed according to regulations, they find their working conditions so unsuitable that they are forced to quit. Their complaints are frequently ignored, as are their pleas to be permitted to work at home.* Welfare workers find that at times it takes a lot of pressure to make the placements directed by VTEK, and that in some instances administrators can ignore them.[14]

There is a growing concern about other aspects of invalid placements.

---

* The only group for whom it is claimed that the problem of job placement has been "solved" are the blind, the majority of whom work in VOS, not in state enterprises. Between 1955 and 1960, the proportion of working blind among the total number of blind increased by nearly 20 per cent. During this period, the number of blind working in VOS enterprises rose by 48.1 per cent and in other establishments by 6.1 per cent, while the percentage working in producers' cooperatives, collective farms, and state farms declined. (See *484*, pp. 5–6.)

Many are not good for the invalids' health, or are not at a level commensurate with their qualifications; there is inequality of treatment of people with the same kinds of handicaps. This adds to the impression that production plans are more important than invalids. It is not surprising, therefore, that welfare personnel are urging VOS and VOG to employ the Group III blind and deaf instead of sending them to state establishments, and that an all-Russian invalids' society be organized to improve the position of the disabled in the labor force.[15]

It is claimed that in spite of these difficulties, throughout the postwar years approximately 70 per cent of all disabled have been returned to productive work. On the basis of data for the RSFSR, and assuming that the distribution of invalids among the three disability groups and the proportions working are the same in the other republics, it may be estimated that for the country as a whole the number currently working is about 4 million. (In 1964, data for fourteen republics—Moldavia excluded—indicated that 3.9 million pensioners were working. However, this included not only the disabled but also the retired aged, who were not disabled but were working.[16] The 70 per cent claim is high if it applies only to those who are *invalid* pensioners.)

Work Incentives. As already explained, one of the central ideas in Soviet helping methods is that work, appropriate to the individual's state of health, aids in the regeneration process, improves the moral and physical condition of the invalid, and satisfies his natural urge to participate in his country's development. When conditions suitable to the character of the invalid's defect are created, he may be involved in productive activity without harm, and generally with a good effect on his health. This philosophy is based on the Pavlovian dictum "Work gives great satisfaction, and it is essential to open the way to this joy for the sick person, leading him step by step into work activity." At the same time it is very useful to the Soviet regime in meeting its need for manpower.

Indications abound that over long periods work therapy became a form of pressure rather than treatment, undoubtedly resulting in hardships and suffering for many disabled persons. The wretched plight of the disabled and handicapped during the early post-Revolutionary era drove them to work at anything they could. The launching of the first five-year plan in 1928 elevated work to a virtue, and enabled invalids by working hard to raise their pitifully low pensions to a subsistence level. By 1930, job placement, rather than other kinds of help, was assigned top priority in welfare policy—with no concern shown about how the drive for "productive" labor affected psychological and social adjustment.[17] Apparently it was assumed that once the disabled person was sufficiently healed to work and had been taught the skills for a specific job, other things would take care of themselves.[18] The major function of the Central Scientific Research Institute of Expertise on Work Ability and Organization of Labor (Tsentral'nyi Nauchno-issledovatel'skii Institut Ekspertizy Trudosposobnosti i Organizatsii Truda—TSIETIN), organized in Moscow in 1930 and placed within the RSFSR Ministry of Social Welfare, was to show how "methods of work must change" in order that more invalids could be placed in jobs. Pressure to produce was intensified during World War II.

Although it has been relaxed somewhat since 1956, this pressure has not been abandoned by any means. For example, it was not until 1959 that it became possible to pay the blind on an hourly or weekly basis, rather than on a piece-work basis, although it had been known for a long time that piece work led to fatigue, nervous strain, and, in some cases, weakening of the remaining vision. Not until 1959 was a shortened work week introduced for those blind who were forbidden by medical directives to do full-time work. At present, there is a drive to "raise the consciousness" of the blind to such heights that work will become a spiritual necessity for them.

That the consciousness of many has not yet been raised to this level is clear. Even many Group III invalids prefer not to work in regular jobs if "social conditions" permit—a preference often interpreted by the authorities as laziness. There are endless exhortations to be strict with "parasites" and "social anomalies"—the carriers of the capitalist past— among the handicapped as well as among able-bodied workers.[19] Some are helped to resume productive lives through work therapy, but for the majority, the most potent incentive is the low pension rates. In addition, as a result of the upward curve of the economy, enough jobs are being generated for everyone; invalids know that mastering some type of skill within their physical and mental capacities is not merely an academic exercise, but will probably enable them to secure employment. And when this goal is achieved, not only do they find themselves in a better economic position, but also they are more highly valued for doing their share in building the new society.

Prostheses and Special Appliances. These are supplied by research institutes—in Moscow (TSIETIN), Leningrad (Leningradskii Nauchnoissledovatel'skii Institut Ekspertizy Trudosposobnosti i Organizatsii Truda—LIETIN), and an affiliate of the Moscow Institute in Rostov-on-Don—and by prostheses-manufacturing establishments.* For the hand-

---

* The institutes provide treatment, but only for cases useful in research, study, or the training of students. The prostheses available to ordinary invalids leave much to be desired, as I discovered through personal contact with a war veteran whose arm was amputated from below the elbow. All that had been given to him was a "piece of wood" (*dereviashka*) that he found useless.

icapped from the wage and salaried group, payment—when required— is made by the social insurance system. But up to 1965 most peasant mutual aid societies did not finance the purchase of prostheses, and most peasants could not afford to pay for them themselves. In some cases, even when money was at hand, poor coordination between welfare and medical authorities made it almost impossible to obtain the needed service. Since 1965, complex prostheses have been paid for by the farm insurance fund; simple types (orthopedic shoes, for example) must be paid for by the individual. In recent years, concern for those living in remote areas has led to action: in accordance with a 1964 decree, prostheses-manufacturing establishments are organizing small hospitals in which both children and adults can receive treatment, as well as be provided with prostheses. Of special benefit to those in isolated communities is the traveling prostheses workshop; this facility serves people who are recovering from major medical treatment or are suffering from relatively "minor" ailments.

The All-Russian Societies for the Blind and the Deaf. These two societies—VOS and VOG—given official status and included in the system of invalids' cooperatives in 1923 and 1926, respectively, came into being through the efforts of the blind and deaf themselves. The histories of the societies are replete with difficulties, setbacks, and disappointments. They persisted because of their conviction that only by separating themselves from the rest of the disabled could they hope for assistance in meeting their special needs. Consistently, their objectives have been enriching the "daily lives" of their members and "raising their ideological, political, educational, and technical level, drawing them into the ranks of active builders of communism."[20] Throughout, emphasis has been on the need to take their handicaps into account, but not to exaggerate them.[21]

There have been various difficulties involved in building up the membership of these societies. These have included a lack of reliable data concerning the number and whereabouts of the blind and deaf, a shortage of trained personnel, poor administration, and, at times, the overbearing attitude of welfare authorities. Obstacles were especially formidable in rural areas, where the blind and deaf were widely scattered, with sometimes only one or two living in a village. Growth was erratic until after World War II, when these groups benefited from the attention and resources devoted to war veterans. VOS membership rose from 9 to 95 per cent of all the blind between 1941 and 1965; VOG membership increased from less than a third of the country's deaf in 1938 to about 85 per cent in 1965. The societies' ability to furnish suitable employment to their members was strengthened when they were given permission to control production in their own establishments, were freed from taxation on profits, and were provided with government subsidies. The subsidies were not withdrawn until 1952, when the societies were deemed to have achieved a sound economic position.

Data on membership of the two societies and the number of their training-producing establishments in 1963 are shown in Table 9. The top organs in the societies are republic administrations, elected for four years; the hierarchy then descends to the regional, district, and city levels. The republic offices maintain contact with foreign countries, including entering into world federations organized by the handicapped groups. Membership is open to the blind and the deaf who have reached age 14, and confers privileges such as freedom from taxation, free public transportation, and assistance in case of acute need.[22]

The societies' economic position has been improving steadily, and although the major portion of their resources goes into capital investment, they have been spending relatively more on social services in recent years than in the past. They keep statistics on the handicapped, make sure that blind and deaf children attend special schools, place adults in jobs in their own enterprises or in state industry, provide for

TABLE 9

MEMBERSHIP OF THE ALL-RUSSIAN SOCIETIES FOR THE BLIND AND THE DEAF, AND
THE NUMBER OF TRAINING-PRODUCING ENTERPRISES UNDER THEIR
JURISDICTION IN 1963, BY REPUBLIC

Republic	Members in VOS and VOG	Number of VOS and VOG Training-Producing Enterprises
Russia	270,000	339
Ukraine	27,650	116
Belorussia	19,186	26
Kazakhstan	10,577	35
Azerbaidzhan	6,328	8
Latvia	3,292	7
Armenia	3,259	13
Estonia	2,063	7
Turkmenia	810	5
Uzbekistan	13,680	33
Grusiia	4,889	34
Lithuania	4,003	8
Kirgiziia	2,685	8
Tadzhikistan	1,973	10
TOTAL	370,395	649

Source: *125*, pp. 4–12 and 4–9, respectively. Data for Moldavia not available.

medical care, and organize daily life assistance by building housing, issuing loans, giving relief, and attending to cultural and recreational needs.* In all of these undertakings, the societies are aided by their monthly publications: *Zhizn' Slepykh* (Life of the Blind), started in 1924, and *Zhizn' Glukhikh* (Life of the Deaf), started in 1933. An important ally is the bureau for the deaf within the central trade union organization, set up in 1936. The societies have succeeded in centralizing the social services for the blind and the deaf; others in the community who need similar services have no specific place to which they can turn. There remains, however, the persistent problem of the vast difference in the services for the urban as compared to the rural handicapped.

An Evaluation of Soviet Rehabilitation Services. One of the strengths of the Soviet rehabilitation system is the inclusion of a union member, with knowledge of the work processes involved in different occupations, in each Medico-Labor Expert Commission; he can help to determine as precisely as possible what kind of work an invalid has the capacity to do and what kind of working conditions he requires.† The union member can follow through on VTEK directives, in this way reinforcing the work of the factory medical staff. On the basis of experience that has shown that VTEK physicians should have specific preparation for their work, in addition to basic training in medicine, specialized training for them, beyond short in-service courses, is being made widely available.[23] The original notion that it is desirable to have numerous local VTEKs so that they are easily accessible to the disabled has been discarded. It was found that this resulted in weak commissions, because neither the requisite number of qualified physicians could be found nor adequate diagnostic facilities provided. A movement toward consolidation was initiated in 1946, leading to interdistrict and specialized VTEKs, e.g., for invalids suffering from tuberculosis, psychic disorders, and eye diseases. At the same time, procedures for continual review of activities were introduced, contributing significantly to a general rise in quality of service. Also, a considerable amount of research has been done in recent years toward developing practical techniques for determining invalidity and for formulating treatment and work plans.[24] An emphasis on "socialist humanism" has imbued the vocational rehabilitation ser-

---

* Among the many activities that provide a richer life for those who cannot hear, special mention should be made of "The Theater of Mime," opened in Moscow in 1962. Its company includes about 90 actors, all deaf, who speak in mime, with an interpreter on stage giving a running commentary on the action.

† It is reported that at times the presence of the trade union member prevents the expert physicians from losing their tempers when invalids oppose their recommendations. He frequently has a similar calming effect on invalids whose attitude toward the medical experts is one of scarcely concealed contempt (357, p. 59).

vices with a humane and individualized approach, which has helped to meet the needs of the disabled more effectively both from the standpoint of the regime and of the disabled themselves.[25]

Soviet personnel have always maintained that vocational rehabilitation must be an integrated process that coordinates economic, medical, and vocational services in such a way as to have the greatest possible impact on the problems faced by disabled individuals.[26] But to this day, the integration has not been wholly successful: medical authorities make many incorrect referrals to VTEK; members of commissions are often unfamiliar with pension law; in some instances, the commission's union member is absent or ineffectual; quite often, whether or not the invalid works and what he does depends on what he himself decides to do or what the management wants rather than on what the experts recommend.[27] As a result, instead of reaping the benefits of an integrated process, the handicapped person often finds himself pulled in different directions by the various groups involved in the process—the referring physicians, VTEKs, the organizations of the handicapped, the employing establishments, and the social welfare authorities. The emphasis on work therapy, and the limited qualifications of some Soviet welfare personnel, often obscure the fact that some of the disabled need help at a deeper emotional level than supportive therapy can provide. The presence of a neuropathologist in VTEK means little in this respect: the most that can be assumed is that if psychic disturbances reach unmanageable proportions, the invalid will be referred to a community mental health clinic. Nothing helpful will be undertaken in connection with less acute symptoms.

Institutional Services

"Homes" for the disabled and the aged, often housing the two groups under the same roof, have existed from the beginning of the Soviet regime. But during most of the years prior to the period after World War II, they were inadequate and overcrowded in the extreme.[28] The great impetus for increasing facilities and raising standards was given by World War II: care for war invalids—including orphaned and crippled children—disabled for any work and without homes and families, had to be provided. Expanded and improved facilities gradually became available to labor invalids as well. In the RSFSR, for example, the number of beds in such institutions increased by 189 per cent between 1945 and 1957.[29] Nevertheless, the expansion has not been commensurate with the need,[30] and the achievement of acceptable standards in the homes has been difficult. The problem of selecting those who should be sent to the homes from among the numerous applicants has been a vexing one, in spite of many directives. Some welfare ministries, it seems, send people to the homes without taking into account the state of their health. As a result, invalids who should be sent to specialized homes are placed in homes of a general type. According to one invalid, the home in which he is an inmate contains six "chronic psychotics" who wreck routine and make life unbearable for the other inmates; requests to have them transferred have been ignored for months.[31] Alcoholics and drug addicts also "ruin the peace ... steal, beg, insult those around them."[32] In many homes there is a lack of recreational activities and workshops.[33]

A major shortcoming is the poor quality of personnel employed by the homes. Many are people who have failed in other jobs or have been guilty of unethical conduct; many waste public funds and make life miserable for their subordinates. The district departments of social welfare often close their eyes to the situation. Control over the homes is weak, and there is no "patronage" by trade union, Party, or Komsomol organizations.[34] Frequently, the situation is exacerbated by inadequate allocations and uneven distribution of available resources between regions and different types of homes.[35]

The number of inmates in institutions for the aged and disabled, whether measured in relation to the total number of pensioners or to the total number of aged in the population, has always been small. Thus, in 1958, there were only 1,055 institutions with 135,000 inmates for the aged and disabled. Of these, 609 homes with 91,000 inmates were located in the RSFSR; peasant mutual aid societies in the whole country supported only 69 homes.[36] In 1965, when more than 14 million persons were receiving old age and disability pensions, there were only 1,290 institutions with 210,000 inmates.[37] Institutional placement has always lagged behind demand. In July 1962, for example, in the RSFSR alone, 20,000 applicants were on waiting lists. Currently there are many more applicants than places, according to the RSFSR Minister of Social Welfare, and the problem is considered one of the major ones confronting social welfare authorities.[38] There is little movement from institutions into the community, not only because most of the inmates need constant attendance and do not have families, but also because there is an acute shortage of decent housing. The strain on institutions has also been increased by the changing character of the Soviet family: children no longer hesitate to place their aged parents in homes. Often the proviso that relatives must be unable to provide care is disregarded.

Data on the number of aged and disabled in institutions, the number of homes, annual expenditures, and amounts spent per inmate per month are available for 1963 for 14 of the republics. They are given in Table 10.

TABLE 10

THE AGED AND THE DISABLED IN INSTITUTIONS IN 1963, BY NUMBER OF INSTITUTIONS,
ANNUAL EXPENDITURES, AND AMOUNTS SPENT PER INMATE PER
MONTH, BY REPUBLICS

	Number of Institutions	Number of Inmates	Annual Expenditures (*in rubles*)	Amount Spent per Inmate per Month (*in rubles*)
Russia	758	130,876	99,220,000	63.09
Ukraine	223	35,700	22,593,000	52.73
Belorussia	73	10,000	6,000,000	50.00
Kazakhstan	34	5,735	3,938,400	57.22
Azerbaidzhan	10	1,125	822,300	60.91
Latvia	73	7,670	4,267,100	46.36
Armenia	4	850	483,000	47.35
Estonia	39	4,400	2,749,000	52.06
Turkmenia	6	835	554,800	55.36
Uzbekistan	31	2,830	1,604,400	47.24
Grusiia	8	810	573,000	58.95
Lithuania	40	5,600	3,665,000	54.53
Kirgiziia	12	1,393	947,900	56.70
Tadzhikistan	8	1,140	703,200	51.40
TOTALS	1,319	208,964	148,121,100	59.00 (Avg.)

Source: *125*, pp. 4–12 and 4–9, respectively. Data for Moldavia not available.

It will be noted that these types of facilities are found in every republic and that the differences in monthly expenditures per inmate between republics are not as great as for invalid trainees, ranging from a low of 46 rubles per month in Latvia to a high of 63 rubles in the RSFSR. (The average monthly wage of a Soviet industrial worker at this time was about 85–90 rubles.) This seems to indicate that the need to provide decent care for the aged and the disabled is more widely recognized and accepted than the need for training of the "most difficult" disabled (see Table 8).

Considerable progress has by now been made toward removing young invalids from the homes. Most of them live in separate facilities where they can get an education, as well as custodial and medical care. It also appears that most of the aged and disabled suffering from mental conditions have been placed in mental institutions. The rest have been classified into those afflicted by "general" causes who are ambulatory, the tubercular, and the bedridden.[39] While they are in the homes (as well as in hospitals and sanatoria), pensioners have their pensions reduced in accordance with a standard formula that leaves only pocket money.

Quite a number are engaged in useful work—cultivating institutional gardens and orchards, raising pigs and chickens, sewing garments, overseeing libraries and reading rooms and recreation halls, participating in institutional government. It is emphasized that such work increases the material resources available to the inmates and helps them fulfill their desire not to be a burden to society.[40]

The several homes for the aged and disabled visited by the author in three of the republics were similar in physical arrangements. Most were located on the outskirts of towns, in pleasant natural settings, often surrounded by woods, gardens, or orchards. There was usually a wing for each sex (married couples can live in either wing), and as a rule two to four in a room. The buildings were two-story structures, and most rooms had windows. While very modest, furnishings were clean and adequate, but toilet and bathing facilities were of poor quality. Food seemed to be plentiful and suited to the needs of old and sick people. Medical facilities ranged from barely adequate to fairly well-appointed clinics. In most homes, there were modest libraries, social rooms, a hall for movies, stage performances, and lectures, and radios. There were either no television sets or only one for the whole institution.*

* See Appendix E for a description of a rather unique home for the aged opened in 1964 near Tashkent.

II

Income Maintenance Programs

The Pension Law of July 14, 1956, for workers and employees, preceded by considerable discussion and publicity in the press, represented a genuine leap forward: it ushered in a new era in income security, and still remains the single most important piece of Soviet legislation in this domain. It rectified the most serious injustices prevalent prior to its passage; at the same time, it merged the social security system in producers' cooperatives into the general one for workers and employees—a logical outcome of the absorption of these cooperatives by state industry. How desperately the 1956 reforms were needed can be judged by the fact that the minimum old-age pension was set at a level almost 50 per cent above the *maximum* sum generally allowed previously, while the minimum invalidity pension was raised to six times its former amount. On the average, old-age pensions rose 100 per cent, invalidity pensions 50 per cent, and pensions for loss of the family breadwinner 64 per cent. The greatest increases were for low-paid workers: for them, pensions increased almost three times. The increase in the provisions was reflected almost at once in the proportion of pensioners who remained at work: on January 1, 1956, 60 per cent of them were working; by January 1958, this percentage had dropped to 20.[1]

The favoritism shown to the privileged prior to 1956 was eliminated, the distinctions in the new law being based upon conditions of work only. The most liberal treatment was given to those employed underground, in unhealthy occupations, in hot shops, and under hazardous conditions. Minimums and maximums set on benefits for each kind of pension made the huge differences that existed earlier impossible. Length of employment, as well as its continuity, are now taken into account in calculating benefits. Coverage was appreciably broadened by removing a number of limitations. It now extends to most of the workers in the industrial sector, as well as to their dependents. The only present exclusions of significance are persons who do temporary and casual work for private employers, members of nomadic tribes, some individual huntsmen and fishermen, and church personnel. The combined impact of these liberalizations was to raise annual social insurance expenditures by 1.3 billion rubles immediately. Between 1955 and 1961 the broadened coverage and increased benefits raised annual expenditures from 2.6 to 7.7 billion rubles—a jump from 16.9 to 30.1 per cent of "collective" funds. This meant an increase in the average expenditure per worker from 54.6 rubles to 102.5 rubles.[2]

The Soviet state social insurance system provides compensation for temporary loss of income due to illness, accident, pregnancy, or childbirth; pensions in cases of prolonged or permanent disability, or old age; funeral benefits; and pensions to dependent survivors of deceased workers. In addition, long-service pensions are paid to certain types of officeholders, such as educators, agronomists, and veterinarians, to flying personnel, and to performing artists. A pension may be awarded to any citizen, regardless of occupational status, for extraordinary contributions to society, and since 1956 pensions have been granted in cases of the death or disablement of any individual in circumstances connected with the performance of public duties or an attempt to save another person's life. Social insurance also pays for visits to spas and other health facilities. Military pensions for current draftees (*srochnye*) are paid by ministries of social welfare from their own budgets (rather than from social insurance funds transferred to them by trade unions), but servicemen who were wage earners and salaried employees before World War II, or who entered the labor force after demobilization, are covered by social insurance; their military service is counted as employment for purposes of determining their eligibility for a social insurance grant or pension and the amount of the pension. Members of the regular army have a separate pension system.

Pensions for Old Age, Disability, and Death of Workers and Employees

Old-age retirement is based upon sex, working conditions, and the physical condition of the worker.[3] For men in ordinary work, the minimum retirement age is 60; for women, 55. For both, these ages are lowered by five years if their work has been difficult or "dangerous" (such as underground mining). Further reductions in age are made for two groups of handicapped—the blind and dwarfs; other handicapped persons are denied this privileged position, apparently a culturally determined distinction. Mothers who have given birth to and raised at least five children to the age of eight may retire at 50. The employment requirement under general circumstances is 25 years for men and 20 years for women. Again, it is lowered if the work is difficult or dangerous, if the worker is handicapped (a blind woman needs to work only ten years), or if the worker is a mother who has raised at least five children (her employment requirement is only 15 years).

With regard to disability, the Soviets from the very beginning adopted the principle of compensating for the loss of wages sustained rather than for the physical or mental harm involved. This principle is still used in assigning invalids to one of the three invalidity groups, i.e., Group I— persons who are almost completely unfit for any work and who usually require constant attendance, Group II—persons who are unfit for any regular occupation, but who do not require special care and may be capable of work under special conditions or at home, and Group III— persons who because they are partially disabled have suffered a significant decline in their earning capacity. Whether the disability is work-connected, war-connected, or brought on by general causes is not a factor in the assignment to an invalidity group. However, the nature of the cause does enter into the determination of the amount of the pension that the invalid will receive. Those disabled by work-related causes have less difficulty than others in meeting conditions of eligibility, and are given more generous pensions.*

In some cases it is very difficult to determine whether or not a disabling condition is work-connected; an additional complication is that the list of occupational diseases is very seldom up to date. In this situation the interests of the individual and the state do not coincide: they "see the problem differently." To the individual and his dependents, it seems unfair that he should receive less when he is disabled by non-work-connected causes, because his loss of income is the same; to the state such differentiation seems fair, because the disability is brought on by conditions outside the state's control. For those disabled by nonoccupational causes, the period of employment required to be eligible for a pension ranges from two years for men 20 to 22 years old (and one year for women in this age group) to 20 years for men who are over 60 and 15 years for women who are over 55. For persons who have worked in

---

* Invalidity pensions are paid until the invalid's health improves to the point where he is no longer entitled to the pension, or until he dies.

dangerous occupations, the period of employment required is reduced so that it ranges from one to 14 years. For those disabled by occupational causes, no set period of employment is required.

Among survivors considered to be dependent are fathers, mothers, and spouses who have reached the age of 60 if male, or 55 if female (or any age if disabled); children (own or adopted), brothers, sisters, and grandchildren under 16, or under 18 if in school (or any age if they had become invalids before reaching 16 or 18); parents or spouses caring for children, brothers, sisters, or grandchildren of the deceased who are less than eight years old; grandparents. (Years of employment required of workers in order for these survivors to receive pensions are the same as for disability pensions.) Children who are dependent on both parents are eligible for a pension on the death of either even if the surviving parent is working. Full orphans are awarded pensions based on the total earnings of both parents, if both were working; the rates are those applicable in work-related cases, whether or not the death of either parent was work-connected. The same is true for orphans of unmarried mothers, except that the earnings of the mother only are considered. The middle-aged widow finds herself in a disadvantaged position. If she has no child capable of supporting her, she may obtain a pension as a survivor at the age of 55 or if she becomes disabled within five years after her husband's death. Usually, however, the only way for most such widows to maintain themselves is to work, and the length of employment requirement may permanently bar them from a pension based on their own earnings.

For social insurance purposes, almost all types of work are considered employment, as are periods spent in technical and higher educational institutions and in the armed forces. A retirement test is used to determine eligibility for old-age and disability pensions. But this is not applicable to Group I invalids and survivors: both are permitted to keep all their earnings without any reduction in pensions. Since 1964, persons in certain economic sectors and occupations have been allowed to earn twice as much as those in ordinary work and still receive at least 50 per cent of their pensions. In this way the Soviets have used the pension system to further the objectives of the regime, by encouraging people to work in sectors considered important to the economy. The same may be said of increments for long periods of continuous employment—a way to discourage labor turnover.

Social insurance is financed entirely by the employing enterprises and institutions. They contribute to the social insurance fund an amount equal to a certain percentage of their total payroll. This percentage is fixed for each industry, but varies between industries according to the risk that work in them entails, and is adjusted from time to time as conditions change. The total payroll includes regular pay, overtime pay, the value of payments in kind, and commissions—in short, everything paid by employers to workers. The rates for individual enterprises and employers are established by the All-Union Central Committee of Trade Unions in cooperation with the various interested state bureaus and the Ministry of Finance.

Since 1938 social insurance funds have been collected and spent in accordance with a single, centralized plan. Centralized budgeting has apparently been used for purposes of equalization, made necessary by the unequal premium rates in the different industries. In this way the central organization makes certain that every insured person, regardless of the industry or locale in which he is employed, enjoys an equal opportunity for benefits. Since 1956, the availability of needed funds has been guaranteed both by the growth of the economy and by the practice of making up any deficits from the general budget of the USSR.[4]

With the exception of a few lump-sum payments, benefits in the Soviet scheme are based upon previous earnings rather than upon need or contributions. Thus, the Soviets are still operating on the principle "To each according to his work" rather than "To each according to his needs." However, in almost no case do benefits equal the amount the beneficiary earned when he was an active member of the labor force. In this respect the Soviet regime seems to adhere to the famous principle enunciated by the English Poor Law commissioners in 1834 (and since then applied to the social security systems of all capitalist countries) that publicly assured income should never exceed the earnings of the lowest category of independent workers. Behind it is the fear that a liberal publicly assured income will, by reducing the economic penalty for not working, discourage initiative and cause a decline in national output. On the other hand, attainment of the security objective requires the assurance of a level of consumption reasonably comparable to that to which the beneficiary has been accustomed. Various devices are used in an attempt to achieve this objective. The benefit formula is weighted in favor of the low wage earners and those who have suffered the greatest loss of work ability; minimum benefits are established; dependents' allowances are paid to retired old-age pensioners and to Group I and II invalids who have completely withdrawn from work; and a partial pension (not lower than one-fourth of what the full pension would have been) is granted to aged, disabled, and survivors who do not qualify for full pensions.

These devices are part of an overall policy aimed at achieving a national minimum below which no Soviet citizen ought to fall. They are needed, it is maintained, because the transition to a communist society is still in progress; when it is completed, the ideal "To each according to his needs" will be achieved, and current inequalities and the devices used to minimize them will be eliminated. (In 1927 it was prophesied that in a fully developed communist society social insurance would disappear, passing into the broader phenomenon of social "guarantee.")[5] This postponement does not stem from economic considerations alone; it also involves a failure to transform the Soviet citizen into the "new Soviet man." Soviet planners are still afraid that publicly assured income based upon need rather than upon previous earnings would so reduce the economic penalty for not working at top efficiency that it would cause a decline in national output. Thus, economic rewards, instead of motivation generated by lofty ideological convictions, are still relied upon to sustain the economy.[6]

Table 11 presents data for 1963 on the number of pensioners in 14 of the republics, average amounts paid each pensioner per month, and

TABLE 11

SOCIAL SECURITY IN 1963: NUMBER OF PENSIONERS, AVERAGE AMOUNT PAID
EACH PENSIONER PER MONTH, AND TOTAL COST, BY REPUBLICS

	Total Number of Pensioners	Number of Working Pensioners	Number of Non-working Pensioners	Amount Spent on Nonworking Pensioners (*in rubles*)	Average Monthly Benefit of Non-working Pensioner (*in rubles*)
Russia	14,096,981	2,704,157	11,392,824	4,537,302,000	33.19
Ukraine	3,625,005	624,521	3,000,484	1,172,820,000	32.57
Belorussia	629,000	126,768	502,232	155,000,000	25.71
Kazakhstan	800,000	—	800,000(?)	250,000,000	26.04
Azerbaidzhan ...	242,257	60,637	181,620	78,033,000	35.80
Latvia	231,098	53,790	177,308	71,913,000	33.79
Armenia	149,129	27,950	121,179	50,450,000	34.60
Estonia	134,000	30,000	104,000	42,940,000	34.40
Turkmenia	79,775	11,909	67,866	2,112,000	25.93
Uzbekistan	435,139	98,540	336,599	127,800,000	31.64
Grusiia	338,357	90,712	247,645	87,230,000	29.35
Lithuania	153,000	35,000	118,000	39,335,000	27.78
Kirgiziia	127,545	21,420	106,125	39,519,100	31.03
Tadzhikistan	75,564	20,260	55,304	16,275,000	24.52
USSR	21,116,593	3,905,664	17,211,182	6,670,729,100	32.30

Source: *125*, pp. 4–12 and 4–9 respectively. Data for Moldavia are not available.

All ruble values are given in terms of the "old" Soviet currency used before the monetary revaluation of January 1961.

total costs. (An entire survivor family is counted as one pensioner, and dependents of those receiving pensions are not counted separately.) As can be seen in the table, the average monthly benefit of a nonworking pensioner in 1963 for the country as a whole was only 32.3 rubles. The minimum wage at the time was 45 rubles per month. (In November 1967 it was raised to 60 rubles per month.) If the minimum wage is regarded as the poverty line below which nobody ought to fall, then pensions provided only about two-thirds of the amount considered necessary for minimum decency. They provided only about *one*-third of the average wage of a worker in the labor force—95 rubles per month. Of course, the average amounts received by different groups of pensioners varied: in 1958, they ranged from 55 rubles per month for a Group I invalid disabled by work-connected causes to 21 rubles per month for a single survivor. The most numerous group—old-age pensioners—received 47 rubles per month.[7] The 32.3 ruble monthly average is explained by the relatively low pension for survivor families, as well as by the inclusion of war pensioners (who make up about half the total of nonworking pensioners), who receive average payments of about 27 rubles per month. In November 1967, the pensions for Group I and II invalids were raised 15 rubles per month, while the maximum for Group II invalids was raised to 30 rubles per month. With these increases the average pension was equal to 60 per cent of earnings. (Old-age pensions were equal to 70 per cent of earnings.) The generally modest pension amounts help to explain why most of the complaints from pensioners can be summed up in the statement "We want more money,"[8] and why many of the aged and disabled try to work as long as possible.*

Benefits for Temporary Inability to Work

In order to receive a sickness benefit, a worker must present a doctor's certificate of illness.[9] There is no waiting period for benefits and no limitation on their duration: they continue until the worker gets well or is transferred to the disability pension roll. The amount of the benefit depends on average daily earnings and on the number of continuous years of service with the employing enterprise: the longer the service,

* For example, in a Leningrad telephone exchange, an old woman insisted upon continuing to work as a telephone operator even though influenza required her to apply mustard plasters every night and dose herself with medicines. The woman was within three months of retirement. Staying home because of illness meant receiving sick benefits at the rate of 80–90 per cent of full pay, and since sick benefits are counted as wages, the earnings on the basis of which her old-age pension was to be calculated would be lower. The telephone exchange decided to help the woman by granting her a sort of vacation without pay (*otgul*). This would not be reflected in her wages, and she would be able to make up the time later on, when she was well. The reason she was given such considerate treatment was that she had a long and uninterrupted work record and was about to receive the Order of Lenin.

the higher the benefit rate, ranging from 50 per cent of earnings for those with less than five years of employment, 80 per cent for those with five to eight years, and 100 per cent for those with more than eight years. The only restriction is that persons who are not trade union members (very few are not) receive only 50 per cent of what union members would normally receive. As a result of post-1956 liberalizations, a person who left a job of his own accord can no longer be punished by requiring that he complete six months of employment at his new job before he is eligible for sickness benefits: he now qualifies for benefits on the very first day of his new job. However, a drunkard with no dependents can be deprived of benefits for the entire period of temporary incapacity; if he has dependents he receives no benefits for the first ten days and only 50 per cent of the normal rate thereafter. The maximum daily benefit is ten rubles; the minimum monthly benefit is 30 rubles (except in rural localities, where it is 10 per cent lower).

The principles that govern pregnancy and childbirth benefits are identical with those that govern sickness insurance. Benefits start eight weeks before birth and continue through eight weeks after birth, with an additional two weeks if there is a plural birth or an abnormal confinement. There are differences in the ratio of the benefit to average earnings: the benefit is equal to two-thirds of the average earnings for those who have worked less than one year in the employing enterprise, and is equal to 100 per cent of the average earnings for those who have worked a total of at least three years, of which at least two were in the enterprise presently employing them. Women under 18 are treated more generously than older ones. The only reduction is for those who are not trade union members—to two-thirds of earnings, regardless of length of service.

The same principles also apply to benefits for work-connected injuries and diseases. The benefit in all instances is 100 per cent of average earnings, with the same minimums as apply in sickness benefits and with no maximum on the daily rate. Trade union membership is not considered.

Social Insurance for Collective Farmers

The 1956 pension reform was concerned solely with workers and employees. The situation of collective farmers and their dependents was left unchanged: they continued to be dependent on mutual aid funds.[10] However, some farms had no funds as late as 1957,* others were ineffec-

---

*In the entire RSFSR, which had a population of 117 million in 1956, of whom perhaps 35 to 40 million were peasants, there were only 24,000 mutual aid funds, uniting 5 million members and with a budget of 60 million rubles. The funds helped to repair homes of invalids and of survivors of military personnel, bought cattle and feed for the needy, organized trips to spas for invalids and the seriously ill, cared for 23,000 orphans,

tive because of their precarious "outside-the-law" position, and still others refused pensions to those indisputably entitled to them because "they had several able-bodied members in the family or a sufficient income."[11] Since there was no machinery for equalization in the form of an all-Russian fund or a contribution from the USSR budget, the kind, amounts, and duration of benefits that individual peasants could get depended on the material situation of each farm. Hence, the poorest farms, which normally have the highest percentage of persons who quickly become needy when unable to work, had the most meager resources for social assistance. The only peasants who could receive pensions from the state system were those who acquired a right to them through service in an industrial enterprise or on a state farm. However, the farmer who transferred to covered employment after middle age found it very difficult to build up a long enough work record to qualify for a state pension.

Proposals for bringing the collective farm population into the social insurance system, or at least for the formation of an all-Union or all-Republic fund to which each farm would be obliged to contribute, had not been lacking, but up to 1964 nothing had been done about them.[12] This was attributed to the greater complexities of administering insurance for the "self-employed," to the desire to preserve the tradition of mutual aid in peasant communities, and to the theory that, legally, collective farms are independent entities that are not subject to certain central controls. In 1964 a fundamental reform was finally made. It should be noted that as of January of that year, the total number of pensioners in the country was 26 million. Of these, 23.3 million were within the state social insurance system, and only 2.6 million were receiving benefits from collective farms.[13] Even in the RSFSR, which usually leads in social welfare matters, only 25 per cent of the eligible aged and disabled collective farm members were receiving a pension—a truly sad commentary on the mutual aid system for the peasants, lauded by the regime for 43 years.

The decision concerning the reform was announced to the country in a speech by Premier Khrushchev, who conceded that "practice shows that in the pension system for the collective farm members, we still do not have a strictly determined order." What was needed, he continued, was an all-Union centralized fund into which all collective farms would put a portion of their income: 2 per cent in 1964 and 4 per cent from then on. (The state would make up the difference between the amount the farms contributed and the amount necessary to pay the pensions.) He hastened to add that the farmer who was more productive would be

---

supported 69 homes for 1,000 aged and disabled, and in seven districts gave monthly grants, in money and in kind, to invalids suffering from work-connected injuries (*83*, pp. 38–40).

better provided for in his old age: there would be no egalitarianism. In this way, the pension system would motivate farmers to greater productivity.[14] A law embodying these features was passed in July 1964, to become operative in January 1965. But certain groups within the collective farm membership were singled out for full social insurance coverage to begin in October 1964—collective farm chairmen, specialists, and workers in mechanized occupations.

Even though social insurance for the farmers was to be more restricted and less generous than the system for workers and employees, it was estimated that 6.5 million persons (rather than the 2.6 million who received benefits up to that time) would be eligible in 1965. In 1966, 8.3 million would be receiving benefits. The pensions were much higher than the ones paid by mutual aid funds, and were more firmly guaranteed. For old-age pensioners, retirement age was based upon sex only: 65 for men and 60 for women. The employment requirement was not adjusted according to working conditions or the physical condition of the individual: it was 25 years for men and 20 for women. Women who had given birth to five or more children and reared them to the age of eight were entitled to old-age pensions when they reached the age of 55 and had worked at least 15 years.

As for disability pensions, only Group I and II invalids were eligible. Those disabled by occupational injury or disease were granted pensions regardless of how long they had worked. For those disabled by nonoccupational causes, the required period of employment ranged from one year for those under 20 to 20 years for men and 15 years for women who were over 60. The eligible survivors were the same as in the state system, except that the old-age requirement for surviving fathers, mothers, wives, and husbands was 65 for men and 60 for women. The benefit system did not allow weighting in favor of the low wage earner, nor did it include other devices used in the state insurance system to assure the adequacy of the minimum benefits, which were quite low. The minimum and maximum benefits for old-age pensions were fixed at 12 and 102 rubles a month, respectively (as compared to 30 and 120 rubles for workers and employees); disability pensions were 15 rubles a month for Group I and 12 rubles for Group II invalids; for survivors they were 15 rubles a month for three or more dependents, 13 rubles for two, and nine rubles for one. If disability or loss of income resulted from occupational injury or disease, 20 per cent was added.

Pensions were based upon average monthly earnings for work on the collective farm during any five successive years (the years being chosen by the pension applicant) from the 15 years preceding application. For those who had worked for less than 15 years, pensions were based upon the average monthly earnings on the farm during the time worked. Payments in kind were calculated in monetary terms.* Those aged who had worked long and hard on the average would get 30-40 rubles per month when they retired (about as much as the minimum pension paid to a worker or employee). No sickness benefits were available for farmers. However, there was a benefit for pregnancy and childbirth if the mother had a three-year work record: it applied to the eight weeks before and the eight weeks after birth, and ten weeks after delivery if the birth was multiple or complicated.

Social welfare personnel almost always explained the less generous provisions for farmers, as compared with those for workers and employees, by saying "Not everything at once!" They predicted liberalizations in the future, and pointed out that the increasing mechanization of farms was making the position of more and more farm workers equivalent to that of industrial workers—as far as social insurance is concerned. The activity of mutual aid societies in the area of income maintenance would gradually cease, to the relief of all concerned. The societies would concentrate on "welfare" functions: aid to the needy not covered by insurance, arrangements for orphans, housework for disabled pensioners, loans for special purposes, and administration of homes for the aged.†

A number of difficulties, more or less peculiar to life and work on

---

* The computations of earnings on the basis of which the pension was calculated were often so involved that they taxed the ingenuity of even sophisticated and experienced personnel, as is evident from the numerous instructions and guides that were published. (See, for example, *404*, pp. 4–13.) There were three kinds of payments to consider in the total on which the pension was based: (1) the number of days during which the individual fulfilled the norm: these were called "labor-days" and had a definite monetary value; (2) payments in kind: here only grain, milk, meat, sugar beets, and sunflower seeds were counted, and they were evaluated according to their worth in retail prices at the time of payment; (3) any sums that the individual was paid for production over the norm.

† The predicted liberalizations were made on the fiftieth anniversary of the Revolution, in November 1967. For old-age pensioners, retirement age was lowered by five years, making it the same as that for workers and employees. Group III disability pensions were added, but only for injuries and diseases having occupational causes: for nonoccupational disabilities, only Group I and Group II disability pensions were available. Group I and Group II invalids who had been disabled from childhood and had reached 16 were brought into the system, whatever the cause that disabled them. They are to receive a flat monthly grant of 16 rubles. Minimum disability benefits for the disabled in Groups I and II were raised so that the range is now from 12 rubles per month for a Group III invalid to 30 rubles per month for a Group I invalid disabled from occupational causes. The category of eligible survivors was broadened to include grandparents, the age requirement being 60 for men and 55 for women. A pensioner can now choose any five successive years of earnings from the ten (rather than from the 15) that preceded application. The cumulative effect of these liberalizations is to bring the social insurance system of collective farm members closer to that of workers and employees. It suggests that the two will eventually merge into a single system for the country's entire work force.

collective farms, have had to be dealt with in setting this new social security system in motion. Many old people have no documents for proving
their age or length of employment: they never existed or were destroyed
in the war. Witnesses must be used, and these are not always reliable.
Especially erroneous have been "mass fixations" of work periods by witnesses, which have been resorted to in some places to expedite matters.
Some collective farm pension committees, although presumably they
had the data at hand needed to arrive at correct conclusions, have provided incorrect information about work records because they wanted
to include people who might otherwise be ineligible.[15] In other cases,
these committees have deliberately raised the average earnings on which
pensions were calculated, resulting in overpayments. Some executives
high in the administrative hierarchy, it is complained, have been slow
to react and sometimes have taken no measures to recover overpayments.
While in some farms, lists with the names of those who have reached pen-
sionable age or would reach it within a few months are posted in order
"to avoid errors and to keep loafers from receiving pensions,"[16] in others
little effort has been made to obtain the necessary information and documents. Delays have been reported in examinations by Medico-Labor
Expert Commissions; in some districts, pregnancy and birth benefits
were still not being paid eight months after the law went into effect.[17]

These problems have not been easy to deal with, as is shown by the
fact that in the RSFSR, the number of overpayments and underpayments
uncovered in 1966 was significantly higher than in 1965.[18] Numerous
1967 reports indicate that the work of collective farm pension commissions leaves much to be desired. Instead of doing the work with which
they are charged, many commissions leave it to the local departments of
social welfare; many have not yet mastered the legal intricacies of their
work; many go through the motions but avoid making substantive decisions; many leave everything to the chairman; and in some localities,
members simply absent themselves.

Public Assistance

Final approval of public assistance is by local soviets; getting together
necessary documents and making recommendations about eligibility are
the responsibility of local welfare departments, who also make the payment to the recipient. There appears to be no consistent rationale for the
amounts paid in flat grants; rather, they seem to be related to the general level of living in the applicant's place of residence and, to some extent, to what the needy person had been used to. Amounts differ in the
different republics: in the RSFSR they were finally raised in 1957 (they
had remained unchanged between 1935 and 1957) to 10 rubles per month

for those living in urban communities and 8.5 rubles per month for those in rural areas. In Latvia, they may reach 15 rubles per month, and in Armenia 10–15 rubles. The RSFSR amounts, it will be noted, are still below the minimum set for collective farmers eligible for social security benefits, and even the highest amount is only one-fourth of the current minimum wage. Thus, public assistance, financed from local funds, keeps its clients substantially below the poverty line; by requiring them to prove destitution, as well as age or disability, it also humiliates them. In addition, whenever an aid recipient becomes a landowner, or gets income from relatives or from some other source,* or gets well enough so that he can work, aid is stopped.[19] In spite of these severe limitations, outdoor relief has eased life for many poor people who otherwise would have suffered even more acutely—especially old and disabled widows who depended on their husbands and do not have work records of their own for social insurance purposes.† Sometimes this assistance is given in spite of complaints by administrators that the recipients are undeserving people who had not worked when they were able-bodied.[20]

As throughout the 1928–55 period, help for people whose basic needs are not met by pensions and outdoor relief can come from only three sources: local welfare departments, whose budgets include some money for "single-time" payments; social organizations such as VOS, VOG, KOV, Veterans of Labor, and Parents' Committees; trade unions, which help those currently or formerly employed through loans. Although single-time grants are supposed to be used only for unusual needs, in fact one family or person will often receive such grants several times a year to meet recurring needs. A great deal seems to depend on how concerned social welfare personnel are about the well-being of helpless people.[21] Local welfare offices can do a variety of things with the funds at their disposal: give extra help to children of invalids and pensioners,[22]

---

* Enforcement of the "source of income" and the "responsible relatives" limitations frequently creates severe hardships. For instance, ownership of a plot of ground is regarded as a "source of income," even though the aged person does not have the strength to cultivate it. A grown son who lives far away and has heavy responsibilities in his own family is considered a "responsible relative." In some cases the help from "sources of income" and from "responsible relatives" is so negligible that it is not sufficient to sustain life, but there is no machinery for regular supplementation (*40*, p. 19).

† It is interesting to note that of the four suggestions for liberalization of income maintenance provisions made by republic ministers of social welfare at the end of 1963, three were concerned with public assistance. One proposal was that partial pensions be granted to those with insufficient work records who have *no sources of subsistence,* and who presumably are now destitute or are receiving only public assistance. Another proposal was that prostheses should be made available free to those *who are receiving grants from local budgets:* apparently these people are now going without them. A third proposal was that assistance grants be paid through the mails like pension benefits, instead of requiring the recipients to come in for them (*125*, pp. 4–12 and 4–9, respectively). [Emphases mine.]

give an extra allowance to an unmarried mother. These funds provide a way, albeit a narrow one, for dealing with the rigidities and inadequacies of the social welfare system, if the welfare workers are imbued with socialist humanism and are ingenious and imaginative. But even then, the absence of an obligation to provide supplementary assistance in a consistent and rational manner can be hard on many people.

No information is provided by the authorities as to how much is distributed in the form of single-time grants; nor is it possible to calculate how much aid is given by the social organizations and the trade unions. However, a careful reading of the evidence gives one the impression that these types of aid alleviate only the severest want, and that administrative discretion, long ago discarded in social insurance determinations, is still an important element in treatment accorded to the most disadvantaged group. This explains in part why indoor relief, in the form of homes for the aged and disabled, is so important in the public assistance system. Although legally these homes are supposed to serve people on pensions (substituting pensions in kind for pensions in money), in fact nonpensioned destitute persons are accepted. Furthermore, although the regulations say that among pensioners it is those who are "alone" who have priority for institutional care, it is obvious that the homes accept many who are not alone but whose entire worldly resources added to their pensions do not yield enough for the barest existence. These factors undoubtedly contribute to the growth in the number of these homes, to the waiting lists of those wishing to get in, and to plans for their future expansion.

Family Allowances

The only segment of the social security system that has remained totally unchanged since 1947 is family allowances. Current monthly benefits, ranging from four rubles for the fourth child to 15 rubles for the eleventh and subsequent children, mean that by the time the child reaches age five, when allowances stop for legitimate children, the mother will have collected 257 rubles for a fourth child, 373 for a fifth, 436 for a sixth, and 970 rubles for the eleventh and following. Thus, the fourth child's allowances during the entire five years will come to only two months of average wages, and the eleventh child's to about seven months of such wages. It has been calculated that in families in which there are four children, and the youngest child is between one and four years old, the yearly payment will represent only 4.4 per cent of the average wage, but that this percentage rises sharply for those recipients who have more than four living children: to 12.3 per cent of the average wage for the year in which a fifth child is born and the fourth child is less than five years old, and to 41.2 per cent of the average wage in the year when a tenth child is born and two other children are eligible for payments.[23]

On the average, in 1963 each mother of "many children" received 10.8 rubles per month.[24] Although in the aggregate family allowances add up to a sizable sum, since 1958 this sum has constituted a decreasing proportion of the national income: in 1963 family allowances payments amounted to only 0.28 per cent of national income, whereas in 1958 they had amounted to 0.42 per cent.[25] However, these payments are probably quite a help to children in peasant households, where incomes are still low.

Various explanations have been offered for the failure to increase allowance amounts since 1947, to provide allowances for the first two children of married mothers, and to continue payments for eligible children beyond the age of five. One is the previously noted fact that although individual amounts are modest, in the aggregate allowances constitute a large sum (in 1963, mothers received 452.3 million rubles in fourteen republics); another is that mothers receiving allowances are entitled to many privileges that add substantially to their well-being— for example, they have first priority in placing their children in preschool facilities, and pay nothing or very little for such care; a third is that the overall standard of living has improved. On the other hand, with regard to mothers of illegitimate children, Soviet society is concerned with the loose morals that it is felt unmarried motherhood represents, and many question the desirability of helping the unmarried mother even to the extent that she is being helped now—though they would deny wishing to punish the children for the misdeeds of their parents.

In spite of their shortcomings, the income maintenance programs discussed above undeniably exert a beneficial influence on the lives of Soviet citizens—both as aid received here and now and as a guarantee of the care that will be given by the state in time of need. Everywhere people openly express or imply their gratitude to the state that provides for them in old age, in sickness, in bereavement, even in death. Everywhere they voice confidence that the state's provisions will be better and more generous in the future. The sense of security bestowed by these programs, albeit in return for their doing their utmost in the common undertaking, is unmistakable.

And we would say to the enemies of freedom, whatever the magnificent ends they propose—the brotherhood of man, the kingdom of saints, "from each according to his ability, to each according to his needs"—they miss just this essential point: that man is greater than the social purposes to which he can be put. He must not be kicked about even with the most high-minded objectives. He is not a means or an instrument. He is an end in himself.

—Adlai Stevenson

12

Past, Present, and Future—
Summary and Conclusions

The history of social welfare in Russia records many changes in theory and practice—changes which, as in other societies, have been more rapid or profound in some periods than in others, and have essentially continued or departed from traditional ways of dealing with social problems. In this concluding chapter, the strengths and weaknesses of Soviet welfare policies will be assessed, what they reveal about the nature of Soviet society will be discussed, and the ways in which they have influenced Soviet society and in turn been influenced by it will be analyzed. The major Soviet welfare achievements will then be compared briefly with developments in the United States. This assessment and comparison will be the basis of some speculation about what these two countries can learn from each other and what the Soviet experience indicates about the problems to be faced by the underdeveloped countries that wish to attain decent levels of social well-being at the same time as they industrialize—hopefully to the advancement of social welfare in all these countries.

The Past

In tsarist times, stipulations in the poor laws that want must be relieved were so vague and resources to implement them so meager that most poor people could not rely on the state to alleviate even the most acute suffering. Whether they were helped or not depended on fortuitous circumstances beyond their control. If they were not helped, the indigent had no way of appealing to higher authority, no power to force the responsible organs to give them assistance. As a final resort, they could beg—and this they did, in many instances, in spite of the cruel punishment that this entailed. The only exception was the group of workers (about a fifth of those employed for hire) who had a right to benefits under the social insurance laws. In their case, however, compensation was paid only for sickness and work-connected injuries, they themselves had to contribute a substantial part of the benefits they received, the sums they were given were low in comparison to wages, and they had only a minor voice in the administration of the benefits.

Because public provision was inadequate and uncertain, many needy people sought aid from private charitable societies. Forced to concentrate on relieving immediate suffering, these societies spent relatively insignificant sums on preventive and treatment-oriented programs. As is true of all private charitable organizations, they could not offer assistance to all who needed help or provide protection against all the contingencies that made it necessary for people to seek help. Their boards of directors determined intake policies, eligibility requirements, and the kinds and amounts of aid that would be provided. With membership on these boards open exclusively to upper class contributors, it is not surprising that a considerable proportion of privately supported charitable facilities were available only to the "deserving" poor, the definition of "deserving" embodying the philosophy and objectives of the donors. In the public sector as well, prejudice and discrimination ruled. With no fair-hearings machinery available, the decisions of local officials were supreme, however capricious or injurious some of them might be. As a rule, the assistance given, both under public and private auspices, was in kind, for the most part as support in institutions, and occasionally as commodities to be used at home. Traditionally, assistance in kind is unpopular with the recipients. It is used by the donors when they wish aid to be such that it is sought only in the most desperate circumstances, and when their basic assumption is that those who seek aid are incapable of efficiently managing their affairs.

Under the tsars of the nineteenth century, the Ministry of Interior was responsible for supervising all public and private poor relief. Its influence on day-to-day operations, however, was negligible, because the central government made no grants-in-aid to the local authorities, set no standards, and used its licensing power in a formal and inflexible manner. The management of local relief by an uncontrolled multitude of uncoordinated public and private agencies was characterized by variations in kinds and amounts of aid available to people in similar circumstances. In matters of pauperism, begging, and vagrancy, the police rather than welfare authorities had jurisdiction, and they invariably resorted to repressive and often cruel methods. Community participation in any meaningful sense was either prohibited or allowed only in a limited sphere. With regard to social insurance, the central council encouraged a uniform interpretation of the law, and was able to make its power tangibly felt through its right to conduct hearings on appeal. Nevertheless, eligibility requirements and amounts of benefits varied between localities because the resources of sickness funds and accident insurance brotherhoods were determined by the financial conditions of the industrial establishments in which they were located.

With reference to the quality of welfare services in pre-Revolutionary Russia, the literature is almost wholly devoid of anything but pious exhortations. This fact, combined with the general tone of the materials available, makes it clear that no training of any kind was required (or available) for welfare work. All welfare activity was permeated by the "charity" approach, with the benevolence of those who carried it on being constantly extolled, frequently in exaggerated terms. There is no mistaking the condescension—sometimes genuinely kind,[1] but often coldly indifferent—on the part of the donors and officials toward those who received. At best, they assumed that poor people were so weak-willed or simple that they could not be extricated from perpetual dependency; at worst, they humiliated and treated with cruelty those who could not defend themselves. On the one hand, poverty was an inevitable part of the economic system, and the workings of this system were identified with the laws of nature and were not to be tampered with; on the other hand, poverty was the result of improvidence on the part of the poor for which they were to be punished, not helped. It is obvious that the possibilities for rehabilitation of the poor and the socially handicapped remained largely unexplored. Rigid in their attitudes, many officials were loath to experiment or even to introduce already tested innovations. In children's institutions, both the physical and the educational standards were low. For children from the lower social classes, institutional care bordered on exploitation.

At the close of the tsarist era, Russia was undoubtedly behind the other industrializing countries of Europe in all aspects of social welfare. At the beginning of the twentieth century none of these countries could be said to have done much toward alleviating the misery and suffering of its people, or preventing individual and family disorganization, but Russia was behind all of them—quantitatively, qualitatively, and philosophically. Her welfare efforts, in spite of their considerable size in absolute terms, had little impact on massive social problems deeply rooted in tradition, such as alcoholism, corruption, poverty, prostitution, vicious child labor practices, and illegitimacy. These massive problems were passed on to the Soviet regime. That the Soviets did not remain complacent or inactive with regard to them has been amply documented in the preceding text. Let us now attempt to assess what has been accomplished and at what human cost.

The Present

What can be considered the *major advances* in social welfare made during fifty years of Soviet power?

Indisputably, one major advance has been a steady broadening of the category of those with a legal right to comprehensive income assistance, and thus freedom from degrading means tests and humiliating charity. The movement toward the guarantee of a decent minimum income has been furthered by the all-inclusive nature of the coverage offered by social insurance, the rising level of insurance benefits, and the reduction in the number of people in the rural population with inadequate protection. If a citizen is a worker or employee or a dependent of a worker or employee, his assistance will come from the state social insurance system and will be paid for jointly by his employing establishment and the state; if he is a member of a collective farm or a dependent of such a member, his assistance will come from the collective farm system of social insurance and will be paid for jointly by the farm and the state; if he falls outside both of these groups and is in need, his assistance will be a flat grant financed from local revenues or placement in an institution in which he will receive complete support at state expense. These provisions protect him against most of the contingencies in industrial societies that interrupt, diminish, or cut off income.

Especially generous, from the point of view of eligibility and benefit rates, are provisions for expectant mothers. The privileged position of mothers and children in Soviet society is further strengthened by children's allowances, available for both urban and rural children. These allowances are granted because a decent income for families of all sizes cannot be guaranteed by a wage system based on the product of a man's labor and not on the size of his family. Flat assistance grants and institutional care—the catchall provisions underpinning social insurance—represent a recognition by the regime that an undeviating adherence to the "according-to-his-work" principle for income security purposes results in dire poverty for some to which they ought not to be abandoned. In all welfare arrangements (with the exception of institutional care), assistance is given in the form of money, so that beneficiaries retain the power to regulate their own affairs and are not set apart from the rest of the population by being deprived of the ability to make monetary transactions.

In sum, the Soviets have firmly established the general principle of public responsibility for income maintenance; they have discarded the old, inadequate poor laws and replaced them with a modern scheme of social security—a scheme based on the assumption that the role of social welfare institutions is to ensure individual fulfillment, rather than to treat the abnormal or pathological conditions found in modern society. During this transformation they have adhered to the fundamental idea that economic security can best be provided for the vast majority—the employable—by guaranteeing full employment through economic planning. On the other hand, they have recognized that eliminating the fear of income loss so that it is no longer a factor in promoting job stability and good workmanship creates the problem of maintaining incentive. Unwilling to rely on coercive measures, especially in the past decade, Soviet authorities have endeavored to use the provision of economic rewards to motivate workers to act voluntarily in the manner desired by the state, that is, to maintain and increase incentives that contribute to an upward productivity curve. Although this approach results in some injustices, care has been taken to produce an equitable situation for the majority, and the system now operates with no serious clash between the needs of the regime and the needs of the individual.[2]

Another major advance is the creation of new social services, steadily extended to wider segments of the population and differentiated in accordance with individual needs. These services help people take greater advantage of what the society has to offer, and provide an institutionalized method for facilitating social adjustment and for intervening in cases of social dysfunction. They have been made more accessible by reducing costs to economically weak groups and by setting up facilities close to where people live. Consistent with their drive to lift the masses out of poverty, the Soviets have insisted that the main function of these services, as well as of the entire welfare system, is to make and keep people productive. Methods for achieving this objective have been formulated: they are addressed primarily to the rational elements in individual and social behavior, and utilize group relationships and work therapy as the major tools in treatment.

Services have been created for young and old, for the physically disabled and handicapped and the emotionally disturbed, for those whose maladjustments threaten society openly, and for those whose problems have more subtle injurious effects. On many occasions treatment methods are weakened by an excessive reliance on work and group pressures; on the whole, however, considerable success has been achieved by programs involving the aged, disabled, handicapped, delinquent, alcoholic, mentally retarded, and mentally ill. An impressive number of them are benefiting economically, physically, emotionally, and socially by being taught skills and placed in part-time and full-time jobs. Since 1930 it has been obligatory for employing establishments to hire them when directed to do so by welfare and educational authorities, and for the most part jobs for them have been plentiful. The desire to make these services more effective has led to a recognition of the need to individualize treatment programs, to strive for deeper therapeutic effects, and to develop capacities to handle interpersonal relations more successfully.

In social welfare administration, a number of important gains have been made. While state control of public welfare agencies and all allied voluntary groups exemplifies the totalitarian character of Soviet society, it has a positive side: the conviction that welfare services are too important to the general well-being to be left to the sporadic and uncertain activities of voluntary groups. All major social welfare functions have become part of the on-going responsibilities of state organs, are included in planning budgets, and are allotted resources on a regular basis. Social welfare agencies have come to occupy a permanent place within the structure of government. This has resulted from (and has contributed to) a clarification of functions. Administrative decentralization—a pronounced feature of the Soviet welfare scene—permits some control at the local level, but the Party remains the final determiner of policy.

Local responsibility has also been advanced by the Party's promotion of the idea of community participation. Here, as in other areas of Soviet life, the Party has combined coercion and guidance with an educational campaign to explain why such effort is desirable and necessary. On the one hand, involvement of large numbers of people in voluntary welfare activities is a way of getting work done without increasing government expenses; on the other, volunteers often provide simple, supportive therapy that helps people with "daily living" and assures them of the society's readiness to stand by them in time of trouble. In some instances community participation helps people when everything else fails. The exercise of social responsibility by the community, although permitted only within limits strictly defined by the state, has widened the social welfare base and has brought welfare closer to home. This, in turn, has generated a growing interest in welfare programs, has opened a channel for pressure from below, and has provided additional opportunity for initiative and creativity—features that mitigate somewhat the pressure of state demands on the individual.

Planning in welfare has meant a more rational use of resources, avoidance of duplication of efforts, a steadier progress toward defined objectives, and less costly administration. It is widely supported by both welfare personnel and the citizenry. There is less approval of the way administrators handle welfare "cheating," i.e., the receipt of publicly supplied income by able-bodied persons. Unless a person can claim that he is unable to work for medical reasons, he is not given economic aid, but is given a job, or is paid to train for a job. It does not matter if the person involved is a mother of young children, married or unmarried, who wants to stay home and care for them, or is a seasonal worker who wants to wait until employment in his own line is available. In the Soviet view, welfare "cheating" is to be blamed on "human nature" that has not yet become "communist" rather than on ambivalence on the part of the regime about how welfare recipients ought to behave or on its failure to provide work, education, or medical care.

There is no doubt that the Soviet welfare effort has been strengthened and advanced by the guidance it has obtained from science and its decreasing reliance on casual improvisation. During the last decade, in particular, the area in which research and investigation are permitted has been broadened, in order to produce the knowledge essential to the management of social welfare in modern industrialized societies. Present research on small groups and on work therapy, as well as on the meaning of physical and mental handicaps for the individual, will probably be especially helpful. Social welfare has become an integral part of the Soviets' scientifically oriented culture, in striking contrast to its place in the tradition-weighted, eternal-verities-oriented and superstition-laden era of the tsars.

Tied to the scientific approach is an emphasis on prevention. The effort to achieve an acceptable economic level and essential social services for all is in itself a preventive program of major proportions. There are also important efforts to create a more informed and more genuinely involved community. A more direct type of prevention is the concern shown for the well-being of mothers and children, a concern that starts from the time the child is conceived and continues until he reaches maturity; it takes in all aspects of his life, and its objective is to give him the opportunity to reach his full potential. The Soviet regime's willingness to devote extensive resources to the care, education, and upbringing of "defective" children (youngsters who at best can never be as productive as the nondefective) is an especially vivid proof of a desire to give all of the country's children a good start. The Soviets' accomplishments in raising women from their submerged state in tsarist times—economic, social, cultural, and legal—have been substantial.

While there are still troublesome problems in connection with the selection, training, utilization, and retention of social welfare personnel, progress has nevertheless been appreciable. Efforts are being made to specify qualifications for welfare work that will be more precise than a vague listing of benevolent attributes. Certain educational credentials are being insisted upon in many instances, and in-service training and training institutes are being widely used to improve work performance and keep workers abreast of new developments. There is an awareness that traits other than intellectual and rational—the personality elements that create what the Russians call "character"—are of prime importance. Considerable experience has been gained in the use of indigenous nonprofessionals, and in coordinating their activities with community participation programs.

Genuine progress is evident in the growing emphasis on "socialist humanism": the realization that people who need help must be provided for in a kind and dignified manner. In socialist humanism the human being is regarded as the most important element in the rehabilitation process. Organizational innovations, achievements of science and technology, and education of the public to the significance of what welfare can do are to be utilized to give each individual, with his special needs, the best welfare service at the society's disposal, and to do this patiently and considerately, without delays and complications. This new attitude has tended to give treatment a deeper significance for both the individual and society. At the same time, it has introduced some flexibility into rigid bureaucratic procedures, and indirectly opened a way for the community to have a voice in welfare matters.

The transformations and achievements in social welfare since 1917 represent substantial progress: the metamorphosis of a backward, punitive system to one that compares favorably with those in other advanced countries. That this has been achieved in the relatively short period of 50 years, in the midst of rapid industrialization and of monstrously devastating social upheavals and wars, makes the transformation even more impressive. If continued, it will further enrich the lives of the people, make more genuine the guarantee of material and social aid, and increase the dignity of the individual in Soviet society.

What can be said about the *price that has been paid* for this progress? From the point of view of the masses, the price in human suffering has been enormous. One of the major reasons for this is that throughout the 1917–66 period, and to a lesser degree today, the working population has lived "under conditions characteristic of economically backward countries."[3] Sums allocated for social insurance during the first 12 post-Revolutionary years were meager in the extreme. After the first five-year plan, greater resources became available, but welfare programs were severely limited by being subordinated to economic and production goals. The right to assistance in case of need was largely an empty promise, its irony underscored by the sporadic welfare handouts given only in cases of the most abject poverty, and even then only in trifling amounts. The resulting serious deprivation for the majority of the urban aged, disabled, and handicapped was only slightly alleviated by funds that they themselves were able to scrape together for mutual protection. The government, while loudly proclaiming the right of these unfortunate people to security against the vicissitudes of modern life, was in fact spending relatively little on them. It was not until the passage of the 1956 pension law, almost 40 years after the Revolution, that there was a genuine movement toward achieving a decent minimum income for the industrial segment of the population.

However, the deprivations experienced by workers and employees pale in significance when compared to the suffering endured by the peasantry, who constituted a majority of the population until the 1960's. Forced to rely upon the uncertain and paltry resources of mutual aid funds, the helpless among them undoubtedly suffered acutely in most of the rural communities—despite glowing official accounts about the high level of social security benefits on a few prosperous collective farms. Their situation was exacerbated by their total exclusion from the rudimentary public assistance program (a policy continued up to the present) and by the absence of effective avenues of appeal from the decisions of mutual aid committees. The Soviet regime insisted upon making mutual aid the main line of defense against peasant income loss; it also attempted to use it as a weapon in the collectivization drive. The latter function was inappropriate to a welfare scheme, and the former was far beyond the resources and powers of mutual aid. It was not until 1965 that the sham of mutual aid as a way of securing against income loss was finally admitted, and a system of social security, somewhat less complete and generous than that for industrial workers, introduced. Mutual aid is now only an adjunct, additive in character, to the state system of economic assistance.

It must be remembered that insurance benefits have never been available to those considered to be opposed to the Soviet regime. Sorely needed help was denied in the early days of the regime to the "socially inimical," and pensions were taken away from people who had received them under the tsar. In more recent times, hundreds of thousands in corrective labor camps have been excluded from the social security system, and the "kulaks" from mutual aid societies. When one realizes that these same people for the most part had whatever material assets they possessed confiscated, and were ineligible for jobs in state agencies and organs, one begins to sense the terrible ordeal they have had to endure—both physical and social.

In the high cost of Soviet social welfare progress must be included the lost and stunted lives of millions of homeless and, later, "unsupervised" children. As has been shown, the overwhelming majority of these children did not get even elementary care on a continuing basis, in spite of endless decrees, meetings, and plans. Their plight was the effect of a series of social upheavals that wrought unprecedented havoc upon family life—a havoc for which the welfare measures enacted prior to the late 1950's were on the whole only a feeble antidote. Added to this was the destructive impact on family life of low living standards, official labor policies, and many years of Party propaganda against the "reactionary" nature of family authority.

Nor should the almost desperate predicament of the disabled and the handicapped during the first 30 post-Revolutionary years be forgotten. They were left to depend almost entirely on their own efforts; the regime did not become interested in them until the 1930's, and then primarily as a potential source of manpower. Reliance on a mass approach, and an overriding concern for making the disabled "productive," resulted in a difficult existence for many and much suffering—economic, social, and emotional. State organs showed little concern for those who through no fault of their own, but because of the lack of knowledge and skill of their "trainers," could not become productive. Only the collective of the handicapped themselves consistently pushed for better facilities and greater resources in the first post-Revolutionary decade; this collective also tried to ease the often intolerable pressures of the industrialization and collectivization drives of the 1928–41 period by offering cultural activities and relaxation. It was not until after World War II that the disabled began to enjoy the benefits of the improvement in the economic position of the country and of the constructive new ideas and methods concerning rehabilitation.

There is no doubt that the price of Soviet social welfare progress, like the progress itself, reflected the operation of large social forces—some deliberately unleashed by the regime, others of a cataclysmic nature beyond the regime's control.

What are some of the *major weaknesses* of present-day Soviet welfare practice? One weakness is that social services by a responsible agency are not available at all for those confronted with certain kinds of social problems, such as difficulties that arise when childless married couples do not get along or, in the case of unmarried parents, from the lack of legal marital status. Welfare services are not uniformly available throughout the country. The rural population does not begin to receive the benefits and services that the urban population enjoys. Income-maintenance programs do not cover all losses of income, and the benefits they provide are often inadequate. For example, there is no unemployment compensation, because Soviet authorities insist that there is no unemployment as long as job openings in the economy as a whole exceed the number of workers available to fill them, as is the case in Russia today.* They refuse to recognize that people who are having a hard time finding employment are not helped by the availability of work in some distant place to which they are unable or unwilling to go.

In addition, as noted above, social insurance benefits are frequently inadequate. Current Soviet pensions are equal to only a fraction of the minimum wage and to an even smaller fraction of the average wage. It is clear that pensioners, on the average, are living below the standard they enjoyed before the loss of income against which they were insured.† This is especially true of survivors: the meagerness of their benefits belies the regime's alleged concern for large families, and underscores its use of the social insurance system to motivate people to work. The restrictive features of family allowances—with respect to extent of coverage and duration and amounts of benefits—make them least helpful to the most disadvantaged children.

These weaknesses in Soviet welfare practice indicate that so far Soviet ingenuity, limited by economic, political, and moral considerations, has failed to devise a system flexible enough to assure the meeting of all need as a matter of right. Nor have the Soviets created a system that offsets through benefits the income inadequacies that existed during productive years. The benefit formula requires that benefits be calculated in relation to former earnings. Hence, people whose earnings were low receive low benefits, a hardship that is only partially relieved by the establishment of minimums below which no benefit is permitted to fall. This method of determining benefits, operative almost without interruption throughout 1917–68, has tended to perpetuate economic differences between

---

* That frictional unemployment exists is not disputed. Enterprises shut down; staffs are reduced; people quit their jobs to find more suitable or more remunerative work, either on their own or at the request of management. However, the fact that there is no unemployment compensation undoubtedly has acted as an incentive to remain on the job or to actively seek new employment.

† In Russia "no investments by individuals in the equities or debt obligation of industrial and commercial organizations are permitted, and wage and salary levels for rank-and-file workers are generally so low in comparison with living costs as to minimize the possibility of substantial savings of any type—home ownership, individual savings and insurance, and employer- or union-sponsored supplementary pensions.... Therefore, a pension that would be at all adequate would have to be quite close to full wages" (*453*, pp. vii–viii, 7).

population groups, which in turn have contributed to the formation of classes in a supposedly classless society. It is indeed a black mark against "socialist humanism" that to this day the Soviet public assistance program offers only the feeblest ministrations to needy persons excluded from social insurance, and to those whose insurance benefits are too low for them to maintain a decent standard of living. The silence with respect to this aspect of welfare administration, in contrast to the abundance of materials available concerning social insurance, is evidence of the Soviet regime's embarrassment over the fact that it has neither eliminated want nor devised a system for making it vanish when it appears.

The Soviets have also failed in their struggle to deal with "social anomalies." While improvement in the economic, social, and educational condition of the people has reduced appreciably the massive problems inherited from tsarism, life under the Soviets has engendered a new set of social problems. Efforts to treat the "socially anomalous," born and raised under socialism, on the basis of a "remnants of capitalism" theory have failed. The next step has been to find out what is wrong with the socialist conditions of life, since in the Soviet view these conditions completely mold the personality and determine all its characteristics. In this investigation certain aspects of the so-called "socialism to communism" period have been exposed that, it is said, affected people adversely. An effort is also being made to understand why the same conditions of life affect people differently and are perceived by them differently. Implicit in these new studies is the recognition that more is required to return some people to a productive life than recourse to the rational elements in behavior, as expressed in the notions of the educational value of work, socialization, group pressure, and self-control—the legacy from Makarenko that has constituted the arsenal of treatment tools for Soviet welfare personnel for the past 30 years. However, the view that some conflicts require dealing with the "unconscious" is still not widely accepted.

The social services provided for children reveal the contradictions in the regime's position concerning the family. On the one hand, it would like to remove an ever-increasing number of children from families to community institutions, because this would free mothers for work, would provide rearing by professionals rather than by parents, and would result in more children being raised as "new Soviet men" rather than as "individualists." On the other hand, it is faced with the fact that full-time institutional care is very expensive, and that "something irreplaceably valuable in the personality and moral development of the child"[4] may be lost if the family's role in child-rearing is drastically diminished. Parents, on the whole, want to keep their children with them (while at the same time they are eager for better facilities and services for their children), and many educators are not in agreement with the official ideology. How to give the child an upbringing that is social and collective and at the same time keeps the family intimately involved remains to be determined.

Administrative inefficiencies in Soviet welfare programs are apparent everywhere. Services often originate far away from the area or person they are intended for, adding to the frustrations of the poor and sick. Mistakes are not always rectified by the appeals machinery, especially when this involves the exercise of judgment on the part of incompetent administrators, which increases the possibility of unjust decisions. There are also evidences of rigidity, a tendency to ignore needs that have not been planned for, a failure to recognize genuine differences in individuals, and an adherence to outmoded ways of doing things. Research often deals with problems that are of importance only to administrators, and neglects problems of importance to welfare recipients. Experimentation whose outcomes might threaten preconceived notions is often avoided. There are few evaluative analyses, which means, among other things, that poor practices and programs are continued for many years without modifications. Advances in knowledge often remain unincorporated into welfare practices for extended periods. Red tape prevents even the most devoted and able administrators and workers from making their ministrations prompt and effective. Mass operations, such as calculation and issuance of social insurance benefits, are handicapped by reliance on hand processes in the absence of machines.

Many Soviet welfare personnel are underpaid, overworked, and poorly trained. Positions in the welfare field have not been made attractive in terms of salary, status, or opportunity for advancement; hence, turnover is still high in some areas. In-service training, while extensive, is uneven in quality. Many administrators are political appointees who are skilled neither in administration nor in the technical aspects of welfare services. Progress toward greater recognition for social welfare agencies and personnel is hampered by their exclusion from the highest levels of government. This accounts in part for the insufficiency of the resources allocated to welfare, resulting, for example, in an inadequate number of institutional facilities for the aged and invalided, in overcrowding of schools for the retarded, and in the generally shabby condition of many welfare offices and facilities.

The effect of these weaknesses is to substantially reduce the social welfare agencies' ability to prevent "social anomalies" and to "return to productive life everyone who has strayed" from it. In almost every welfare program the substance of what is done falls far short of what the policies are designed to accomplish. It is often difficult to carry out these policies either because they are inconsistent with other programs sanctioned by the regime, or because they are in conflict with the needs of those who require welfare services.

What does the preceding analysis reveal about the *major historical continuities and discontinuities* between the pre- and post-Revolutionary functions, problems, and processes of social welfare in the Soviet Union? Just as small, simple societies fulfill the same basic social functions as large, complex ones, so in both the pre- and post-Revolutionary periods social welfare's functions in the Soviet Union have remained the same— to provide services that support and enhance individual and social life, to create conditions essential to the harmonious interaction of individuals and their social environment, and to alleviate or contribute to the alleviation of social problems. The problems have also remained essentially the same: those generated by the social environment, such as poverty, and those originating from internal factors, such as emotional deprivation. Both obstruct the individual in his efforts to use constructively what the environment has to offer. But with modernization there has been a shift in welfare emphasis from a concern with visible, immediate suffering to a concern with creating the proper conditions for the development of human resources—in other words, from efforts to meet welfare needs as they arise to efforts to prevent the conditions that produce such needs. This emphasis on the development of human resources has required not only a more complete program for meeting basic needs— economic, health, educational, and recreational—but also a recognition that therapy cannot be successful without the support that a substantial fulfillment of basic needs provides.

Changes in welfare programs and practices took place in both the pre- and post-Revolutionary periods, but in the latter the rate of change has been much more rapid and has had much wider and more durable effects. Use has been made of a rational and planned approach to solving social problems—an approach that relies on science rather than on traditions and superstitions, and on goal-oriented comprehensive programs rather than on piecemeal and sporadic responses. In this respect, the Soviet welfare system has moved far away indeed from its pre-Revolutionary counterpart, for throughout its structure there is apparent an effort to institutionalize a rational and planned approach, to train welfare personnel to utilize it in the development of programs, and to devise appropriate techniques for its application.

At the same time, a continuity between the two periods is evident, especially up to 1956, with regard to change: in both there is resistance to the idea of accepting change as normal and to using the tensions and stresses it produces as opportunities for innovation. In the tsarist period, rigidity made the welfare system a barrier to change. Coercion was used to suppress conflicts and to prevent innovations until intolerable conditions, which often led to violence, forced modifications. (The inability of the welfare system to alleviate widespread suffering contributed greatly to the development of the movement that led to the 1917 revolution.) The Soviet regime also has opposed change that challenges its ideological and political assumptions. It too has used coercion to prevent innovation. There has been a gradual advance from opposing change to regulating and controlling it, but it has been slow and painful. It was not until 1956 that the government became appreciably more flexible in its handling of welfare problems and permitted innovations aimed primarily at meeting human needs rather than with meeting state requirements.[5]

It is clear that such flexibility, and the innovations it permits, will continue to be necessary. Social welfare programs, grounded in the philosophy of socialist humanism, are likely to conflict with programs in other fields where there is little concern for the well-being of socially weak groups. Because of the highly complex nature of the components of human development with which welfare programs are concerned, they may be unable to bring about change as rapidly as is possible in other types of programs, and the results of its activities may be more difficult to predict. To the extent that social welfare's values, objectives, and methods are antagonistic to the aims of the regime, to that extent the changes that welfare requires may be subordinated to changes in other programs more consistent with the regime's general goals.

Soviet welfare organizations in their early phase bore a marked resemblance to their pre-Revolutionary predecessors. Immediately after the Revolution, the government tried to merge all welfare organizations into a single bureaucracy. When this proved impractical, separate divisions were reestablished, but these were always subject to control by a central organ. As in tsarist times, control at first was by decree, but as before this resulted in the creation of a vast bureaucracy, reduced effectiveness and efficiency, and increased alienation and apathy.

In recent years, there has been a pronounced willingness to decentralize welfare administration, which is contributing to a decrease in alienation and to an increase in the desire of young people to seek careers within the welfare system. Although the Soviet welfare bureaucracy encourages adherence to rules and regulations for their own sake, it is no longer as inflexible in applying them. There is increasing recognition that organizations develop special needs that cannot always be met by a reliance upon organizational norms, and that maximizing staff productivity through controls and minimizing the dissatisfaction that controls often engender are equally important. Soviet welfare administrators are becoming more skilled at using authority, as well as at using the noneconomic rewards and sanctions that can so significantly affect staff behavior and productivity. Control through norms that require visible conformity is becoming less important; administrators are beginning to rely more upon the development of a sense of responsibility, integrity, and loyalty. The aim is to generate the highest possible degree of commitment—to capitalize on self-oriented interests rather than to depend upon force for compliance. This greater awareness of the range of motives that can underlie compliance is contributing to the professionalization of Soviet welfare services, as well as to an appreciation of the significant role of personal qualities in determining the effectiveness of staff. It has advanced the humanist point of view, which was so lacking in the pre-Revolutionary scene.

However, as yet most Soviet welfare agencies are only partially staffed by professionals, among them many whose training has been brief and unsystematic. Consequently, professional work in welfare settings is subject to considerable control by persons occupying higher positions in the hierarchy, whether or not they are professionals. While other Soviet organizations rely to some degree on other administrative units in the hierarchy in order to fulfill the functions assigned to them, Soviet welfare agencies, because of their semiprofessional status, do not find it easy to obtain cooperation, nor do they often win in the inter-organizational power struggles that determine the allocation of scarce resources. Among other things, this results in less of an access to the material and symbolic rewards that the society has to offer—which was true of welfare agencies in the tsarist era as well.

What at first appears to be a major change wrought by the Revolution—the subordination of voluntary agencies to state control—on closer examination turns out to be a difference in form rather than in content. In pre-Revolutionary Russia, voluntary agencies were administered by persons identified with the state, and the distance between the state and the community remained great and unbridged. The voluntary agencies that have developed in the Soviet period are closely allied with state institutions and are entrusted with the performance of only minor functions. Both the tsarist and the Soviet regimes have regarded voluntary agencies as adjuncts to the state, and what they have been able to achieve has often been despite, rather than because of, the central authorities. Community participation in the Soviet period, as an effort to bridge the distance between the state and the community, has been only partially successful. In both the tsarist and Soviet periods there have been tensions in the relationships between recipients of welfare services and the state. In both the recipient has found it easier to work with the welfare worker who "bends the rules" than with the worker who rigidly follows the rules.

Soviet welfare organizations have encouraged the development of informal relationships to an appreciably greater extent than was the case in the tsarist period. At times informal groups have even hindered the achievement of state goals. On occasion they have wielded enough influence to bring about changes in the formal welfare structure, in its rules and procedures. Here and there informal leaders have challenged those whose leadership is exercised through formal, organizational positions. Thus, as American social scientists have noted, the individual through his informal relationships may be able to bring about changes in structures where the individual seemingly is of little importance. Similarly, organizations that are internally undemocratic may, by avoiding wasteful internal strife, be more effective than democratic groups in attaining democratic goals.

An area in which discontinuity between the two periods is sharp is the extent of personal involvement of people in social welfare. As noted, in the pre-Revolutionary period individual donations of goods and money for welfare purposes were widespread. But they represented for the most part a desire to do one's duty as a Christian (and in the case of many of the largest donors, to gain prestige and power) and at the same time avoid personal involvement. In the Soviet period, individual donations of goods and money for welfare purposes (except in emergencies such as World War II) have almost completely ceased. People who need assistance now receive it from public, that is, collective funds. However, the termination of this kind of individual assistance has led to greater emphasis on personal involvement when participating in welfare activities. An indigenous nonprofessional who assists welfare personnel in work with the aged, a member of a patronage committee attached to a children's institution, or a volunteer who involves himself in the daily life of a blind person is expected to be warm and understanding. This kind of involvement is more likely to lead to the development of a more constructive and enduring welfare system than the "giving" of pre-Revolutionary days, even when kind and generous, ever could have.

This analysis of the continuity and discontinuity between social welfare as it developed in tsarist Russia and Soviet societies helps us to see more clearly some of its present characteristics. In recognizing the influence of the environment on the personality and yet insisting that the individual is expected to meet society's demands, Soviet welfare appears to regard human nature as a mixture of good and evil that is subject to change through both external and internal influences. In its reliance on the rational powers and work-oriented treatment methods to develop human potential, Soviet welfare rejects the view that suffering automatically confers a right to assistance on the afflicted person, whether or not he acts to extricate himself from it. Rather, it follows the principle that only those who help themselves are entitled to help from others. This is vividly illustrated in the treatment of the physically disabled. Rehabilitation is based on the assumption that the disabled individual wants to get well and wants to make the most of his capacities within the restrictions set by his impairment. The emphasis is on the healthy aspects of his personality and life situation rather than on the limitations imposed by his disability; while it is conceded that these limitations may result in behavior that is different from the behavior of normal persons, it is insisted that they will not produce motivations that will be different from those of normal people. It is on this basis that the disabled person is taught to see his role in the community. The community, in turn, is taught to accept the unusual behavior that may result from disability, but is led to expect that the disabled person will play an active part in community life, not merely suffer. Mutual acceptance, rather than isolation and rejection, is the objective.

Another illustration of this approach in welfare practice is the treatment of juvenile delinquents. Insofar as their deviance is intolerable to the community, delinquents become outcasts and suffer. Soviet welfare workers recognize that standards for judging deviance vary from one community to another and from one set of judges to another. It is generally agreed that internal factors frequently cause deviance, among which are a low degree of commitment to approved goals, and acquired abilities that are low in comparison to potential capacities. (There is less agreement on the relation of innate capacity to deviance.) These views are reflected in rehabilitation practices primarily through the non-judgmental attitudes of welfare personnel that protect the delinquent from destructive group pressures. It is assumed that the deviant wants to re-enter society and to prepare himself for constructive participation by modifying his behavior in accordance with social norms, rather than to continue the suffering that his deviance imposes. It is on the basis of these assumptions that he is allowed to return to society, and that his reentry is explained to the community. This explanation decreases community hostility; at the same time it obligates the community to act to minimize the effects of its intolerance on the individual's sense of identity, status, and career chances. It may even make the community realize that group standards on the basis of which rewards and punishments are meted out are not invariably right from the individual deviant's point of view, and that unless they are changed, the resistance to them will continue. However, more often than in the case of the disabled, both remain ambivalent about mutual acceptance: sometimes the community's relations with the deviant are free of tension, and it supports a reasonable treatment program; at other times, guilt feelings and hostility are generated that incline the group to develop punitive attitudes.

Another illustration of the Soviet philosophy of social welfare is the child-rearing techniques it encourages. Within families and in settings outside the home, welfare practice is designed to condition the child for responsible social participation, to prepare him for the tasks that are expected of him according to his capacity. The child is encouraged to work to make a contribution to society. His work is measured by standards appropriate to his strength and skill; in this way he learns how to make a sensible evaluation of his achievement. Because adults likewise are expected to contribute to society through work, this approach arouses in the child the desire to share adult responsibility, to connect his world with the world of adults. It also helps the child to perceive discipline as reasonable and desirable rather than as a method for forcing him into submission and subjecting him to the dominance of adults. It is by orienting the child to what Florence R. Kluckhohn calls "doing"—rather than to "being" or "being-in-becoming"—that Soviet welfare strives to achieve continuity during the life cycle. This orientation also seems to echo Piaget's teaching that for the child a sense of ethics and justice is anchored first in acceptance of adult authority, to be replaced at a later stage by acceptance of social interdependence, and, finally, of social solidarity. Preparation of children for sexual experience is a more complex matter. This presents special, difficult problems for welfare, just as for the society as a whole. The assumption that children do not become interested in sexual experience until they have matured physically does not seem to make it any easier for the Soviet welfare worker to deal with the essential problem posed long ago by Ruth Benedict—namely, that the child be taught nothing he must unlearn later. Welfare workers stress the reproductive rather than the pleasurable aspects of sex, but it is not clear that this emphasis prevents the child from associating sex with wickedness.

Soviet welfare practice involves the assumption that the family remains one of the most important systems for imposing culture patterns on the individual. Like the society, social welfare places a high value on family self-sufficiency and independence when these attributes are coupled with the ability to meet social expectations. Welfare practice reflects the changes, especially geographic and social mobility, that have made of the contemporary Soviet family a modified extended unit linked to the social structure by friendships and kin contacts, and have eliminated some of its so-called "traditional" functions. Of special concern to Soviet welfare agencies are families that do not fulfill their functions of emotional support, socialization, and social control. In some families, husband-wife and parent-child relationships have been adversely affected by the individualism that modernization fosters; in others, there are signs of apathy and alienation because significant emotional ties severed by family mobility have not been replaced. Soviet welfare agencies, increasingly aware of these problems, have become less inclined to condemn and to make demands that are beyond families' ability to meet. A greater appreciation of the parents' role in the life of their children and a more realistic appraisal of the difficulties experienced by parents in fulfilling this role have led welfare agencies to expand their protective, supportive, and complementary services, and to replace the family only as a last resort.

The collectivist philosophy of the Soviet regime is best exemplified in the welfare system's use of small groups to influence the individual. Less successful has been the use of community participation. On the one hand, social participation by large groups is facilitated by the fact that it contributes to the drive for modernization that is an unmistakable feature of Soviet culture. On the other hand, such mass participation is hindered by social stratification—an equally prominent feature of the Soviet social scene. Social stratification leads to apathy and hostility on the part of those with less prestige and fewer privileges, and lessens their motivation to participate. This situation is exacerbated by the fact that Soviet citizens are denied the power to make decisions in many major areas of life, to question judgments handed down from above, and to effectively influence their social circumstances. The Soviet regime demands of its people a high degree of order, unity, and acquiescence; it stresses adjustment to conditions determined by those in power, those "who know best."

Soviet social welfare programs have of course had an influence on Soviet culture; although it is often obscure, it is nonetheless discernible. While these programs have relied heavily on environmental influences, they have directed attention to the importance of dealing with internal factors. In this way, social welfare practice has led to a recognition that inherent capacities have an importance almost equal to that of environment in determining an individual's potentialities for development. While acknowledging man's ability to control his behavior by use of reason, social welfare personnel have noted that there are limits to what reason, in combination with science and technology, can do. In this way, they have made the society aware of the need to make allowances for the "unconscious," the irrational, and the unpredictable. Dedicated to helping troubled, poor, and handicapped people here and now, social welfare has shown the importance of present as opposed to future-oriented needs, as well as the importance of feelings, desires, and impulses that are not clearly in line with the social concept of "success" toward which everyone is expected to strive. In this way, it has helped to create a pluralistic view of life. Increasingly concerned with people as many-faceted and unique individuals, rather than as undifferentiated producers and consumers, social welfare on occasion places a higher value on individual than on group considerations. In this way, it has broadened somewhat the area for individual independence and has shown that demands for cooperative action are not appropriate in all circumstances, but only as a response to group problems. Social welfare has also maintained that cooperative action should be required only after it has been ascertained that the claims of other individuals upon one's time and resources are legitimate, as opposed to having to prove to one's fellows and to oneself that one has good cause for not committing one's time and resources to community efforts. Social welfare has contributed to the opening of channels of communication between the Party and government leaders and those who experience the deficiencies of welfare policies in their daily lives—those at the bottom of the social ladder. Discussion of welfare problems is more widespread and proposals from ordinary citizens concerning them more numerous than in many other areas of Soviet life, often preventing an unceremonious imposition of policy from above. There can be no doubt that social welfare is contributing to the democratization of Soviet society.

The Future

What can the United States and the Soviet Union learn from each other's experience with social welfare?

An attempt to answer this question should be preceded by noting that the progress in social welfare for which the Russian people have paid such a high price is unique in the sense that the Soviets had much less to work with when they came to power in 1917 than did the Western democracies at that time, they had to fight a costly civil war from which they did not recover for almost a decade, and they were met with hostility, rather than with offers of assistance, from almost all directions. But it is not unique in the sense that they have accomplished more in the 50 years that followed their assumption of power than has any other nation. On the contrary, Soviet progress has been matched by advances in the welfare field occurring throughout the world in the twentieth century.

In the United States, for example, the right to a decent standard of living was acknowledged by the Social Security Act of 1935 (since extended in almost every session of Congress), and clearly established as a national policy in the antipoverty and economic opportunity legislation of 1964. Legislation of the past 30 years has resulted in higher benefits, a broadening of the philosophy of human rights, and the provision of more effective social services. Included in this general advance have been arrangements for public assistance to needy persons who do not qualify for social insurance and for those whose social insurance grants fall below a decent minimum standard. Public welfare agencies make cash payments to millions of needy persons, administer publicly financed medical care and health services for large numbers, provide child welfare services, give employment counseling, place employable needy persons in work and training programs and administer such programs, and provide a variety of special services for the aged and the disabled, whether needy or not. All this has combined to give government a dominant role in social welfare: in 1965–66, tax revenues paid for 85.4 per cent of all expenditures on social insurance, public assistance, and social services. Social welfare expenditures as a percentage of the gross national product rose from 9.3 in 1934–35 to 12.3 in 1965–66.[6] In recent years, and especially since 1964, there has been a pronounced emphasis on programs that aim to increase employability and the capacity for self-support and self-care. At the same time, voluntary agencies have strengthened the services that they are uniquely qualified to offer. (However, there is a need to coordinate public welfare activities with those in the voluntary sector.) Treatment methods have become more effective in returning people to productive lives, as well as in assisting them to achieve richer social relationships. A profession of social work has been developed, with a special body of knowledge taught to selected students in postgraduate courses in universities throughout the country. Funds for social work research have become increasingly abundant, so that much important new knowledge is being acquired. Closer association between social work, other professions, and the social sciences is bearing fruit in deepened insights into social problems and more effective welfare practices. Old ways of doing things are being reexamined and changed in order to deal with new conditions, and community acceptance and understanding of social work are gradually increasing.

Similar developments have taken place in other Western democracies. The Beveridge Report that appeared in England in 1942 has exerted a profound influence on that country's entire system of social services. It put an end to the rule of poor laws, substituting for them a comprehensive system of income maintenance for every risk that diminishes, inter-

rupts, or cuts off income in industrial societies; it led to the establishment of a national health service that provides an impressive array of
medical benefits; and it resulted in the creation of a program of family
allowances. England has also developed a constructive network of social
services for families and children based upon experimentation and research findings. Especially significant have been its contributions to
knowledge about what children need from parents in order to develop
properly, and how what children need can best be provided when their
own parents are unable to fulfill their roles adequately. France's program
of family allowances is one of its major achievements in social welfare.
Not only has French society accepted the idea that children are entitled
to security, but it believes that children should be privileged beneficiaries.
Sweden has led in developing singularly constructive attitudes toward
persons suffering the consequences of deviant behavior—such as delinquents and unmarried mothers—and in creating for such persons therapeutic services that are readily accessible and do not involve humiliation
or hostility.

It should also be emphasized that the weaknesses that exist in the Soviet welfare system are not unique. For example, these same weaknesses
exist in the United States, though sometimes in a modified form. In the
United States there are many more social services available in urban than
in rural communities.[7] Some services are so inadequate that they can
have only a feeble impact.* Social insurance provisions do not cover all
people for all risks,[8] and are often inadequate in amount or in duration,
or both.[9] Unlike all other major industrial countries, the United States
still does not have family allowances, which contributes to the fact that
many children continue to be "born under the poorest circumstances,
live in the most unhealthful homes, and have access to only the most
limited cultural and educational opportunities."[10] In 1966, after an unprecedented period of prosperity and steadily rising income, a fourth
of the nation's children were living in poverty or in conditions only
barely above the poverty line. Public assistance very seldom provides
needy families with funds adequate for a standard of living as high as
the poverty minimum. (This standard varies widely from state to state.)
There are arbitrary differences in the treatment of different categories
of needy persons—a situation that places children at an especially serious disadvantage. The methods for determining eligibility and amount
of assistance are humiliating and demoralizing. In the view of some, the
detailed information these methods require constitutes an invasion of

---

* For example, in 1965 public school enrollment exceeded 41,000,000. In 1960 there
were 2,370 school social workers. Hence, the national average was about one social worker
for every 14,000 children enrolled in the public schools.

the legal and constitutional rights of needy people that results in a system of family law for the public assistance client different from that which applies to the rest of the community. All this discourages efforts at self-support, tends to immobilize people in poverty, and diminishes resources that should be spent on constructive social services, backed up by the provision of education, medical care, recreation, and work. It is no wonder that experts consider the government itself "a major source of the poverty on which it has declared unconditional war."[11] It is also held by many that the administrative structure of welfare programs in the United States is clumsy in the extreme. Some critics note that the involvement of two and often three levels of government in program administration, and the proliferation of special purpose federal grants-in-aid, each with its own terms, requirements, and methods of assuring conformity, restrict the freedom of the states and localities to develop their own policies and involve an appalling amount of red tape. The federal role is too large, or too concerned with minutiae. Other critics claim, on the contrary, that the federal government does not play as great a role as its financial commitments and national responsibilities demand. All seem to agree, however, that the help offered by income-maintenance programs in the United States is not equally available to all those whose economic and social condition falls below the "poverty" level; in many instances it is not provided in such a way as to best serve the interests either of those helped or of the society as a whole; and the organizational and jurisdictional arrangements that prevail do not lend themselves to the development of the most effective policies.[12]

There is widespread concern in the United States about the "ineffectiveness" of social workers in handling social problems and preventing the conditions that breed them. The objectives of social workers are criticized for being vague,[13] and new ways are being sought "to meet social and economic needs in programs of enhancement, prevention, and rehabilitation that do not depend so heavily upon individualized professional social work services."[14] It is observed that many low income people cannot grasp the notion that a person can improve his circumstances through a better understanding of himself and of the way he contributes to his own problems. Nor do they have the middle class background necessary to benefit from social work techniques that are based upon introspection, insight, and verbalization. Social workers are being urged to make wider use of the technique of "learning-by-doing," rather than strictly verbal approaches to problem-solving,[15] and to stress self-help possibilities among low income people.[16] Recent research has cast doubt on the notion that depriving a young child of maternal care *necessarily* has grave permanent effects,[17] and has shown that many children are undersocialized when forced to depend entirely on their own parents for social stimulation. It is now believed that even infants benefit from a wide range of experience outside the immediate family—experience that quickens their imaginations as well as contributes to their emotional and social growth.

The social work profession has not significantly affected the quality of welfare services in the United States, and social workers have not been assigned positions of leadership in a number of endeavors that are clearly social welfare programs.[18] A comparison of the salaries of social workers with the salaries paid to holders of master's degrees in both technical and nontechnical positions in business and industry shows that, despite similarities in preparatory education, the starting salaries in business and industry are considerably higher than in social work. In addition, dissatisfaction with social work education is evident. There are too few professionals for the needs at hand, and social workers are being warned that "if we hesitate to experiment and effect indicated changes, the profession of social work could lose the confidence of the community and be relegated to a narrow service and clerical role."[19]

One thing about social welfare that the Soviet Union and the United States can learn from each other is that there will always be a considerable difference between the "ideal" welfare system planned and the system that actually emerges in the process of implementing the model. This is so not only because in a dynamic society the "ideal" is always being modified, but also because no society can exercise complete control over social development. A second thing to be learned is that it is increasing industrialization, rather than "democracy" or "totalitarianism," that will primarily determine the nature of the society of the future—a future in which all advanced countries will face more or less the same social problems.[20] Many of the changes that come with industrialization, such as a rise in educational standards, secularization, increasing occupational specialization, and the dominance of science, are likely to lead to wider recognition of the need for effective social services. Other changes, such as increases in social and geographic mobility, a decline in the role of the family, and the physical and psychological strains of modernization, may make social welfare's task more difficult. A third thing that the two societies can learn from each other is that there will always be a need for a social welfare system. Social welfare helps create a social climate that gives people a sense of security, order, identity, and belonging, and thereby fulfills basic needs.[21] Social welfare is a response to the human condition, and the growing complexity of life resulting from industrialization increases the necessity for it.

Certain aspects of social work experience in the United States might be instructive for Soviet welfare personnel. One is the American willingness to investigate, experiment, and evaluate, no matter what the consequences for the "establishment," and the concern above all with the needs and possibilities of people rather than with ideologies. For example, the Soviets might do well to study American programs of short-term foster family care, adoption, and integrated services for "defective" children—programs that have not always come up to expectations, but which nevertheless have been beneficial for many children. This may increase Soviet awareness of what can be accomplished through a variety of approaches.

In addition, the Soviets might benefit from studying the ways diagnosis is used in the United States for gaining a deeper understanding of the client, and for determining a treatment for him that will have lasting effects. It might be helpful for them to note that in American treatment procedures a considerable amount of freedom is encouraged in purely personal matters, while protection is provided against fears and anxieties that may arise when individuals attempt to act on their own. Soviet welfare personnel might increase their knowledge of emotional processes and see how this knowledge can be incorporated into the client-worker relationship, where it becomes an additional tool in treatment. Acquaintance with the American method of community organization, and all that it implies with regard to social change, social participation, and social goals, might yield many useful insights as well.

Another area in which American experience might be helpful to Soviet welfare personnel is in the establishment of a profession of social work—a development that the differentiation of functions inherent in modernization appears to make inevitable. Study of professional social work organizations and social work education in the United States will reveal how professional functions can be precisely differentiated and rationally distributed among personnel with different skills, as well as how these skills can be taught.

American welfare personnel might find it instructive to observe Soviet methods for incorporating into social welfare the notion that first priority should be assigned to making the basic system function properly, as opposed to emphasizing the rehabilitation of those with problems. Also of value would be a study of the Soviet methods for achieving comprehensiveness in their welfare programs. This might be helpful in facilitating the shift, currently in progress in the United States, from stress on changing the personality to changing the conditions of life, from concern with personal maladjustments to concern with social maladjustments.

Americans might also benefit by studying Soviet programs for children whose parents are unable to fulfill their proper roles in an increasingly complex society. Especially profitable might be studies of long-term foster family care, semi-institutional arrangements such as extended-day schools, and institutional care for infants and children. Insight into what can be achieved by the latter might encourage Americans to look upon institutions not merely as a last resort, but as the best setting for certain kinds of children with certain kinds of problems.

Americans might do well to observe how Soviet welfare personnel translate concepts such as "improving social functioning" or "strengthening family life" into practices that bear directly on problems presented by clients. It might be equally beneficial to see how the Soviets use the conscious elements of the personality in the therapeutic process, and how they strengthen the influence of reason in the person being treated. It might also be useful to compare their use of the direct, assertive approach that protects the client from being left on his own with the more subtle, insight-oriented procedures that sometimes leave the client confused and vulnerable. Observation of the effects of work therapy might also be of value to welfare personnel in the United States. It might help them to deal with one of the worst effects of automation—the isolation of a growing number of people from a form of social participation whose positive values cannot be easily replaced; it may even enable them to answer the question whether man must work to live decently.[22]

Finally, what does the Soviet experience suggest for underdeveloped countries that wish to attain decent levels of social well-being at the same time as they industrialize?

Perhaps the first lesson to be learned from the Soviet experience is that the transformation of traditional, agrarian societies into modern, industrial states is in many ways an immensely destructive process. Not only are governments, ruling classes, and systems of belief destroyed, but social institutions, personal values, and the psychological security of the individual are undermined. Social scientists have found that even in societies that were the first to modernize, where change has taken place gradually over a period of many generations, the destructive effects of modernization are quite pronounced. In the Soviet Union, which modernized rapidly and under great pressure, a huge price was exacted. At some points, traditional institutions and values were destroyed before modern replacements were available. Developing countries can learn from this that it is essential to provide some protection against the destructive impact of industrialization. If decent levels of social well-being are to be attained simultaneously with industrialization, resources must be allocated to social welfare on a continuing basis, rather than sporadically.

Whether or not totalitarianism is inevitable for an underdeveloped country intent on rapid industrialization is still a debatable question. However, many social scientists agree—and Soviet experience supports the view—that efforts to industrialize rapidly strengthen the totalitarian components in a system of rule. Soviet experience also shows that such strengthening is accompanied by an undercurrent of discontent with the sacrifices that have to be borne, and that aspirations for individual well-being can be only temporarily suppressed, not eliminated. Industrialization creates a revolution of rising expectations. Much of Soviet social welfare progress has been a response to these expectations; the fact that the regime is constantly promising higher levels of well-being for all in the not-too-distant future indicates that these expectations continue to rise, and that no government that wishes to remain in power can ignore them. For underdeveloped countries this means that the better part of wisdom—from the point of view of ensuring government stability, as well as from concern with social well-being—is to build adequate social welfare provisions into the basic machinery of the body politic, rather than to treat such provision as something to be wrested from the state under pressure.

Industrialization entails urbanization, and this, among other things, means that the family, no longer rural and extended, cannot care for the sick, the aged, and the incompetent, and cannot provide formal education for the young, work for the handicapped, or recreation. Not only does the state have to take over these functions, but in the Soviet view, it should. The Soviets have not permitted voluntary welfare organizations to significantly diminish the power and authority of the state in the welfare field: as already noted, such organizations are for the most part adjuncts to the state rather than independent, self-governing bodies. This takeover of welfare functions obligates the state to guarantee the citizen's welfare, and most Soviet citizens believe that what makes the Soviet form of government more desirable than the "capitalist" form is that the former is willing and able to meet people's welfare needs, whereas the latter purportedly neither can nor wishes to do so. To a considerable extent this explains why there has been wider approval among the people of what the government has done in the welfare field than of what it has done in other sectors, such as agriculture or foreign policy. What underdeveloped countries can learn from Soviet experience is that the significance of industrialization for the ordinary citizen will center primarily on what it can do to promote his individual well-being. The Soviet experience also demonstrates that conditions that usually accompany industrialization—especially a falling birth rate and a growing demand for highly trained personnel—require that people live longer and that they remain healthy, contented, and engaged in socially useful work. This means that the state has to be prepared to steadily expand its welfare services, and that it cannot lightly ignore welfare considerations in favor of others that may seem weightier to the leaders, such as solidifying or extending their own power.

Underdeveloped countries can learn from Soviet experience that in the division of resources between welfare services aimed primarily at meeting immediate needs and services aimed at developing human potential and preventing social problems (assuming resources are insufficient to finance both adequately) emphasis ought to be placed on the latter. Programs for dealing with immediate needs cannot be effective unless they are integrated with basic services accessible to all. Most important, Soviet experience teaches that welfare services must be administered in a manner acceptable to the recipients: welfare assistance is not acceptable to people who need help if material values are emphasized at the expense of the dignity of the individual and if those who can no longer contribute to the wealth of the community are seen as burdensome and unimportant.

Underdeveloped countries can learn from the Soviets that it is inadvisable to attempt to use the welfare system primarily for ideological or political purposes. Nor should the system be forced to adhere rigidly to a view of man that makes impossible a diversity of approaches to social problems. The Soviet view of man fails to treat adequately all of man's essential attributes and their relation to each other; this is also true of other views of man. Neither the concept of the non-existent "Soviet man" nor the equally nebulous "true Christian" enables a society to achieve a satisfactory balance between the fulfillment of personal and social needs. Social welfare must be based upon a concept of man broad enough to allow for a diversity of approaches to the problems people face, without resulting in chaos, which itself leads to instability and violence.

Underdeveloped countries, with their more "traditional" family patterns, have much to learn from Soviet experience with regard to family welfare policy. They can see that changes brought about by industrialization inevitably lead to greater freedom for women, to a decline in parental authority, and to increased social and geographic mobility—all factors that may weaken family ties. However, Soviet experience shows that it is unwise to attempt to replace the constructive influence of family life—especially of the warm, rich texture of emotional experience that it alone can offer—by rearing children in state institutions. Rather, underdeveloped countries should stress, as the Soviets now do, the development of programs that help parents to fulfill their roles more effectively and to derive greater satisfaction from it. Community facilities should be sufficiently diversified and accessible that all parents can use them. Equally important, it should be made clear that these facilities are made available primarily for the welfare of the children, and not for purposes of indoctrination by those in power.

That the achievement of desired results in social welfare is facilitated by careful planning—a process that involves compromise and sometimes the sacrifice of short-range gains that are incompatible with long-range or overall goals—is clearly apparent from Soviet experience. However, the Soviets have not yet shown how planning can be used to motivate people to take the initiative and to be creative, rather than to acquiesce in a manner that in some instances borders on apathy. Nor have they succeeded in developing plans that meet the variety of needs people have; rather they ignore those needs that do not fit into pre-established categories. That much is to be gained from decentralized welfare administration, when it is coupled with access to the financial resources of the central government, is also evident from the Soviet experience. However, welfare practice in the Soviet Union indicates that there must be a certain amount of central control in order to prevent local communities from becoming complacent and from regarding local difficulties as permanent obstacles to change. Soviet central organs have contributed much by setting standards, disseminating knowledge, and stimulating experimentation.

Since welfare services in underdeveloped countries will be plagued by acute shortages of professional personnel, Soviet experience with in-service training and with the use of indigenous nonprofessionals can be instructive for them. These countries might also profit by investigating the possibilities of community participation as a way of providing simple supportive services to people who need outside emotional sustenance in order to handle their daily affairs. However, the underdeveloped countries need to be made aware of the difficulties, vividly demonstrated by Soviet experience, involved in making community participation a genuinely constructive method for providing mutual aid rather than a method for exerting punitive group pressures and for justifying intrusions into private life.

In the background of all these speculations about the future of social welfare is the awesome possibility of nuclear war. Fear of such war not only threatens what has been achieved with difficulty, but diverts needed resources, saps the will, and stifles the imagination needed for the achievement of higher standards of well-being for all people and the fulfillment of man's highest aspirations. The preservation of peace is thus the primary concern of social welfare everywhere, as it has been ever since men recognized that their survival and progress depended on what they can do for, and not against, each other.

Appendixes

Appendixes

Appendix A

A CLINICAL FACILITY FOR NERVOUS CHILDREN

This facility near Moscow for nervous children suffering from "improper" social conditions is under the direction of a young female physician. It serves children from grades 1 to 4 inclusive, with two sections for each grade. The children are admitted from Moscow and its suburbs, via referral from psycho-neurological outpatient facilities; they are considered normal children, intellectually and physically. The staff consists of doctors with a specialization in "nervous" conditions, a speech therapist, nurses, and teachers. There are two consultants who come on alternate weeks, though sometimes they are present together. They handle between 10 and 12 cases each month. Classes average 18 to 23 children, and the upbringers, who are in charge before and after classes, are responsible for about 10 children each. Altogether, there are 15 teachers and upbringers for 106 children. During the regular school year, children stay for three months; in summer, they stay for six weeks. The object is to give each child a thorough diagnostic examination. Treatment consists of medication, corrective physical exercises, an individualized pedagogical program, and individual psychotherapy when indicated (group psychotherapy is not practiced). Parents are usually consulted, but no treatment of them is attempted: they serve only as a source of information about a child's developmental history and school achievement. A case study of a child who was suspected of mental retardation is given below.

Pavlik: Age 10, First Grade Repeater

At one time Pavlik had rickets; he is now suffering from an organic defect of the palate that makes his speech difficult to understand; he is enuretic.

At times he cries bitterly when asked about his mother, who is in jail for stealing money from her place of employment; at other times he is almost boastful about her incarceration. He bothers the other children, disorganizes their games; he does not participate in group activities; he always has a silly smile on his face; he shrugs his shoulders when he is asked questions; he makes a peculiar movement of closing and opening his lips; when somebody praises him or is kind to him (as when he was ill and spent some time in the isolation ward, or when he was praised for completing a small task in the classroom), he becomes extremely grateful, and will stroke and kiss the hand of the person who was kind.

P.'s father is an alcoholic, and is known to have beaten and mistreated the boy. The boy's maternal grandmother has come to Moscow to stay with the father and the boy. When P. was asked what his father does, he answered that his father sings at the Bolshoi Theater: in fact, the father is a carpenter at the Bolshoi.

P. is a small, pale, hunched child—rather pathetic. When brought in for examination, where he was surrounded by more than a dozen women clad in white, he was altogether unable to perform: he froze, and only his lips moved in his peculiar smacking motion. He could not smile. The whole experience was an obvious torture for him; it was almost unbearable—the tension and the unhappiness. The consultant pronounced the boy retarded, and the plan made for him was to return him to his family and to have him attend a "special" school. It was suggested by the consultant that during his remaining time in the facility the boy be treated with "a little psychotherapy."

Examination of the record and questions to the chief physician established that neither the boy's father, mother, or grandmother had been seen. Information about the boy's social circumstances had been given by a neighbor woman. I asked whether the diagnosis of retardation might not be premature, since the consultant herself had suggested that the boy might be reacting to trauma produced by his mother's incarceration. I also expressed concern about the decision to return the child "home," without the slightest knowledge about what this might mean for him. I asked whether a foster home—*patronat*—could be considered, since it was agreed that P. was a love-starved youngster who had had a very bare and deprived existence. The chief physician and the consultant conceded that after a period of warm, individualized care, a more correct determination of P.'s intellectual status could be made. They grasped the possibilities, but this was for the future, perhaps—not for P.

Comment. Note should be taken of the relative paucity of background social data, as compared, for example, with a carefully detailed medical history. The case makes clear that treatment may be severely hampered by lack of diversified resources and administrative rigidity. The child is sent back home because substitute parental homes do not exist, and not because it is the best place for him; he is sent to a "special" school because such a school is available, and not because the diagnosis of retardation is firm. The treatment plan also shows that some decisions are determined by considerations other than the child's welfare: the fact that the boy's father could support him played a role, but the quality of interpersonal relationships in the home was ignored. (In the case of children suspected of mental retardation, there are no published norms, and psychological examiners are expected to make clinical judgments on the basis of their experience. Observation makes clear that some of the factors that enter into these judgments are culturally determined, reflecting what the child learned or did not learn in his home.)

Appendix B

Case Study of an Adopted Boy Suspected of Mental Retardation

Twenty-two staff members and trainees of the Institute of Defectology in Moscow participated in a conference concerning Tolia; it was led by a retardation specialist. She stated that T., age 8, was repeating first grade for the third time. He had been under care at the Institute for a year and had been the subject of a similar conference once before. A physician and a special education teacher who had been working intensively with the boy for the past year gave detailed reports that dealt exclusively with the technical aspects of their experience with him.

The conference lasted three hours and developed into a heated argument concerning the diagnosis—infantilism: some took the position that the boy's inability to read and do arithmetic problems at his age level was due to organic damage to the brain; others, including the retardation specialist, insisted that no organic damage was present, but that the normal development of certain brain functions had been arrested. It turned out that they were not quite sure that they were all agreed on the definition of "organic," "functional," and "arrested development"; hence, it was possible they were not using these terms in the same way. It was decided that a special conference on the general subject of retardation was needed, to which authorities in the field should be invited.

The following significant facts emerged:

1. T. spent the first four and one-half years of his life in a children's home. Then his present parents adopted him. Sometime after adoption, he spent six months in a boarding kindergarten, where he remained full time except for weekends. No information was provided about why this arrangement had been made or how the child had reacted to it.

2. All agreed that T. was "typical" of the children who come from "homes." (The Institute staff had had considerable experience with such children.) Children in these institutions are not raised in as constructive an environment as children who live in their own homes. They are less developed from a social point of view, even though their intellectual growth may not be impaired.

3. No data concerning T. were furnished by the home, which, like many others, had poor records. (Note: The boy was placed in the institution in 1956, that is, ten years after the war. Wartime pressures and disorganization could not have been the cause for the total lack of information.) Neither were data of any kind available about the adoption itself and post-adoptive developments, some of which, at least, could have been given by the adoptive parents themselves. It was explained that at the time the family consisted of the father, mother, and maternal grandmother. The mother was a very competent teacher who had been completely cooperative in carrying out the instructions of the special education teacher about helping the boy with his homework; the grandmother cared for the boy when he came home from school. Not a word was said about the father—nobody had ever talked with him. As a matter of fact, the discussion of the social milieu took exactly three minutes. When one of the conference participants, a psychologist, briefly referred to this paucity of information, nobody paid attention to her. A young woman, a trainee, sitting next to me said: "Please, let's not bring in the parents." She wanted to stick strictly to technical matters, medical and pedagogical.

4. The grandmother, who had brought the boy in, was asked to come into the conference room, at which point the retardation specialist requested that she not be "traumatized," without further explaining what she meant. The grandmother, a tall, gray woman, relatively well dressed, was obviously nervous and embarrassed; nobody offered her a chair, and she sat down on a windowsill. In answer to a question about the boy's studies at home, she said that it was the mother who worked with him—not she. She was allowed to leave after this—the whole futile episode taking about two minutes.

5. While nobody had any illusions about the boy's ability to achieve in a regular school setting, it was decided to continue the current arrangement for the present—chiefly, it seemed, because the mother was willing to work with him intensively at home. During the past year—that is, while the current arrangement was in progress—the boy was said to have become more "rational" in his attitude toward his schoolwork; he still lacked motivation, however.

Appendix C

A BOARDING SCHOOL FOR MUSICALLY GIFTED CHILDREN IN LENINGRAD

This school is administered by the RSFSR Ministry of Education. It was founded in 1948 and is one of 12 such schools in the republic. According to the director, in the whole country there are about 20 such schools.

In March of each year a committee of teachers from the school visits the children's homes and the boarding schools in the 18 regions that come within its jurisdiction, in order to make their selection. They usually select about 200 children, who arrive at the school in June, to be further evaluated by the entire faculty. About 30 children are chosen to remain at the school; the other 170 return to the institutions from which they came.

Currently, there are 300 students at the school, ranging in age from 7 to 18, and divided almost evenly between girls and boys. Since each child attends regular school as well, he carries a double load. Those in the first three grades spend about two hours daily on music, grades 4–6 three hours daily, and grades 6–11 more than three hours. The director said that this heavy schedule does not seem to affect the children adversely; she attributes this to the fact that they are well-fed and spend summer and winter vacations in the country where there is opportunity to work outdoors.

Most of the children are either orphans or come from homes that cannot give them an appropriate upbringing. The others are admitted to the school because their own communities do not offer musical training; their parents pay in accordance with a sliding scale. For the most part, however, expenses are borne by the state. There are 100 teachers, including 20 upbringers, both men and women. Some of the music teachers come from the famous Leningrad Conservatory. There is a doctor, as well as several nurses, and the usual administrative and service personnel. Altogether there are about 500 people either living or working in the school.

The selection committees make mistakes, of course: children considered gifted often turn out to be quite ordinary. These children are returned to the institutions from which they came after two years of musical education. The director does not think this is a traumatic experience for them because their regular school training has not been interrupted. Those who remain at the school are required to become proficient on at least one instrument and must play in ensembles and study musical theory and history.

The students impressed me by the seriousness of their work in music. Many are bright in academic work as well; none fail. Upon graduation, a third, chosen via open competition, enter the Leningrad Conservatory. The other two-thirds become teachers of music in secondary schools or members of orchestras and musical ensembles.

The director said that many of the children are difficult to raise because they are temperamental and have a tendency to think too highly of themselves. She finds them sensitive, and deals with them gently. She thinks that doing farmwork in summer is a good antidote against their becoming self-centered. She said that there is a good collective spirit in the school and that there are no sex problems. The physical plant is extremely old and wretched. However, it was a relief to see, in addition to the usual pictures of Lenin, many portraits of great composers. There has been hope for a new building for some time, but so far nothing has come of it. The director impressed me as being a "motherly" person (she had lost her husband in the Finnish war when she was 23; she has two sons who are sailors) who is genuinely fond of her charges. She also appeared to be a good organizer and a very hard worker. The children appeared generally subdued, simply dressed.

Appendix D
Moscow School for the Deaf

In about 1965, the four schools for the deaf that served Moscow were combined into one. It is located in a new section of the city, characterized by large apartment buildings—all of the same kind—and by the absence of paved streets and sidewalks and landscaping. The school owns a pioneer camp set in beautiful natural surroundings, but the cabins have become so dilapidated that the children are taken to other resorts for the summer. It is hoped that the school will soon have a new country home.

The institution plant does not include living rooms, as distinct from classrooms and sleeping quarters. The director explained that the original plans included living rooms, but the pressure of numbers made it necessary to eliminate them. All pupils who are deaf and cannot learn in mass schools must be accepted. The director hopes that a new building with living rooms will be added to the institution.

Parents pay according to a sliding scale: from nothing for families whose earnings average less than 30 rubles per person per month to 40 rubles per month per student for families whose average earnings are 200 rubles per person or more.

The following attitudes toward parents are evident:

1. The child's family is very important—in fact, irreplaceable. Hence, work toward a close and constructive relationship between parents and child is given major attention and support.

2. Work with parents begins in the kindergarten and continues throughout the child's education at the school. It takes varied forms: individual teachers discuss a particular child's problems with the parents (usually the mother); there are group discussions at which teachers, upbringers, and invited persons participate; literature is provided; there is an active parents' committee that assists school personnel in specific activities—staying with the children at night, helping to keep the school clean, attending classes to learn more about techniques of instruction, dealing with parents who lack interest in their children's progress. Once every year, the children arrange a festive occasion for the mothers for which all preparations, including the making of food, are carried out by the children; they also arrange the graduation exercises. The pleasure that the parents express on these occasions contributes to the child's feeling that his family cares deeply about him.

3. Older students, who can get around by themselves, live at home so that they can have a reasonably normal family life. With regard to the younger children, the director feels that despite working mothers and the hardships of "daily living," a child can nevertheless be brought up in the family if the parents are genuinely interested and if they are helped to organize home activities so that the child is included in them. The important factor is the

quality of family life: it must be a situation in which the child is a full-fledged member who shares the burdens as well as the joys.

4. All the younger children go home on Saturday, and many families are encouraged to take them home in the middle of the week. Some parents are not able to do a good job of upbringing, and for their children the institution is a good place, but most parents are a good influence.

5. In working with parents, the main problem is their feeling that demands on deaf children cannot approximate what is expected of "normal" children. The best way to convince them that this is an error is to show them their children in action. At graduation exercises most parents usually cry for joy; they have never imagined that their handicapped children could participate in life so fully.

Appendix E

HOME FOR THE AGED: TASHKENT, UZBEK REPUBLIC

The home is a two-story building, with several wings connected by corridors; it is surrounded by six hectares of apple orchards and vineyards, their produce used for the inmates and, if there is a surplus, for sale. The building is quite poorly constructed, and toilet facilities, by American standards, are scandalous. The rooms, each for two persons, have windows, a small clothes closet, and a sink with running hot and cold water. Some of the tables in the rooms are covered with newspapers. There is a radio in each room, but no television in the entire institution. On each floor there is a poorly equipped kitchen and a small, bare sitting room. The library contains nothing but newspapers. The main meal on the day of my visit consisted of good soup, terrible macaroni with a few small pieces of meat, fruit jelly, and tea. The kitchen in which the meals are cooked has electric boilers, a bread cutter, one broken dishwasher, and one refrigerator (used only in the hottest weather). The dining room has a stage and a piano: it also serves as a recreation hall.

This is a rest home for pensioners who have outstanding work records. They are selected for entry by a special committee and are permitted to keep their entire pensions while in the home. The length of stay is three months. In very exceptional cases a pensioner may remain six months, and in a few cases he may come two years in a row. Such exceptions are made for health reasons. There are 250 "resting ones," of whom 138 are women. The staff is supposed to consist of 78 persons, but currently there are 18 vacancies. There is one doctor, one doctor's assistant, one chief nurse, and four assistant nurses. The rest of the staff are administrative and service personnel. The director is a retired tank corps officer who impressed me as a man of discipline who gets things done, and yet who is quite humanitarian and has some insight into people and their problems. He seemed to have the respect of the staff and inmates. In fact, several old ladies praised him highly in his presence.

Inmates are expected to make their own beds and to work outdoors four hours a day, if their health permits.

I was struck by the fact that among the 250 inmates there were only four Uzbek men and one Uzbek woman; the population is almost solidly Russian. The old people were quite lively and very patriotic. They had lived long enough to have experienced both the old and the new regimes, and to be able to compare the two. Several of them told me that nowhere in the world do old people live as well as in the Soviet Union and that there are no pensions for old people from the working class in the United States. I calmly informed them that such pensions exist in the United States and that, in coverage of people, the American system is more extensive than that which existed in the Soviet Union prior to 1965. I suggested that they ask the minister of social welfare of the Uzbek Republic, who had been in the United States, to tell them about the American system. Later, the director and those who accompanied me to the home, begged me to forgive the old people for their ignorance and thanked me for my restraint and kindness in answering them.

Notes

The numbers in italics refer to listings in the Bibliography, pp. 261–91.

Preface

1. *487*, p. iii.
2. *449*, p. 6.
3. *447*, p. 105.
4. *487*, p. vii.
5. *455*, p. 7.
6. *262*, pp. 3–14.
7. *307*, p. 572.

Chapter 1

1. Unless otherwise indicated, the analysis of welfare developments to the end of Catherine's reign is based on *146*, pp. 2–176.

2. *91*, pp. 6–9.

3. *181*, p. 3.

4. *475*, II, 114.

5. Unless otherwise indicated, the material concerning illegitimate children in this chapter is based on *140*.

6. This estimate is based on a variety of data, such as the exact number of children admitted to the Moscow Home and the number that died in the years 1764–67 and 1880–89; exact figures on admissions and deaths in the St. Petersburg Home from the year of its founding until 1905; expenditures by each home in 1904; survival rates for scattered years; the number of children under care for various years; and the number sent to work in factories (*140*; *188*, pp. 58–61; *97*, VII (1895), pp. 274–80; *91*; *93*, pp. 10–11). For a more detailed account of the provisions for illegitimate children under Peter and Catherine, see *242*, pp. 82–96.

7. *332*, pp. 296–302.

8. *97*, XXX (1900), 653, 656–57.

9. *158*, p. 55.

10. *98*, VI, 18; *91*, pp. 42–43.

11. *335*.

12. *268*, pp. 22–43; *400*, p. 603.

13. *52*, X, 62–64.

14. *355*, II, 409–10.

15. *91*, p. 26.

16. *503*, p. 8.

17. *194*, p. 4.

18. *379*, pp. 5–29.

19. *103*, pp. 126–35. Here the regulations governing guardianship, foster care, and adoption in rural communities are explained.

20. *301*, pp. 38–39; *300*, p. 87; *265*, pp. 24–25.

21. *97*, XXV (1898), 482; *98*, XXXIII (1915), 584; *385*, p. 184.

22. *424*, pp. 18–19.

23. *134*, pp. 254–55; *463*, pp. 155–56, 198–200.

24. *465*, I, 437; *191*, pp. 176–77.

25. *439*, p. 110.

26. *22*, pp. 5–6.

27. *226*, pp. 25–30; *269*, pp. 5–6, 13–17; *224*, p. 18.

28. *467*, pp. 75–76; *76*, pp. 5–7; *222*, p. 241; *108*, p. 26n.

29. *342*.

30. *123*, p. 19.

31. See previous references on social insurance. See also *34*, p. 46.

32. *343*, pp. 5–21; *7*, p. 85. For provisions of the 1912 law, see *225*.

33. *479*, pp. 1–3; *195*, p. 8; *439*, pp. 51–52.

34. *316*, p. 5.   35. *161*; *372*.

36. *274*, pp. 7–15, 17–18.   37. *126*, pp. 26–27.

38. The three laws were those of July 25, October 11, and October 17, 1917. See also *473*, pp. 43–45, and *226*, p. 65. Domestics, employees in mercantile establishments and offices, and government, railroad and agricultural workers remained excluded. See *Trud*, April 22, 1922, p. 2.

39. *Voprosy Strakhovaniia*, No. 6–7, pp. 3–4; *470*, pp. 5–6.

40. *158*, p. 50.   41. *335*, pp. 139–40, *347*.

42. *98*, VI, 19.   43. *300*, pp. 7–8.

44. *118*, pp. 3–14.

Chapter 2

1. *60*, p. 3.

2. *9*, p. 5.

3. *509*, pp. 713–28.

4. This paragraph is based on *36*, pp. 79–91. Quotations are from pp. 79 and 90, respectively.

5. *413*, pp. 20–21.

6. *235*, p. 3.

7. *327*, pp. 359, 361–62, 433–34. For a discussion of reflexology by an American scholar, see *230*, pp. 70–73.

8. *139*, p. 9.

9. *392*, p. 14.

10. *15*, "Predislovie" (Introduction), I (1959), 5.

11. *155*, p. 20.   12. *266*, II (1960), 120.

13. *360*, p. 12.   14. *216*, I, 14–15, 20, 25, 34.

15. *462*, p. 33.   16. *Ibid.*, pp. 187–88, 191.

17. *391*, pp. 184–85.   18. *89*, p. 3.

19. *267*, pp. 12, 13.   20. *211*, pp. 38–39.

21. *353*, p. 126.

22. *203*, II (1960), 62. So far, motivation has only rarely been used as an experimental category. Similarly, most of the experiments in children's thinking, imagi-

nation, concept formation, and skills appear to have been designed with teaching objectives in mind. See *110*, p. 102.

23. *260*, p. 254.

24. *376*, p. 7.

25. *156*, p. 44.

26. *94*, p. 165.

27. *90*, pp. 129–30. See *37*, pp. 134–42, for a discussion of certain aspects of the "Russian national character" as seen by Western scholars.

28. *67*, pp. 307–8, 311.

29. *64*, p. 42; *255*.

30. *384*, pp. 133, 151–52.

31. *229*, pp. 227–33.

Chapter 3

1. This concept of the family has always been defended by Soviet authorities who have written on marriage and the family. Among them are *417*, p. 5; *418*, p. 5; *171*, pp. 65–66; *172*, p. 20; *173*, p. 66; *174*, pp. 53–63; *176*, pp. 135–36; *398*. Among Western scholars who have tended to support it may be included *325*, pp. 29–35; *364*, p. 7; *239*, pp. 297–301; *47*, p. 331.

2. Sources of information about legal provisions affecting the family enacted from 1917 to 1956 are *148*, pp. 189–94; *131*, pp. 530–35; *239*; *136*, pp. 246–72; *179*.

3. Some of the better sources for detailed accounts of these laws and regulations are *1*; *2*, pp. 136–60; *358*.

4. *192*, pp. 96–97.

5. *47*, p. 336.

6. *130*, II, 248–78; *135*, p. 424; *396*, pp. 83–94; *474*, pp. 3–5.

7. *206*, p. 28; *460*, p. 11; *458*, pp. 3–27.

8. *126*, p. 107; *501*, pp. 5–15; *85*, pp. 71, 117–18; *20*, pp. 10–30, 120–22; *150*, p. 70; *499*, pp. 55, 60, 61.

9. *189*, p. 9.

10. *202*, p. 1. An account of the famine may be found in *109*.

11. *287*, pp. 126–30.

12. *408*, pp. 52, 64, 71; *457*, pp. 3–14; *394*; *25*, p. 23.

13. *28*, p. 557.

14. *419*, p. 109.

15. *206*, p. 7.

16. *228*, p. 121.

17. *19*, pp. 3–54.

18. Figures for the years 1917–28 are given in *506*, pp. 91–93.

19. There is an enormous amount of material on the homeless. A sampling giving different interpretations of the situation would include *298*, pp. 6–17; *42*; *104*, p. 50; *247*; *382*; *505*; *285*, pp. 3–7; *480*.

20. *367*, pp. 17–19.

21. *43*, pp. 11, 12, 45. On the work of the homes in the Ukraine, see *194*. Another good account is *186*, pp. 52–53, 159.

22. *36*, pp. 41–42.

23. *325*, p. 29.

24. *187*, pp. 45, 58.

25. *297*, pp. 98, 104.

26. *311*, pp. 1, 3.

27. *337*, pp. 3, 7–10.

28. *452*, p. 21.

29. In addition to the literature cited in note 19, especially interesting references include *198*, p. 4; *281*, pp. 4–5; *427*.

30. *93*, pp. 45, 65–66, 107.

31. *261*, p. 9.

32. *393*, pp. 8–32.

33. *421*, p. 6.

34. *175*, pp. 70–71.

35. *277*, pp. 13–15; *215*, pp. 4–5; *176*, pp. 203–4; *398*, p. 147; *322*, pp. 26–27.

36. *173*, p. 94; *284*, pp. 7, 14–15.
37. *418*, p. 10.

Chapter 4

Parts of the material in this chapter are drawn from my earlier publications. See especially *241*, pp. 523–34; *244*, pp. 191–205.

1. *492*; *493*; *Voprosy Strakhovaniia*, No. 9, February 22, 1923, p. 3; *101*, p. 15; *494*, pp. 4–5; *157*, p. 1; *99*, p. 10; *197*, pp. 5–7; *45*; *196*.
2. *213*, p. 427; *24*, pp. 8–9.
3. A voluminous literature on social insurance is available. Among the most helpful works are *196*; *34*; *338*; *147*; *410*; *163*; *1*.
4. *473*. The first extension of social insurance—the introduction of unemployment compensation for some employees in the low and middle income groups—was passed on December 11, 1917. On December 22, 1917 such benefits were extended to all employed persons in these income groups and paid maternity leave was lengthened to 16 weeks.
5. *504*, p. 29.
6. *314*, pp. 14–15; *351*, pp. 10–11; *Voprosy Sotsial'nogo Obespecheniia (VSO)*, No. 11, June 1, 1926, p. 9; *296*, pp. 1–3; *264*, p. 1; *512*, pp. 22–26; *497*, pp. 3–6; *150*; *504*; *471*.

7. *472*, p. 15.	8. *272*; *300*.
9. *270*, p. 14.	10. *338*, p. 145.
11. *101*, p. 15.	12. *96*, p. 11.
13. *403*, pp. 1–3.	14. *153*; *149*.
15. *271*, p. 10.	16. *299*.
17. *205*, p. 1.	18. *167*, p. 8.

19. Decree of the All-Russian Executive Committee and the Soviet of People's Commissars, USSR—"About Approving the Regulation Concerning the People's Commissariat of Social Welfare," reprinted in full in *VSO*, No. 9–10, 1926.
20. *VSO*, No. 2, January 15, 1927, p. 1.
21. *Ibid.*, No. 8, April 15, 1926, p. 2; *295*, pp. 1–3; *VSO*, No. 13, July 1, 1928, p. 4.
22. *66*, pp. 4–5.
23. The number of unemployed fell from 1.6 million in 1928 to 240,000 in 1930. See *442*, p. 247.
24. *Voprosy Strakhovaniia*, No. 9, March 20, 1931, pp. 4–6.
25. *55*, p. 24.
26. *VSO*, No. 2, May 15, 1930, pp. 1–2.
27. *31*, p. 5.
28. *21*; *318*.
29. *Sotsial'noe Obespechenie (SO)*, No. 1, January 1931, pp. 27–28.
30. *VSO*, November 1929, pp. 14–15.
31. *329*, p. 40.
32. *393*, pp. 8–32; *453*, pp. 36, 66.

Chapter 5

1. *Current Digest of the Soviet Press*, Vol. 12 (1960): No. 13, p. 43; No. 30, p. 33; No. 36, p. 13; No. 38, p. 14; No. 51, p. 38.

2. *386*.	3. *50*, p. 20.
4. *374*, p. 16.	5. *234*, p. 150.

6. *291*, p. 305; *106*, pp. 12–13. See also *38*.

7. *110*, p. 109.   8. *58*, Vol. 2, p. 223.

9. *35*, pp. 14, 16, 31; *292*, p. 17.   10. *232*, pp. 98–99.

11. *383*, p. 6.

12. Apparently led by A. B. Sakharov; see *360* and *361*; similar studies, less carefully thought out, are discussed in *284*, pp. 7–17.

13. *361*, pp. 162, 172.   14. *Ibid.*

15. *206*, p. 4.   16. *406*, p. 16.

17. *115*, p. 20.   18. *128*; *71*; *366*; *330*.

19. *193*, pp. 43–52.   20. *72*, p. 101.

21. *409*, p. 156.   22. *176*, pp. 258, 259.

23. *369*, p. 11.   24. *79*, p. 602.

25. *239*, pp. 162–63.

26. *Literaturnaia Gazeta*, April 2, 1960, p. 2; *Pravda*, December 19, 1963, p. 6.

27. Statement by Khrushchev in *Pravda*, May 9, 1956.

28. *166*, p. 4.   29. *54*, p. 6.

30. *Pravda*, March 8, 1963, p. 2.   31. *236*.

Chapter 6

1. *214*, pp. 9, 15, 19, 125, 137, 139, 164, 179; *170*. Since accounts from other republics are few and sketchy and since most of them modeled their services on those of the Russian Republic (RSFSR), discussion is confined to the latter, unless otherwise indicated.

2. *494*, pp. 4–5.   3. *81*, pp. 95–96.

4. *273*, p. 39.   5. *205*, p. 1.

6. *VSO*, No. 24, December 15, 1929, p. 3, and No. 6, March 15, 1930, p. 1.

7. For example, one compilation of social insurance laws was a book of 743 pages of single-spaced double columns: *119*.

8. *209*, p. 6.   9. *434*, p. 28; *445*, p. 23.

10. *164*, pp. 82–83.   11. *258*, p. 26.

12. *Okhrana Truda i Sotsial'noe Strakhovanie*, No. 6, December 1958, p. 64, and No. 5, May 1965, pp. 38–39; *352*, pp. 55–56.

13. *249*, pp. 33–34; *125*, pp. 4–12, 4–9, respectively.

14. *40*, p. 19.

15. *377*, p. 27.

16. *Zhizn' Slepykh*, No. 9, September 1958, p. 1.

17. *125*, pp. 4–12, 4–9, respectively. The Moldavian minister was not heard from —reason not given.

18. *121*, p. 7; *120*, p. 11; *219*, p. 56; *395*, pp. 52–53.

19. *124*, pp. 19–20; *420*, pp. 56–57; *Trud*, August 27, 1955, p. 2; *Okhrana Truda i Sotsial'noe Strakhovanie*, No. 10, October 1965, p. 11.

20. *Okhrana Truda i Sotsial'noe Strakhovanie*, No. 6, June 1958, pp. 21 and 23, and No. 8, August 1958, p. 28.

21. *299*, pp. 9–33; *300*, pp. 10–16; *VSO:* No. 2, January 15, 1926, p. 2; No. 9–10, May 15, 1926, pp. 10–11; No. 15, August 1, 1926, p. 3; No. 16, August 15, 1928, p. 5; No. 24, December 15, 1928, p. 1; No. 10, May 15, 1929, p. 3; No. 7, July 1933, pp. 6–10; *Voprosy Strakhovaniia*, No. 43, October 20, 1925, pp. 5–6; *SO:* No. 1, January 1931, p. 21; No. 1, January 1934, pp. 2–4; No. 7–8, July–August 1935, pp. 4–6. See also a sad but nevertheless delightful account by two Soviet satirists—*145*, pp. 55–66.

22. *302*, pp. 37–38.
23. *SO*, No. 2, February 1957, p. 8.
24. *339*, p. 18.   25. *312*, p. 3.
26. *33*, p. 15.   27. *483*, p. 14.
28. *164*, p. 84.   29. *92A*, pp. 2–5.
30. *302*, p. 5. See also *152*, pp. 91–92.
31. *204*, pp. 32–34; *483*, p. 14; *SO*, No. 4, April 1961, pp. 8, 13, 57.
32. *483*, p. 16.   33. *428*, p. 34.
34. *288*, p. 42; *208*, p. 14.   35. *SO*, No. 1, January 1966, pp. 1–3.
36. *SO*, No. 10, September 1963, pp. 12–13.
37. *484*, p. 11.
38. *347*, pp. 49, 54; *280*, pp. 25, 34. There is no later edition of this manual.
39. *114*, p. 6; *46*, p. 209; *75*, pp. 84, 117, 124–27, 141–42, 157.
40. *12*, p. 33; *56*, p. 2.   41. *193*, p. 48.
42. *443*, pp. 149, 79–80.   43. *142*, pp. 13–14.
44. *90*, p. 238.

Chapter 7

1. *425*, pp. 3, 12.   2. *51*, p. 5.
3. *75*, pp. 43, 85.   4. *180*, p. 166.
5. *155*, p. 21.   6. *217*, p. 31.
7. *107*, p. 90.   8. *253*, pp. 59, 60, 65–66.
9. *514*, p. 16.   10. *183*, pp. 38–39.
11. *387*, pp. 112–15.   12. *Ibid.*, pp. 99–110.
13. *59*, pp. 87–113.   14. *Ibid.*, pp. 171–200.

Chapter 8

1. *469*, p. 24; *279*; *294*, pp. 54–55; *156*, pp. 50, 51, 52, 70–71.
2. *Trud:* April 16, 1935, pp. 2–3; August 24, 1940, p. 3; June 17, 1953, p. 2; July 2, 1955, p. 3; *340*, p. 2; *388*, pp. 137, 139–40.
3. *466*; *144*; *290*, p. 2; *340*, pp. 1–3.
4. *310*, p. 15.
5. This refers to the RSFSR regulation. As is usually the case, it has been copied by other republics. See, for example, *333*.
6. *47*, p. 286; *48*, p. 35; *220*, pp. 222–34; *154*.
7. *Trud:* March 9, 1935, p. 4; November 30, 1952, p. 2; April 19, 1953, p. 3; December 15, 1953, p. 2; August 29, 1954, p. 3; September 24, 1954, p. 3; November 19, 1954, p. 2; *Komsomol'skaia Pravda:* February 1, 1953, p. 3; July 19, 1953, p. 2; *256*, p. 194.
8. *345*, p. 4.   9. *398*, p. 81.
10. *482*, pp. 381–82.   11. *156*, pp. 50, 52, 70–71.
12. *405*, pp. 54–55.   13. *114*, p. 6.
14. *Ibid.*, p. 23.
15. *San Francisco Chronicle,* "Comrades' Courts Given More Power," March 14, 1965.
16. *47*, p. 83.   17. *220*, pp. 222–34.
18. *41*, p. 8.   19. *334*, p. 19; *422*, p. 71; *32*, p. 16.
20. *59*, p. 85.   21. *360*, pp. 20–21; *233*, p. 17.
22. *173*, p. 56; *345*, p. 4.

23. A report in *Komsomol'skaia Pravda*, July 28, 1960, p. 1—only one of many similar accounts (cited in *166*, p. 137).

24. *334,* p. 32.
25. *Ibid.,* p. 41.
26. *422,* p. 37.
27. *231,* pp. 79–82; *169,* pp. 10–11.
28. *419,* pp. 49–50.
29. *173,* pp. 95–96; *9,* p. 25.
30. *414,* p. 7.
31. *390,* pp. 73–94.
32. *Izvestiia,* June 30, 1963, p. 6.
33. *322,* p. 27.
34. *511,* pp. 3–4.
35. *114,* p. 14.
36. *Ibid.*
37. *502,* pp. 283, 282.
38. *113,* p. 8.
39. *138,* p. 8.
40. *503,* pp. 8–9.
41. *177.*
42. *89,* p. 4; *183,* pp. 38–39.

Chapter 9

1. *373,* p. 65; *159,* p. 107; *329,* p. 51.
2. *387, passim.*
3. *212,* pp. 12, 28, 44, 104, 123, 135–36.
4. *201.*
5. *13,* p. 190.
6. *176,* p. 268. See also *389,* p. 176.
7. In 1955, 116,553 children were attending special schools (and presumably living at home), while 381,185 were in homes and boarding schools. In 1950, the comparable numbers were 116,336 and 635,913. Hence, there seems to have taken place a rise in proportion accommodated in special schools as the total number of the defective has diminished. See *451,* p. 129.

8. *44,* p. 15; *189,* p. 185; *190,* pp. 114–48; *1,* pp. 65–69; *489,* p. 24.

9. *317,* pp. 17–26.

10. *321,* pp. 16–17.

11. *387,* p. 86. For descriptions and discussion of cooperative activities, see *387,* pp. 18–146; *184,* pp. 44–91 *passim; Komsomol'skaia Pravda,* January 10, 1953, p. 3; *217,* pp. 28–65; *322,* pp. 26–34; *468, passim.*

12. *Pravda,* October 12, 1962, p. 3.

13. With regard to preschool education, see *46,* p. 143. For information concerning summer camps, see *227,* p. 5; *218,* pp. 55–56; *178,* p. 373; *Pravda,* June 21, 1962, p. 4.

14. *130,* pp. 11, 248, 278; *182,* p. 27.
15. *417,* pp. 189, 190; *419,* p. 90.
16. *358,* p. 245.
17. *419,* p. 88.
18. *450,* pp. 11–90; *416.*
19. *278,* pp. 7–9.

20. *Sem'ia i Shkola:* 1947, No. 1, p. 35; 1955, No. 6, p. 25; 1956, No. 11, pp. 27–28; 1958, No. 5, p. 32; 1959, No. 1, pp. 17–19; 1959, No. 7, pp. 14–15; 1959, No. 9, p. 14; 1959, No. 12, p. 11. For a discussion of adoption practice in the United States, see *245,* pp. 205–29.

21. *143; 252; 323; 275; 324; 156; 80; 177; 68; 414; 511; 427.*

22. There are also sanatorium-type homes for children, ages 7–15, under the Ministry of Health. The length of stay depends on the child's physical condition. With regard to two experimental boarding schools, see *375,* p. 26.

23. *10,* p. 10.

24. *176,* p. 267. The new journal *Shkola-Internat* (Boarding School) which began in 1961, discontinued publication in 1965, and was succeeded by *Vospitanie* (Upbringing), another indication of the fall from favor of the boarding schools.

25. *100,* p. 3; *95,* p. 9.

26. *378,* p. 40; *306,* pp. 35–38; *95,* pp. 5–14; *132,* pp. 40–48; *199,* pp. 35–36; *346,* pp. 34–37; *259,* pp. 38–39.

27. *90.*

28. *491,* p. 220; *328,* p. 434.

29. *380,* p. 3; *86,* p. 14.

30. *265,* pp. 28–29.

31. *88,* pp. 3–6; *142,* pp. 13–14.

32. *90,* pp. 226–28.

33. *87,* p. 4; *88,* pp. 3–6.

34. *89,* p. 4.

35. Material about the rights of unmarried mothers is based on *189,* pp. 41, 136, 180; *190,* pp. 31, 91, 94–98; *1,* pp. 24–25, 31, 34; *358,* pp. 44–45.

36. *Sem'ia i Shkola:* No. 6, 1955, p. 23; No. 9, 1963, p. 26.

37. See a description of one such facility in *388.*

38. *281,* pp. 5, 12; *186.*

39. *362,* p. 91.

40. *50,* p. 23; *Komsomol'skaia Pravda,* July 28, 1960, p. 1; *Pravda,* January 13, 1965, p. 2.

41. *356,* p. 1.

42. *347,* pp. 54–55, 98.

43. *39,* pp. 6–8.

44. *154; 334,* pp. 5–14.

45. *454,* p. 1.

46. The materials upon which this estimate is based are of many kinds. *Pravda* of January 24, 1964, p. 2, gave the total number of children receiving their education in boarding schools, extended-day schools, and extended-day groups organized in regular schools in 1963. Entry 1 in Table 6 is based on the number of unmarried mothers reported to be receiving allowances for their children in 1963 (*444,* p. 512). (It should be added that the number of illegitimate children in entry 1 probably represents less than half the total number of such children in 1963. To the number in this entry must be added illegitimate children between ages 12 and 18 living with their mothers and no longer eligible for allowances; others whose mothers had not applied for allowances because of ignorance, indifference, or shame; some whose fathers were providing support under "Section 43" or were raising them; and some whose mothers placed them in institutions. Painstaking calculations, going back to the number of unmarried mothers in 1945, yield a total of 5 to 5.5 million illegitimate children, ages 0–18, living in the country in 1963. This is quite consistent with the 4.8 million in 1964 suggested by an American publication [*373,* p. 65], but rather difficult to reconcile with another American estimate published in 1963 of 8 million for 1957 [*159,* p. 115], even allowing for the fact that there was an unusually high number of illegitimate children in 1957.) The number of children in entry 2 in Table 6 was calculated on the basis of field findings that during the past few years, of all normal children who do not live in their own homes, 40 per cent are placed in institutions and 60 per cent in substitute homes. (These percentages are substantiated by 1958 data in *347,* pp. 46–47.) The division of this number for entries 3 and 4 in Table 6 was made by adjusting the number in each of these two types of facilities in 1962 (*Pravda,* March 8, 1963, p. 2) by the increase in boarding school enrollment in 1963 (*444,* p. 517), and by taking into account the fact that since 1962 extended-day facilities have been multiplying at a more rapid rate than boarding schools (*347,* p. 14). In estimating entry 5 in Table 6, the starting point was the number of children, both normal and defective, in "homes" in 1956 (*78,* p. 70); defective children were then excluded and the number of normal children projected to 1963 for the country as a whole on the basis of field information concerning the number in the RSFSR in 1960 and in the Buriat ASSR in 1963 (*275,* p. 5). Entry 6 is based on the official figure of defective children educated in 1963 (*444,* p. 556), and the assumption that most of the schools educating the defective were boarding schools. The number in entry 7 is projected from field findings in 1960 in the RSFSR. The number of "nervous" children in entry 8 is projected from Skolnick (*388*) and my own findings in the field.

Chapter 10

1. *395*, pp. 57–58.
2. *466*, pp. 3, 6, 9, 14.
3. *82*, p. 45.
4. *436A*, pp. 27–32.
5. *433*, p. 26; *434*, pp. 28–36; *435*, pp. 34–39; *436*, pp. 14–19; *436A*, pp. 27–32.
6. *30*, p. 21; *430*, pp. 8–9.
7. *Zhizn' Glukhikh*, No. 10, October 1959, p. 5; *485*, p. 1.
8. *300*, p. 15; *301*, pp. 22–23; *205*, p. 1; *VSO*: No. 7, April 1, 1926, p. 16; No. 1, January 1, 1928, p. 6; No. 13, July 1, 1928, p. 4; No. 2, January 15, 1929, p. 1.
9. The 1927 figure is from *VSO*, No. 2, January 15, 1929, p. 1; the 1958 figure is from *167*, p. 5.
10. *411*, pp. 18–19; *301*, p. 16. The impact of the first five-year-plan on the placement of invalids is reflected in the following figures for the RSFSR: in 1929–30, 26,000 were placed; in 1931, 147,000; in 1932, 225,000; in 1933–34, 334,561.
11. *4*, p. 140.
12. *302*, pp. 3–13, 57.
13. *309*, p. 36.
14. *SO*, No. 3, March 1965, p. 31.
15. *SO*, No. 12, December 1964, pp. 36–38, and No. 1, January 1966, p. 33; *Sovetskaiia Iustitsiia*, No. 5, May 1965, pp. 10–12.
16. *125*, pp. 4–12 and 4–9. Here the employed group is shown as "working pensioners."
17. *VSO*: No. 22, November 15, 1929, p. 9; No. 1, January 1, 1930, p. 1; No. 7–8, April 15, 1930, *passim*; No. 21–22, November 15, 1930, p. 1.
18. *VSO*: No. 7, July 1931, p. 8; No. 3–4, March–April 1933, pp. 1–6; No. 5, May 1933, p. 3; No. 11, November 1934, p. 3; No. 1, November 1935, p. 18; No. 8, August 1936, p. 2; No. 6, June 1940, pp. 3–6; *Zhizn' Glukhonemykh*, No. 1, June 1933, p. 2; No. 1, January 1941, p. 11; *151*, p. 641.
19. *Zhizn' Glukhikh*, No. 1, January 1964, p. 9.
20. *165*, p. 191; *Zhizn' Slepykh*, No. 11, November 1957, p. 14.
21. *Zhizn' Slepykh*, No. 4, April 1960, p. 3; *24*, p. 70; *167*, p. 4; *289*, p. 5.
22. *300*, p. 50; *VSO*, No. 6, June 1931, p. 8; *315*, p. 6; *Zhizn' Glukhikh*, No. 10, June 1938, p. 15; *412*, pp. 31–32.
23. *435*, p. 35; *432*, p. 29; *429*, p. 30; *251*, p. 22; *341*, pp. 18–20.
24. *127*, p. 31; *513*, p. 2. The major publication, a journal, is *Protezirovanie i Protezostroenie*.
25. *410*, pp. 419, 423; *152*, pp. 18–218; *431*, pp. 28, 31.
26. *151*, p. 638; *448*, p. 14.
27. *464*, pp. 37–39; *SO*, No. 12, December 1965, p. 27, and No. 1, January 1966, p. 3; *510*, pp. 29–30; *435*, p. 37; *432*, p. 29; *250*, p. 20.
28. *205*, pp. 1–2; *300*, pp. 13, 20, 35. That progress was slow and erratic is painfully clear: see *301*, p. 9; *SO*, No. 11, November 1938, p. 60.
29. *SO*, No. 12, December 1957, p. 25.
30. *370*, p. 61.
31. *11*, pp. 36–38; *200*, p. 38. In 1965, of the 13 homes for aged and invalids under the Moscow department of social welfare, only two were for adult psychotics—one for men, the other for women. See also *446*, p. 62; *141*, p. 41.
32. *SO*, No. 1, January 1966, p. 33.
33. *SO*, No. 6, June 1965, pp. 38, 42, and No. 6, June 1957, p. 41.
34. *305*, pp. 33–34; *53*, pp. 1–4; *319*, p. 56; *SO*, No. 9, September 1963, p. 41.
35. *476*, pp. 37–38; *477*, pp. 61–65.
36. *24*, pp. 49, 52.

37. *236.*
39. *273,* p. 51.

38. *237,* p. 30.
40. *348,* p. 23.

Chapter 11

1. *Okhrana Truda i Sotsial'noe Strakhovanie,* No. 4, October 1958, p. 13.
2. *122,* pp. 3–5.
3. For a detailed discussion, see *453,* pp. 34–44, 50–51.
4. *165; 5,* pp. 2–6.
5. *498,* pp. 12–16.
6. *426,* p. 10; *117.*
7. *453,* p. 81.
8. *481,* pp. 26–27. During 1958 VTEKs of the RSFSR reexamined 183,000 persons, largely in connection with complaints. A serious failure to respond to the complaint of an invalid was described in *Izvestiia,* under the heading "Porok Serdtsa" (A Failure of the Heart). A discussion of the case and the resulting regulation imposed by the RSFSR Minister of Social Welfare appears in *SO,* No. 1, January 1962, pp. 22–23.
9. The discussion in this section is based upon *453,* pp. 52–53.
10. *508,* pp. 40–41; *207,* pp. 25–27.
11. *49,* pp. 38–39; *SO:* No. 7, July 1957, p. 52; No. 9, September 1956, p. 60; No. 8, August 1965, pp. 12–13.
12. *477,* p. 71; *6,* pp. 22–24; *371,* pp. 1–4.
13. *444,* p. 512.
14. *Pravda,* February 15, 1964, pp. 4–5.
15. *SO,* No. 3, March 1965, p. 5, and No. 10, October 1965, pp. 11–12.
16. *SO,* No. 10, October 1965, pp. 13–14.
17. *SO,* No. 8, August 1965, p. 13.
18. *195A,* p. 12.
19. *402,* pp. 275–79.
20. *SO,* No. 10, October 1962, p. 3.
21. *495,* p. 7.
22. *254,* p. 54.
23. *137A,* p. 155.
24. *125,* pp. 4–12 and 409, respectively. I made the necessary calculations.
25. *137A,* p. 155.

Chapter 12

1. In addition to the genuinely humane persons mentioned in Chapter 1, such as Betsky, see *74,* pp. 84–100, for examples of truly devoted, unselfish, and sacrificing attitudes on the part of helpers of the unfortunate.
2. *352A,* pp. 104–24.
3. *365,* p. 592.
4. *13,* pp. 157–58.
5. *63A,* pp. 202–32.
6. *263,* pp. 21 and 9.
7. *454,* pp. 4, 5.
8. *455,* p. 21.
9. *293.*
10. For benefit amounts, see *Social Security Bulletin,* May 1966, p. 1f. For duration of unemployment benefits and percentage of wages they represent, see *293,* p. 188.
11. *243,* p. 134.
12. *456,* p. xii.
13. *486,* p. 23.
14. *238,* p. 188.
15. *455,* p. 57.
16. *70,* pp. 15–16; *168,* pp. 68–74.
17. *57,* p. 46; *488,* pp. 13, 14, 25, 98–99.
18. *69,* pp. 29–41.
19. *221,* p. 3.
20. *64,* p. ix; *137; 356,* p. 1.
21. *72,* pp. 89–91, 99–100, 109, 113.
22. *423,* p. 15.

Bibliography

1. Abramova, A. A. Okhrana trudovykh prav zhenshchin v SSSR (Protection of women's labor rights in the USSR). Moscow, 1954.

2. ——— "Razvitie zakonodatel'stva ob okhrane truda zhenshchin" (Development of legal provisions concerning protection of women's labor), in N. G. Aleksandrov, ed., Novoe v razvitii trudovogo prava v period mezhdu XX i XXII s"ezdami KPSS (New features in the development of labor law between the 20th and the 22nd conference of the Communist Party). Moscow, 1961.

3. Acharkan, V. "Leninskie idei sotsial'nogo obespecheniia" (Lenin's ideas on social security), *Sotsial'noe Obespechenie*, No. 11, November 1956.

4. ——— "O pravovom polozhenii rabotaiushchikh pensionerov" (About the legal position of working pensioners), *Sotsialisticheskii Trud*, No. 4, April 1959.

5. ——— "Konstitutsionnye osnovy sotsial'nogo obespecheniia" (Constitutional bases of social welfare), *Sotsial'noe Obespechenie*, No. 12, December 1960.

6. ——— "Nekotorye voprosy sotsial'nogo obespecheniia kolkhoznikov" (Some questions about the social security of collective farmers), *Sotsial'noe Obespechenie*, No. 8, August 1962.

7. Ainzaft, S. "Professional'noe dvizhenie v Rossii, 1905–1907 g. (Trade union movement in Russia, 1905–1907). Moscow, 1925.

8. ——— Istoriia rabochego i professional'nogo dvizheniia derevoobdelochnikov do revolutsii 1917 goda (The history of the woodworkers' trade union movement prior to the 1917 Revolution). Moscow, 1928.

9. Akademiia obshchestvennykh nauk pri TS. K. KPSS. Osnovy kommunisticheskogo vospitaniia; uchebnoe posobie (The bases of communist upbringing; educational aids). Moscow, 1960.

10. Akademiia pedagogicheskikh nauk RSFSR. V pomoshch rabotnikam shkol-internatov; dokumenty i materialy (To the aid of workers in boarding schools; documents and materials). Moscow, 1956.

11. Alekseev, N. "Kak zhivetsia v vashem dome?" (How is life in your home?), *Sotsial'noe Obespechenie,* No. 10, October 1956.

12. Alpatov, N. I. Shkola-internat; voprosy organizatsii i opyt vospitatel'noi raboty (The boarding school; organizational questions and experience with upbringing work). Moscow, 1958.

13. Alt, Hershel and Edith. The New Soviet Man. His Upbringing and Character Development. New York, 1964.

14. Altaiskii kraevoi otdel narodnogo obrazovaniia. Sbornik materialov pervoi kraevoi konferentsii rabotnikov detskikh domov Altaiskogo kraia, posviashchennoi izucheniiu i tvorcheskomu ispol'zovaniiu v uchebnovospitatel'noi rabote pedagogicheskogo naslediia A. S. Makarenko (Collection of materials of the first regional conference of workers from children's homes in the Altai region, devoted to the study and to the creative use, in education and upbringing, of the pedagogical heritage of A. S. Makarenko). Barnaul, 1951.

15. Anan'ev, B. G., *et al.,* eds. Psikhologicheskaia nauka v SSSR (Psychological science in the USSR). 2 vols. Moscow, 1959–60.

16. Anderson, Raymond H. "Incomes Increase Sharply in Soviet," *New York Times,* January 30, 1967.

17. Ankudinov, A. "Slavnoe" (The fine things of the past), *Okhrana Truda i Sotsial'noe Strakhovanie,* No. 1, January 1962.

18. "An Outline Survey on Soviet Social Services, with Bibliographical References," *American Review of the Soviet Union, 1938–1948,* No. 3–4, October 1947.

19. Ansheles, I. I., S. D. Benenson, and B. S. Utevskii. "Krasnaia Armiia i deti" (The Red Army and children), *Biblioteka "Okhrana Detstva i Detskoe Pravo,"* No. 5, 1932.

20. Ansheles, I. I., V. V. Weisfeld, and Z. L. Mordukhovich. "Trud molodezhi" (The labor of youth), *Biblioteka "Okhrana Detstva i Detskoe Pravo,"* No. 1, 1932.

21. Antipov, N. K. Finansovaia praktika professional'nykh soiuzov (Financial practices of trade unions). Moscow, 1923.

22. Antoshkin, D. V. Ocherk dvizheniia sluzhashchikh v Rossii. So vtoroi poloviny XIX-go veka (A description of the movement among employees in Russia. From the second half of the nineteenth century). Moscow, 1921.

23. —— Kratkii ocherk professional'nogo dvizheniia v Rossii (A short description of the trade union movement in Russia). Moscow, 1928.

24. Aralov, V. A., and A. V. Levshin. Sotsial'noe obespechie v SSSR (Social security in the USSR). Moscow, 1959.

25. Arbore-Ralli, E. Mat' i ditia v Sovetskoi Rossii (Mother and child in Soviet Russia). Moscow, 1920.
26. Arkhipov, A. R., and N. A. Pomanskii. Finansirovanie sotsial'nogo strakhovaniia i sotsial'nogo obespecheniia. Sbornik zakonodatel'nykh i instruktivnykh materialov (The financing of social insurance and social assistance. Collection of legal and instructional materials). Moscow, 1958.
27. Arnautova, G. Ia., ed. Organizatsiia kollektiva vospitannikov v detskom dome (Organization of the children's collective in a children's home). Moscow, 1958.
28. Aronovich, G. A. "Nevrozy istoshcheniia u detei" (Neuroses of malnutrition in children), *Voprosy Izucheniia i Vospitaniia Lichnosti,* No. 4–5, 1922.
29. Astrov, P. I. Russkaia fabrichnaia meditsina. Kritika zakonoproekta komissii gosudarstvennoi Dumy po rabochemu voprosu (Russian factory medicine. Critical analysis of the law proposed by the Duma commission concerning labor questions). Moscow, 1911.
30. Aulov, I. "Na komissii—kolkhozniki" (To the commissions, collective farmers), *Sotsial'noe Obespechenie,* No. 2, February 1962.
31. Avdeev. "Klassovaia bor'ba v derevne i zadachi sotsial'nogo obespecheniia" (The class struggle in the village and the problems of social welfare), *Sotsial'noe Obespechenie,* No. 1, January 1931.
32. Babaev, M. "Vospityvaet kollektiv" (The collective is doing the upbringing), *Okhrana Truda i Sotsial'noe Strakhovanie,* No. 2, February 1962.
33. Balbenkov, M. "Obshchestvennyi kontrol' trudiashchikhsia" (Social control by the toilers), *Sotsial'noe Obespechenie,* No. 1, January 1957.
34. Barit, A., and V. Miliutin. Osnovy sotsial'nogo strakhovaniia (The bases of social insurance). Moscow, 1934.
35. Bassin, F. V. "A Critical Analysis of Freudianism" and "A Rejoinder to Professor Musatti," *The Soviet Review, A Journal of Translations,* Vol. 1, No. 5, December 1960.
36. Bauer, Raymond A. The New Man in Soviet Psychology. Cambridge, Mass., 1952.
37. Bauer, Raymond A., *et al.*, eds. How the Soviet System Works: Cultural, Psychological and Social Themes. Cambridge, Mass., 1956.
38. Bauer, Raymond A., ed. Some Views on Soviet Psychology. Washington, D.C., 1962.
39. Beliaev, N. A. Tseli nakazaniia i sredstva ikh dostizheniia v ispravitel'-notrudovykh uchrezhdeniiakh (Purposes of punishment and the means for achieving them in rehabilitative labor institutions). Leningrad, 1963.
40. Beliakov, F. "O probelakh i neiasnostiakh" (About gaps and unclear areas), *Sotsial'noe Obespechenie,* No. 10, October 1957.
41. Beliakova, Z. "Idet obshchestvennyi sud" (A session of a comrades' court is in progress), *Zhizn' Glukhikh,* No. 1, January 1964.

42. Belykh, G., and L. Panteleev. Respublika bezprizornykh (The republic of the homeless). Riga, 1930.

43. Bem, O. L., and V. I. Kufaev. "Sotsial'no-zapushchennye deti i podrostki i metody raboty s nimi" (Socially neglected children and adolescents and methods of working with them), in Trudnye deti i podrostki i metody raboty s nimi v detucherzhdeniiakh. Po materialam Moskovskogo oblastnogo soveshchaniia zaveduiushchikh detskimi domami, 15–19 dekabria 1933 g. (Difficult children and adolescents and methods of working with them in children's institutions. Materials of the Moscow regional conference of the directors of children's homes held from December 15–19, 1933). Moscow, 1934.

44. Benenson, S. D. "Okhrana materinstva i mladenchestva" (Protection of motherhood and infancy), *Biblioteka "Okhrana Detstva i Detskoe Pravo,"* No. 6, 1932.

45. ——— "Sotsial'noe obespechenie detei" (Social assistance for children), *Biblioteka "Okhrana Detstva i Detskoe Pravo,"* No. 7, 1932.

46. Bereday, George Z. F., William W. Brickman, and Gerald H. Read, eds. The Changing Soviet School: The Comparative Education Society Field Study in the USSR. Boston, 1960.

47. Berman, Harold J. Justice in the USSR: An Interpretation of Soviet Law. Cambridge, Mass., 1963.

48. Berman, N. "Soviet Law Enforcement and the Young Offenders," *American Quarterly on the Soviet Union,* No. 4, April 1940.

49. Boev, Ia. "Bespravnoe polozhenie kassy vzaimopomoshchi" (Outside-the-law position of the mutual aid fund), *Sotsial'noe Obespechenie,* No. 7, July 1956.

50. Boldyrev, E. "The Study and Prevention of Juvenile Delinquency," *The Soviet Review, A Journal of Translations,* Vol. 2, No. 5, May 1961.

51. Boldyrev, N. I., ed. Organizatsiia i vospitanie uchenicheskogo kollektiva (Organization and upbringing of the pupils' collective). Moscow, 1959.

52. Bol'shaia Entsiklopediia (The large encyclopedia). St. Petersburg, 1896–1909, Vol. 10.

53. "Bol'she vnimaniia domam invalidov" (Let us pay more attention to invalids' homes), *Sotsial'noe Obespechenie,* No. 2, February 1957.

54. Bondar, A. D., and A. F. Pacheko, eds. Pervye shagi. Shkoly internaty (First steps. Boarding schools). Moscow, 1958.

55. Bondarenko, V. "Kto Pridet v Internat?" (Who will come to the boarding school?), *Komsomol'skaia Pravda,* April 12, 1961, p. 2.

56. Bondarev, Iu. Tishina, roman (Quiet, a novel). Moscow, 1962.

57. Bowlby, J. Maternal Care and Mental Health. Geneva: World Health Organization, Monograph series, No. 2, Second edition, 1952.

58. Bozhovich, L. I. "Izuchenie lichnosti shkol'nika i problemy vospitaniia" (Study of the schoolchild's personality and problems of upbringing), in B. G. Anan'ev, ed., Psikhologicheskaia nauka v SSSR (The science of psychology in the USSR). Vol. 2. Moscow, 1960.

59. ———, ed. Psikhologicheskoe izuchenie detei v shkole-internate (Psychological study of children in boarding school). Moscow, 1960.

60. ——— "O nekotorykh problemakh i metodakh izucheniia psykhologicheskoi lichnosti shkol'nika" (About certain problems and methods in studying the psychological personality of the pupil), in L. I. Bozhovich, ed., Voprosy psikhologicheskoi lichnosti shkol'nika (Questions concerning the psychological personality of the pupil). Moscow, 1961.

61. Bronner, V. M. La lutte contre la prostitution en URSS (The struggle against prostitution in the USSR). Moscow, 1936.

62. Brusianin, V. V. Deti i pisateli; literaturno-obshchestvennyia paralleli. Deti v proizvedeniakh Chekhova, Leonida Andreeva, Kuprina i Remizova (Children and writers; literary-social parallels. Children in the works of Chekhov, Leonid Andreev, Kuprin and Remizov). Moscow, 1915.

63. Buslaev, N. A. Zabota sovetskoi vlasti o glukhonemykh (Soviet government's care of deaf-mutes). Moscow, 1946.

63A. Brzezinski, Zbigniew, and Samuel P. Huntington. "Policy Making in the U.S.A. and U.S.S.R.," in *Political Power: USA/USSR*. New York, 1964.

64. Cantril, Hadley. Soviet Leaders and Mastery Over Men. New Brunswick, N.J., 1960.

65. Carter, Herbert Dyson. Sin and Science. New York, 1946.

66. Chapman, Janet G. Real Wages in Soviet Russia since 1928. Cambridge, Mass., 1963.

67. Chauncey, Henry. "Some Notes on Education and Psychology in the Soviet Union," *The American Psychologist,* Vol. 14, No. 6, June 1959.

68. Chekerlan, D. L. "V internate dalekogo zapoliar'ia" (In a boarding school in the far north), in Vospitatel'naia rabota detskikh domov (Upbringing work of children's homes). Akademiia Pedagogicheskikh Nauk RSFSR. Moscow, 1961.

69. Chernin, Milton, and Hasseltine B. Taylor. "Principles and Organization of Undergraduate Social Service Education Programs: Content and Supporting Courses," in Regional Institute on Undergraduate Social Service Education. Western Interstate Commission on Higher Education. Boulder, Colo., June 1965.

70. Chilman, Catherine S. "Child-rearing and Family Relationship Patterns of the Very Poor," *Welfare in Review,* Vol. III, January 1965.

71. Chuchelov, N. I. O polovom vospitanii (About sexual upbringing). Moscow, 1964.

72. Communist Party of the USSR. Program of the Communist Party of the Soviet Union. New York, 1961.

73. Curtiss, John S. Church and State in Russia: The Last Years of the Empire, 1900–1917. New York, 1940.

74. ——— "Russian Sisters of Mercy in the Crimea, 1854–1855," *Slavic Review,* Vol. XXV, No. 1, March 1966.

75. Daniushevskii, I. I. Uchebno-vospitatel'naia rabota v detskikh domakh i spetsial'nykh shkolakh (Educational-rearing work in children's homes and special schools). Moscow, 1954.

76. Danskii, B. G. (K. A. Komarovskii), ed. Strakhovanie rabochikh v Rossii i na zapade (Workers' insurance in Russia and in the West). Vol. I. First edition. St. Petersburg, 1913.

77. Danskii, B. G. Dorevolutsionnaia strakhovaia kampaniia (Pre-revolutionary social insurance campaign). Moscow, 1925.

78. Deineko, M. Forty Years of Public Education in the USSR. Facts and Figures. Moscow, 1957.

79. De Jouvenel, Bertrand. "The Logic of Economics," in Abraham Brumberg, ed., Russia under Khrushchev: An Anthology from *Problems of Communism*. New York, 1962.

80. Denisova, G. Ikh bol'shaia sem'ia, k 40-letiiu Chitinskogo detskogo doma, No. 1 (Theirs is a big family, for the 40th anniversary of the Chita children's home No. 1), Chita, 1961.

81. De Palencia, Isabel. Alexandra Kollontay, Ambassadress from Russia. New York, London, Toronto, 1947.

82. Derevnin, M. "Oni khotiat i mogut rabotat'" (They want to and can work), *Sotsial'noe Obespechenie*, No. 5–6, May–June 1956.

83. ———— "Shire razvivat' deiatel'nost' KOV" (Let us develop more extensively the activity of peasant mutual aid societies), *Sotsial'noe Obespechenie*, No. 11, November 1956.

84. "Deviatyii s"ezd VOS" (The ninth conference of the All-Russian Society for the Blind), *Sotsial'noe Obespechenie*, No. 1, January 1960.

85. Dewar, Margaret. Labour Policy in the USSR, 1917–1928. London and New York, 1956.

86. D'iachkov, A. I. "Sostoianie i zadachi nauchno-issledovatel'skoi raboty v oblasti defektologii" (The status of scientific research and questions for research in defectology), in Trudy nauchnoi sessii po defektologii (Work of the scientific session on defectology). Akademiia Pedagogicheskikh Nauk RSFSR. Moscow, 1958.

87. ———— "Razvivat' i formirovat' u uchashchikhsia spetsial'nykh shkol navyki rabotat' samostaiatel'no" (Toward developing and forming skills among students of special schools for working independently), *Spetsial'naia Shkola*, No. 2, 1960.

88. ———— "Osnovy sovetskoi sistemy obucheniia i vospitaniia anomal'nykh detei" (Bases of soviet system of education and rearing of abnormal children), in Tezisy dokladov tret'ei nauchnoi sessii po voprosam defektologii, 22–25 Marta 1960 g. (Theses of the scientific reports on questions of defectology at the third scientific session, March 22–25, 1960). Akademiia Pedagogicheskikh Nauk RSFSR. Moscow, 1960.

89. ———— "O perestroike spetsial'nykh shkol" (About the reorganization of special schools), *Spetsial'naia Shkola*, No. 1, 1960.

90. ————, ed. "Kratkii defektologicheskii slovar'" (A short defectological dictionary). Seen in unpublished manuscript in Moscow, 1965.

91. Direction Generale de l'Economie Locale du Ministere de l'Interieur. L'assistance publique et privee en Russie (Public and private assistance in Russia). St. Petersburg, 1906.

92. Dobrova, A. D. "Osnovnye etapy razvitia sovetskoi shkoly glukhonemykh za 30 let sushchestvovaniia" (Major stages in the development of the Soviet school for the deaf during 30 years of its existence), in Trudy nauchnoi sessii po defektologii (The work of the scientific session on defectology). Akademiia Pedagogicheskikh Nauk RSFSR. Moscow, 1958.

92A. Dolgov, K. M. "Kadram-Bol'she Vnimaniia!" (More attention to personnel!), *Sotsial'noe Obespechenie,* May 1966.

93. Dovgalevskaia, A. I. Semeinoe vospitanie priemnykh detei (Family upbringing of foster and adopted children). Moscow, 1948.

94. Dragunova, T. V. "O nekotorykh psikhologicheskikh osobennostiakh podrostka" (About certain psychological peculiarities of the adolescent), in L. I. Bozhovich, ed., Voprosy psikhologicheskoi lichnosti shkol'nika (Questions concerning the psychological personality of the pupil). Moscow, 1961.

95. Dul'nev, G. M., and M. I. Kuz'mitskaia, eds. Obuchenie i vospitanie umstvenno otstalykh detei (The education and rearing of mentally retarded children). Moscow, 1960.

96. El'tsin, B. Oktiabr'skaia revoliutsiia i perspektivy sotsial'nogo obespecheniia (The October Revolution and the perspectives of social welfare). Moscow, 1921.

97. Entsiklopedicheskii Slovar' (Encyclopaedic Dictionary). Brokgauz and Efron, eds.

98. Entsiklopedicheskii Slovar' (Encyclopaedic Dictionary). Granat and Co. Seventh edition.

99. "Epokhi sotsial'nogo strakhovaniia" (The epochs of social insurance), *Voprosy Strakhovaniia,* No. 29–30, November 7, 1932.

100. Erastova, E. A. Vospitanie slepykh detei v sem'e (The upbringing of blind children in the family). Moscow, 1956.

101. Faingold, B. "Teoriia i praktika sotsstrakha" (The theory and practice of social insurance), *Voprosy Strakhovaniia,* No. 32–33, September 1, 1924.

102. Fediaevsky, V. M., in collaboration with Patty Smith Hill. Nursery School and Parent Education in Soviet Russia. New York, 1936.

103. Feodos'ev, B. Sistematicheskii sbornik otvetov redaktsii zhurnala "Izvestiia Zemskogo Otdela" za 1904–1912 g. (Systematic compilation of answers by the editors of the journal "News from the Zemstvo Section" for the years 1904–1912). St. Petersburg, 1912.

104. Field, Mrs. Alice Withrow. Protection of Women and Children in Soviet Russia. New York, 1932.

105. Field, Mark. "Approaches to Mental Illness in Soviet Society: Some Comparisons and Conjectures," *Social Problems,* Vol. 7, No. 4, Spring 1960.

106. —— Review of M. S. Lebedinskii, ed., Voprosy psikhoterapii (Questions of psychotherapy). Moscow, 1958. In *Contemporary Psychology,* Vol. VI, No. 1, January 1961.

107. —— and Jason Aronson. "Soviet Community Mental Health Services and Work Therapy," *Community Mental Health Journal,* Vol. 1, No. 1, Spring 1965.

108. Fischer, Louis. The Life of Lenin. New York, Evanston, Ill., and London, 1964.

109. Fisher, Harold H. The Famine in Soviet Russia, 1919–1923: The Operations of the American Relief Administration. New York, 1927.

110. Fitzpatrick, William H., and Chester W. DeLong, eds. Soviet Medical Research Related to Human Stress: A Review of the Literature. Washington, D.C., 1961.

111. French materials. Fourteen articles in French, written by staff members of the Russian Ministry of Social Welfare, dealing with the major aspects of the Ministry's work. They were given to the author in 1965 and are in her possession.

112. Fridland, L. S raznykh storon; prostitutsiia v SSSR (From different sides; prostitution in the USSR). Berlin, 1931.

113. Geiger, Kent. "Change, Values and National Integration in the USSR." Unpublished manuscript prepared for presentation at the First National Meeting of the American Association for the Advancement of Slavic Studies, New York, April 1–4, 1964.

114. Gerasiuk, L. I., and P. I. Shpital'nik. Voprosy vospitaniia v detskom dome (Questions of upbringing in children's homes). Moscow, 1956.

115. Gertsenzon, A. A. "The Community's Role in the Prevention and Study of Crime," *The Soviet Review, A Journal of Translations,* Vol. 2, No. 1, January 1961.

116. Glavnoe Politicheskoe Upravlenie RKKA. Posobiia, pensii a l'goty voennosluzhashchim i ikh sem'iam (Grants, pensions and privileges for military personnel and their families). Moscow, 1943.

117. Gokhman, V. Ocherki po strakhovaniiu ot neschastnykh sluchaev (Descriptions about insurance against accidents). Moscow, 1928.

118. Gorbunov, A. V. Bor'ba s nishchenstvom i brodiazhnichestvom (The struggle against begging and vagrancy). Moscow, 1909.

119. Gorbunov, A. I., B. N. Guterman, and A. Ia. Usikov. Deistvuiushchie zakonodatel'stvo po sotsial'nomu strakhovaniiu SSSR i RSFSR (Social insurance laws in force in the USSR and RSFSR). Moscow, 1930.

120. —— and M. Frid'ev. Gosudarstvennoe sotsial'noe strakhovanie v SSSR (State social insurance in the USSR). Moscow, 1938.

121. —— Strakhovoi delegat (The social insurance delegate). Moscow, 1958.

122. —— "Po puti neuklonnogo rosta" (On the road of unceasing growth), *Okhrana Truda i Sotsial'noe Strakhovanie,* No. 9, September 1961.

123. Gordon, Manya. Workers Before and After Lenin. New York, 1941.

124. Gosudarstvennoe sotsial'noe strakhovanie, sbornik ofitsial'nykh materialov (State social insurance, collection of official materials). Moscow, 1959.

125. "Govoriat ministry soiuznykh respublik" (Republic ministers of social welfare speak), *Sotsial'noe Obespechenie,* No. 11, November 1963, and No. 12, December 1963.

126. Grishin, Zin. Pravovoe polozhenie iunosheskogo truda v SSSR (Legal status of the work of adolescents in USSR). Moscow, 1929.

127. Gritskevich, A. "Ukrepliaem sviaz' s praktikoi" (We are strengthening contact with practice), *Sotsial'noe Obespechenie,* No. 2, February 1960.

128. Gromozdov, G. G. Za zdorovyi byt (Toward a healthy life). Moscow, 1964.

129. Grushin, B. "Kak vy provodite svobodnoe vremiia" (How you spend your leisure time), *Komsomol'skaia Pravda,* February 24, 1966.

130. Gsovskii, V. Soviet Civil Law. 2 vols. Ann Arbor, Mich., 1948.

131. —— "Family and Inheritance in Soviet Law," in Alex Inkeles and Kent Geiger, eds., Soviet Society, A Book of Readings. Boston, 1961.

132. Gurevitch, I. S. "Opyt organizatsii spetsial'nykh uchrezhdenii dliia gluboko umstvenno otstalykh detei v SSR (Experience with organizing special facilities for severely retarded children in the USSR), in Dul'nev and Kuz'mitskaia, eds., Obuchenie i vospitanie umstvenno otstalykh detei (The education and rearing of mentally retarded children). Moscow, 1960.

133. Gurskii, Ch. "Doverennyi vrach kassy" (Trusted physician of the fund), *Voprosy Strakhovaniia,* No. 8, 1913.

134. Harcave, Sidney. Russia, A History. Third edition. New York, 1956.

135. Hazard, John N. "The Child Under Soviet Law," *University of Chicago Law Review,* Vol.V, 1937–38.

136. —— Law and Social Change in the USSR. London, 1953.

137. Hechinger, Fred M. "U.S. and Soviet Teaching Methods," *New York Times International Edition,* October 29, 1964.

137A. Heer, David M., and Judith G. Bryden. "Family Allowances and Fertility in the Soviet Union," *Soviet Studies,* XVIII, 2 (October, 1966).

138. Herzberg, Frederick. "U.S. Workers 'Happier' Than Russians, Panel Told," *Focus,* Vol. III, No. 2, February 1966.

139. Hiebsch, Hans. "Introduction," in Soviet Psychology: A Symposium. New York, 1961.

140. Iablokov, N. V. Prizrenie detei v vospitatel'nykh domakh (Care of children in institutions). St. Petersburg, 1901.

141. Iakushev, I. "Razbiraetsia personal'noe delo" (A personal matter is being looked into), *Sotsial'noe Obespechenie,* No. 4, April 1957.

142. Iarmachenko, N. D. "O podgotovke defektologicheskikh kadrov" (About the preparation of defectological personnel), in Tezisy do-

kladov tret'ei nauchnoi sessii po voprosam defektologii, 22–25 Marta 1960 g. (Theses of reports read at the third scientific session on questions of defectology). Akademiia Pedagogicheskikh Nauk RSFSR. Moscow, 1960.

143. Igrunov, Nikolai. Kostry (Camp fires). Belgorod, 1963.

144. Ikonnikov, V., and A. Novozhelov. Sovet pensionerov "Krasnogo Sormova" (Soviet of pensioners of Red Sormovo). Moscow, 1958.

145. Il'f, I. A., and E. Petrov. 12 stul'ev, roman (12 chairs, a novel). Sixth edition. Moscow, 1934.

146. Imeretinska, O. F. (Kniaginia, ed.) Blagotvoritel'naia Rossiia; istoriia gosudarstvennoi, obshchestvennoi i chastnoi blagotvoritel'nosti v Rossii (Charitable Russia; history of state, societal, and private charity in Russia). St. Petersburg, 1901.

147. Iniutin, G. K. Chto daet trudiashchimsia novyi pensionnyi zakon (What the new pension law gives the toilers). Moscow, 1956.

148. Inkeles, Alex, and Raymond A. Bauer. The Soviet Citizen; Daily Life in a Totalitarian Society. Cambridge, Mass., 1959.

149. International Labor Office. Organization of Industry and Labour Conditions in Soviet Russia. Geneva, 1922.

150. International Labor Office. Industrial Life in Soviet Russia, 1917–1923. Geneva, 1924.

151. International Labor Office. International Survey of Social Services, 1933. Geneva, 1936.

152. International Labor Office. The Training and Employment of Disabled Persons: A Preliminary Report. Montreal, 1945.

153. Isaev, A. N. Bezrabotitsa v SSSR i bor'ba s neiu, za period 1917–1924 g.g. (Unemployment in the USSR and the struggle against it, during the period 1917–1924). Moscow, 1924.

154. Iudaev, L. Kogda opuskaiutsia sumerki (When twilight falls). Riazan', 1961.

155. Ivanov, N. V. "A Soviet View of Group Therapy," The Soviet Review, A Journal of Translations, Vol. 2, No. 3, March 1961.

156. Ivanova, A. I., and V. Ia. Korchagina. Obsluzhivaiut sebia sami (Self-care). Moscow, 1962.

157. "Izmeneniia v zakonakh i zadachi strakhkass" (Changes in the law and the problems of social insurance funds), Voprosy Strakhovaniia, No. 40, November 28, 1929.

158. Johnson, William Eugene. The Liquor Problem in Russia. Westerville, Ohio, 1915.

159. Juviler, Peter. "Marriage and Divorce," Survey, A Journal of Soviet and East European Studies. London, No. 48, July 1963.

160. "Kak budet postavleno lechenie rabochikh po zakonu 23 iiuniia 1912 g." (How medical care for the workers will be organized under the law of July 23, 1912), Strakhovanie Rabochikh, No. 1, December 1912.

161. Kakiia pensii i posobiia poluchaiut sem'i ushedshikh na voinu i uvech-nye (Pensions available for the families of conscripted and disabled soldiers). Moscow, 1915.

162. "Kak voznikli 'Voprosy Strakhovaniia'" (How the journal *Questions of Social Insurance* came into being), *Voprosy Strakhovaniia*, No. 45, November 8, 1928.

163. Karavaev, V. V. Posobiia po vremennoi netrudosposobnosti (Grants for temporary disability). Moscow, 1950.

164. ——— "Za dal'neishee sovershenstvovanie pensionnogo zakonodatel'-stva" (Toward further perfecting the pension law), *Sovetskoe Gosudarstvo i Pravo*, No. 3, 1959.

165. ——— Sotsial'noe strakhovanie v SSSR (Social insurance in the USSR). Second edition. Moscow, 1959.

166. Kassof, Allen. The Soviet Youth Program: Regimentation and Rebellion. Cambridge, Mass., 1965.

167. Kats, R. R. Sovetskoe kooperativnoe strakhovanie (Soviet cooperative insurance). Moscow, 1960.

168. Katz, Alfred H. "Application of Self-Help Concepts in Current Social Welfare," *Social Work*, Vol. X, July 1965.

169. Kerbikov, O. V. "The Principles of Mental Hygiene and Prophylaxis and the State of the Mental Health of the Population in the USSR," in Reports of the Members of the Soviet Delegation at the V Congress on Mental Health Defense. Moscow, 1954.

170. Kerimova, L. Razvitie sotsial'nogo obespecheniia v Dagestane za 40 let (Development of social welfare in Dagestan during 40 years). Makhachkala, 1960.

171. Kharchev, A. G. Brak i sem'ia v sovetskom obshchestve (Marriage and the family in Soviet society). Leningrad, 1955.

172. ——— Marksism–Leninism o brake i sem'e (Marxism–Leninism about marriage and the family). Moscow, 1959.

173. ——— Sem'ia v sovetskom obshchestve (The family in Soviet society). Leningrad, 1960.

174. ——— "Sem'ia i kommunism" (The family and communism), *Kommunist*, No. 7, 1960.

175. ——— "O roli sem'i v kommunisticheskom vospitanii" (About the role of the family in communist upbringing), *Sovetskaia Pedagogika*, No. 5, 1963.

176. ——— Brak i sem'ia v SSSR (Marriage and the family in the USSR). Moscow, 1964.

177. Khundadze, A. E. Iz opyta raboty detskikh domov Gruzii (From the experience of children's homes in Gruziia). Tbilisi, 1958.

178. Kiktenko, E. "Social Insurance in 1950," *Soviet Press Translations*, Vol. 5, No. 12, June 15, 1950.

179. Kingsbury, Susan M., and Mildred Fairchild. Factory, Family and Women in the Soviet Union. New York, 1935.

180. Kline, Nathan S. "The Organization of Psychiatric Care and Psychiatric Research in the USSR," *Annals,* New York Academy of Sciences, Vol. 84, Article 4, April 22, 1960.

181. Kliuchevskii, V. O. Dobrye liudi drevnei Rusi (Kind people of ancient Russia). Moscow, 1916.

182. Kodeks zakonov o brake, sem'e i opeke, RSFSR (Code of laws concerning the family, marriage and guardianship). Moscow, 1950.

183. Kolarova, D., K. Tsafarov, and E. Sharankov. "Compulsory Treatment for Chronic Alcoholics," *The Soviet Review, A Journal of Translations,* Vol. 2, No. 10, October 1961.

184. Kolbanovskii, V. N. Kommunisticheskaia moral' i byt (Communist morality and daily life). Moscow, 1955.

185. Kollontai, A. M. Prostitutsiia i mery bor'by s nei (Prostitution and measures to combat it). Moscow, 1921.

186. Kondakov, A. I. Shkola-kommuna, opyt uchebno-vospitatel'noi raboty Znamenskoi shkoly-kommuny Viatskoi gubernii, 1918–1925 (School-commune, the experience of educational-upbringing work of the Znamensk school-commune of Viatsk province, 1918–1925). Moscow, 1961.

187. Konius, E. M. Protection of Motherhood and Childhood in the Soviet Union. Trans. by Vera Fediavsky. Moscow–Leningrad, 1933.

188. ——— Istoki Russkoi pediatrii (Sources of Russian pediatrics). Moscow, 1946.

189. Kopelianskaia, S. E. Sotsial'no-pravovaia pomoshch' materi i rebenku (Socio-legal help for the mother and child). Moscow, 1950.

190. ——— Prava materi i rebenka v SSSR (The rights of mother and child in the USSR). Moscow, 1954.

191. Kornilov, A. A. Modern Russian History, From the Age of Catherine the Great to the End of the Nineteenth Century. New York, 1952.

192. Kostiashkin, E. G. "K istorii prodlennogo dnia v shkole" (History of the extended-day school), *Sovetskaia Pedagogika,* Vol. XXVI, No. 8, August 1962.

193. ——— "Pedagogicheskie aspekty polovogo vospitaniia" (Pedagogical aspects of sexual upbringing), *Sovetskaia Pedagogika,* Vol. XXVIII, No. 7, July 1964.

194. Kovalenko, S. S. Istoriia vozniknoveniia i razvitiia detskikh domov Ukrainskoi SSR v period s 1917 po 1929 god (History of the rise and development of children's homes in the Ukrainian Republic during 1917–1929). Kiev, 1954.

195. Kozhebatkin, A. Bol'nichnye kassy gornykh i gornozavodskikh rabochikh (Sickness funds for workers in foundries and in the mining industry). St. Petersburg, 1914.

196. Krasnopol'skii, A. S. Osnovnye printsipy sovetskogo gosudarstvennogo sotsial'nogo strakhovaniia (Basic principles of Soviet state social insurance). Moscow, 1951.

197. ——— "U istokov Leninskoi strakhovoi programmy" (At the sources

of Lenin's program of social insurance), *Okhrana Truda i Sotsial'noe Strakhovanie,* No. 4, April 1961.

198. Krasnovskaia, I. R. Timbaevskii detskii dom, 1917–1947 (Timbaev children's home, 1917–1947). Kazan', 1947.

199. Kravchik, Ts. "Rabota s umstvenno otstalymi det'mi" (Work with severely retarded children), *Sotsial'noe Obespechenie,* No. 2, February 1961.

200. Krivoshchepov, N. "Narushaetsia poriadok komplektovaniia domov invalidov" (The intake policy in homes for invalids is being violated), *Sotsial'noe Obespechenie,* No. 10, October 1956.

201. Krupianskaia, V. Iu. Selo Viriatino v proshlom i nastoiashchem (The village of Viriatino in the past and in the present). Moscow, 1958.

202. Krupskaia. "Bor'ba s detskoi besprizornost'iu" (The struggle against the homelessness of children), *Pravda,* No. 51, 1923.

203. Krutetskii, V. A. "Problema kharaktera v sovetskoi psikhologii" (The problem of character in Soviet psychology), in B. G. Anan'ev, ed., Psikhologicheskaia nauka v SSSR (Psychological science in the USSR). Vol. 2. Moscow, 1959–60.

204. Krutnikova, M. "Odin den' v priemnoi ministerstva" (One day in the reception room of the Ministry), *Sotsial'noe Obespechenie,* No. 12, December 1956.

205. Ksenofondov. "Zadachi i perspektivy sotsial'nogo obespecheniia" (The problems and perspectives of social welfare), *Voprosy Sotsial'nogo Obespecheniia,* No. 1, January 1, 1926.

206. Kufaev, V. I. Iunye pravonarushiteli (Young lawbreakers). Moscow, 1929.

207. Kuliev, G. "Pensionirovanie kolkhoznikov Saratovskoi oblasti" (Pensions for collective farmers of Saratov region), *Sotsial'noe Obespechenie,* No. 12, December 1961.

208. Kulikov, I. "Chem mogut pomoch pensionery-aktivisty" (How can pensioners-activists be of help?), *Sotsial'noe Obespechenie,* No. 8, August 1957.

209. Kuznetsova, N. I. "Obsuzhdaem nasushchnye voprosy nashei raboty. Vseli u nas khorosho i nezyblemo?" (We are discussing important problems of our work. Is everything all right and firm with us?), *Sotsial'noe Obespechenie,* No. 2, February 1957.

210. "K voprosu o iazyke v bol'nichnykh kassakh" (About the language problem in the administration of sickness funds), *Strakhovanie Rabochikh,* No. 7, June 1913.

211. Lebedinsky, M. S. "General Methodological Problems of Psychotherapy," in Ralph B. Winn, ed., Psychotherapy in the Soviet Union. New York, 1961.

212. Leites, N. S. Ob umstvennoi odarennosti (About the intellectually gifted). Moscow, 1960.

213. Lenin, V. I. Sochineniia (Complete works). Fourth edition. Moscow, 1948.

214. Leningradskaia Vysshaia Partiinaia Shkola. Osnovy sovetskogo gosu-
     darstvennogo prava i sovetskoe stroitel'stvo, lektsii, prochitannye
     slushateliam Leningradskoi vysshei partiinoi shkoly (Bases of Soviet
     state law and Soviet construction, lectures, read to the students of
     the Leningrad Higher Party School). Leningrad, 1961.
215. Leningradskii Ordena Lenina Gosudarstvennyi Universitet imeni A. A.
     Zdhanova. Teoriticheskaia konferentsia, po voprosam bor'by s ob-
     shchestvenno-opasnymi deistviiami nesovershennoletnikh i nevmi-
     niaemykh (Theoretical conference on questions of the struggle
     against socially dangerous acts of juveniles and outcasts). Leningrad,
     February 1956.
216. Leont'ev, A. N. "Ob istoricheskom podkhode v izuchenii psikhiki che-
     loveka (The historical approach to the study of human psychology),
     in B. G. Anan'ev, ed., Psikhologicheskaia nauka v SSSR (Psycho-
     logical science in the USSR). Vol. 1. Moscow, 1959–60.
217. Levin, Deana. Soviet Education Today. New York, 1959.
218. "L'goty predostavliaemye pensioneram" (Privileges available for pen-
     sioners), *Sotsial'noe Obespechenie,* No. 6, June 1961.
219. Liangner, V. Strakhovye delegaty (Social insurance delegates). Mos-
     cow, 1955.
220. Linenburg, G. A. "Rol' tovarishcheskikh sudov v ukreplenii trudovoi
     distsipliny" (Role of comrades' courts in strengthening labor disci-
     pline), in N. G. Aleksandrov, ed., Novoe v razvitii trudovogo prava
     v period mezhdu XX i XXII s"ezdami KPSS (New features in the
     development of labor law during the period between the 20th and
     22nd conference of the Communist Party). Moscow, 1961.
221. Linford, Alton A. "The Future of Social Work Education," *Social Ser-
     vice Administration Newsletter,* School of Social Service Adminis-
     tration of the University of Chicago, Vol. XIII, No. 1, Spring 1966.
222. Litvinov-Falinskii, V. P. Otvetstvennost' predprinimatelei za uvech'ia
     i smert' rabochikh po deistvuiushchim v Rossii zakonam (Responsi-
     bility of employers for injuries and deaths of workers according to
     laws operative in Russia). St. Petersburg, 1903.
223. —— Novyi zakon o voznagrazhdenii uvechnykh rabochikh (The
     new law on rewarding workers who suffered accidents). St. Peters-
     burg, 1904.
224. —— Novye zakony o strakhovanii rabochikh (New laws on workers'
     insurance). St. Petersburg, 1912.
225. —— Kak a dlia chego strakhuiutsia rabochie. Populiarnoe izlozhenie
     zakonov 23 Iiunia 1912 g. o strakhovanii rabochikh s prilozheniem:
     1. Polnogo teksta strakhovykh zakonov; 2. Normal'nogo ustava bol'-
     nichnykh kass (How and why workers are insured. A popular pre-
     sentation of the laws of June 23, 1912, about insuring workers, with
     appendices: 1. Full text of the insurance laws; 2. Model regulations
     concerning sickness funds). Second edition. St. Petersburg, 1913.

226. Liubimov, V. Sotsial'noe strakhovanie v proshlom i nastoiashchem (Social insurance in the past and in the present). Moscow, 1925.
227. Liubimova, V. Soviet Children at Summer Camp. Moscow, 1955.
228. Liublinskii, P. I. "Voprosy sotsial'noi pomoshchi materiam i ikh mladentsam" (Questions of social assistance for mothers and their infants), *Voprosy pediatrii, pedalogii, i okhrany materinstva i detstva*, No. 1, 1929.
229. London, Ivan. "Contemporary Psychology in the Soviet Union," *Science*, Vol. 114, No. 2957, August 31, 1951.
230. ———— "Soviet Psychology and Psychiatry," *Bulletin of the Atomic Scientists*, Vol. VIII, No. 2, March 1952.
231. ———— "Therapy in Soviet Psychiatric Hospitals," *The American Psychologist*, Vol. 8, February 1953.
232. ———— Review of S. L. Rubinshtein, Bytie i soznanie (Being and consciousness), Moscow, 1957. In *Contemporary Psychology*, Vol. V, No. 3, March 1960.
233. Loory, Stuart H. "Crackdown on Russian Drunkards: Families to Turn Them In," *San Francisco Sunday Examiner and Chronicle*, October 31, 1965.
234. Luria, A. R., ed. The Mentally Retarded Child. Essays Based on a Study of the Peculiarities of the Higher Nervous Functioning of Child-oligophrenics. Translated from the Russian by W. P. Robinson; edited by Brian Kirman. New York, 1963.
235. ———— and V. I. Lubovskii, eds. Metody issledovaniia detei pri otbore vo vspomogatel'nye shkoly (Methods of investigation for selecting children for auxiliary schools). Moscow, 1964.
236. Lykova, L., Minister of Social Welfare of the RSFSR in 1965. *See* French materials.
237. ———— Social Security in the USSR. Moscow, ca. 1965.
238. Macdonald, Mary E. "Reunion at Vocational High. An Analysis of Girls at Vocational High: An Experiment in Social Work Intervention," *Social Service Review*, Vol. XL, No. 2, June 1966.
239. Mace, David and Vera. The Soviet Family. New York, 1963.
240. Madison, Bernice. "Contributions and Problems of Soviet Welfare Institutions," *Social Problems*, Vol. VII, No. 4, Spring 1960.
241. ———— "The Organization of Welfare Services," in Cyril E. Black, ed., The Transformation of Russian Society: Aspects of Social Change Since 1861. Cambridge, Mass., 1960.
242. ———— "Russia's Illegitimate Children Before and After the Revolution," *Slavic Review*, Vol. XXII, No. 1, March 1963.
243. ———— "Canadian Family Allowances and Their Major Social Implications," *Journal of Marriage and the Family*, Vol. XXVI, May 1964.
244. ———— "Social Welfare: Soviet Model," *Social Service Review*, Vol. XXXVIII, No. 2, June 1964.
245. ———— "Adoption—Yesterday, Today, and Tomorrow," in Social Work

Practice, 1965: Selected Papers, 92nd Annual Forum. New York and London, 1965.

246. Makarenko, A. S. Learning to Live; Flags on the Battlements. Moscow, 1953.

247. —— The Road to Life. Moscow, 1955.

248. —— A Book for Parents. Moscow, 1957.

249. Makarovskaia, Ia. "Nekotorye voprosy snizheniia invalidnosti" (Certain questions in lowering the rate of invalidity), *Okhrana Truda i Sotsial'noe Strakhovanie,* No. 1, January 1966.

250. Makkaveiskii, P., and M. Magaril. "Bol'nogo napravliaut na VTEK" (The sick person is referred to the Medico-Labor Expert Commission), *Sotsial'noe Obespechenie,* No. 9, September 1960.

251. Makkaveiskii, P. "Novyi institut nachal rabotu" (The new institute has begun working), *Sotsial'noe Obespechenie,* No. 3, March 1961.

252. Maksimova, E. Pedagogicheskaia proza (Pedagogical prose). Moscow, 1963.

253. March, James G., and Herbert A. Simon. Organizations. Fourth printing. New York, 1963.

254. Mchedlishvili. "Rodina zabotitsia o nikh" (The mother country takes care of them), *Sotsial'noe Obespechenie,* No. 8, August 1956.

255. Mead, Margaret. Soviet Attitudes Toward Authority: An Interdisciplinary Approach to Problems of Soviet Character. New York, 1951.

256. Mead, Margaret, and Elena Calas. "Child-Training Ideals in a Post-Revolutionary Context," in Margaret Mead and Martha Wolfenstein, eds., Childhood in Contemporary Cultures. Chicago, 1955.

257. Medynskii, G. Chest'. Povest' (Honor. A story). Petrozavodsk, 1961.

258. Meimukhin, A. "Proverka aktov pervichnogo osvidetel'stvovaniia neobkhodima" (It is essential to check through the findings of initial examinations), *Sotsial'noe Obespechenie,* No. 8, August 1961.

259. Melekhov, D. "Lechenie i trudovoe vospitanie neotdelimy" (Medical treatment and work education are inseparable), *Sotsial'noe Obespechenie,* No. 5, May 1961.

260. Menchinskaia, N. A. "Individual'nye razlichiia shkol'nikov v protsesse usvoeniia znanii" (Individual differences among students in the process of mastering knowledge), in D. N. Bogoiavlenskii and N. A. Menchinskaia, Psikhologiia usvoeniia znanii v shkole (Psychology of the mastery of knowledge in school). Moscow, 1959.

261. Mendel'son, G. A. Otvetstvennost' za proizvodstvo nezakonnogo aborta po sovetskomu ugolovnomu pravu (Responsibility for performing illegal abortions in Soviet criminal law). Moscow, 1957.

262. Merriam, Ida C. "Social Welfare Expenditures, 1963–64," *Social Security Bulletin,* Vol. XXVII, No. 10, October 1964.

263. —— "Social Welfare Expenditures, 1965–66," *Social Security Bulletin,* Vol. XXIX, No. 2, December 1966.

264. "Metody raboty" (Methods of work), *Voprosy Sotsial'nogo Obespecheniia,* No. 21–22, November 15, 1930.

265. Miakotina, M. S., and M. I. Zemtzova, eds. Obuchenie i vospitanie slepykh detei (The education and upbringing of blind children). Moscow, 1956.

266. Miasishchev, V. N. "Osnovnye problemy i sovremennoe sostoianie psy-khologicheskikh otnoshenii cheloveka" (Major problems and current state of man's psychological relations), in B. G. Anan'ev, ed., Psikho-logicheskaiia nauka v SSSR (Psychological science in the USSR). Vol. 2. Moscow, 1959–60.

267. —— "Certain Theoretical Questions of Psychotherapy," in Ralph B. Winn, ed., Psychotherapy in the Soviet Union. New York, 1961.

268. Mikhailov, D. Krasnyi krest i sestry miloserdiia v Rossii a zagranitsei (Red Cross and nurses in Russia and abroad). Petrograd–Kiev, 1914.

269. Milanov, Iu. Kak voznikli profsoiuzy v Rossii (The rise of trade unions in Russia). Moscow, 1929.

270. Miliutin, N. A. Kommuna i sotsial'noe strakhovanie (The commune and social insurance). Petrograd, 1918.

271. —— Organizatsiia sotsial'noi vzaimopomoshchi v derevne (Organi-zation of social mutual aid in the village). Moscow, 1921.

272. —— Itogi i perspektivy sotsial'nogo strakhovaniia (Results and pros-pects of social insurance). Moscow, 1922.

273. Mil'man, A. Sh. Upravlenie zdravookhraneniem i sotsial'nym obespe-cheniem v SSSR (Administration of health services and social wel-fare in the USSR). Baku, 1960.

274. Ministerstvo Narodnogo Prosveshcheniia. Otdel Promyshlennykh Uchi-lishch. Materialy po organizatsii remeslennago i professional'nago obucheniia uvechnykh voinov (Materials concerning the organiza-tion of trade and professional training for maimed warriors). Petro-grad, 1916.

275. Ministerstvo Prosveshcheniia Buriatskoi ASSR. Iz opyta raboty shkol-internatov i detskikh domov (From the experience of boarding schools and children's homes). Ulan-Ude, 1963.

276. Ministerstvo Prosveshcheniia Kazakhskoi SSR. Otdel Detskikh Domov. Sbornik materialov respublikanskogo soveshchaniia po rabote det-skikh domov, 10–15 Dekabria 1949 goda (Collection of materials on the republic conference concerning the work of children's insti-tutions, December 10–15, 1949). Alma-Ata, 1950.

277. Ministerstvo Prosveshcheniia Kazakhskoi SSR. Sbornik rukovodia-shchikh, instruktivnykh i metodicheskikh materialov po voprosam okhrany detstva (Collection of administrative, instructional, and methodological materials on questions concerning the protection of children). Alma-Ata, 1959.

278. Ministerstvo Prosveshcheniia Moldavskoi SSR. Instruktivno-metodi-cheskoe pis'mo o rabote po okhrane prav detstva (Instructional-methodological letter about the work of protection of the rights of children). N.d., but after XXI Party conference.

279. Ministerstvo Prosveshcheniia RSFSR. Upravlenie detskikh domov. Iz

opyta raboty popechitel'skikh sovetov detskikh domov (From the experience of patronage committees in children's institutions). Moscow, 1951.

280. Ministerstvo Prosveshcheniia RSFSR. Upravlenie detskikh domov. Spravochnik po voprosam okhrany detstva (Reference book on questions concerning protection of childhood). Third edition. Moscow, 1956.

281. Ministerstvo Prosveshcheniia RSFSR. Detskii gorodok v Nizhnem Tagile (Children's village in Nizhnii Tagil'). Moscow, 1963.

282. Ministerstvo Vnutrennikh Del SSSR. Otdel Detskikh Kolonii. S putevkoi v zhizn'. Rasskazy byvshikh vospitannikov detskikh kolonii (With a travel ticket to life. Accounts by former inmates of children's colonies). Moscow, 1959.

283. Ministerstvo Zdravookhraneniia RSFSR. Psikhoterapiia v kompleksnom lechenii bol'nykh epilepsiei, metodicheskoe pis'mo (Psychotherapy as a part of methods employed in treating epileptics, a methodological letter). Moscow, 1964.

284. Min'kovskii, G. M. Osobennosti rassledovaniia i sudebnogo razbiratel'stva del o nesovershennoletnikh (Peculiarities of investigation and court study of the cases of minors). Moscow, 1959.

285. Mirandov, A. F. Maksimovka. Shkola dlia nravstvenno defektivnykh detei (Maksimovka. The school for morally defective children). Simbirsk, 1921.

286. Mokhova, K. V. O vospitanii v sem'e (About upbringing in the family). Moscow, 1954.

287. Moskovskii Kabinet po Izucheniiu Lichnosti Prestupnika i Prestupnosti. Nishchenstvo i bezprizornost' (Begging and homelessness). Moscow, 1929.

288. Mozharev, I. "Aktivnye pomoshchniki" (Active helpers), *Sotsial'noe Obespechenie,* No. 8, August 1956.

289. Murav'eva, N. A. "Itogi raboty za 1959 god i ocherednye zadachi organov sotsial'nogo obespecheniia" (Results of work during 1959 and current problems of the organs of social welfare), *Sotsial'noe Obespechenie,* No. 7, July 1960.

290. —— "Velichestvennye perspektivy" (Gigantic perspectives), *Sotsial'noe Obespechenie,* No. 1, January 1962.

291. Murray, Henry A., Mark A. May, and Hadley Cantril. "Some Glimpses of Soviet Psychology," *The American Psychologist,* Vol. 14, No. 6, June 1959.

292. Musatti, Cesare L. "An Answer to F. V. Bassin's Criticism of Freudianism," *The Soviet Review, A Journal of Translations,* Vol. 1, No. 5, December 1960.

293. Myers, Robert J., FSA, FCAS. Social Insurance and Allied Government Programs. Homewood, Ill., 1965.

294. Myshkov, S. Sovety sotsial'nogo strakhovaniia na predpriiatiiakh (Social insurance soviets in industrial establishments). Moscow, 1951.

295. Nagovitsyn, I. "Sostoianie sotsial'nogo obespecheniia v SSSR i ego per-

spektivy" (The situation in social welfare in the USSR and its perspectives), *Voprosy Sotsial'nogo Obespecheniia*, No. 7, April 1, 1927.

296. —— "Itogi V-go vserossiiskogo soveshchaniia rabotnikov sotsial'nogo obespecheniia" (Results of the fifth all-Russian conference of social assistance workers), *Voprosy Sotsial'nogo Obespecheniia*, No. 9-10, May 15, 1928.

297. Narodnyi Komissariat Finansov RSFSR. Sektor Ucheta i Statistiki. Ispolnenie mestnykh biudzhetov RSFSR za 1935 g. (The carrying out of the local budgets in RSFSR, for 1935). Moscow, 1937.

298. Narodnyi Komissariat Prosveshcheniia RSFSR. Bezprizornye v trudovykh kommunakh (The homeless in labor colonies). Moscow, 1926.

299. Narodnyi Komissariat Sotsial'nogo Obespecheniia RSFSR. Sotsial'noe obespechenie za piat' let, 30 Apr. 1918 g.–30 Apr. 1923 g. (Social welfare during five years, April 30 1918–April 30, 1923). Moscow, 1923.

300. Narodnyi Komissariat Sotsial'nogo Obespecheniia RSFSR. Sotsial'noe obespechenie v RSFSR k desiatoi godovshchine oktiabria (Social welfare in the Russian Republic at the tenth anniversary of the Revolution). Moscow, 1927.

301. Narodnyi Komissariat Sotsial'nogo Obespecheniia RSFSR. Sotsial'noe obespechenie v Sovetskom Soiuze (Social welfare in the Soviet Union). Moscow, 1936.

302. Narodnyi Komissariat Sotsial'nogo Obespecheniia RSFSR. Ocherednye zadachi organov sotsial'nogo obespecheniia. Materialy vserossiiskogo soveshchaniia rukovodiashchikh rabotnikov sotsial'nogo obespecheniia, Mai 1945 g. (Current problems faced by social welfare organs. Materials of the all-Russian conference of leading social welfare workers, May 1945). Moscow, 1945.

303. "Nashi zadachi" (Our problems), *Strakhovanie Rabochikh*, No. 1, December 1912.

304. "Navstrechu V vsemirnomu kongressu profsoiuzov" (Greetings to the Fifth World Trade Union Congress), *Okhrana Truda i Sotsial'noe Strakhovanie*, No. 7, July 1961.

305. Nazarov, A. "Za vneshnim blagopoluchiem" (Behind outward wellbeing), *Sotsial'noe Obespechenie*, No. 1, January 1957.

306. "Ne tol'ko vospityvat' no i lechit' " (Not only to rear, but also to treat), *Sotsial'noe Obespechenie*, No. 12, December 1960.

307. Nove, Alec. "Social Welfare in the USSR," in Abraham Brumberg, ed., Russia Under Khrushchev: An Anthology from *Problems of Communism*. New York, 1962.

308. Obshchestvo po rasprostraneniiu politicheskikh i nauchnykh znanii RSFSR. Vospitanie detei v sem'e (The upbringing of children in the family). Leningrad, 1959.

309. "Obsuzhdaiutsia vazhnye problemy truda i byta invalidov" (Important problems concerning the work and the daily life of invalids are being discussed), *Sotsial'noe Obespechenie*, No. 9, August 1961.

310. "Obsuzhdenie opyta raboty obshchestvennykh sovetov pri meditsinskikh uchrezhdeniiakh v MGSPS" (Discussion of the experience of social soviets at medical facilities in MGSPS), *Okhrana Truda i Sotsial'noe Strakhovanie*, No. 1, January 1962.

311. Ob usilenii bor'by s detskoi beznadzornost'iu (About intensifying the struggle against lack of supervision for children). Lenizdat, 1940.

312. "O chutkosti" (About sensitivity), *Sotsial'noe Obespechenie*, No. 10, September 1956.

313. "O iazyke v bol'nichnykh kassakh—iuridicheskaia zametka" (About the language problem in the administration of sickness funds—a legal note), *Strakhovanie Rabochikh*, No. 9, August 1913.

314. "O strakhovanii krest'ianstva" (About insuring the peasants), *Voprosy Sotsial'nogo Obespecheniia*, No. 7, April 1, 1926.

315. Ostroumov, S. S., and K. P. Plotnikov. Trudovoe ustroistvo invalidov otechestvennoi voiny v kooperatsii invalidov (Job placement of war invalids in invalids' cooperatives). Moscow, 1947.

316. "Otkrytie bol'nichnykh kass" (The opening of sickness funds), *Voprosy Strakhovaniia*, No. 4, 1916.

317. Ozeretsky, N. I. "The Paths of Development of Child Psychiatry in the USSR," in Reports of the Members of the Soviet Delegation at the V Congress on Mental Health Defense. Moscow, 1954.

318. Palepa, V. Kassy vzaimopomoshchi: sbornik materialov (Mutual aid funds: a collection of materials). Kharkov, 1935.

319. Panov, V. "Razumno raskhodovat' gosudarstvennye sredstva" (Let us spend government funds wisely), *Sotsial'noe Obespechenie*, No. 9, September 1957.

320. Panova, V. F. Serezha, Valia, Volodia, Evdokiia (Serezha, Valia, Volodia, Evdokiia). Leningrad, 1961.

321. Pechernikova, I. A. Shkola i sem'ia (The school and the family). Moscow, 1952.

322. —— Vospitanie distsiplinirovannosti u podrostka v sem'e (The nurture of discipline among adolescents in the family). Moscow, 1956.

323. Penzenskii Oblastnoi Otdel Narodnogo Obrazovaniia, Institut Usovershenstvovaniia Uchitelei. Splochenie detskogo kollektiva, iz opyta raboty shkol-internatov i detskikh domov (Strengthening the children's collective, from the experience of boarding schools and children's homes). Penza, 1961.

324. Permskii Oblastnoi Institut Usovershenstvovaniia Uchitelei. Iz opyta raboty pedagogicheskogo kollektiva Dobrianskogo doma (From the experience of the pedagogical collective in the Dobriansk children's home). Kudymkar, 1960.

325. Petersen, William. "The Evolution of Soviet Family Policy," *Problems of Communism*, Vol. 5, September–October 1956.

326. Petrishchev, A. B. Iz istorii kabakov v Rossii (From the history of dram shops in Russia). Petrograd–Moscow, 1917.

327. Petrovskii, A. V. "Ob osnovnykh napravleniiakh v russkoi psykhologii

nachala XX v." (About the major directions of Russian psychology in the beginning of the twentieth century), in M. V. Sokolov, ed., Iz istorii Russkoi psikhologii (From the history of Russian psychology). Moscow, 1961.

328. Pevzner, M. S. "Klinicheskii i patofizicheskii analiz osnovnogo simptoma pri oligophrenii" (Clinical and pathological-physical analysis of the basic symptom in mental retardation), in Trudy nauchnoi sessii po defektologii (The works of the scientific session on defectology). Akademiia Pedagogicheskikh Nauk RSFSR. Moscow, 1958.

329. Pierre, A. Les femmes en Union Sovietique (Women in the Soviet Union). Paris, 1960.

330. Piradova, M. D. Iunosha i devushka (The young man and the young girl). Moscow, 1965.

331. Pogozhev, A. V. Uchet chislennosti i sostava rabochikh v Rossii (The number and composition of workers in Russia). St. Petersburg, 1906.

332. Poliakoff, Vladimir. Mother Dear: The Empress Marie of Russia and Her Times. New York, 1926.

333. Polozhenie o komissiiakh po delam nesovershennoletnikh (Regulations concerning minors' commissions). Erevan, 1961.

334. Polozkov, F. A. Obshchestvennost' v bor'be s narushiteliami sotsialisticheskogo poriadka (Community participation in the struggle against breakers of socialist order). Kuibyshev, 1961.

335. Popechitel'stvo o domakh trudoliubiia i rabotnykh domakh. Otchet po trudovoi pomoshchi. Trudovaia pomoshch v guberniiakh Kazanskoi, Viatskoi i Simbirskoi ... okazanaia v 1899 godu (Report on work relief. Work relief rendered in the Kazan, Viatsk, and Simbirsk provinces in 1899). St. Petersburg, 1900.

336. Posnanskii, N. F. "Heredity and the Materialist Theory," in Soviet Psychology: A Symposium. New York, 1961.

337. Potalak, P. V. Institut trudovogo vospitaniia "Novaia Zhizn' " Narkomprosa RSFSR (The institute for labor upbringing named "New Life" of the People's Commissariat of Education of the RSFSR). Moscow, 1940.

338. Pototskii, V. M. Strakhovoe ustroistvo v SSSR (The social insurance system in the USSR). Moscow, 1927.

339. Potrachkov, G. "Gde zhe nam uchit'sia?" (Where are we to study?), Sotsial'noe Obespechenie, No. 8, August 1957.

340. "Povyshat' rol' obshchestvennosti v upravlenii sotsial'nym strakhovaniem" (Let us raise the role of community participation in the administration of social insurance), Okhrana Truda i Sotsial'noe Strakhovanie, No. 2, February 1962.

341. Pozdniakov, I. "Kak my povyshaem ekspertnuiu kvalifikatsiiu. Respublikanskaia VTEK osushchestvliaet metodicheskoe rukovodstvo" (How we raise the qualifications of experts. The Republic Medico-Labor Expert Commission carries out methodological leadership), Sotsial'noe Obespechenie, No. 4, April 1961.

342. Pravila o voznagrazhdenii poterpevshikh vsledstvie neschastnykh slu-chaev rabochikh i sluzhashchikh, a ravno chlenov ikh semeistv v predpriiatiiakh fabrichno-zavodskoi, gornoi i gornozavodskoi pro-myshlennosti (Regulations concerning payments to workers and em-ployees and their families for accidents in factories, mines, and foun-dries). St. Petersburg, 1903.

343. Predkal'n, A. I. "Mytarstva strakhovykh zakonov" (The trying experi-ences of social insurance), in B. G. Danskii, ed., Dorevoliutsionnaia strakhovaia kampaniia (The pre-revolutionary social insurance cam-paign). Moscow, 1925.

344. Press, A. A. Strakhovanie rabochikh v Rossii (Workers' social insurance in Russia). St. Petersburg, 1900.

345. Privalskii, V., and A. Spektorov. "Spravedlivyi, tovarishcheskii" (Just, comradely), *Izvestiia,* June 1, 1963.

346. "Problemy vospitaniia umstvenno otstalykh detei" (The problems of rearing severely retarded children), *Sotsial'noe Obespechenie,* No. 3, March 1961.

347. Pronina, V. S. Rol' mestnykh sovetov v dele preduprezhdeniia pravo-narushenii nesovershennoletnikh (The role of local soviets in pre-venting lawbreaking among minors). Moscow, 1961.

348. "Puti razvitiia uchrezhdenii sotsial'nogo obespecheniia" (Ways of de-veloping social welfare), *Sotsial'noe Obespechenie,* No. 12, December 1959.

349. Queen, Stuart Alfred. Social Work in the Light of History. Philadelphia and London, 1922.

350. "Rabochaia strakhovaia programma" (Workers' insurance program), *Voprosy Strakhovaniia,* No. 4, 1916.

351. "Rabotniki sobesa" (Welfare workers), *Voprosy Sotsial'nogo Obespe-cheniia,* No. 9–10, May 15, 1926.

352. Reshetnikov, A. "Navesti poriadok v raspredelenii putevok" (We must bring order into the assignment of travel orders), *Okhrana Truda i Sotsial'noe Strakhovanie,* No. 6, June 1959.

352A. Rimlinger, Gaston V. "Social Security, Incentives, and Controls in the U.S. and U.S.S.R.," *Comparative Studies in Society and History.* The Hague, 1961.

353. Rokhlin, Leon. Soviet Medicine in the Fight Against Mental Diseases. London, 1959.

354. Roshchin, V. N., and M. P. Lashin. "The Study and Treatment of Crime," *The Soviet Review, A Journal of Translations,* Vol. 2, No. 1, January 1961.

355. Rozanov, V. V. Semeinyi vopros v Rossii (The family question in Russia). 2 vols. St. Petersburg, 1903.

356. Rukeyser, William S. "Jobless Russians. Soviet Unemployment, Not Supposed to Exist, Runs Near U.S. Rate," *The Wall Street Journal,* Vol. LXXIV, No. 95, May 16, 1966.

357. Rulev, N. "Chetvertaia podpis'" (The fourth signature), *Okhrana Truda i Sotsial'noe Strakhovanie,* No. 3, March 1959.

358. Rumiantseva, M., A. Pergament, and G. Gromova. Spravochnik zhenshchiny-rabotnitsy; prava zhenshchiny po sovetskomu zakonodatel'stvu (A book of references for the woman worker; the rights of women in Soviet law). Moscow, 1963.

359. Sablin, V. "Slov—reki, del—rucheiki" (Rivers of words, tiny brooks of deeds), *Okhrana Truda i Sotsial'noe Strakhovanie,* No. 6, June 1960.

360. Sakharov, A. B. O lichnosti prestupnika i prichinakh prestupnosti v SSSR (The personality of the criminal and reasons for crime in the USSR). Moscow, 1961.

361. —— O polnom preodolenii perezhitkov kapitalizma v soznanii i povedenii liudei (Toward the complete overcoming of survivals of capitalism in the consciousness and the behavior of people). Moscow, 1963.

362. —— Kogda sudiat mal'chishku (When the adolescent boy is being judged). Moscow, 1964.

363. Samoilov, F. N. Po sledam minuvshego (In the footsteps of the past). Moscow, 1948.

364. Schlesinger, Rudolf. Changing Attitudes in Soviet Russia. Volume on The Family in the USSR. London, 1949.

365. Schwartz, Solomon M. "Why the Changes?," in Abraham Brumberg, ed., Russia Under Khrushchev: An Anthology from *Problems of Communism*. New York, 1962.

366. Selezneva, E. D. Protivo-zachatochnye sredstva (Contraceptives). Second edition. Moscow, 1964.

367. Semashko, N. Desiat' let bor'by za detstvo (Ten years of struggle on behalf of childhood). Moscow, 1931.

368. —— Health Protection in the USSR. London, 1934.

369. —— Public Health in the USSR. London, 1946.

370. Semenov, N. "Nuzhen internat dlia prestarelykh" (A home for the aged is needed), *Sotsial'noe Obespechenie,* No. 12, December 1956.

371. "Semiletka blagosostoianiia" (The seven-year plan for the well-being of the people), *Sotsial'noe Obespechenie,* No. 1, January 1959.

372. Severin, G. V., ed. Ranenye ofitsery i nizhnie chiny, ikh evakuatsiia, denezhnoe i veshchevoe dovol'stvie, pensionnyia prava, a takzhe obezpechenie semei lits, prizvannykh na voinu. Sbornik zakonov i rasporiazhenii (Wounded officers and lower ranks, their evacuation, support in money and in kind, their pension rights, and support for families of conscripts. Collection of laws and regulations). Petrograd, 1914.

373. "Sex in Russia," *Newsweek,* October 19, 1964.

374. Shabad, Theodore. "Soviet Riot Stirs Drive for Police. More Protection Asked as Juvenile Crime Soars," *New York Times,* June 27, 1965.

375. —— "Tadzik School Forward-Looking," *New York Times,* November 28, 1965.
376. Shabunin, K. G. Pedagogicheskii kollektiv detskogo doma. Iz opyta raboty pedagogicheskogo kollektiva Dobrianskogo detskogo doma (Pedagogical collective in a children's home. The experience of the pedagogical collective of the Dobriansk children's home). Kudymkar, 1960.
377. Shaldurov, S. "Praktika podskazyvaet" (Practice suggests), *Sotsial'noe Obespechenie,* No. 9, September 1957.
378. Sharapov, M. "Otvet upravleniia trudovogo i bytovogo ustroistva invalidov na predlozheniia chitatelei" (The answer of the bureau for the placement into jobs and arranging daily life for invalids to the suggestions of readers), *Sotsial'noe Obespechenie,* No. 12, December 1960.
379. Shcherbinin, G. Ia. K voprosy ob organizatsii zemledel'cheskikh priiutov dlia sel'skikh sirot (The problem of organizing asylums for rural orphans). Petrograd, 1915.
380. Shif, Zh. I., and A. N. Smirnova, eds. Opyt otbora uchashchikhsia vo vspomogatel'nye shkoly (Experience with selecting children for auxiliary schools). Moscow, 1964.
381. Shipov, V. "Inspektora, ikh dela i zaboty" (Welfare inspectors, their work and their cares), *Sotsial'noe Obespechenie,* No. 10, October 1956.
382. Shishkov, V. Ia. Stranniki (Wanderers). Leningrad, 1936.
383. Shtraks, G. M. "On the Problem of Conflict in Socialist Society," *The Soviet Review, A Journal of Translations,* Vol. IV, No. 3, Fall 1963.
384. Shubert, L. Ob obshchestvennoi opasnosti prestupnogo deianiia (About the social danger of a criminal act). Translated from Slovakian by R. P. Razumova; edited by M. A. Gel'fer. Moscow, 1960.
385. Sigerist, Henry E., and Julia Older. Medicine and Health in the Soviet Union. New York, 1947.
386. Simirenko, Alex. "Recent Developments in Soviet Sociology: A Decade." Unpublished manuscript read at the Far Western Slavic Association meeting at the University of California at Berkeley, April 30, 1966, and in my possession.
387. Skatkin, L. N., ed. Sodruzhestvo shkoly i sem'i (Friendship between the school and the family). Moscow, 1956.
388. Skolnick, Alec. "Some Psychiatric Aspects of the 'New Soviet Child,'" *Bulletin of the Menninger Clinic,* Vol. 28, No. 3, May 1964.
389. Slavina, L. S. "Rol' sem'i v formirovanii otnosheniia shkol'nika k ucheniiu v shkole" (Role of the family in forming the schoolchild's attitude toward study in school), in L. I. Bozhovich, ed., Voprosy psikhologii shkol'nika (Questions concerning the psychology of the pupil). Moscow, 1951.
390. —— "K psikhologicheskoi kharakteristike truda shkol'nika v sem'e" (The psychological characteristics of housework done by pupils in

their families), in L. I. Bozhovich, ed., Voprosy psikhologii lichnosti shkol'nika (Questions concerning the psychological personality of the pupil). Moscow, 1961.

391. Smirnov, A. A. "Child Psychology," in Brian Simon, ed., Psychology in the Soviet Union. London, 1957.

392. —— "The Development of Soviet Psychology," in Soviet Psychology: A Symposium. New York, 1961.

393. Smith, Anna Kalet. Health and Welfare Services for Mothers and Children in the USSR. Washington, D.C., 1945.

394. Sokolov, Boris. Spasaite detei! O detiakh sovetskoi rossii (Save the children! About the children of Soviet Russia). Prague, 1921.

395. Sokolova, E. Po pochinu strakhovogo aktiva (In the footsteps of the social insurance group of activists). Moscow, 1958.

396. Soloveitchik, S. "Family Law and Inheritance Law in the USSR," *University of Kansas City Law Review,* Vol. XV, 1946–47.

397. Solov'ev, B. "Organisatsiia bol'nichnoi kassy" (Organizing a sickness fund), in B. G. Danskii, ed., Strakhovanie rabochikh v Rossii i na zapade (Workers' insurance in Russia and in the West). Vol. 1, First edition. St. Petersburg, 1913.

398. Solov'ev, N. Sem'ia v sovetskom obshchestve (The family in Soviet society). Moscow, 1962.

399. Sol'skaia, Olga. Rabotnitsa i strakhovanie (The woman worker and social insurance). St. Petersburg, 1913.

400. Sorok let sovetskogo zdravookhraneniia (Forty years of Soviet health protection). Moscow, 1957.

401. Sosnovy, Timothy. The Housing Problem in the Soviet Union. David I. Goldstein, ed. New York, 1954.

402. Sotsial'noe Obespechenie i Strakhovanie v SSSR, Sbornik ofitsial'nykh dokumentov (Social welfare and social insurance in the USSR. Manual of official documents). Moscow, 1964.

403. "Sotsial'noe obespechenie za piat' let bez Lenina" (Social welfare during the five years without Lenin), *Voprosy Sotsial'nogo Obespechenia,* No. 2, January 15, 1929.

404. "Sovetam sotsial'nogo obespecheniia kolkhoznikov" (For the agricultural social insurance soviets), *Sotsial'noe Obespechenie,* No. 3, March 1965.

405. Sovety sotsial'nogo strakhovaniia na predpriiatiiakh (Social insurance soviets in industrial establishments). Moscow, 1951.

406. Stevens, Edmund. "Crime in Russia's New Society—Figures Given," *San Francisco Chronicle,* November 26, 1965.

407. "Strakhovaia kampaniia ili boikom?" (Social insurance campaign or a boycott?), *Strakhovanie Rabochikh,* No. 5, April 1913.

408. Strong, Anna Louise. Children of Revolution: Story of the John Reed Children's Colony on the Volga.... Seattle, 1925.

409. Strumilin, S. Nasha zhizn' cherez 20 let (Our life in twenty years). Moscow, 1964.

410. Studenkin, Vlasov, Evtikhiev. Sovetskoe administrativnoe pravo (Soviet administrative law). Moscow, 1950.
411. Sutiagin, P., ed. 30 let VOG (Thirty years of the All-Russian Society for the Deaf). Moscow, 1957.
412. Sutiagin, P. "VII s"ezd VOG" (The seventh conference of the All-Russian Society for the Deaf), *Sotsial'noe Obespechenie,* No. 9, September 1959.
413. Svadkovskii, I. F., ed. Protiv pedologicheskikh izvrashchenii v pedagogike (Against pedological distortions in pedagogy). Leningrad, 1938.
414. Svadkovskii, I. F. Zapiski vospitatelia (The diary of an upbringer). Moscow, 1963.
415. Sverdlov, G. M. "The Development of Soviet Family Law," *Soviet Press Translations,* Vol. 3, No. 16, September 15, 1948.
416. ——— Usynovlenie po sovetskomu pravu (Adoption in Soviet law). Moscow, 1951.
417. ——— Sovetskoe semeinoe pravo (Soviet family law). Moscow, 1951.
418. ——— Marriage and the Family in the USSR. Moscow, 1956.
419. ——— Prava grazhdan v sem'e (Family rights of citizens). Moscow, 1963.
420. Syrovarov, A. I., and I. V. Khokhlachev. Gosudarstvennoe sotsial'noe strakhovanie, ispolnenie biudzheta, uchet i otchetnost' (Social insurance, executing the budget, accounting and accountability). Moscow, 1957.
421. Tadevosian, V. S. Prava i obiazannosti roditelei v sovetskom gosudarstve (The rights and duties of parents in the Soviet state). Moscow, 1947.
422. Tadzhikskii Gosudarstvennyi Universitet, Verkhovnyi Sud, MVD i Iuridicheskaia Komissiia pri Sovete Ministrov Tadzhikskoi SSR. Materialy nauchnoi konferentsii po voprosam o roli obshchestvennosti v bor'be s prestupnost'iu i narusheniiami obshchestvennogo poriadka (Materials of the scientific conference dealing with questions of the role of community participation in the struggle against crime and the breaking of social order). Stalinabad, 1961.
423. "Text of President's Economic Report Outlining the Nation's Gains and Problems," *New York Times,* January 27, 1967.
424. Timasheff, N. S. One Hundred Years of Probation, 1841–1941. New York, 1943.
425. Tokmakov, L. K. Psikhologicheskie osnovy individual'nogo podkhoda k vospitannikam detskikh domov (Psychological bases for an individualized approach to children brought up in children's homes). Moscow, 1953.
426. Tolkunova, V. N. Pensionnoe obespechenie rabochikh i sluzhashchikh v SSSR, lektsiia dlia studentov VIUZI (Pensions for workers and employees in the USSR, lecture read to students of higher law institute). Moscow, 1957.

427. Torbeeva, A. S. Nasha sem'ia (Our family). Minsk, 1955.

428. Tret'iakov, A. "V novykh usloviiakh rabotat' po-novomu" (In new conditions, let us work in new ways), *Sotsial'noe Obespechenie*, No. 7, July 1956.

429. ————. "Sovershenstvovat' metody i uluchshat' kachestvo ekspertizy" (Toward perfecting the methods and improving the quality of expertise), *Sotsial'noe Obespechenie*, No. 6, June 1959.

430. ———— "Vazhneishie zadachi VTEK" (The most important problems of Medico-Labor Expert Commissions), *Sotsial'noe Obespechenie*, No. 8, August 1959.

431. ———— "Nuzhen tesnyi kontakt" (What is necessary is close cooperation), *Okhrana Truda i Sotsial'noe Strakhovanie*, No. 9, September 1959.

432. ———— "VTE v 1960 godu" (Medico-labor expertise in 1960), *Sotsial'noe Obespechenie*, No. 2, February 1960.

433. ———— "Invalidnost' i ee pokazateli" (Invalidity and its indicators), *Sotsial'noe Obespechenie*, No. 6, June 1960.

434. ———— "Na novye rubezhi" (Toward new heights), *Sotsial'noe Obespechenie*, No. 7, July 1961.

435. ———— "Zakon o gosudarstvennykh pensiiakh i vrachebno-trudovaia ekspertiza" (The law on state pensions and medico-labor expertise), *Sotsial'noe Obespechenie*, No. 10, October 1961.

436. ———— "Neotlozhnye zadachi" (Urgent problems), *Sotsial'noe Obespechenie*, No. 6, June 1962.

436A. ———— "Desiatiletie Zakona o Gosudarstvennykh Pensiiakh i Dinamika Invalidnosti za Eti Gody" (The tenth anniversary of the law on state pensions and the dynamics of invalidity during these years), *Sotsial'noe Obespechenie*, July 1966.

437. ———— *See* French materials.

438. Troinitskii, N. A., ed. Chislennost' i sostav slepykh v Rossii na osnovanii dannykh pervoi vseobshchei perepisi naseleniia Rossiiskoi Imperii 1897 goda (The number and composition of the blind in Russia, on the basis of the first census of the population of the Russian Empire, in 1897). St. Petersburg, 1905.

439. Trutovskii, V. E. Sovremennoe zemstvo (Modern zemstvo). Petrograd, 1915.

440. Tsentral'noe Statisticheskoe Upravlenie SSSR. Itogi perepisi naseleniia 1920 g. Naselenie po odnoletnim vozrastam i vozrastnym gruppam —litsa s fizicheskimi nedostatkami i psikhicheski bol'nye (Results of the 1920 census. Population by one-year differences in age and by age groups—persons with physical handicaps and the mentally ill). Moscow, 1920.

441. Tsentral'noe Statisticheskoe Upravlenie SSSR. Statisticheskii sbornik za 1913–1917 gody (Statistical compilation for the years 1913–1917). Vol. XII, No. 1. Moscow, 1923.

442. Tsentral'noe Statisticheskoe Upravlenie SSSR. Dostizheniia sovetskoi vlasti za 40 let v tsifrakh (Achievements of the Soviet government during 40 years, in figures). Moscow, 1957.

443. Tsentral'noe Statisticheskoe Upravlenie SSSR. Zhenshchiny i deti v SSSR (Women and children in the USSR). Moscow, 1961.

444. Tsentral'noe Upravlenie Narodno–khoziaistvennogo Ucheta. Narodnoe khoziaistvo SSSR v 1963 godu (The national economy of the USSR in 1963). Moscow, 1965.

445. "Tsifry i facty" (Figures and facts), *Sotsial'noe Obespechenie,* No. 10, October 1961.

446. Ul'ianskaia, E. "Nepravil'no zaseliaiutsia doma invalidov" (Placements into homes for invalids are incorrectly made), *Sotsial'noe Obespechenie,* No. 1, January 1957.

447. United Nations, Bureau of Social Affairs. Report on the World Social Situation. New York, 1963.

448. United Nations, Department of Economic and Social Affairs. International Social Service Review, No. 2, March 1957. New York, 1956–59.

449. United Nations, Department of Social Affairs. Training for Social Work. New York, 1950.

450. United Nations, Department of Social Affairs. Study on Adoption of Children. A Study on the Practice and Procedures Related to the Adoption of Children. New York, 1953.

451. UNESCO. Statistics on Special Education. Paris, 1960.

452. United Nations. Second United Nations Congress on the Prevention of Crime and the Treatment of Offenders. Report Prepared by the Secretariat. New York, 1960.

453. United States Department of Health, Education, and Welfare. A Report on Social Security Programs in the Soviet Union. Prepared by the U.S. Team That Visited the USSR Under the East-West Exchange Program in August–September 1958. Washington, D.C., 1960.

454. United States Department of Health, Education, and Welfare. Children's Bureau Statistical Series, No. 72. Child Welfare Statistics— 1962. Washington, D.C., 1963.

455. United States Department of Health, Education, and Welfare. Closing the Gap in Social Work Manpower. Washington, D.C., November 1965.

456. United States Department of Health, Education, and Welfare. Having the Power, We Have the Duty. Report of the Advisory Council on Public Welfare. Washington, D.C., June 29, 1966.

457. Utevskii, B. S. "Bor'ba s detskoi besprizornost'iu" (The struggle against the homelessness of children), *Biblioteka "Okhrana Detstva i Detskoe Pravo,"* No. 4, 1932.

458. ———— Bor'ba s prestupnost'iu nesovershennoletnikh (Struggle against criminality among juveniles). Moscow, 1932.

459. ———— "Detskii dom" (The children's home), *Biblioteka "Okhrana Detstva i Detskoe Pravo,"* No. 3, 1932.

460. ―――― "Nesovershennoletnie pravonarushiteli" (Juvenile delinquents), *Biblioteka "Okhrana Detstva i Detskoe Pravo,"* No. 10, 1932.

461. ―――― "Obshchestvo 'Drug Detei' " (The society "The Friend of Children"), *Biblioteka "Okhrana Detstva i Detskoe Pravo,"* No. 2, 1932.

462. Venable, Vernon. Human Nature: The Marxian View. New York, 1946.

463. Vernadsky, George. A History of Russia. New Haven, Conn., 1929.

464. Vernikov, G. "Nash opyt trudoustroistva bol'nykh" (Our experience with placing the sick in jobs), *Okhrana Truda i Sotsial'noe Strakhovanie,* No. 6, June 1959.

465. Veselovskii, Boris. Istoriia zemstva za sorok let (The history of zemstvo for forty years). 2 vols. St. Petersburg, 1909.

466. Veterany truda. Iz opyta raboty soveta veteranov truda na Staro-Kramatorskom mashinostroitel'nom zavode (Veterans of labor. From the experience of the soviet of labor veterans at the Staro-Kramotorsk machine-building factory. Stalino, 1958.

467. Vigdorchik, N. A. Gosudarstvennoe obespechenie trudiashchikhsia (Government social security for the toilers). Petrograd, n.d.

468. Vigdorova, F. Diary of a Russian Schoolteacher. Trans. by R. Prokofieva. New York, 1960.

469. Vinogradov, N. Health Protection in the Soviet Union, 1917–1957. Moscow, 1957.

470. Vinokurov, A. N. "Novyi zakon o strakhovanii rabochikh ot bolezni i rabochiia strakhovyia trebovaniia" (New laws about insuring the workers against sickness and workers' demands in social insurance), *Voprosy Strakhovaniia,* No. 6–7, October 9, 1917.

471. ―――― Sotsial'noe obespechenie trudiashchikhsia (Social assistance for the workers). Moscow, 1921.

472. ―――― Sotsial'noe obespechenie—ot kapitalizma k kommunizmu (Social assistance—from capitalism to communism). Moscow, 1921.

473. Vishnevetskii, A. Razvitie zakonodatel'stva o sotsial'nom strakhovanii v Rossii (Development of social insurance law in Russia). Second edition. Moscow, 1926.

474. Vishniak, V. I. "Pravovoe polozhenie rebenka v sem'e" (The legal position of the child in the family), *Biblioteka "Okhrana Detstva i Detskoe Pravo,"* No. 2, 1932.

475. Vishniakov, Mel'gunov, Syroerkovskii, eds. Nashe proshloe, razskazy iz Russkoi istorii (Our past, stories from Russian history). 2 vols. Moscow, 1913–1915.

476. Vlasov, S. "Doma prestarelykh kolkhoznikov" (Homes for aged collective farmers), *Sotsial'noe Obespechenie,* No. 1, January 1957.

477. Vlasov, S. N., and A. V. Levshin. Sotsial'noe obespechenie kolkhoznikov (Social assistance of collective farmers). Moscow, 1960.

478. Vnebrachnye deti. Uluchshenie ikh uchasti. Proekt izmeneniia zakona (Illegitimate children. The improvement of their fate. A proposal for changing the law). Moscow, 1910.

479. Voevodin, Peter. "Zakon rodivshiisia pod sotsializmom" (A law born under socialism), *Izvestiia,* July 11, 1956.
480. Voinov, Nicholas. The Waif. New York, 1955.
481. Volkova, A. "Pravil'noe reshenie—etogo malo" (A correct decision—that is not enough), *Sotsial'noe Obespechenie,* No. 6, June 1961.
482. Volkova, E. I., ed. Roditeli i deti. Vospitanie detei v sem'e (Parents and children, children's upbringing in the family). Moscow, 1961.
483. Voskanian, I. "O kul'ture obsluzhivaniia pensionerov" (About the culture of service for pensioners), *Sotsial'noe Obespechenie,* No. 6, June 1961.
484. Vserossiiskoe obshchestvo slepykh v tsifrakh, 1955–1959 (The All-Russian Society for the Blind in figures, 1955–1959). Moscow, 1959.
485. "Vyshe uroven' profobucheniia" (Let us raise the level of professional education), *Sotsial'noe Obespehcenie,* No. 9, September 1960.
486. Wickenden, Elizabeth, and Winifred Bell. Public Welfare: Time for a Change. New York, 1961.
487. Wickenden, Elizabeth. Social Welfare in a Changing World. Washington, D.C., 1965.
488. World Health Organization. Deprivation of Maternal Care. A Reassessment of Its Effects. Public Health Paper 14. Geneva, 1962.
489. World Health Organization. Maternal and Child Health in the USSR. Geneva, 1962.
490. Wortis, Joseph. Soviet Psychiatry. Baltimore, 1950.
491. —— "Mental Retardation in the Soviet Union," *Children,* Vol. 7, No. 6, November–December 1960.
492. Zabelin, A. Teoriia sotsial'nogo obespecheniia (The theory of social assistance). Moscow, 1924.
493. Zabelin, L. V. Teoreticheskie osnovy sotsial'nogo strakhovaniia (Theoretical bases of social insurance). Moscow, 1926.
494. —— "Sotsial'noe obespechenie" (Social assistance), *Voprosy Obespecheniia,* No. 1, January 6, 1927.
495. Zabota o cheloveke—zakon nashei zhizni. Informatsionnoe pis'mo ob opyte raboty Ust'-Labinskogo raionnogo otdela sotsial'nogo obespecheniia, 4 aprelia, 1960 goda (Concern for the human being—that is the law of our life. Informational letter about the experience of the Ust'-Labin district department of social welfare, April 4, 1960). Krasnodar, 1960.
496. "Zadachi rabochego predstavitel'stva v strakhovom sovete" (The problems of the workers' representatives in the insurance soviets), *Voprosy Strakhovaniia,* No. 3, 1916.
497. "Za edinyi chetkii pensionnyi zakon" (Toward a unified, clear-cut pension law), *Voprosy Sotsial'nogo Obespecheniia,* No. 6, June 1940.
498. Zaitsev, L. "Rol' obshchestvennykh fondov v pod"eme blagosostoianiia trudiashchikhsia" (The role of socialized funds in raising the well-being of the toilers), *Okhrana Truda i Sotsial'noe Strakhovanie,* No. 9, September 1959.

499. Zaitsev, V. Polozhenie truda podrostkov i ego oplata v promyshlennosti (Position in regard to the labor of adolescents in industry and their wages). Moscow, 1924.

500. Zamskii, X. C. "Iz istorii prizreniia, vospitaniia i obucheniia gluboko otstalykh detei" (From the history of care, upbringing, and education of severely retarded children), in Dul'nev and Kuz'mitskaia, eds., Obuchenie i vospitanie umstvenno otstalykh detei (The education and upbringing of mentally retarded children). Moscow, 1960.

501. Zaretskii, M. Organizatsiia truda podrostkov (Organization of the labor of adolescents). Kharkov, 1923.

502. Zemtsova, M. I. Puti kompensatsii slepoty (Ways of compensating for blindness). Moscow, 1956.

503. Zemtsova, M. I., ed. Kniga dlia uchitelia shkoly slepykh (A book for the teacher in a school for the blind). Moscow, 1962.

504. Zen'kovich, V. A. Zadachi sotsial'nogo strakhovaniia sovetskoi Rossii (The problems of social insurance in Soviet Russia). Moscow, 1918.

505. Zenzinov, Vladimir. Besprizornye (The homeless). Paris, 1929.

506. —— Deserted. The Story of the Children Abandoned in Soviet Russia. Trans. by Agnes Platt. London, 1931.

507. Zetkin, Clara. Reminiscences of Lenin. London, 1929.

508. Zhigalko, A. "Pis'mo v redaktsiiu" (A letter to the editors), *Sotsial'noe Obespechenie,* No. 5, May 1961.

509. Zilboorg, Gregory. "Russian Psychiatry—Its Historical and Ideological Background," *Bulletin of the New York Academy of Medicine,* October 1943.

510. Zinov'eva, P. "Bol'she vnimaniia pervichnoi ekspertize" (More attention to initial expert examinations), *Sotsial'noe Obespechenie,* No. 12, December 1960.

511. Ziubin, L. "Predislovie" (Foreword), in Vospitatel'naia rabota detskikh domov (Upbringing work in children's homes). Moscow, 1961.

512. "Znamenatel'nye daty" (Famous dates), *Voprosy Sotsial'nogo Obespecheniia,* No. 10, October 1937.

513. Zvonarev, V. "Segodnia i zavtra sotsial'nogo obespecheniia" (Today and tomorrow of social welfare), *Sotsial'noe Obespechenie,* No. 2, February 1962.

514. Zykov, S. A., ed. Vospitatel'naia rabota v internate shkoly dlia glukhikh detei (Upbringing work in the boarding school for deaf children). Moscow, 1961.

Index